Please Save My Earth

Saki Hiwatari

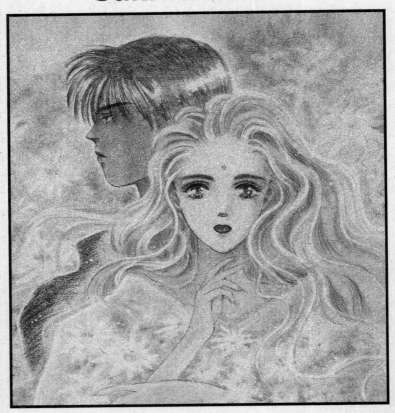

Previous Life [Moon]

Relationship Chart

GYOKURAN
An archaeologist with exemplary conduct—but he also has an inferiority complex toward Shion...

SHION
Gifted engineer and problem child, Gyokuran's boyhood pal lacks social skills but has a strong sense of justice.

MOKUREN
Beautiful, intelligent, sincere, caring, and pure of heart...a biologist and Kiche Sarjalian! ♡

ENJU
An introverted paleontologist with an intense side, she'd go to the ends of the galaxy to pursue Gyokuran!

SHUKAIDO
A stodgy doctor who enjoys afternoon tea with Mokuren, but he could be the most manic of them all...

SHUSURAN
She spent too much time meddling in her best friend Enju's love life, which led to a general distrust of men.

HIIRAGI
He's in charge of the moon mission! Everyone loves him, but he can be quite stubborn... He's a linguist, too! ♡

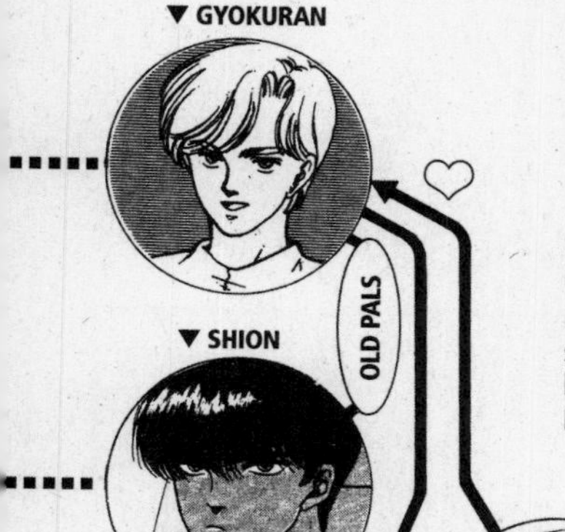
▼ GYOKURAN
OLD PALS
▼ SHION
ENGAGED! ♥

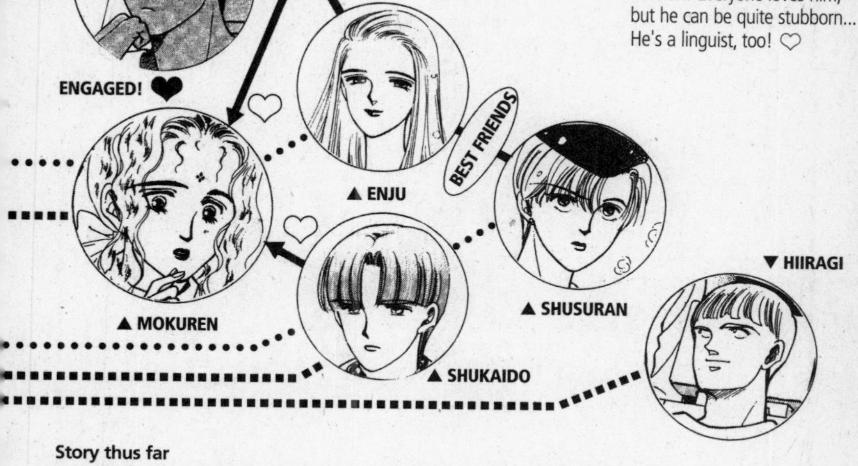
▲ MOKUREN
▲ ENJU
BEST FRIENDS
▲ SHUSURAN
▲ SHUKAIDO
▼ HIIRAGI

Story thus far

Alice and six friends share dreams of their past lives on the moon... Rin, an 8-year-old boy, pretends to be the reborn Shukaido, but is really Shion. Haruhiko (the real Shukaido) is threatened by Rin into pretending *he's* Shion while Rin plots to destroy the moon base. Eventually losing his tight control over the situation, Rin wages a fierce psychic battle with Tamura and Mikuro, Haruhiko's allies. The fight leaves Rin with serious injuries...

Saved by the homeless Boone, and with medical care from Dr. Mori, Rin finally recovers to full health. Going by the name "Ginta," Rin waits patiently for a chance to strike back. Meanwhile, Alice's class goes to Kyoto on a school trip. She, Jinpachi and Issei visit Tamura, but he takes them to see Haruhiko! Haruhiko tells them the truth about Rin and his last

←

Please Save My Earth

Current Life [Earth]

ISSEI
A woman in his previous life, this beauty has fallen in love with Jinpachi, his best friend!

HARUHIKO
A psychic with weak health, he relies on Mr. Tamura for support and still suffers guilt for his previous life. A handsome one-quarter Indian! ♡

SAKURA
A girl from Yokohama who loves taking care of others. She seems aggressive but is really a sweetheart. ♡

DAISUKE
A born leader, he's organized the meetings of the seven moon dreamers at his home in Kawasaki.

JINPACHI
He's fallen in love with Alice, but so far it's been unrequited. He stands for truth, justice and the Japanese way!

RIN
A mischievous, psychic 8-year-old with a crush on Alice, he's out to get the enemy from his previous life, Haruhiko.

ALICE
A shy and quiet teenage girl. ♡ She understands the feelings of animals and plants, but is very timid and sentimental.

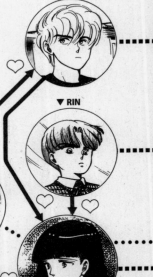

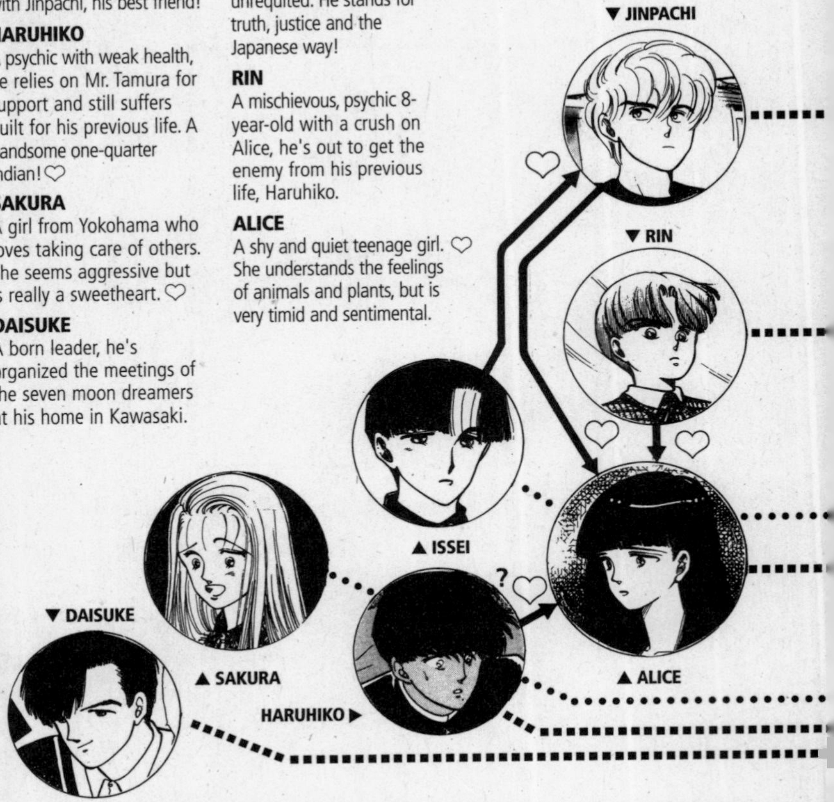

▼ JINPACHI

▼ RIN

▲ ISSEI

▼ DAISUKE

▲ SAKURA

HARUHIKO ▶

▲ ALICE

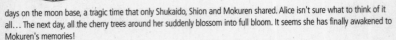

days on the moon base, a tragic time that only Shukaido, Shion and Mokuren shared. Alice isn't sure what to think of it all... The next day, all the cherry trees around her suddenly blossom into full bloom. It seems she has finally awakened to Mokuren's memories!

Mokuren's parents fell in love and renounced their Kiche, but their baby was born with a Kiche on her forehead. The child, Mokuren, is taken away to live in Paradise and forced to live a life she's not used to. Her resentment toward Kiches in general increases. One day, she happens upon a hologram of KK and is enthralled by it. It's a blue planet, just like the color of her father's eyes...

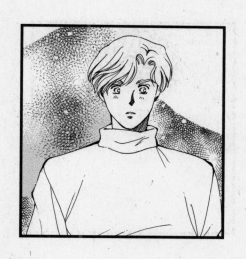
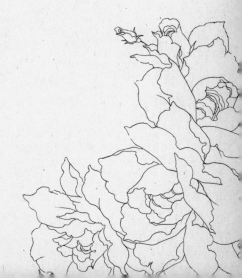

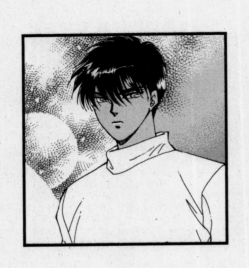
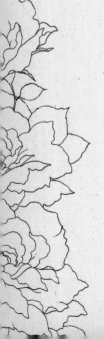

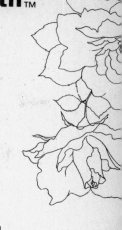

Please Save My Earth™

Vol. #16
Shôjo Edition

Story and Art by
Saki Hiwatari

Translation & English Adaptation Lillian Olsen
Touch-up & Lettering Primary Graphix
Graphic Design Amy Martin
Editor Carrie Shepherd

Managing Editor Annette Roman
Director of Production Noboru Watanabe
Vice President of Publishing Alvin Lu
Sr. Director of Acquisitions Rika Inouye
Vice President of Sales & Marketing Liza Coppola
Publisher Hyoe Narita

Printed in the U.S.A.
Published by VIZ Media, LLC
P.O. Box 77010
San Francisco, CA 94107

10 9 8 7 6 5 4 3 2 1
First printing, May 2006

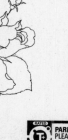

VIZ
MEDIA™

www.viz.com

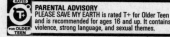

PARENTAL ADVISORY
PLEASE SAVE MY EARTH is rated T+ for Older Teen and is recommended for ages 16 and up. It contains violence, strong language, and sexual themes.

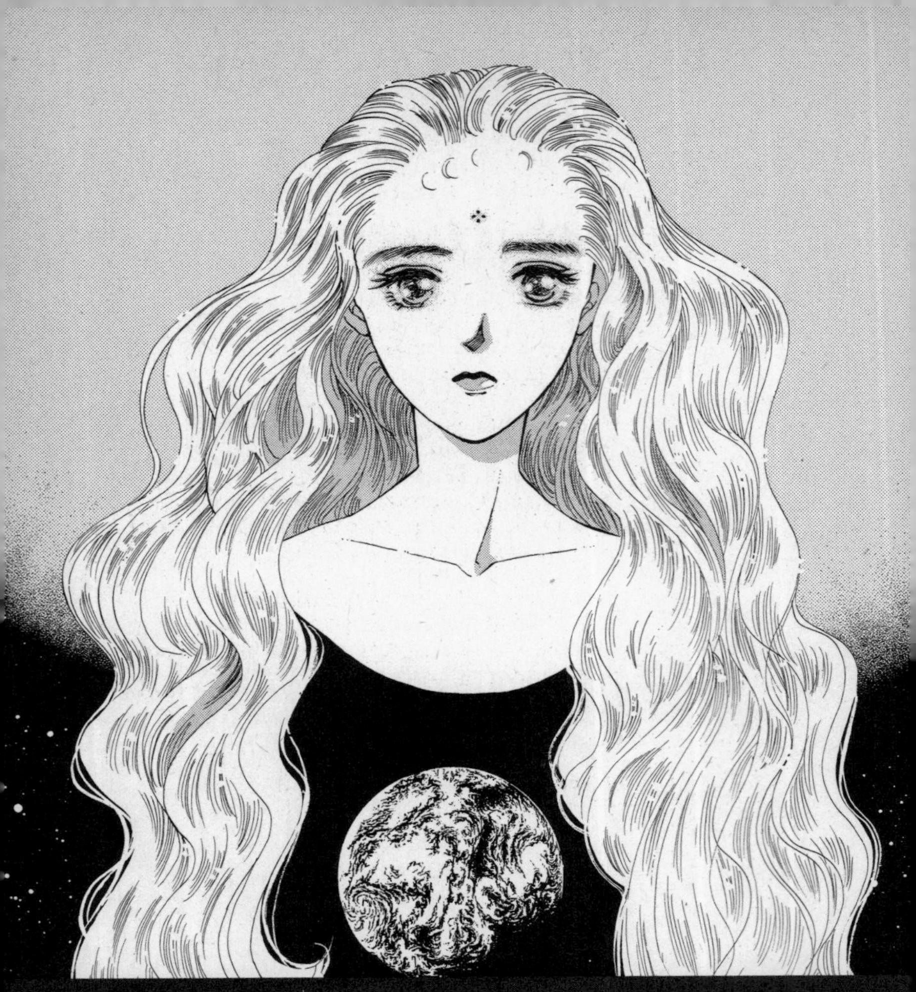

Please Save My Earth™

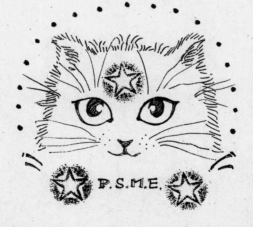

P.S.M.E.

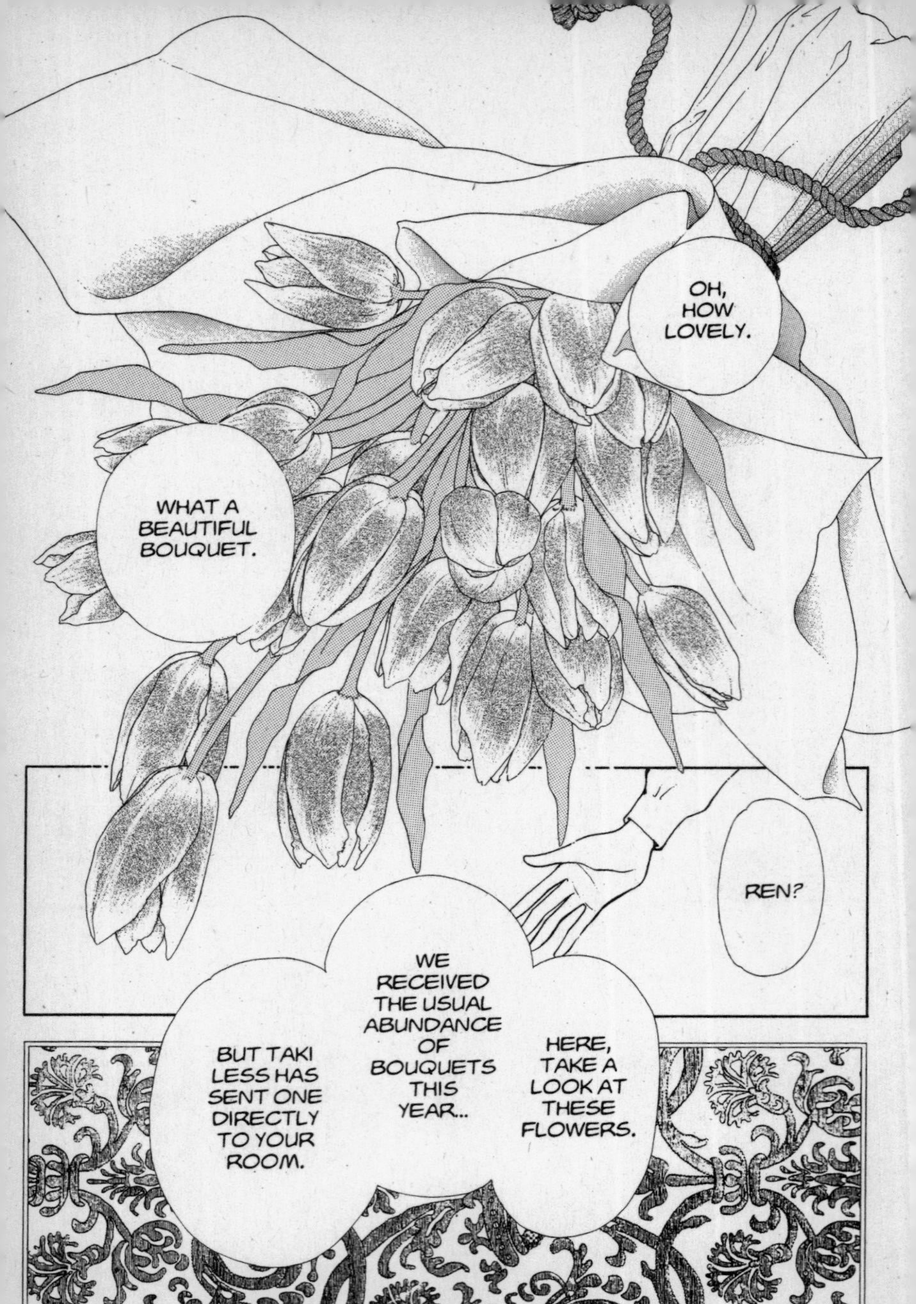
OH, HOW LOVELY.
WHAT A BEAUTIFUL BOUQUET.
REN?
HERE, TAKE A LOOK AT THESE FLOWERS.
WE RECEIVED THE USUAL ABUNDANCE OF BOUQUETS THIS YEAR...
BUT TAKI LESS HAS SENT ONE DIRECTLY TO YOUR ROOM.

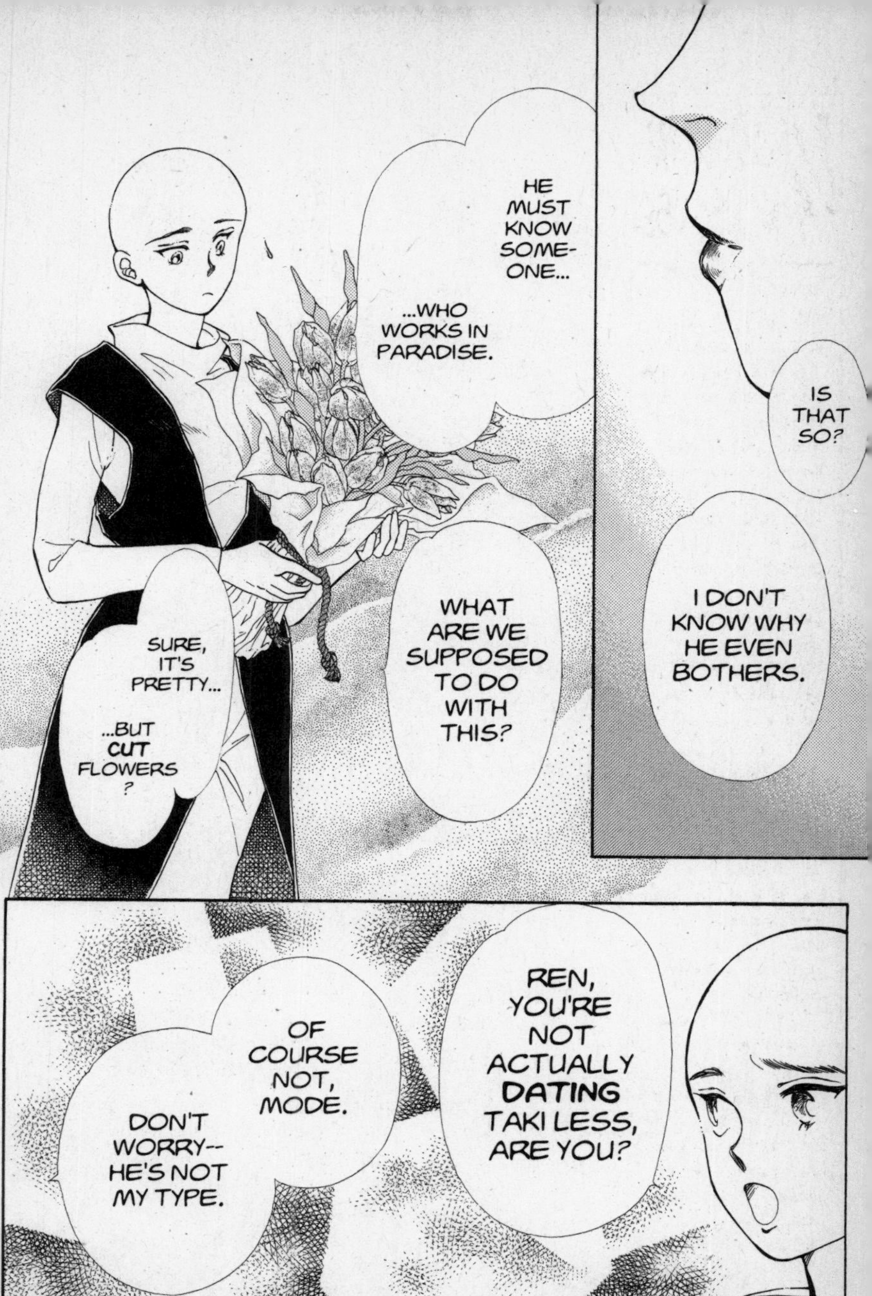
IS THAT SO?
I DON'T KNOW WHY HE EVEN BOTHERS.
HE MUST KNOW SOME-ONE...
...WHO WORKS IN PARADISE.
WHAT ARE WE SUPPOSED TO DO WITH THIS?
SURE, IT'S PRETTY...
...BUT CUT FLOWERS?
REN, YOU'RE NOT ACTUALLY DATING TAKI LESS, ARE YOU?
OF COURSE NOT, MODE.
DON'T WORRY-- HE'S NOT MY TYPE.

1/4 COLUMN NONSENSE

— PART 1 —

Hello! How have you been!?

Time flies. It'll be December already by the time this graphic novel is released... Wow, the year has blown by... I'm in a reflective mood.

I'm actually writing these columns in October. My deadlines will be getting tighter and tighter towards the end of the year, due to the holidays... Argh.

I wonder if I'll be able to survive December. Will I be able to get all my work done?

I don't think I can get any vacation until then...

The year seems to go by extremely fast when you're living deadline to deadline.

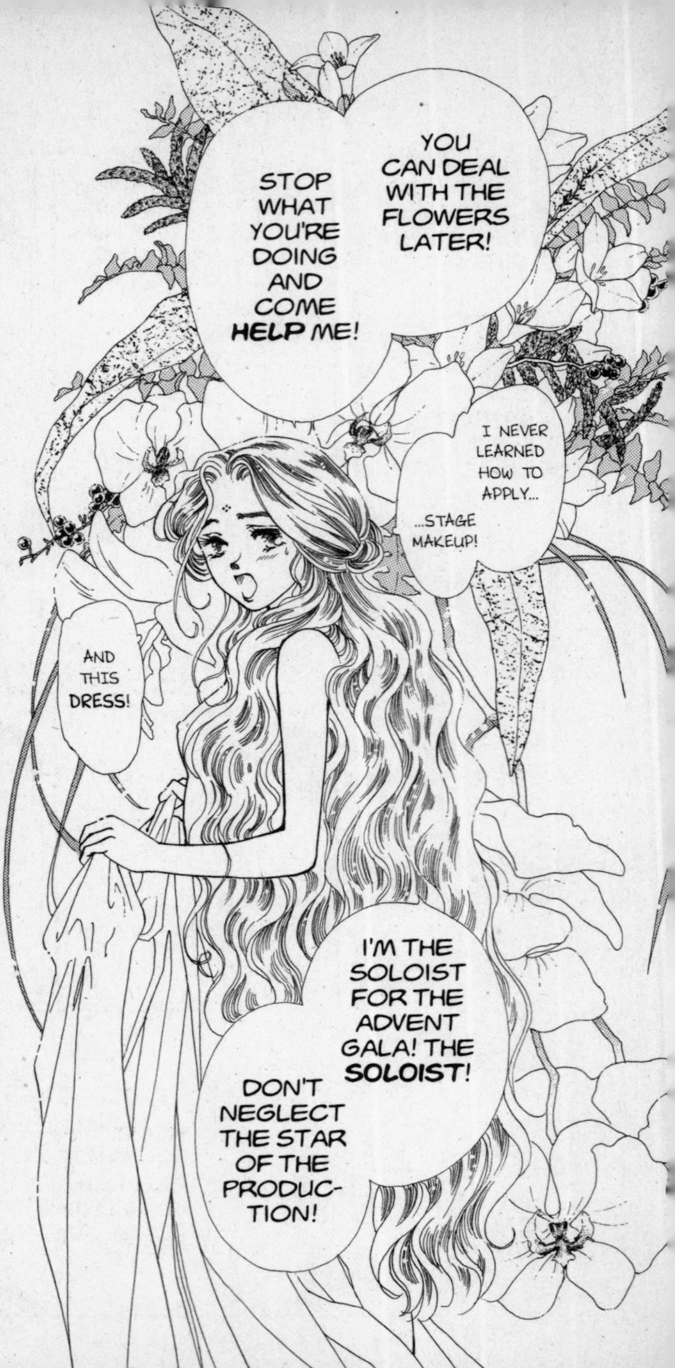
YOU CAN DEAL WITH THE FLOWERS LATER!
STOP WHAT YOU'RE DOING AND COME **HELP** ME!
I NEVER LEARNED HOW TO APPLY... ...STAGE MAKEUP!
AND THIS DRESS!
I'M THE SOLOIST FOR THE ADVENT GALA! THE **SOLOIST**!
DON'T NEGLECT THE STAR OF THE PRODUC-TION!

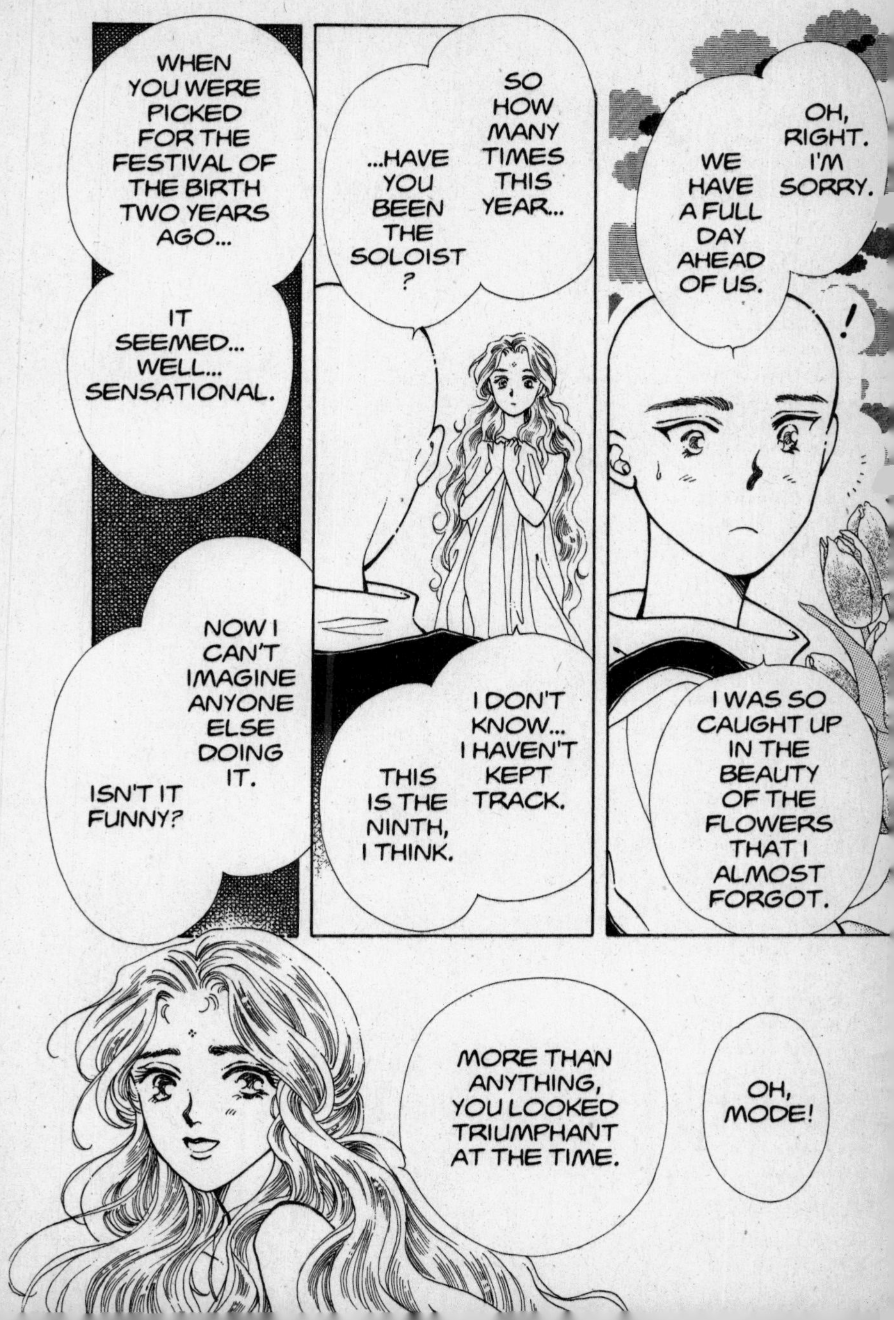
OH, RIGHT. I'M SORRY.
WE HAVE A FULL DAY AHEAD OF US.
!
I WAS SO CAUGHT UP IN THE BEAUTY OF THE FLOWERS THAT I ALMOST FORGOT.
SO HOW MANY TIMES THIS YEAR...
...HAVE YOU BEEN THE SOLOIST?
I DON'T KNOW... I HAVEN'T KEPT TRACK.
THIS IS THE NINTH, I THINK.
WHEN YOU WERE PICKED FOR THE FESTIVAL OF THE BIRTH TWO YEARS AGO...
IT SEEMED... WELL... SENSATIONAL.
NOW I CAN'T IMAGINE ANYONE ELSE DOING IT.
ISN'T IT FUNNY?
OH, MODE!
MORE THAN ANYTHING, YOU LOOKED TRIUMPHANT AT THE TIME.

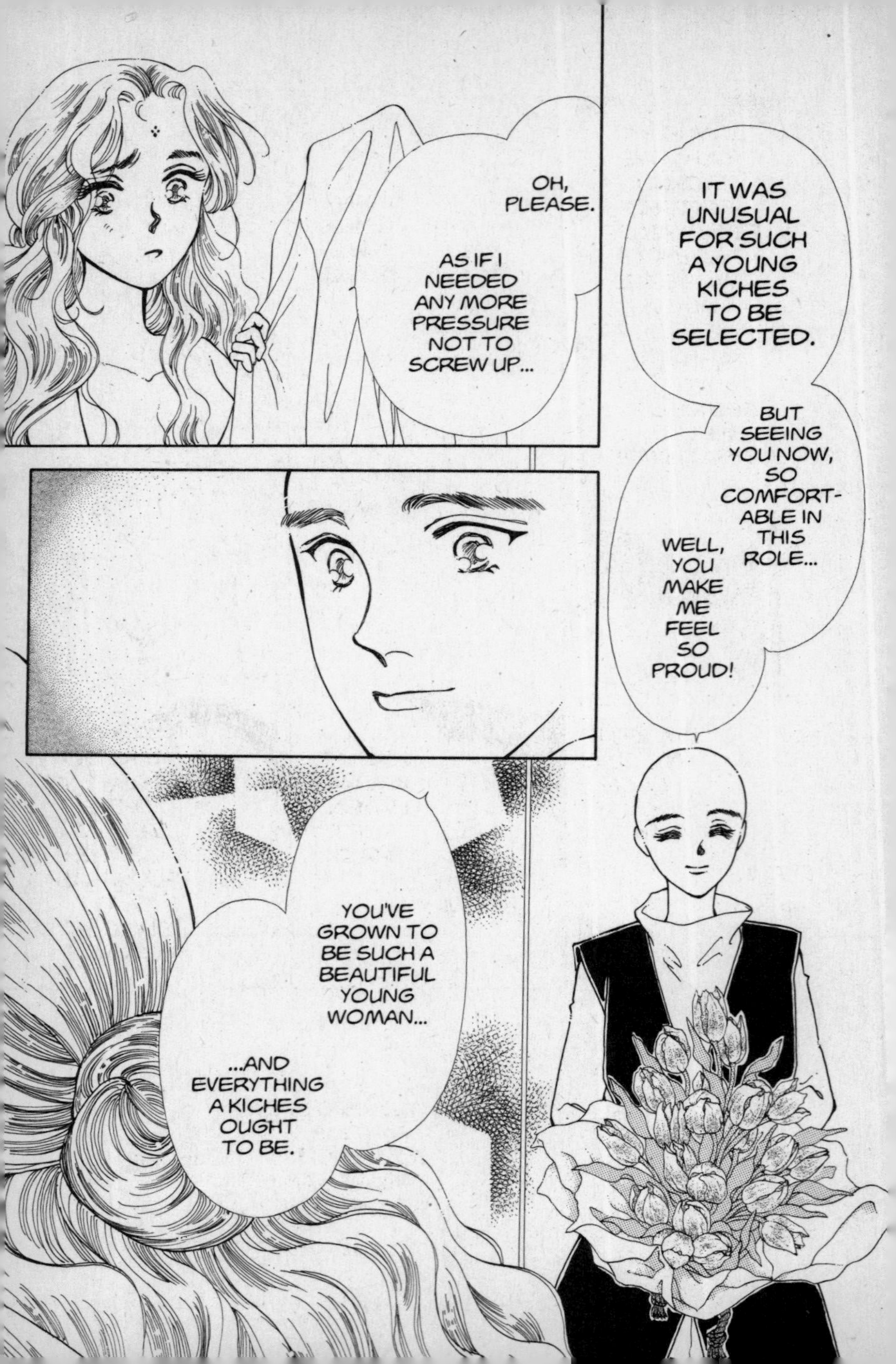
IT WAS UNUSUAL FOR SUCH A YOUNG KICHES TO BE SELECTED.
BUT SEEING YOU NOW, SO COMFORT-ABLE IN THIS ROLE...
WELL, YOU MAKE ME FEEL SO PROUD!
OH, PLEASE.
AS IF I NEEDED ANY MORE PRESSURE NOT TO SCREW UP...
YOU'VE GROWN TO BE SUCH A BEAUTIFUL YOUNG WOMAN...
...AND EVERYTHING A KICHES OUGHT TO BE.

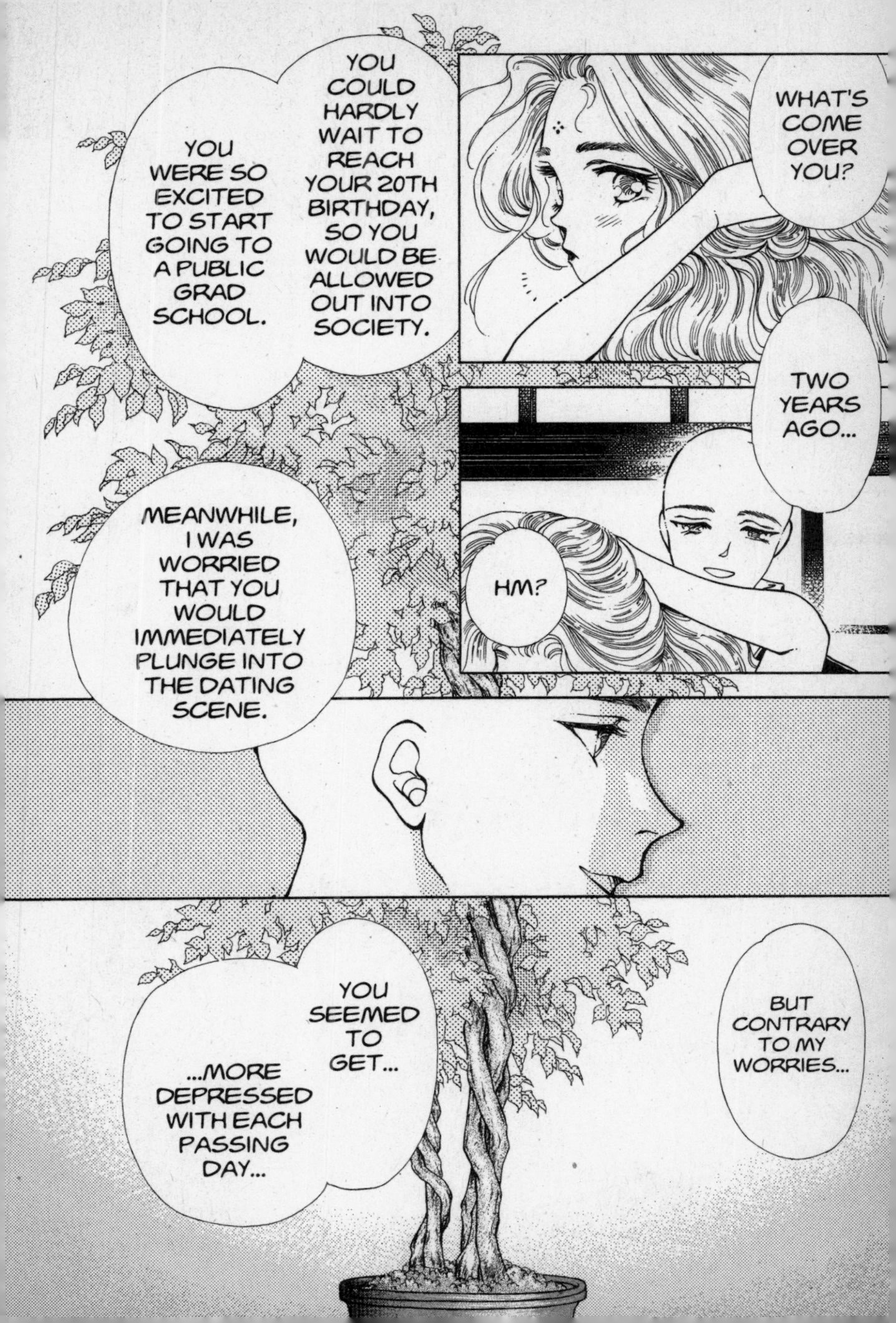
WHAT'S COME OVER YOU?
HM?
TWO YEARS AGO...
YOU WERE SO EXCITED TO START GOING TO A PUBLIC GRAD SCHOOL.
YOU COULD HARDLY WAIT TO REACH YOUR 20TH BIRTHDAY, SO YOU WOULD BE ALLOWED OUT INTO SOCIETY.
MEANWHILE, I WAS WORRIED THAT YOU WOULD IMMEDIATELY PLUNGE INTO THE DATING SCENE.
BUT CONTRARY TO MY WORRIES...
YOU SEEMED TO GET...
...MORE DEPRESSED WITH EACH PASSING DAY...

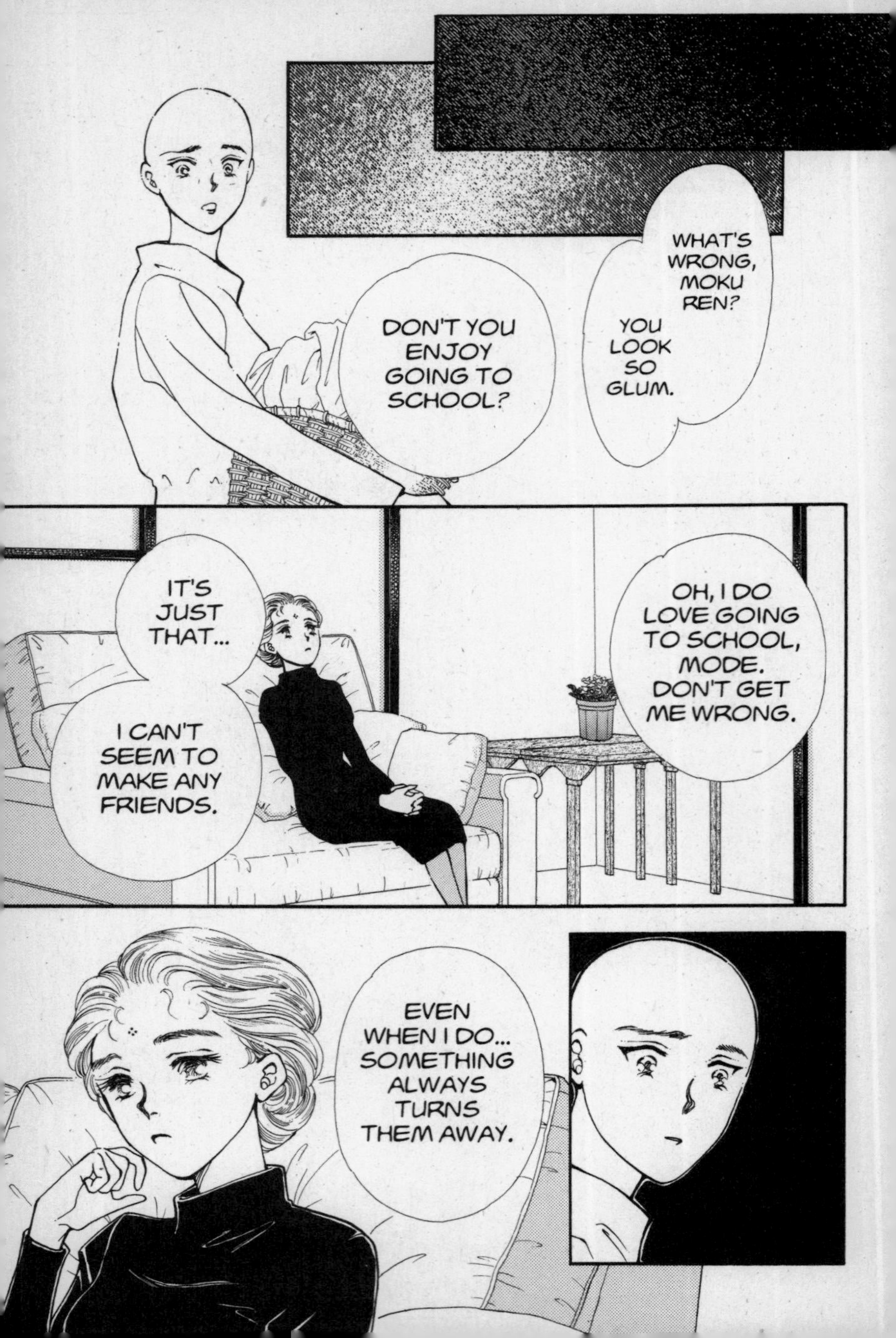
WHAT'S WRONG, MOKU REN? YOU LOOK SO GLUM.
DON'T YOU ENJOY GOING TO SCHOOL?
OH, I DO LOVE GOING TO SCHOOL, MODE. DON'T GET ME WRONG.
IT'S JUST THAT...
I CAN'T SEEM TO MAKE ANY FRIENDS.
EVEN WHEN I DO... SOMETHING ALWAYS TURNS THEM AWAY.

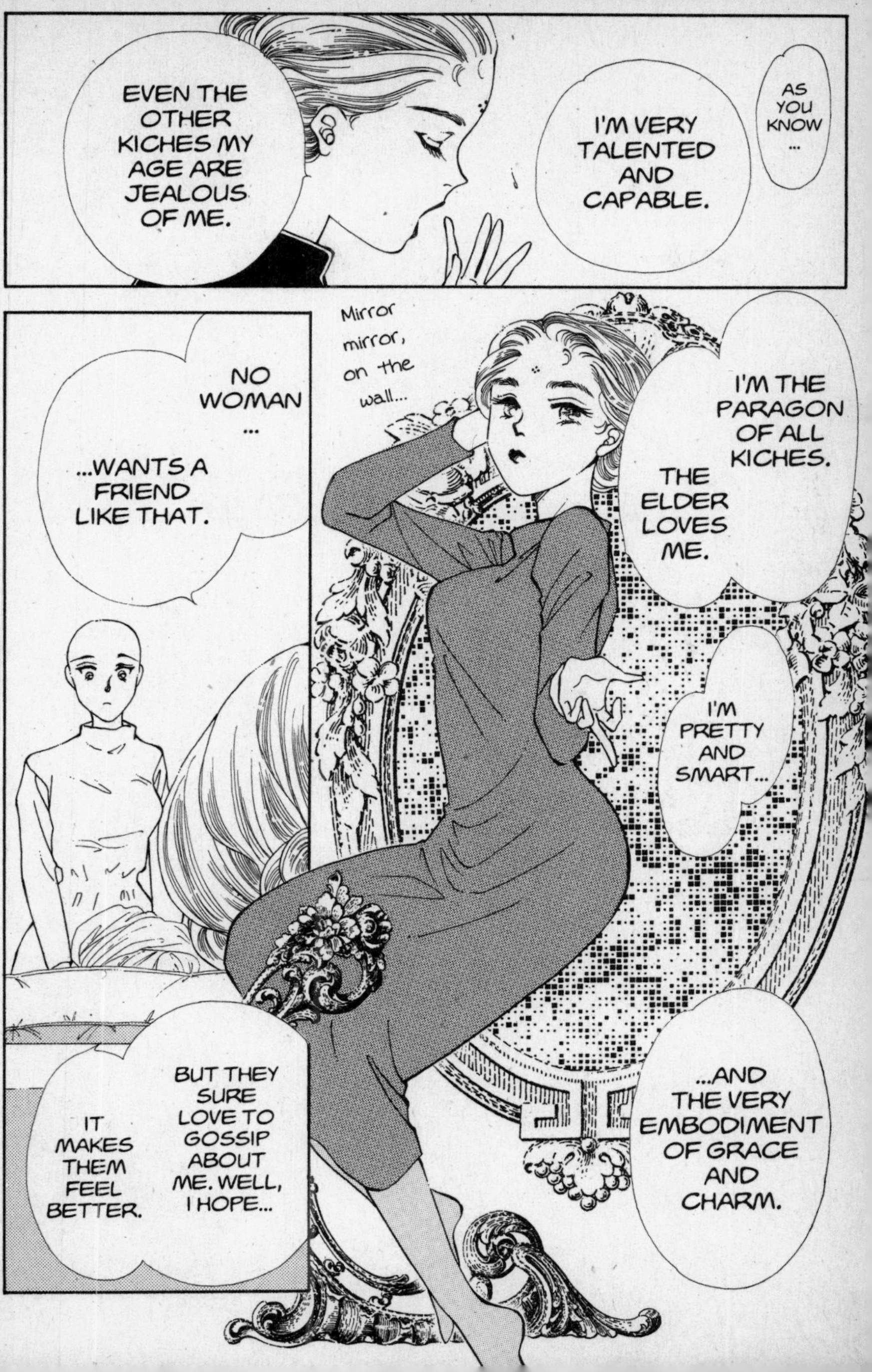
AS YOU KNOW...
I'M VERY TALENTED AND CAPABLE.
EVEN THE OTHER KICHES MY AGE ARE JEALOUS OF ME.
I'M THE PARAGON OF ALL KICHES.
THE ELDER LOVES ME.
Mirror mirror, on the wall...
I'M PRETTY AND SMART...
...AND THE VERY EMBODIMENT OF GRACE AND CHARM.
NO WOMAN...
...WANTS A FRIEND LIKE THAT.
BUT THEY SURE LOVE TO GOSSIP ABOUT ME. WELL, I HOPE...
IT MAKES THEM FEEL BETTER.

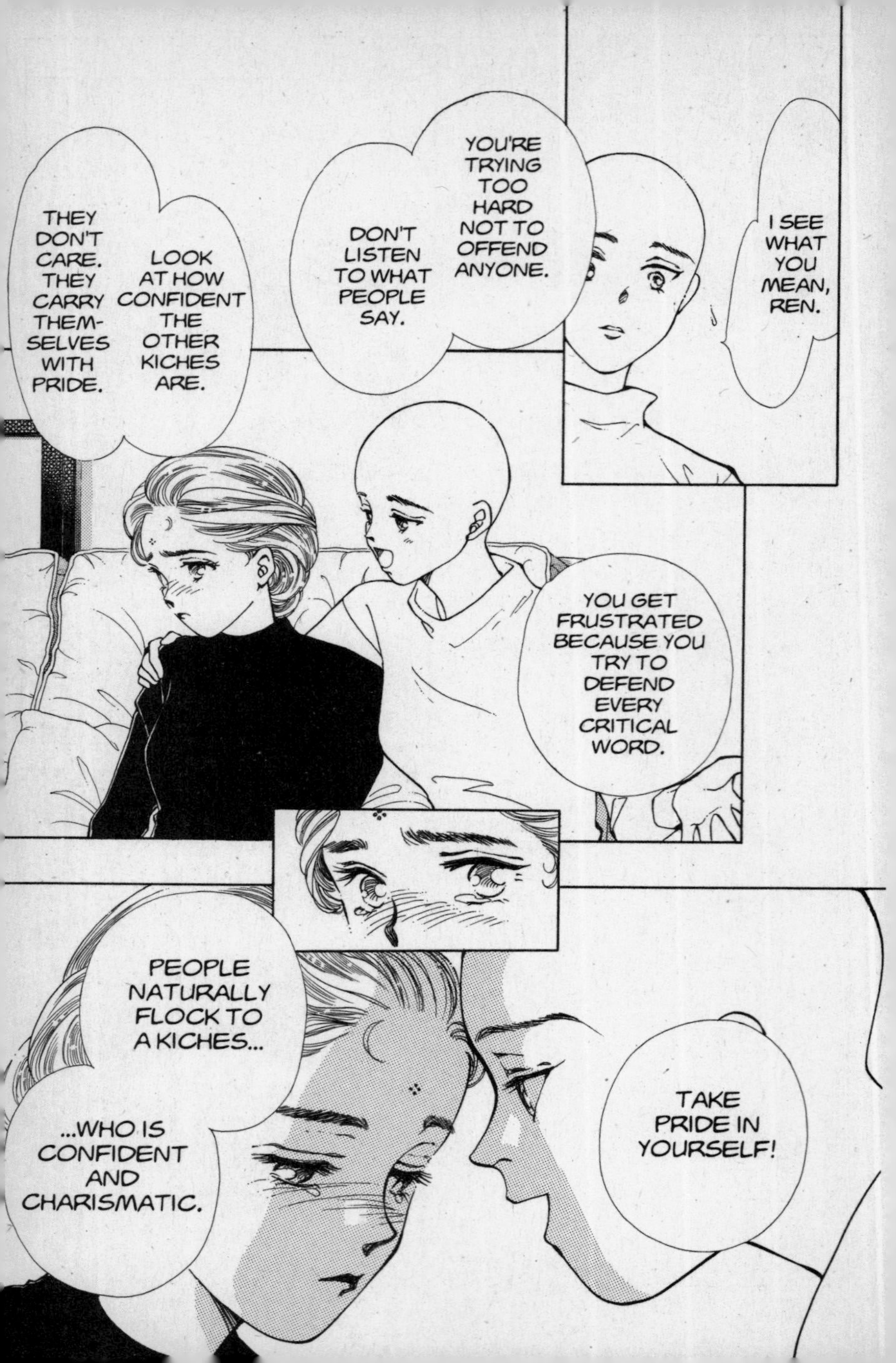
I SEE WHAT YOU MEAN, REN.
YOU'RE TRYING TOO HARD NOT TO OFFEND ANYONE.
DON'T LISTEN TO WHAT PEOPLE SAY.
LOOK AT HOW CONFIDENT THE OTHER KICHES ARE.
THEY DON'T CARE. THEY CARRY THEM-SELVES WITH PRIDE.
YOU GET FRUSTRATED BECAUSE YOU TRY TO DEFEND EVERY CRITICAL WORD.
TAKE PRIDE IN YOURSELF!
PEOPLE NATURALLY FLOCK TO A KICHES...
...WHO IS CONFIDENT AND CHARISMATIC.

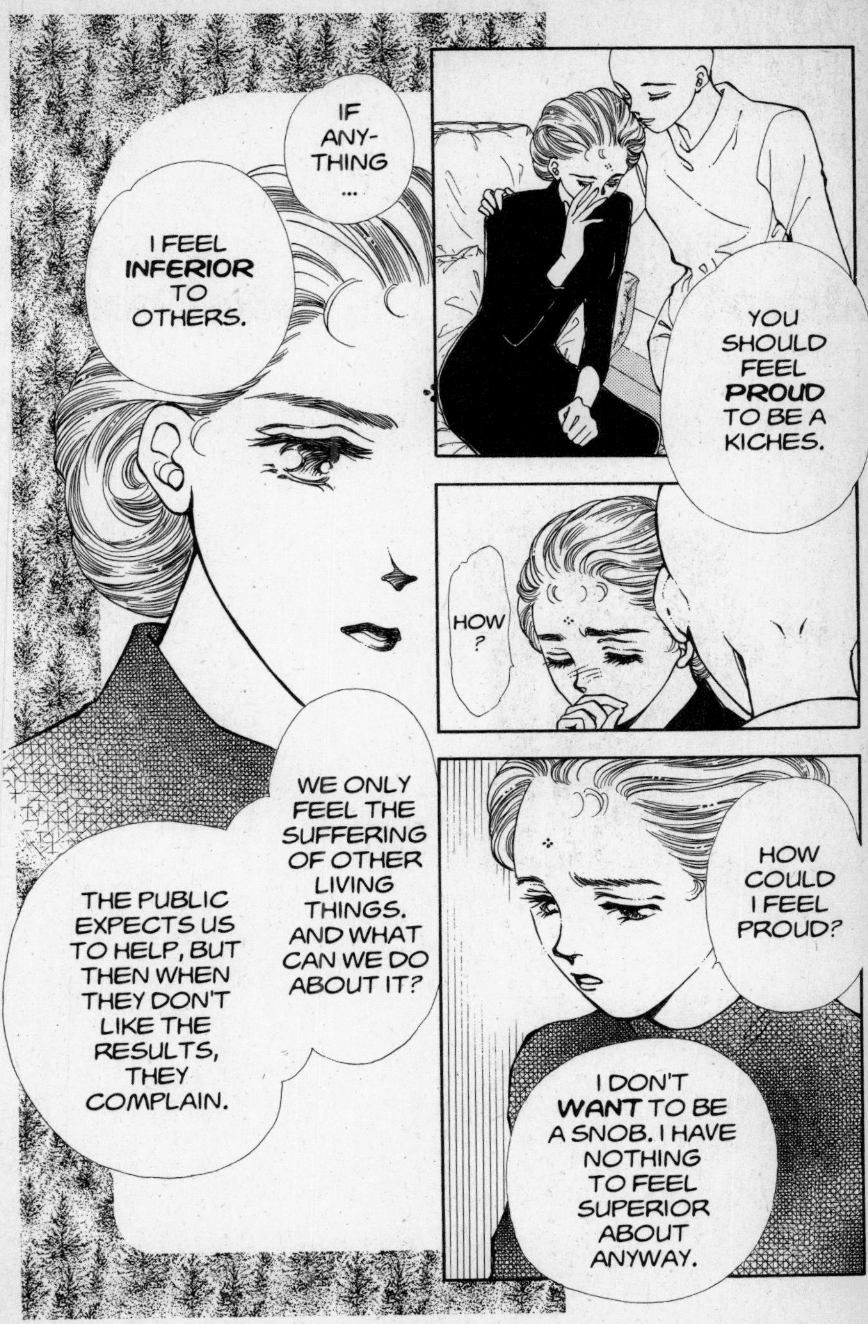
YOU SHOULD FEEL **PROUD** TO BE A KICHES.
HOW?
HOW COULD I FEEL PROUD?
I DON'T **WANT** TO BE A SNOB. I HAVE NOTHING TO FEEL SUPERIOR ABOUT ANYWAY.
IF ANYTHING...
I FEEL **INFERIOR** TO OTHERS.
WE ONLY FEEL THE SUFFERING OF OTHER LIVING THINGS. AND WHAT CAN WE DO ABOUT IT?
THE PUBLIC EXPECTS US TO HELP, BUT THEN WHEN THEY DON'T LIKE THE RESULTS, THEY COMPLAIN.

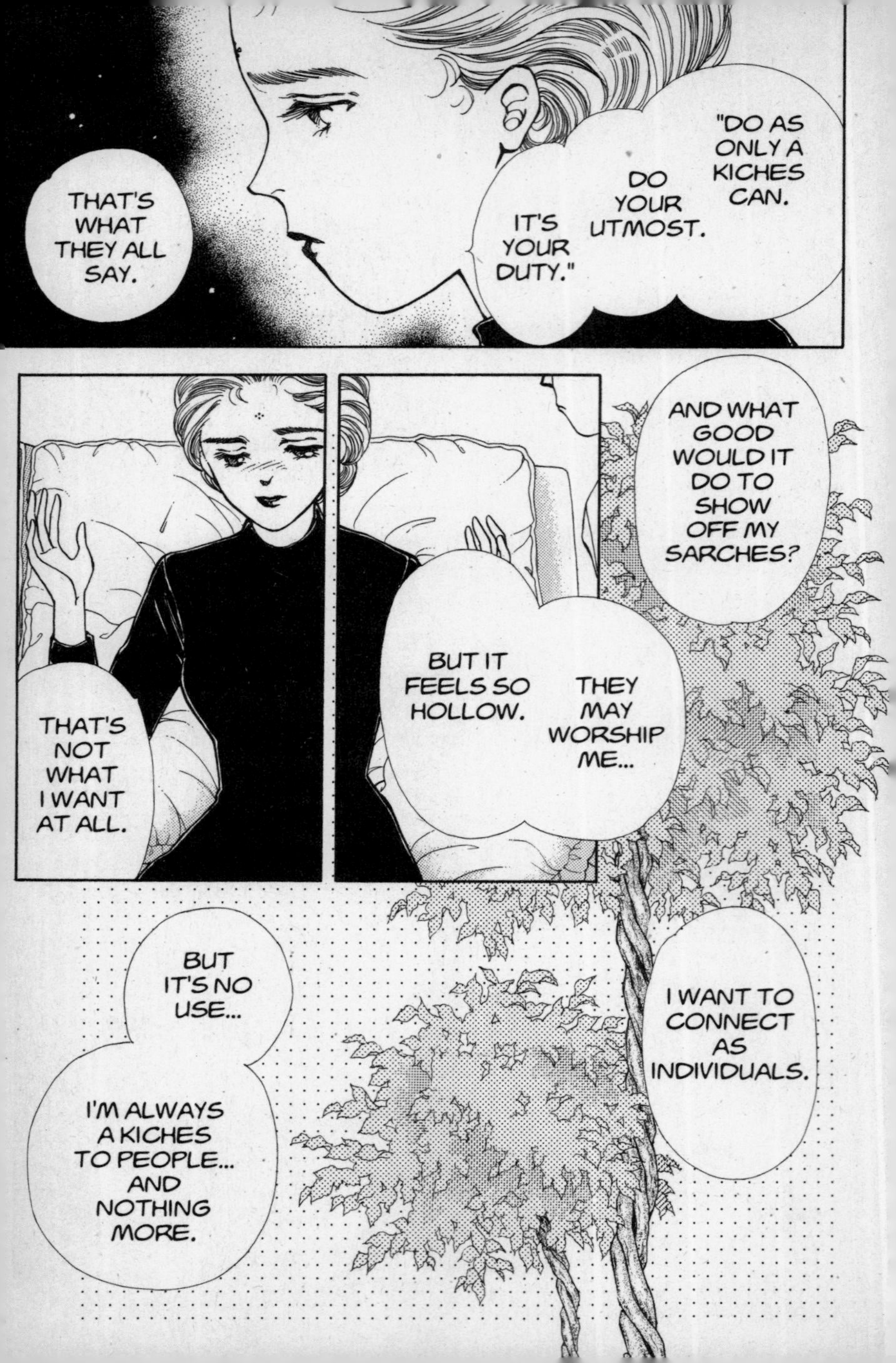
"DO AS ONLY A KICHES CAN.
DO YOUR UTMOST.
IT'S YOUR DUTY."
THAT'S WHAT THEY ALL SAY.
AND WHAT GOOD WOULD IT DO TO SHOW OFF MY SARCHES?
THEY MAY WORSHIP ME...
BUT IT FEELS SO HOLLOW.
THAT'S NOT WHAT I WANT AT ALL.
I WANT TO CONNECT AS INDIVIDUALS.
BUT IT'S NO USE...
I'M ALWAYS A KICHES TO PEOPLE... AND NOTHING MORE.

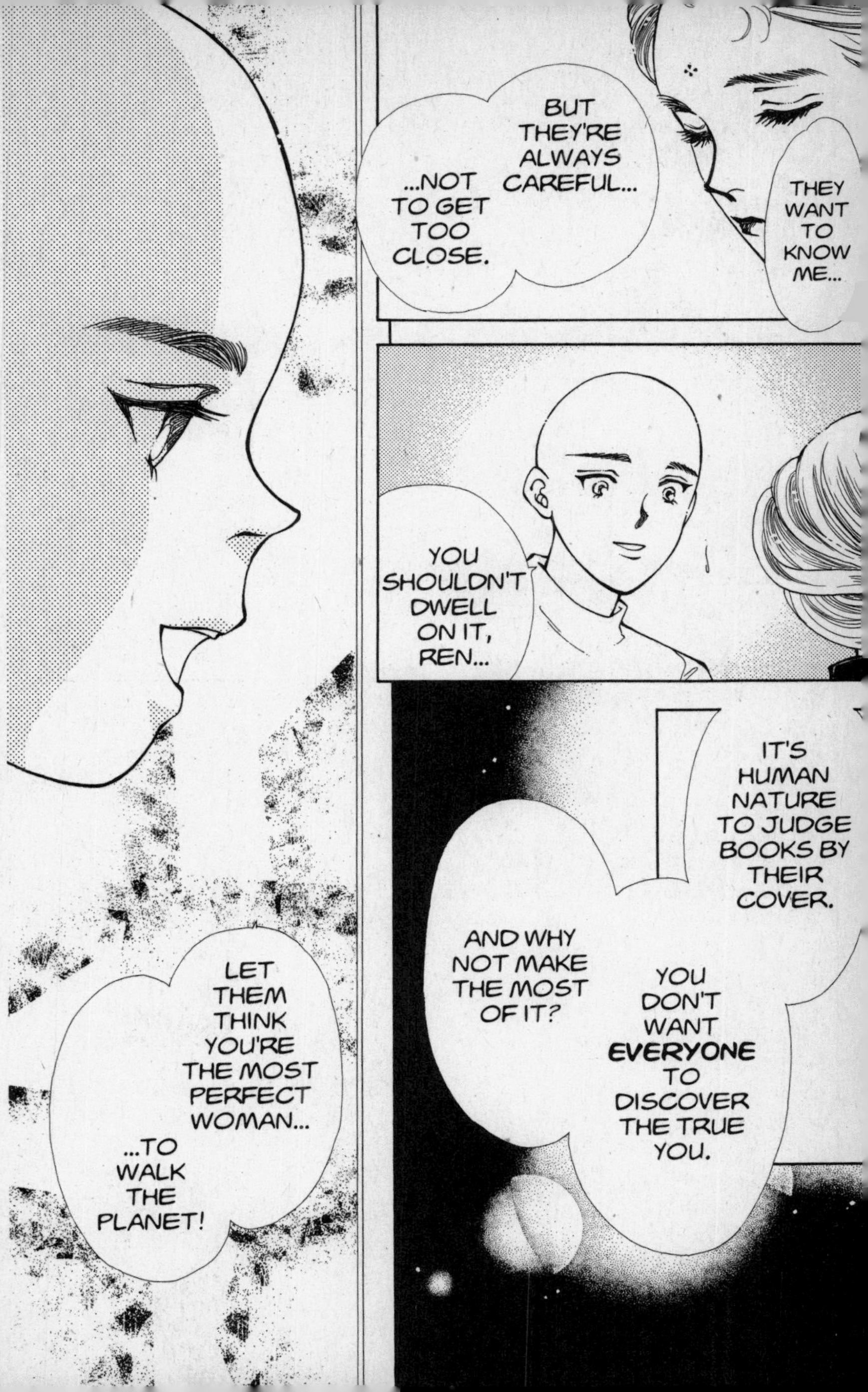
THEY WANT TO KNOW ME...
BUT THEY'RE ALWAYS CAREFUL...
...NOT TO GET TOO CLOSE.
YOU SHOULDN'T DWELL ON IT, REN...
IT'S HUMAN NATURE TO JUDGE BOOKS BY THEIR COVER.
YOU DON'T WANT **EVERYONE** TO DISCOVER THE TRUE YOU.
AND WHY NOT MAKE THE MOST OF IT?
LET THEM THINK YOU'RE THE MOST PERFECT WOMAN...
...TO WALK THE PLANET!

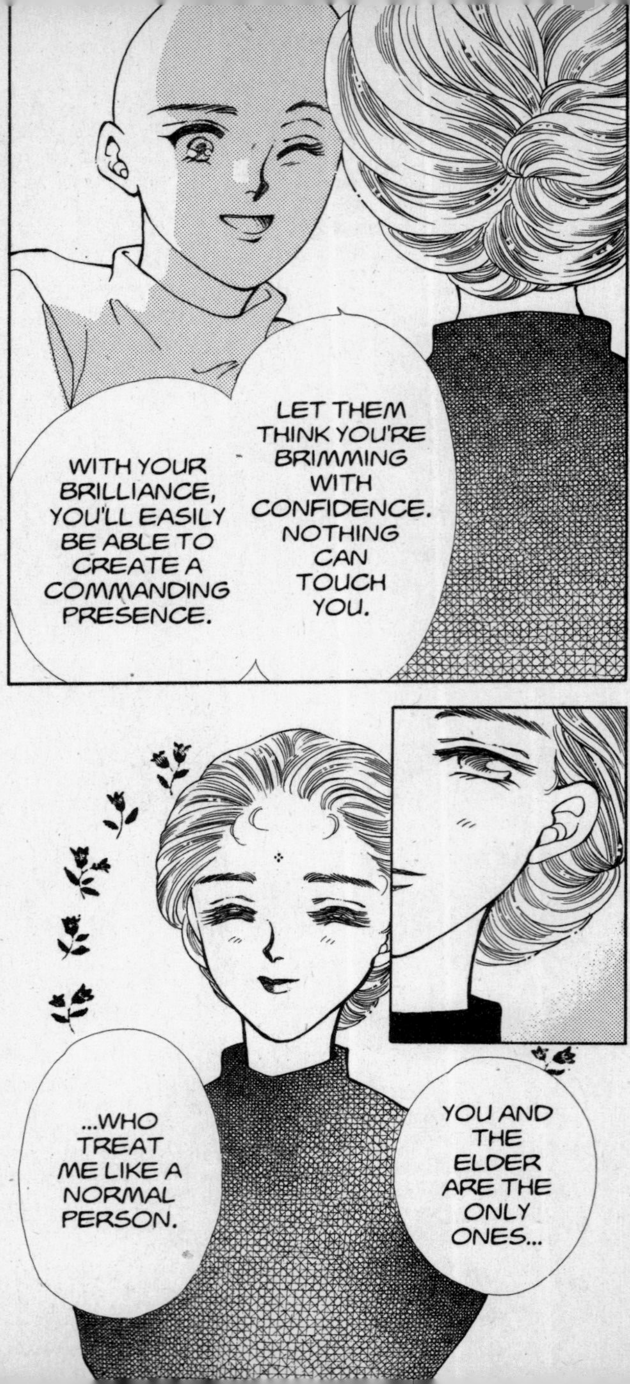
LET THEM THINK YOU'RE BRIMMING WITH CONFIDENCE. NOTHING CAN TOUCH YOU.
WITH YOUR BRILLIANCE, YOU'LL EASILY BE ABLE TO CREATE A COMMANDING PRESENCE.
YOU AND THE ELDER ARE THE ONLY ONES...
...WHO TREAT ME LIKE A NORMAL PERSON.

1/4 COLUMN NONSENSE

PART 2

I did a mini-feature on reader responses to the topic of dieting in vol. 15, and I got more responses to that! Thanks for writing!

One person raised this counterpoint: "Ms. Hiwatari, you thoroughly denounced the girl who wrote about not drinking any water after taking a hot bath at night. Now I feel sorry for her... She's not totally wrong. It's better for your metabolism not to take liquids for two hours after a bath, and you'll be able to lose weight! Though it's not good to deprive yourself of a drink when you really want and need it..."

continued in part 3

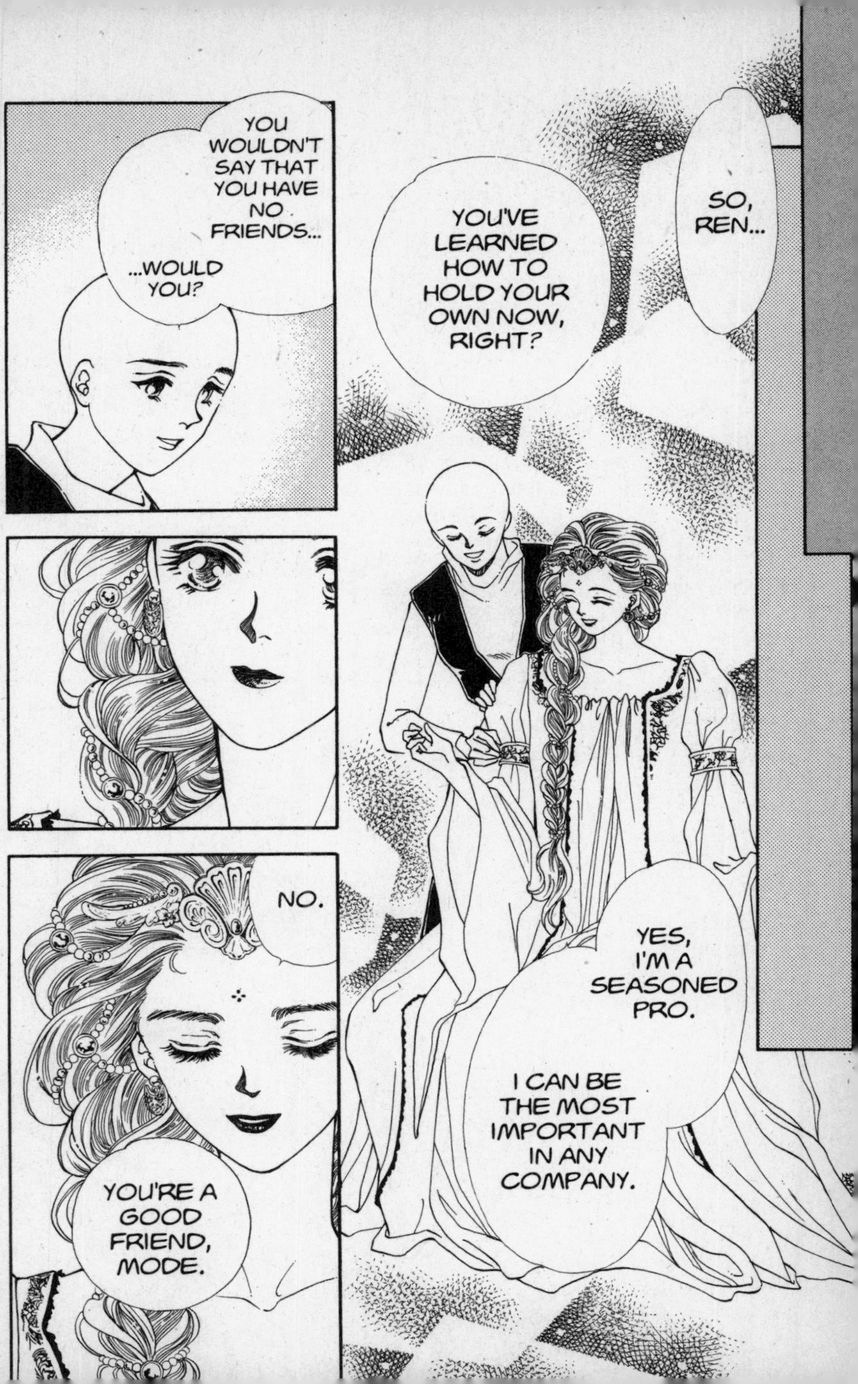
SO, REN...
YOU'VE LEARNED HOW TO HOLD YOUR OWN NOW, RIGHT?
YES, I'M A SEASONED PRO.
I CAN BE THE MOST IMPORTANT IN ANY COMPANY.
YOU WOULDN'T SAY THAT YOU HAVE NO FRIENDS...
...WOULD YOU?
NO.
YOU'RE A GOOD FRIEND, MODE.

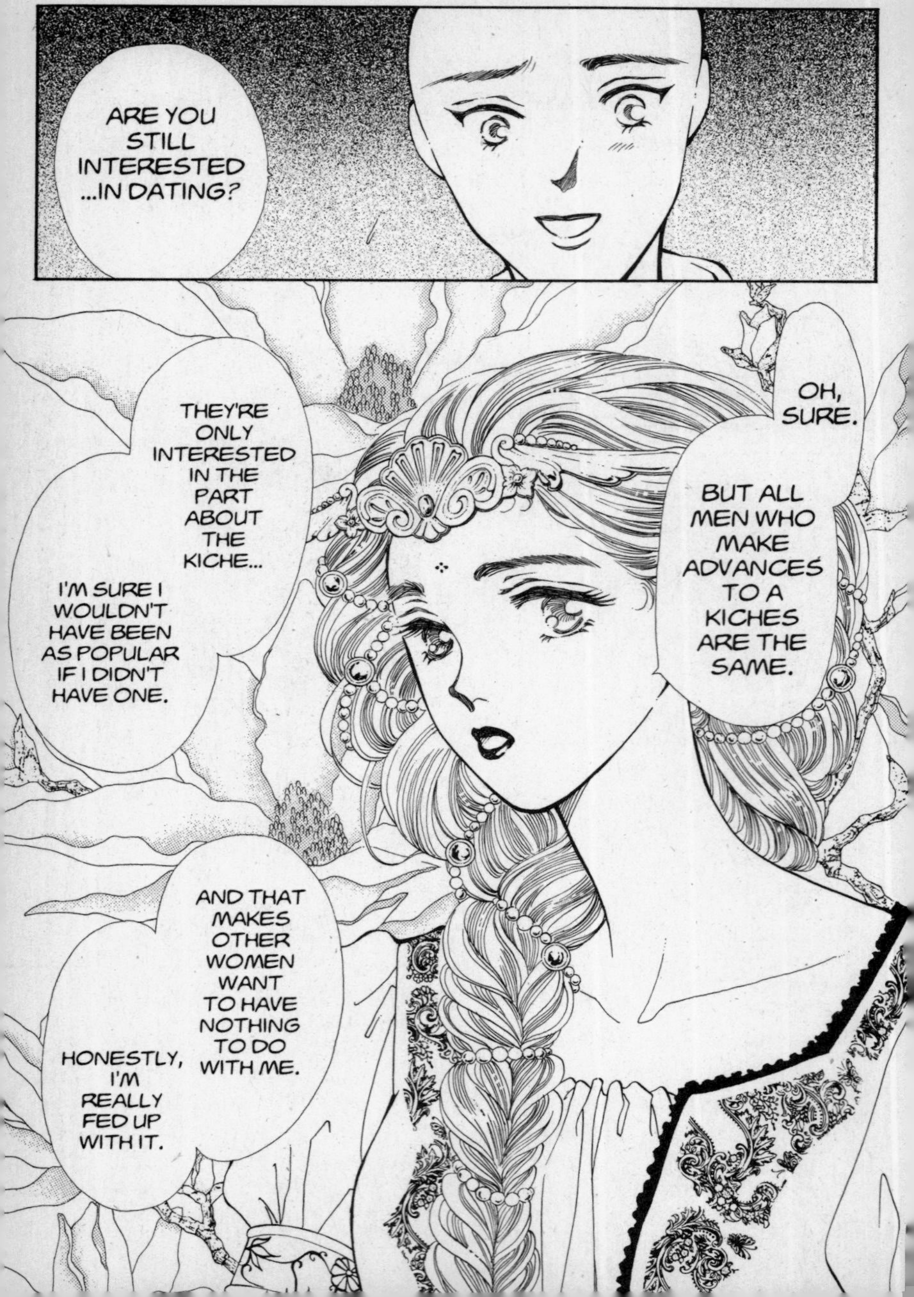
ARE YOU STILL INTERESTED ...IN DATING?
OH, SURE.
BUT ALL MEN WHO MAKE ADVANCES TO A KICHES ARE THE SAME.
THEY'RE ONLY INTERESTED IN THE PART ABOUT THE KICHE...
I'M SURE I WOULDN'T HAVE BEEN AS POPULAR IF I DIDN'T HAVE ONE.
AND THAT MAKES OTHER WOMEN WANT TO HAVE NOTHING TO DO WITH ME.
HONESTLY, I'M REALLY FED UP WITH IT.

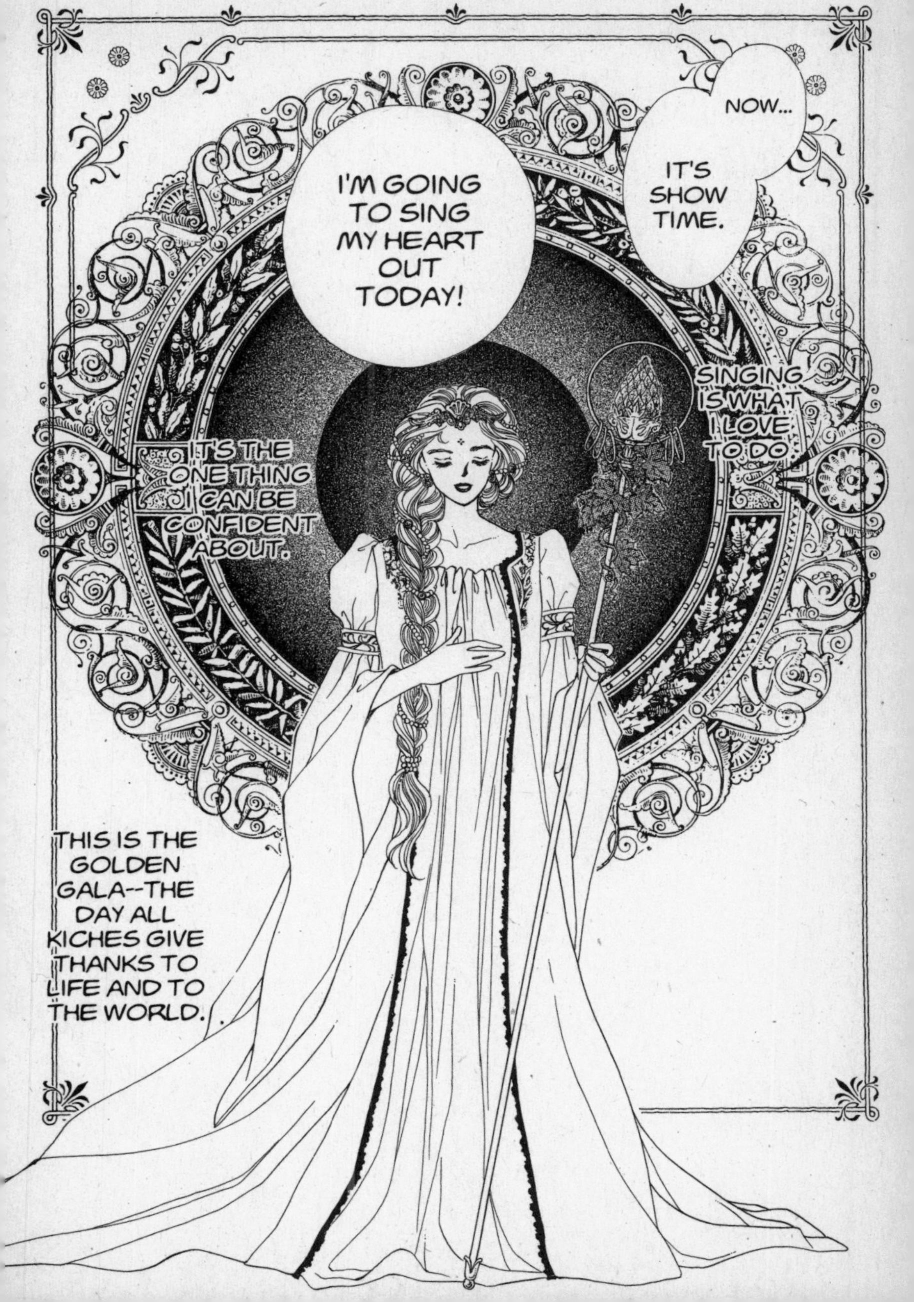
NOW...
IT'S SHOW TIME.
I'M GOING TO SING MY HEART OUT TODAY!
SINGING IS WHAT I LOVE TO DO.
IT'S THE ONE THING I CAN BE CONFIDENT ABOUT.
THIS IS THE GOLDEN GALA--THE DAY ALL KICHES GIVE THANKS TO LIFE AND TO THE WORLD.

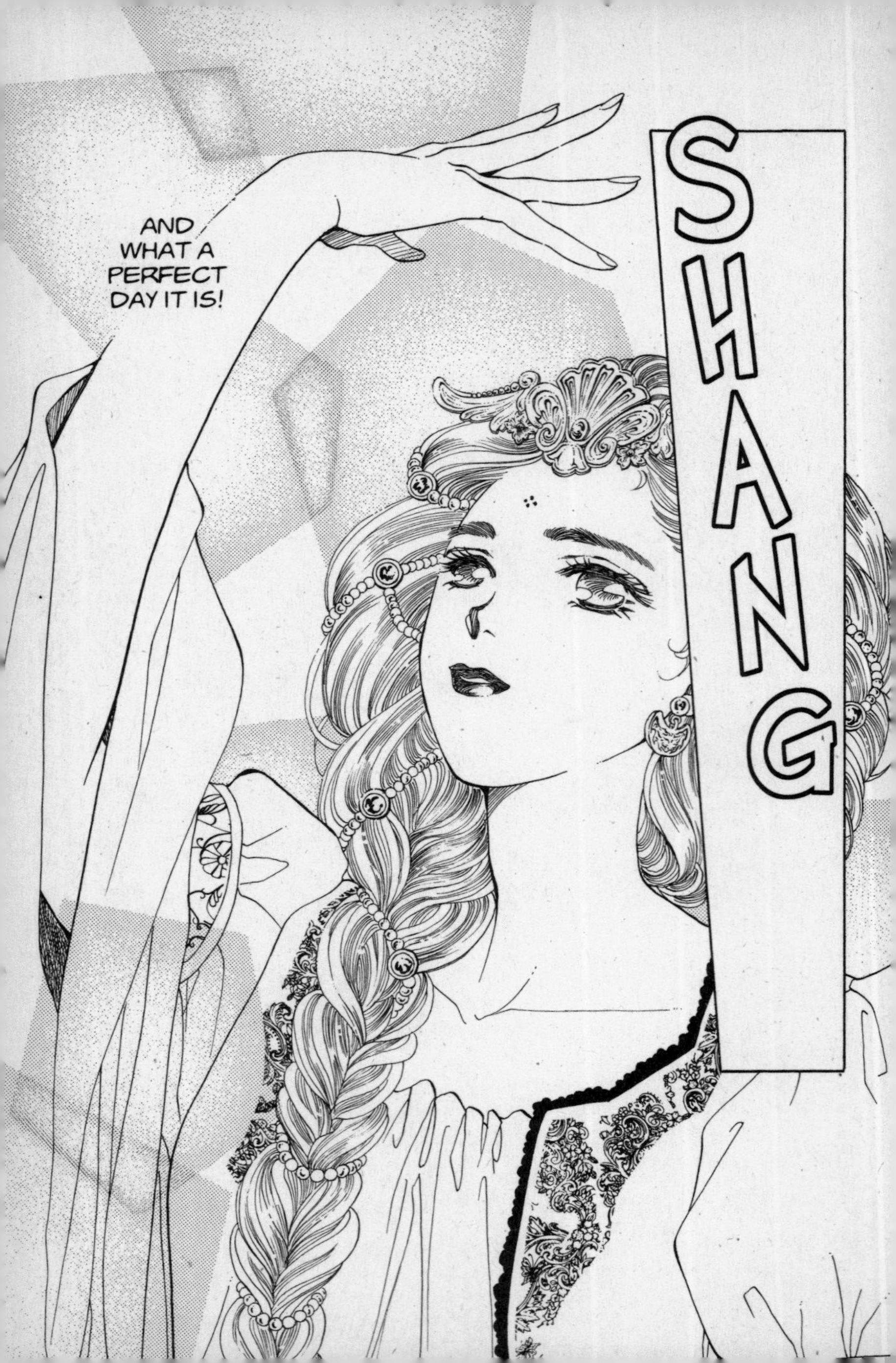
SHANG
AND WHAT A PERFECT DAY IT IS!

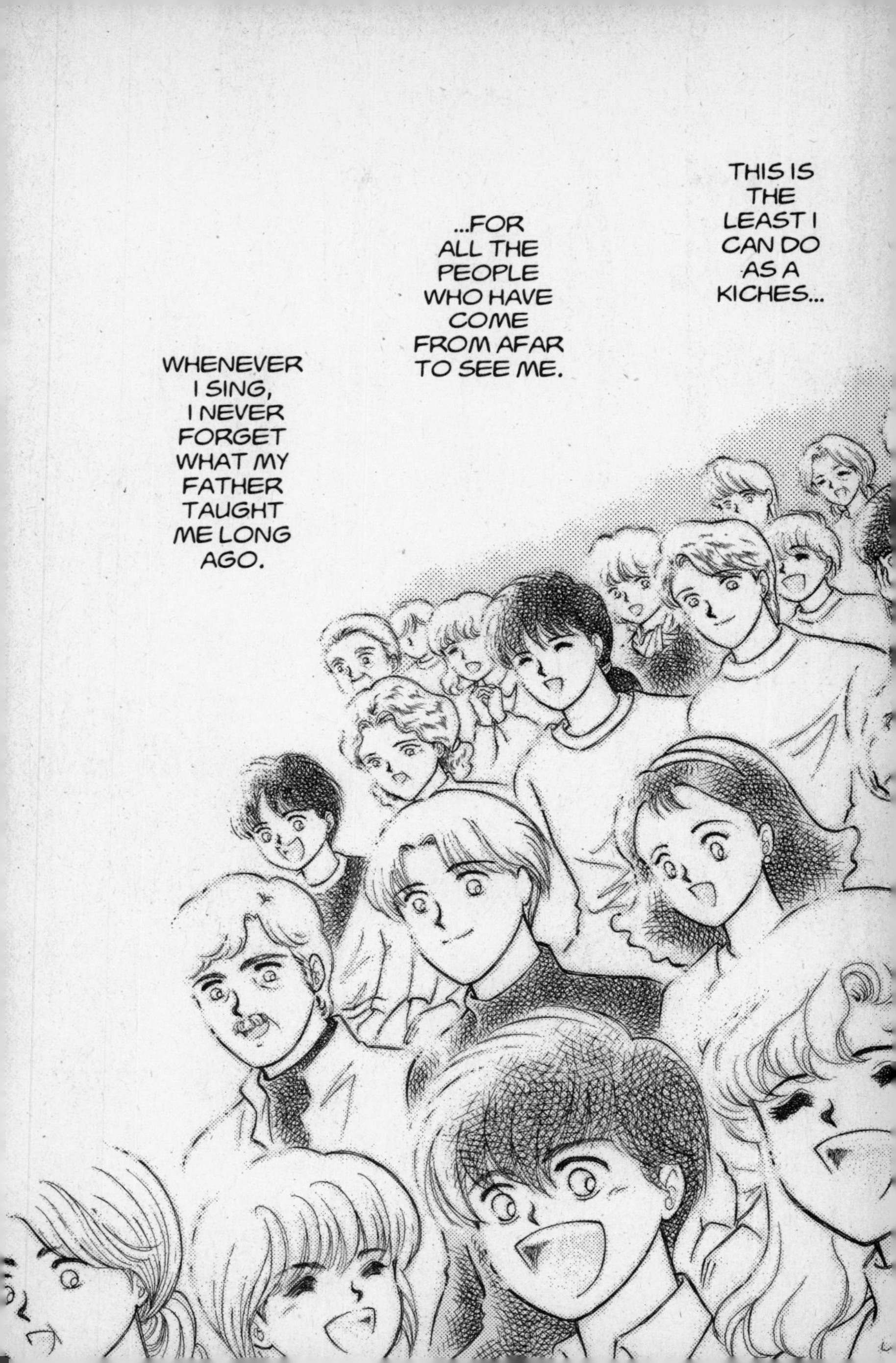
THIS IS THE LEAST I CAN DO AS A KICHES...
...FOR ALL THE PEOPLE WHO HAVE COME FROM AFAR TO SEE ME.
WHENEVER I SING, I NEVER FORGET WHAT MY FATHER TAUGHT ME LONG AGO.

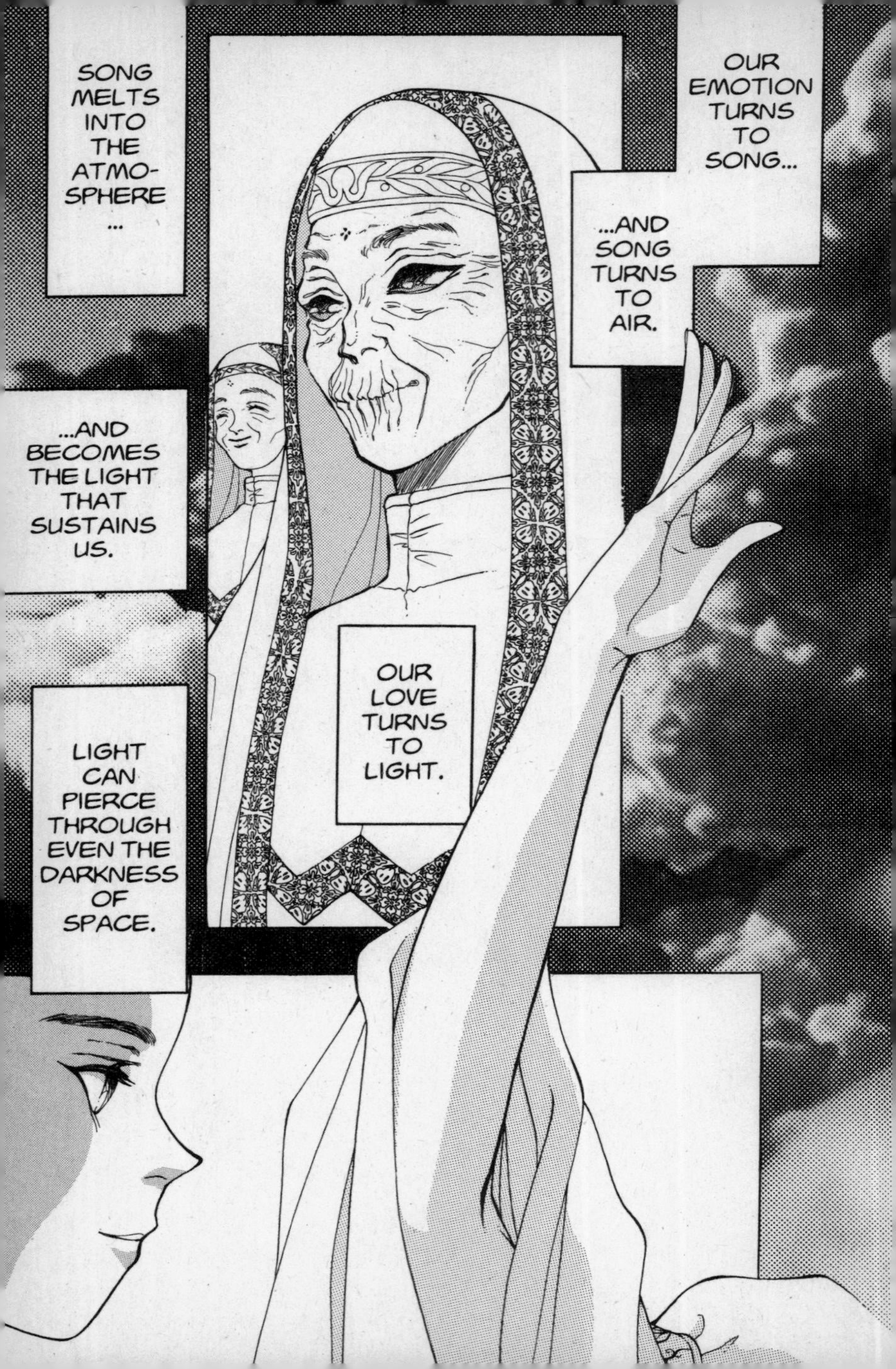
OUR EMOTION TURNS TO SONG...
...AND SONG TURNS TO AIR.
SONG MELTS INTO THE ATMO-SPHERE ...
...AND BECOMES THE LIGHT THAT SUSTAINS US.
OUR LOVE TURNS TO LIGHT.
LIGHT CAN PIERCE THROUGH EVEN THE DARKNESS OF SPACE.

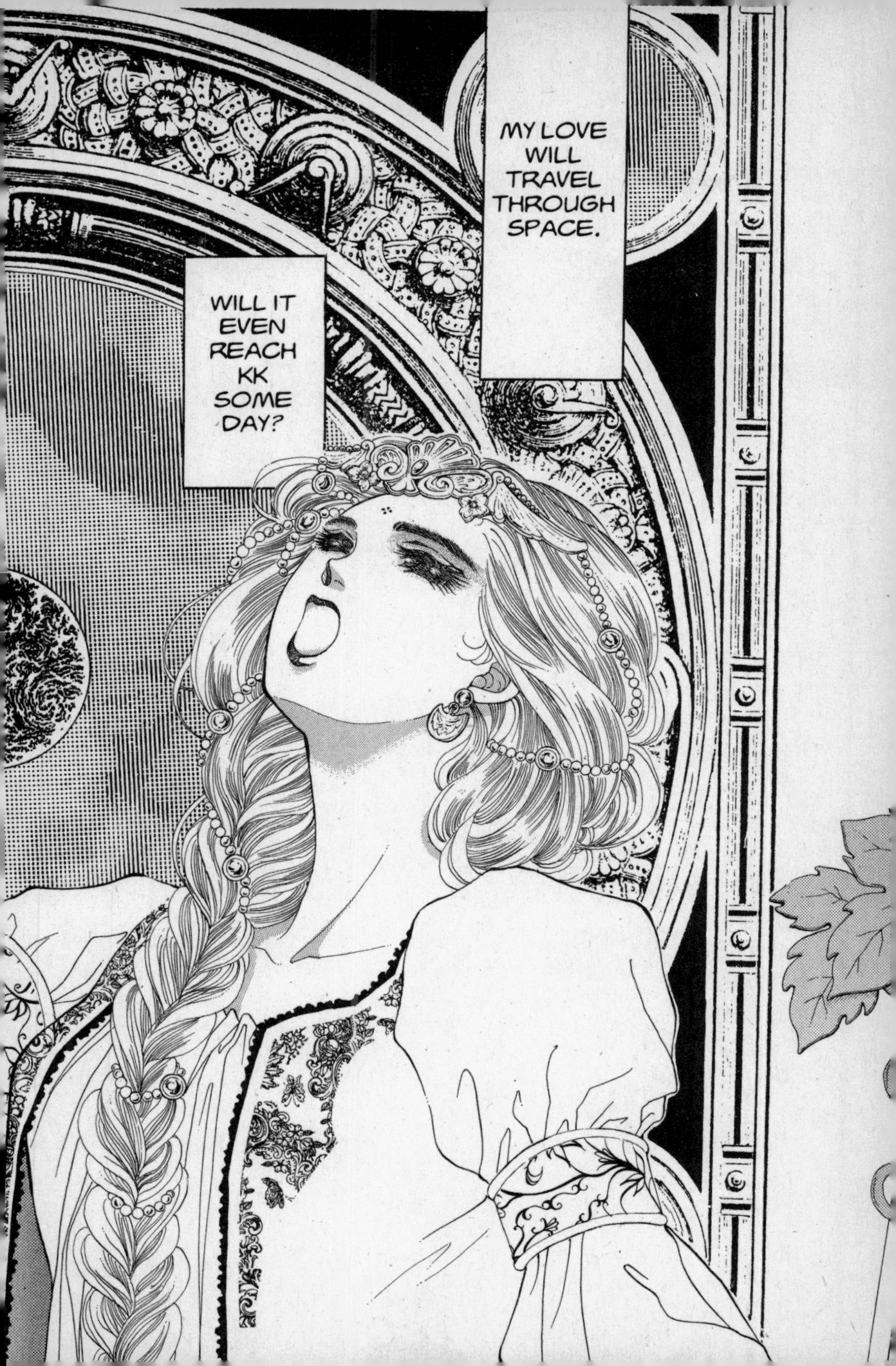
MY LOVE WILL TRAVEL THROUGH SPACE.
WILL IT EVEN REACH KK SOME DAY?

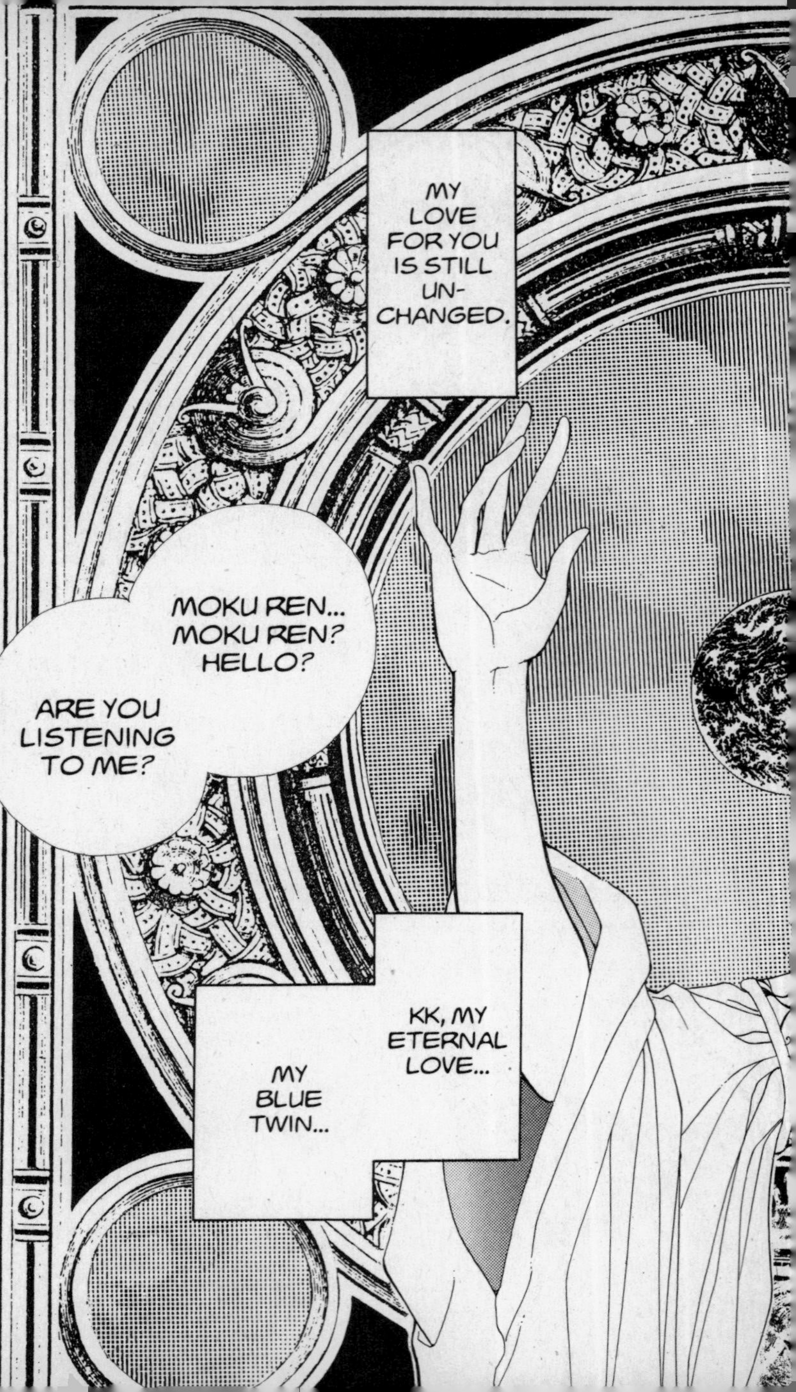
MY LOVE FOR YOU IS STILL UN-CHANGED.
MOKU REN... MOKU REN? HELLO?
ARE YOU LISTENING TO ME?
KK, MY ETERNAL LOVE...
MY BLUE TWIN...

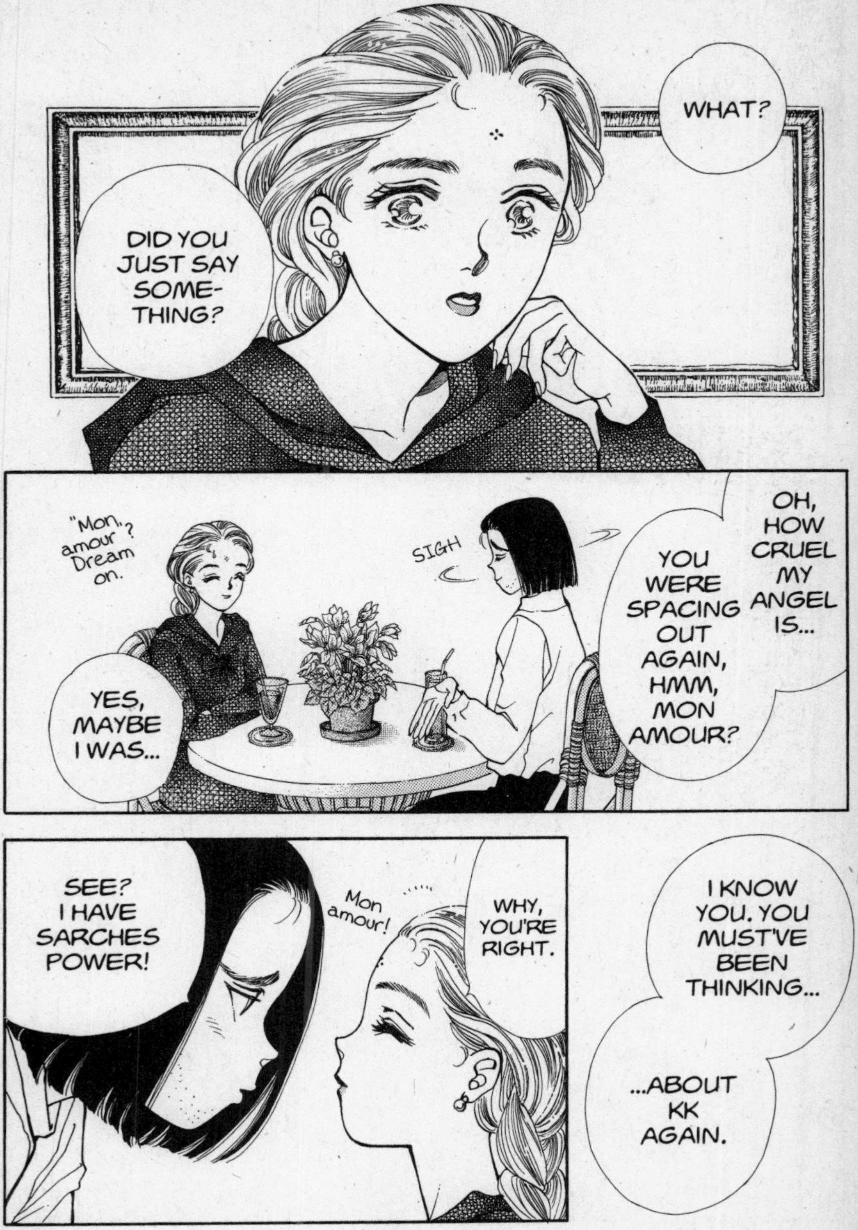
WHAT?
DID YOU JUST SAY SOME-THING?
OH, HOW CRUEL MY ANGEL IS...
YOU WERE SPACING OUT AGAIN, HMM, MON AMOUR?
SIGH
"Mon amour"? Dream on.
YES, MAYBE I WAS...
I KNOW YOU. YOU MUST'VE BEEN THINKING...
...ABOUT KK AGAIN.
WHY, YOU'RE RIGHT.
Mon amour!
SEE? I HAVE SARCHES POWER!

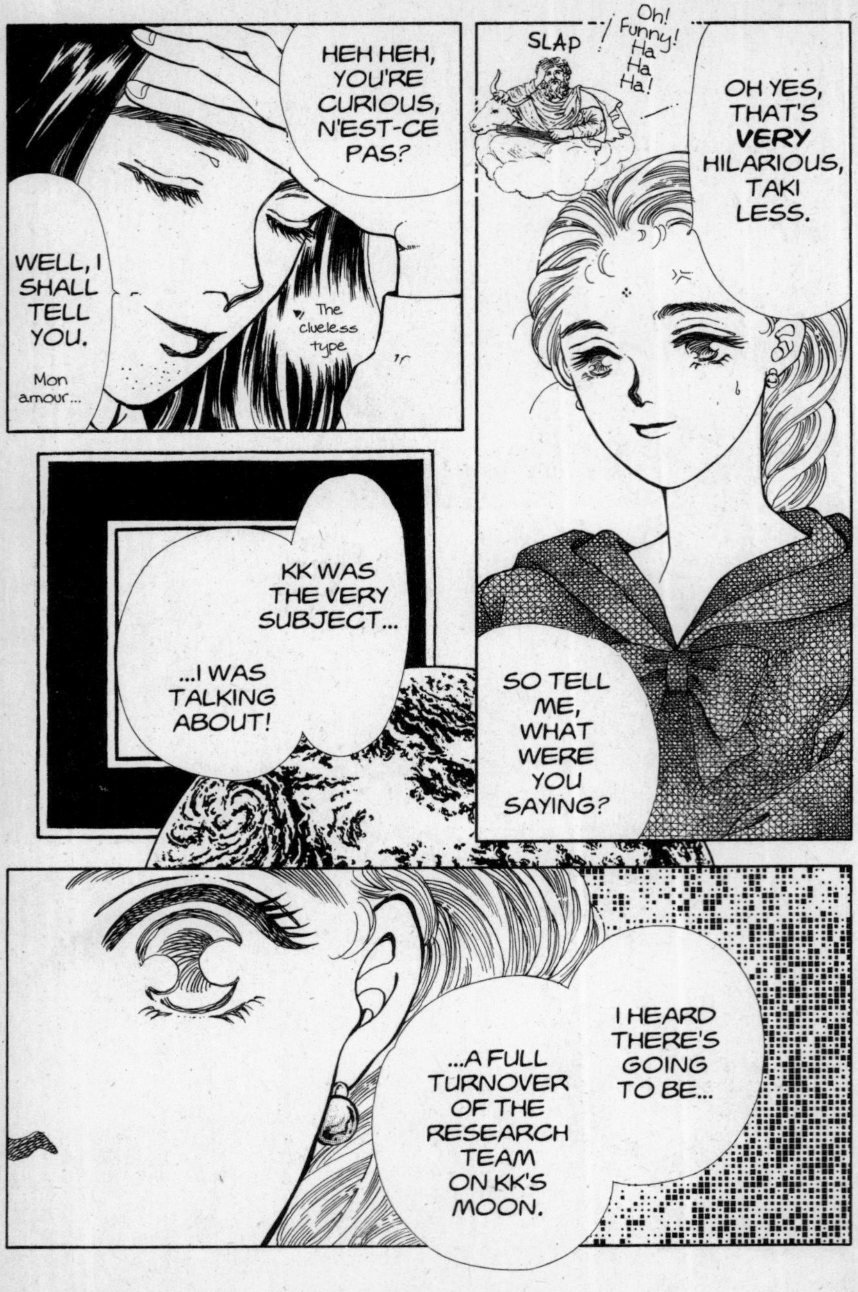

Oh! Funny! Ha Ha Ha!
SLAP
OH YES, THAT'S **VERY** HILARIOUS, TAKI LESS.
SO TELL ME, WHAT WERE YOU SAYING?
HEH HEH, YOU'RE CURIOUS, N'EST-CE PAS?
The clueless type
WELL, I SHALL TELL YOU.
Mon amour...
KK WAS THE VERY SUBJECT...
...I WAS TALKING ABOUT!
I HEARD THERE'S GOING TO BE...
...A FULL TURNOVER OF THE RESEARCH TEAM ON KK'S MOON.

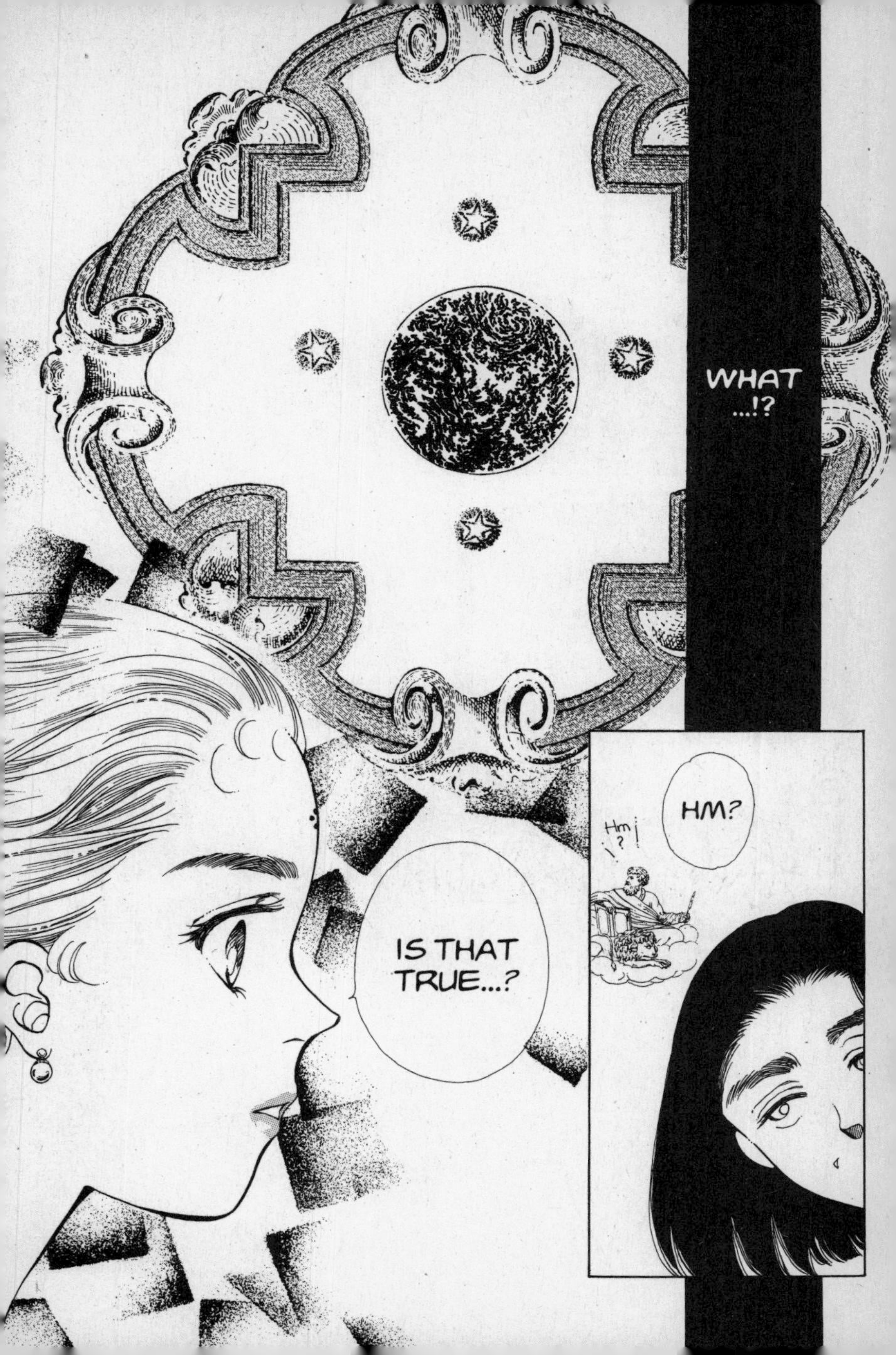
WHAT ...!?
IS THAT TRUE...?
HM?
Hm ?

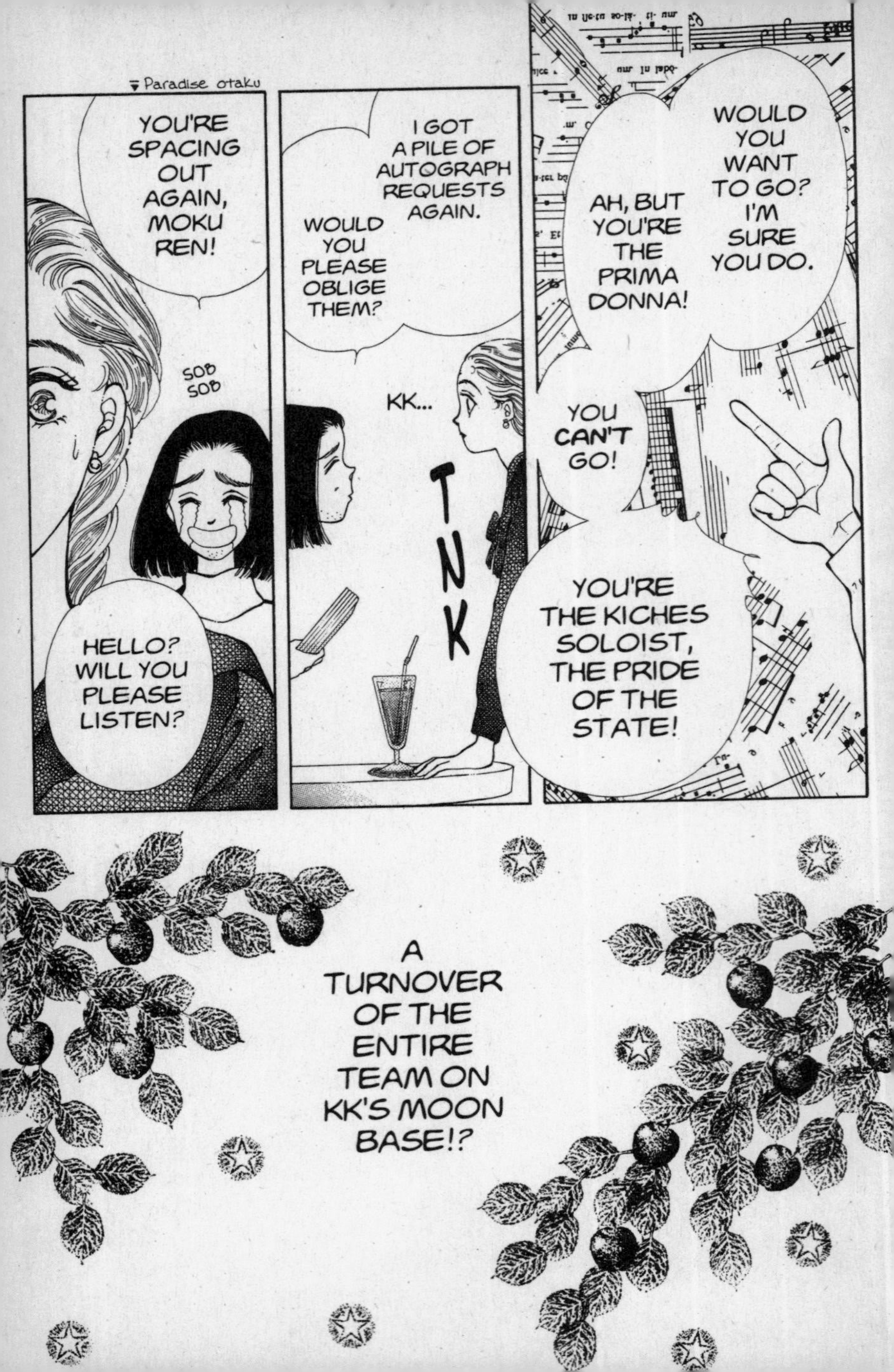
WOULD YOU WANT TO GO? I'M SURE YOU DO.
AH, BUT YOU'RE THE PRIMA DONNA!
YOU CAN'T GO!
YOU'RE THE KICHES SOLOIST, THE PRIDE OF THE STATE!
I GOT A PILE OF AUTOGRAPH REQUESTS AGAIN.
WOULD YOU PLEASE OBLIGE THEM?
KK...
TNK
Paradise otaku
YOU'RE SPACING OUT AGAIN, MOKU REN!
SOB SOB
HELLO? WILL YOU PLEASE LISTEN?
A TURNOVER OF THE ENTIRE TEAM ON KK'S MOON BASE!?

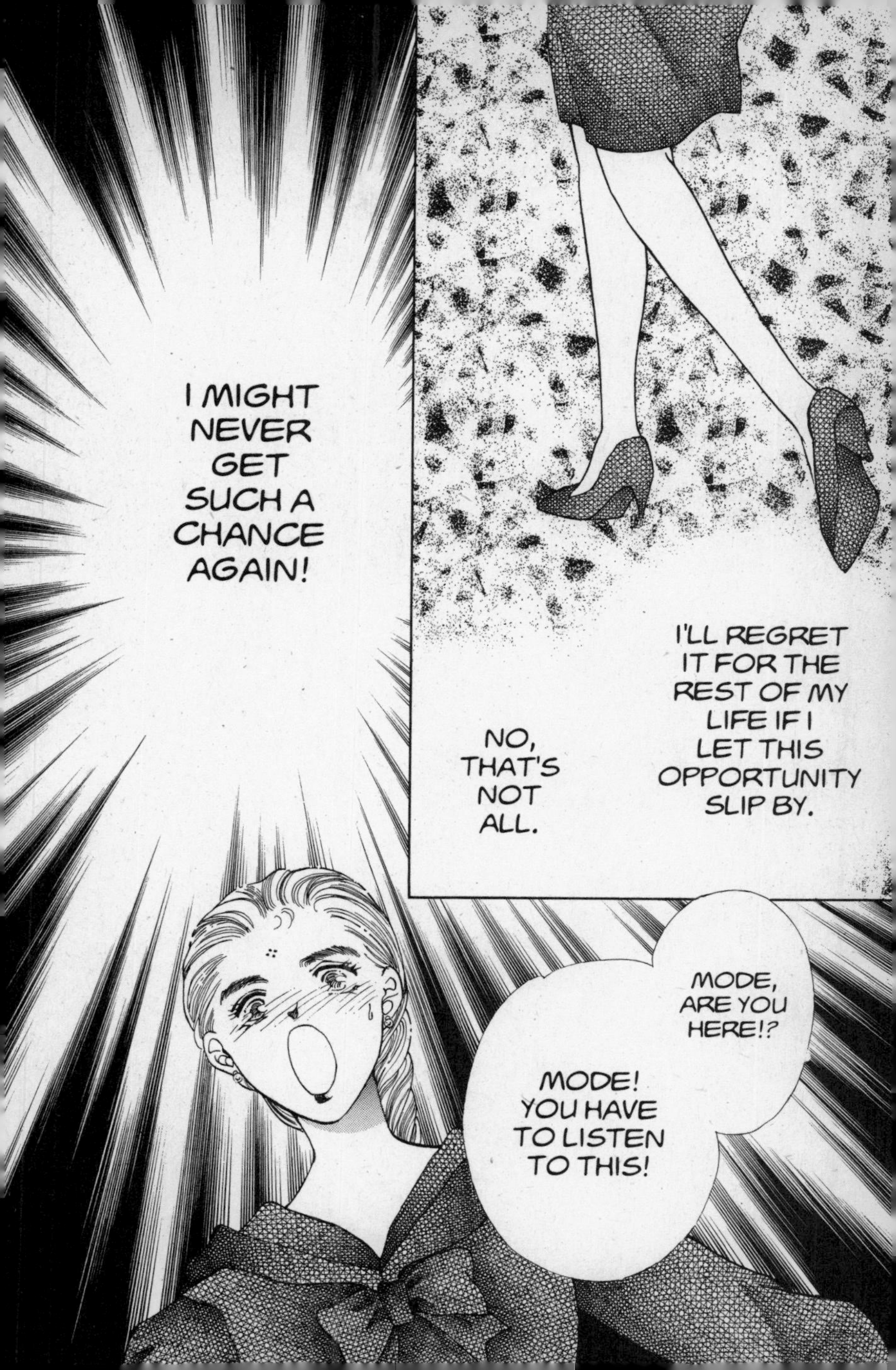
I MIGHT NEVER GET SUCH A CHANCE AGAIN!
NO, THAT'S NOT ALL.
I'LL REGRET IT FOR THE REST OF MY LIFE IF I LET THIS OPPORTUNITY SLIP BY.
MODE, ARE YOU HERE!?
MODE! YOU HAVE TO LISTEN TO THIS!

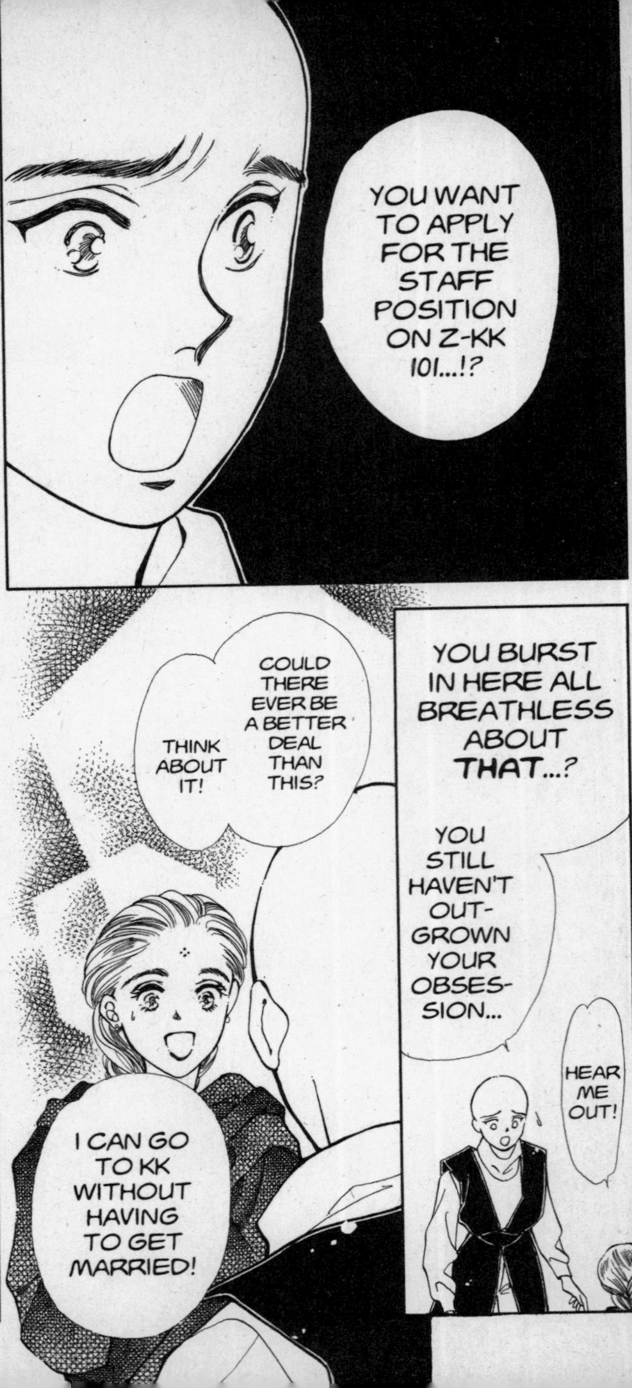
YOU WANT TO APPLY FOR THE STAFF POSITION ON Z-KK 101...!?
YOU BURST IN HERE ALL BREATHLESS ABOUT THAT...?
YOU STILL HAVEN'T OUTGROWN YOUR OBSES-SION...
HEAR ME OUT!
COULD THERE EVER BE A BETTER DEAL THAN THIS?
THINK ABOUT IT!
I CAN GO TO KK WITHOUT HAVING TO GET MARRIED!

1/4 COLUMN NONSENSE

PART 3

So I'm having second thoughts. I'm sorry that I sounded so harsh... It really felt like it wouldn't be good for the body. I read an article in the newspaper or something a while ago about a boy who put on a sauna suit after a bath, and went straight to bed. He got dehydrated, and never woke up, and died...

A lot of people had a lot of different experiences with diets, and it's really a mystery what works and what doesn't.

Anyway, just be careful about diets that may be more harmful than beneficial.

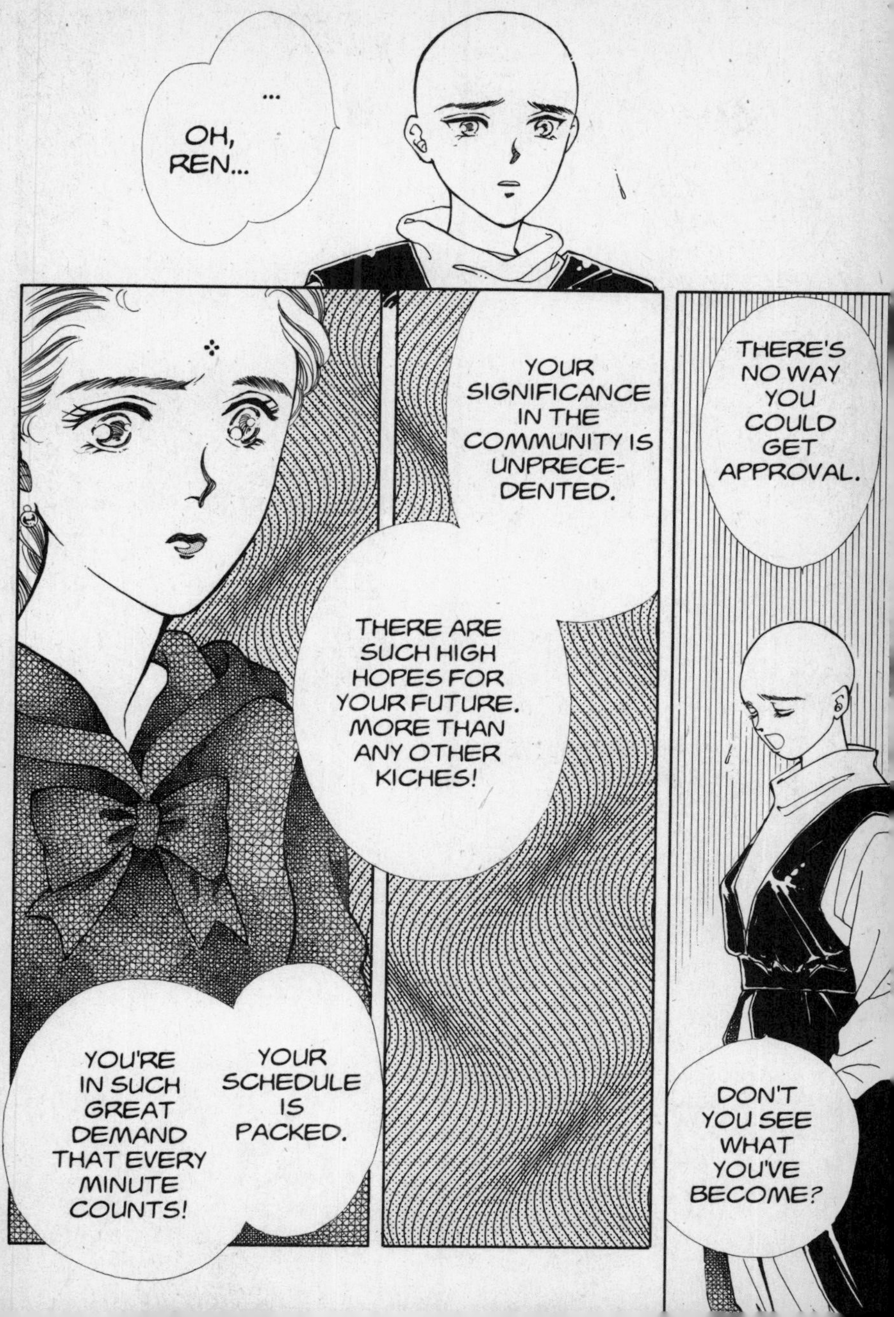
...
OH, REN...
THERE'S NO WAY YOU COULD GET APPROVAL.
DON'T YOU SEE WHAT YOU'VE BECOME?
YOUR SIGNIFICANCE IN THE COMMUNITY IS UNPRECE-DENTED.
THERE ARE SUCH HIGH HOPES FOR YOUR FUTURE. MORE THAN ANY OTHER KICHES!
YOUR SCHEDULE IS PACKED.
YOU'RE IN SUCH GREAT DEMAND THAT EVERY MINUTE COUNTS!

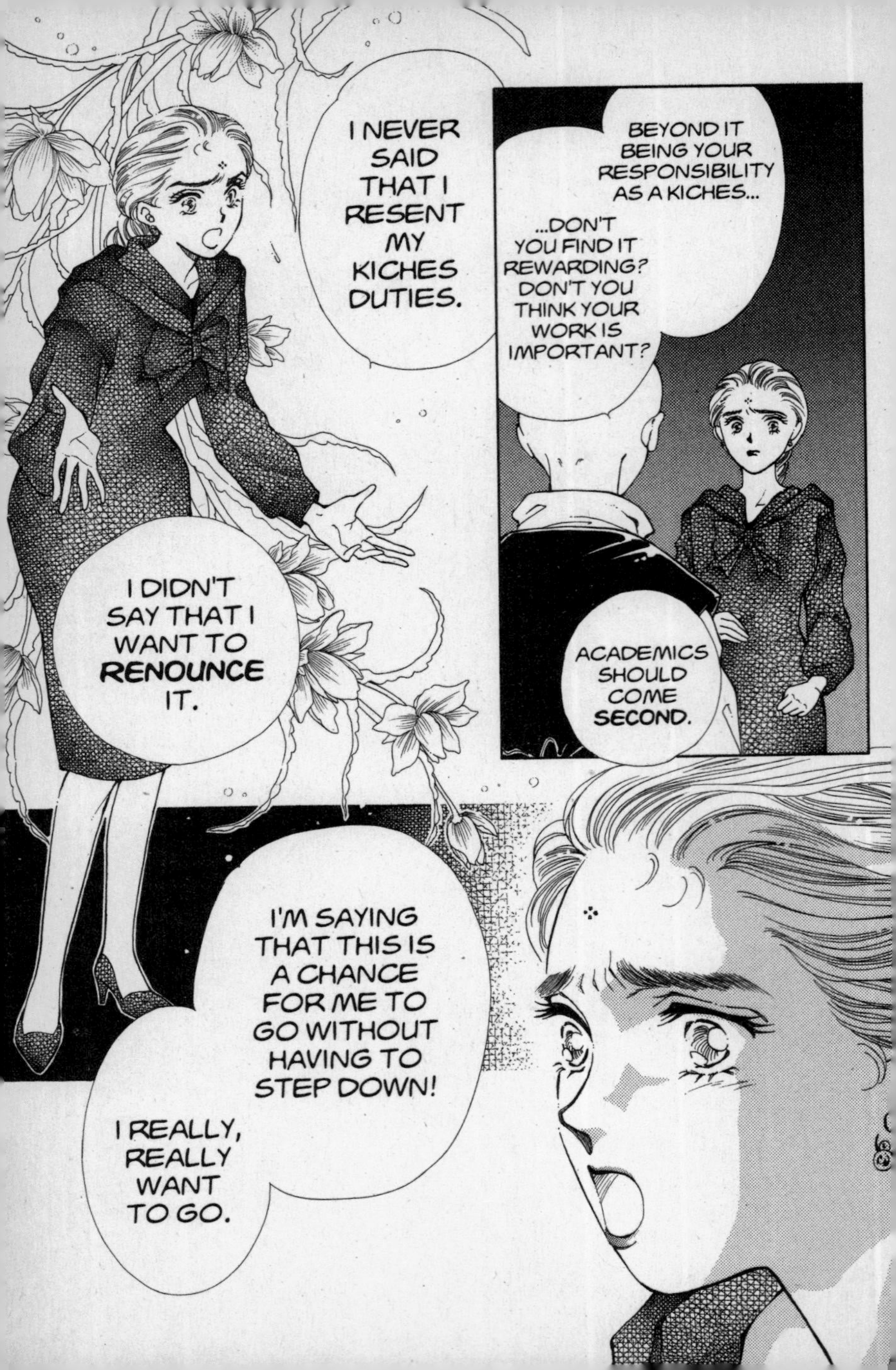
BEYOND IT BEING YOUR RESPONSIBILITY AS A KICHES...
...DON'T YOU FIND IT REWARDING? DON'T YOU THINK YOUR WORK IS IMPORTANT?
ACADEMICS SHOULD COME **SECOND.**
I NEVER SAID THAT I RESENT MY KICHES DUTIES.
I DIDN'T SAY THAT I WANT TO **RENOUNCE** IT.
I'M SAYING THAT THIS IS A CHANCE FOR ME TO GO WITHOUT HAVING TO STEP DOWN!
I REALLY, REALLY WANT TO GO.

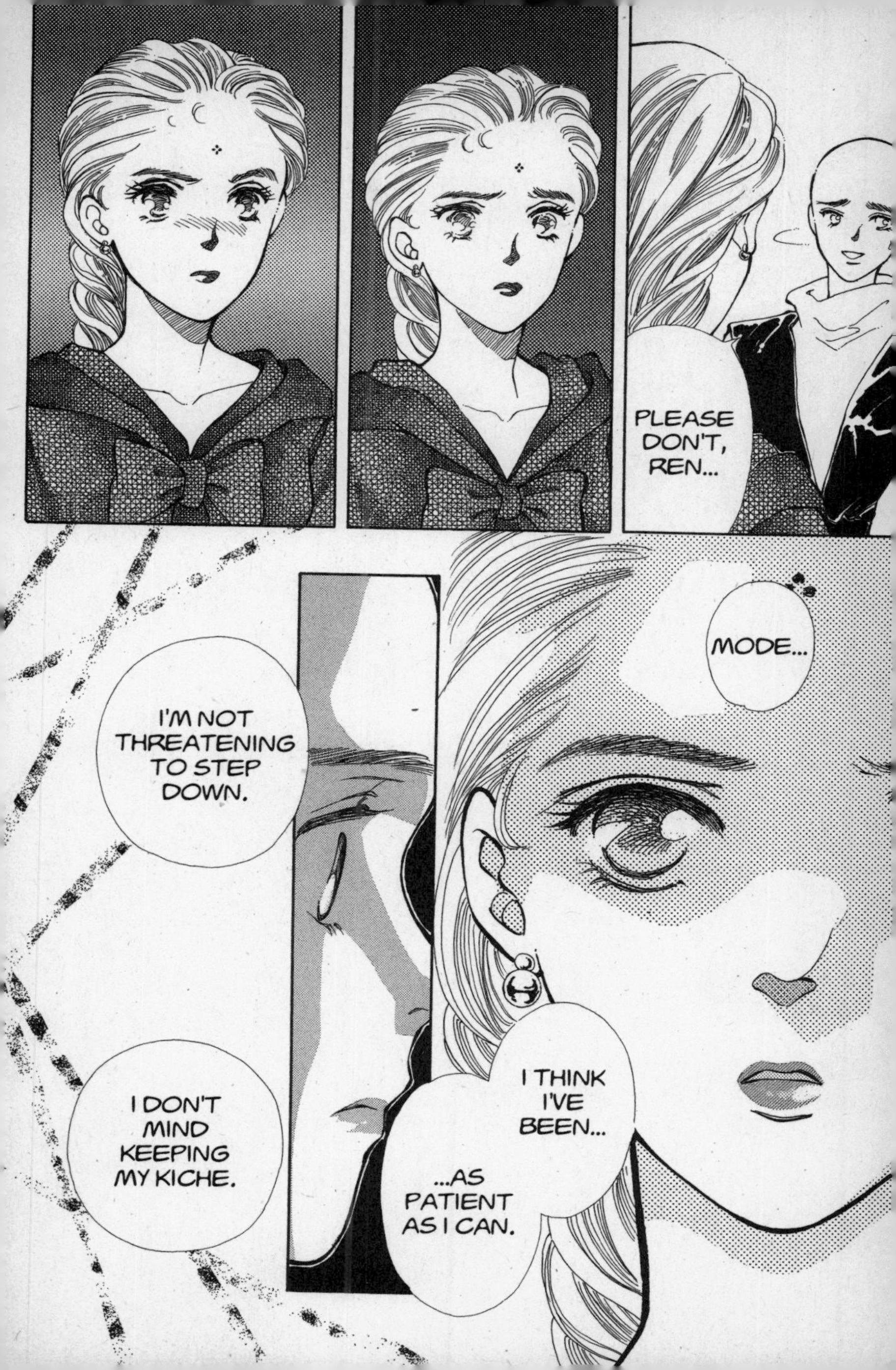
PLEASE DON'T, REN...
MODE...
I THINK I'VE BEEN...
...AS PATIENT AS I CAN.
I'M NOT THREATENING TO STEP DOWN.
I DON'T MIND KEEPING MY KICHE.

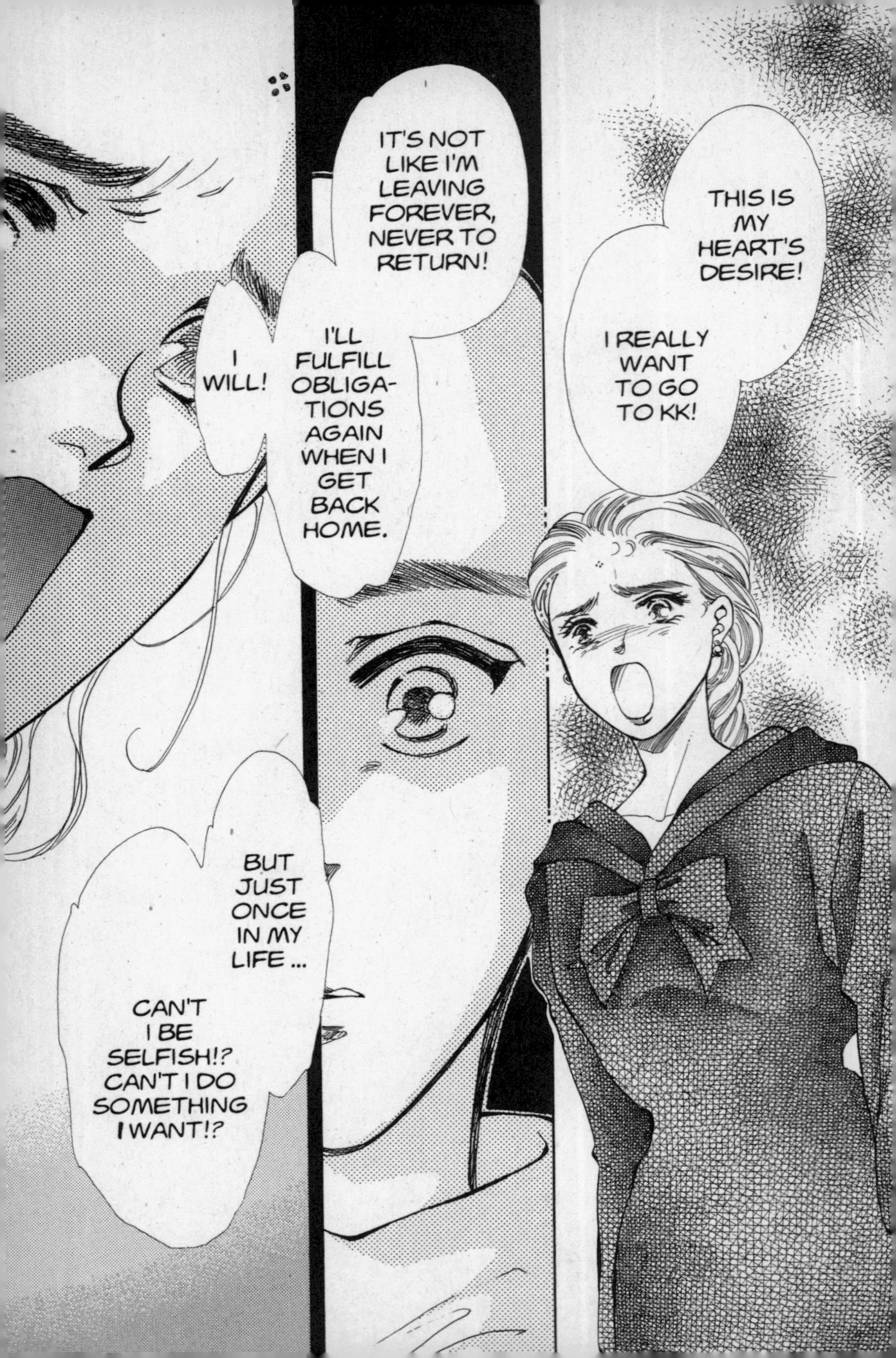
THIS IS MY HEART'S DESIRE!
I REALLY WANT TO GO TO KK!
IT'S NOT LIKE I'M LEAVING FOREVER, NEVER TO RETURN!
I'LL FULFILL OBLIGA-TIONS AGAIN WHEN I GET BACK HOME.
I WILL!
BUT JUST ONCE IN MY LIFE ...
CAN'T I BE SELFISH!? CAN'T I DO SOMETHING I WANT!?

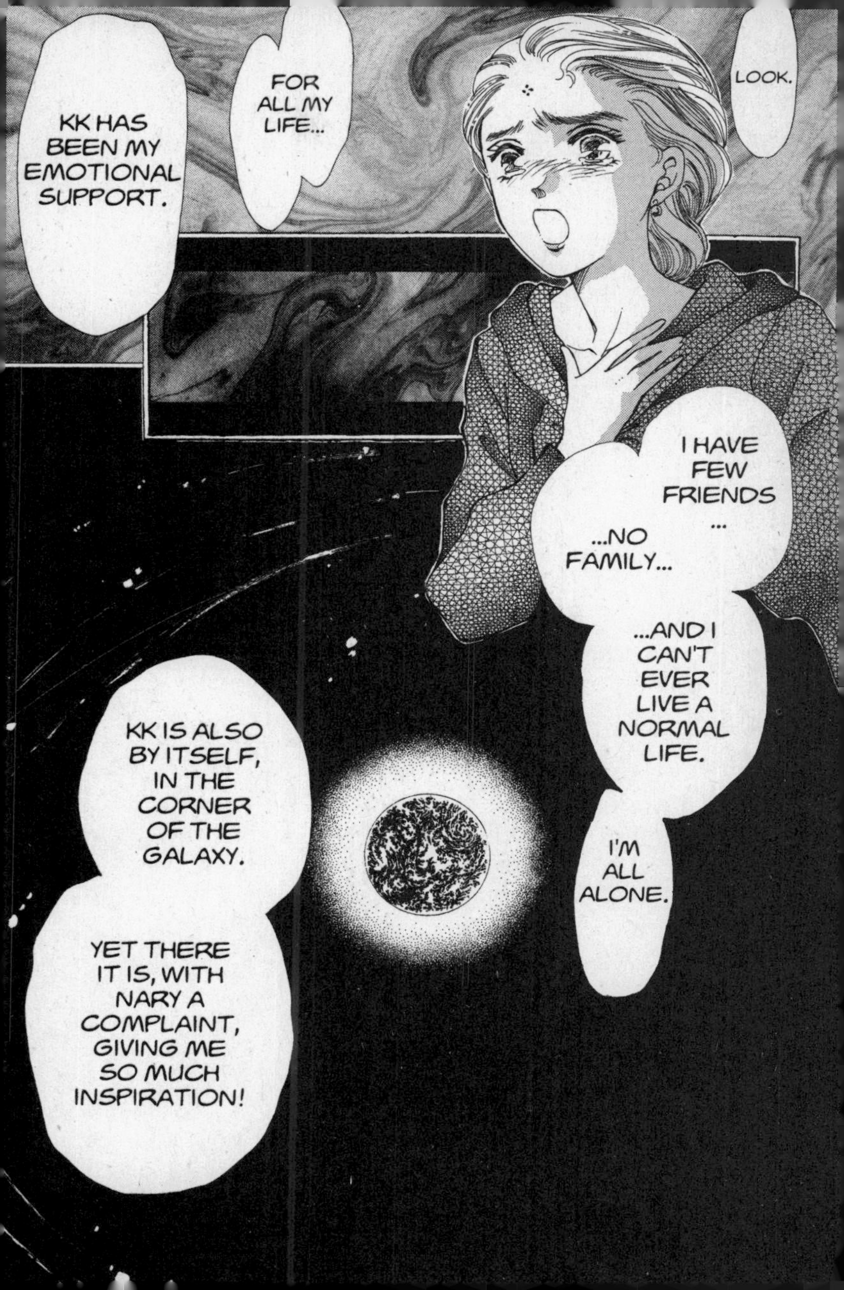
LOOK.
FOR ALL MY LIFE...
KK HAS BEEN MY EMOTIONAL SUPPORT.
I HAVE FEW FRIENDS ...
...NO FAMILY...
...AND I CAN'T EVER LIVE A NORMAL LIFE.
I'M ALL ALONE.
KK IS ALSO BY ITSELF, IN THE CORNER OF THE GALAXY.
YET THERE IT IS, WITH NARY A COMPLAINT, GIVING ME SO MUCH INSPIRATION!

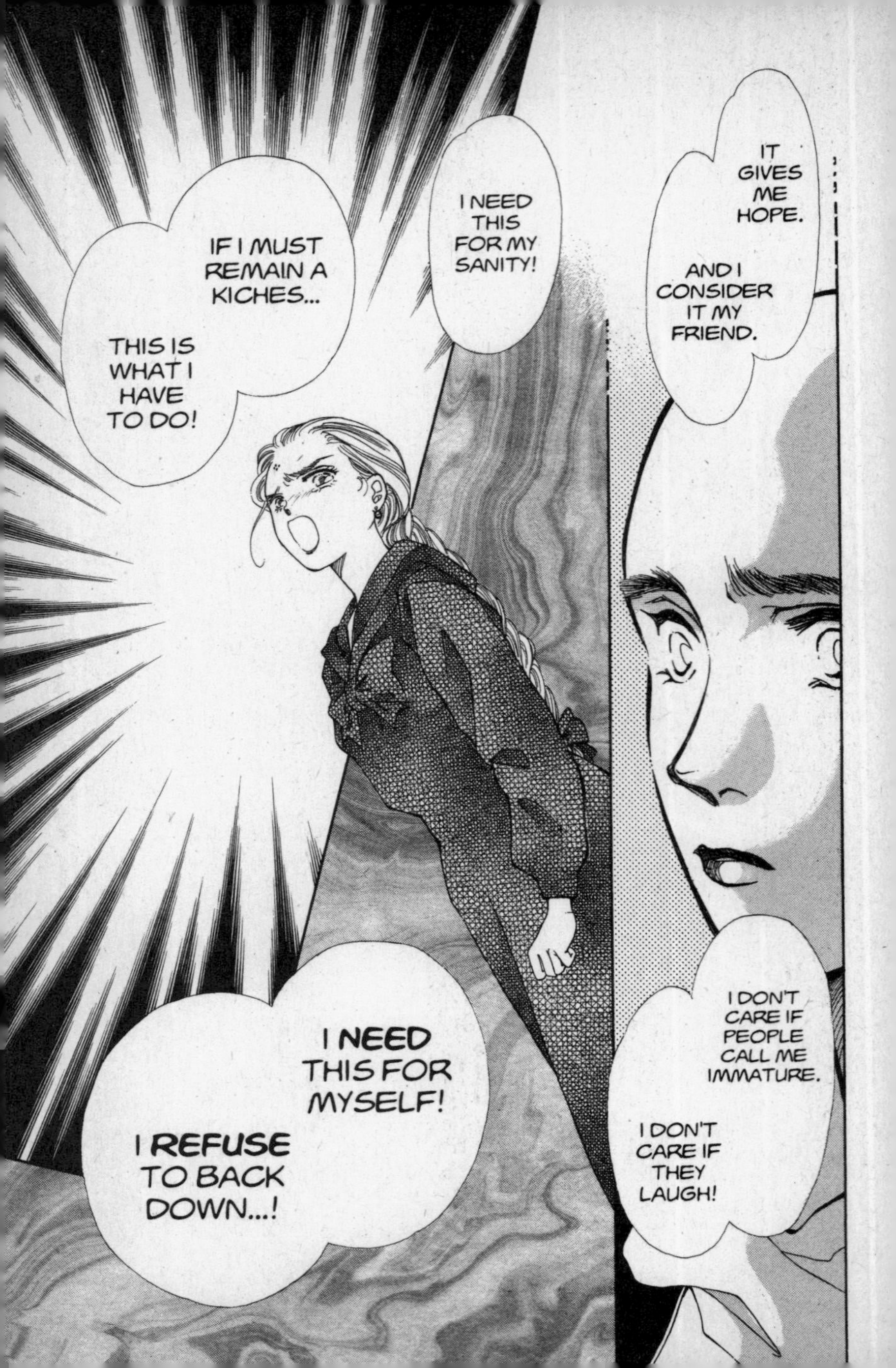
IT GIVES ME HOPE.
AND I CONSIDER IT MY FRIEND.
I DON'T CARE IF PEOPLE CALL ME IMMATURE.
I DON'T CARE IF THEY LAUGH!
I NEED THIS FOR MY SANITY!
IF I MUST REMAIN A KICHES...
THIS IS WHAT I HAVE TO DO!
I **NEED** THIS FOR MYSELF!
I **REFUSE** TO BACK DOWN...!

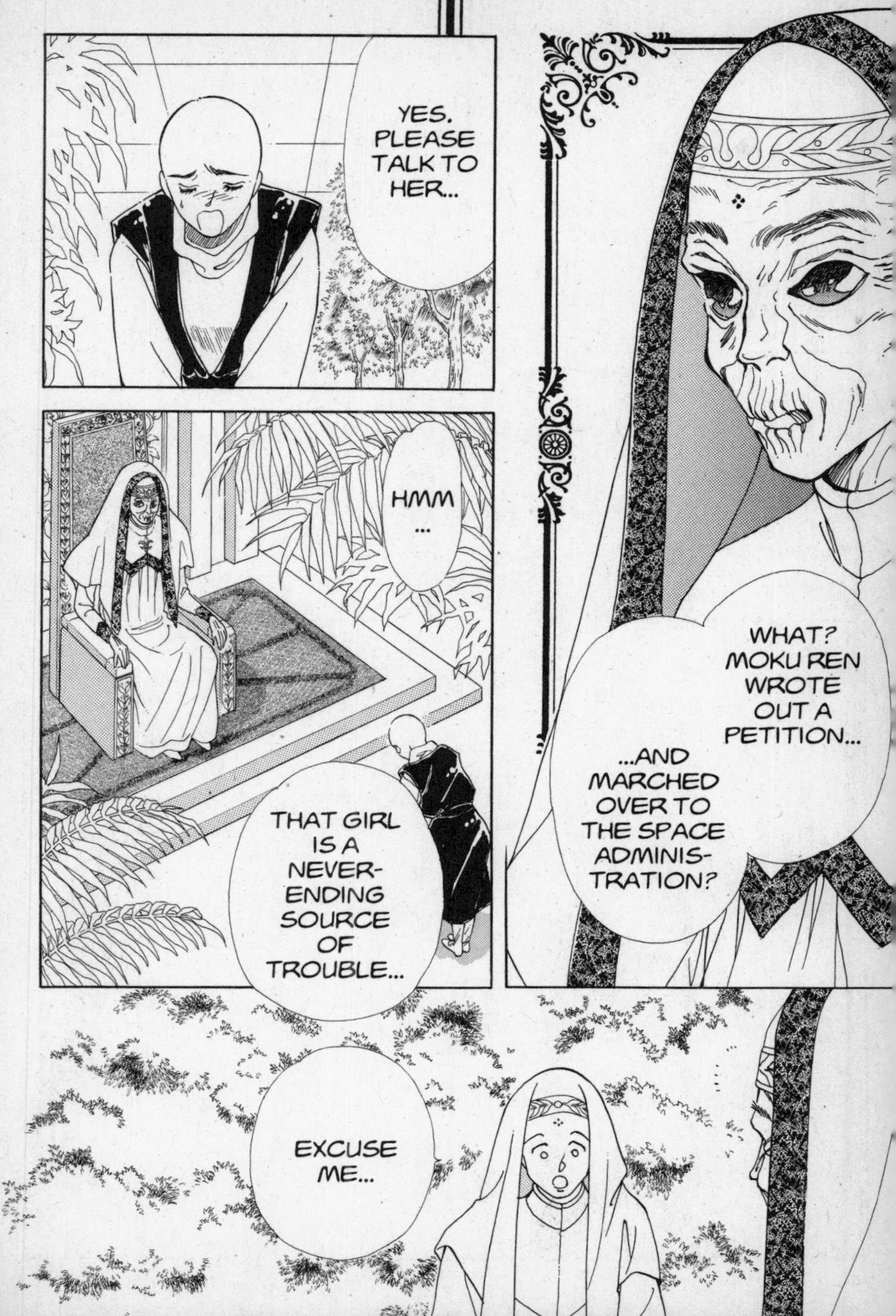
WHAT? MOKU REN WROTE OUT A PETITION...
...AND MARCHED OVER TO THE SPACE ADMINIS-TRATION?
YES. PLEASE TALK TO HER...
HMM ...
THAT GIRL IS A NEVER-ENDING SOURCE OF TROUBLE...
EXCUSE ME...

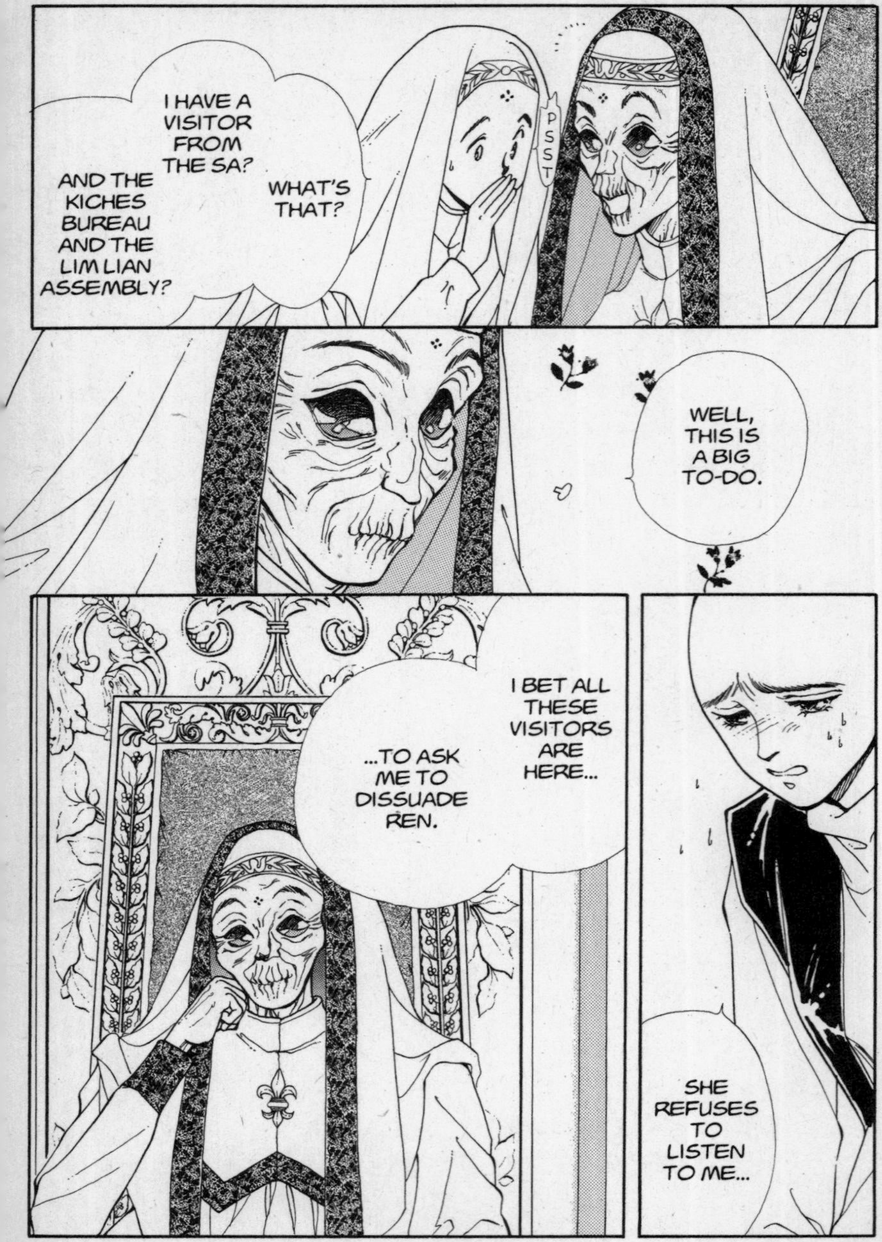
PSST
I HAVE A VISITOR FROM THE SA?
WHAT'S THAT?
AND THE KICHES BUREAU AND THE LIM LIAN ASSEMBLY?
WELL, THIS IS A BIG TO-DO.
SHE REFUSES TO LISTEN TO ME...
I BET ALL THESE VISITORS ARE HERE...
...TO ASK ME TO DISSUADE REN.

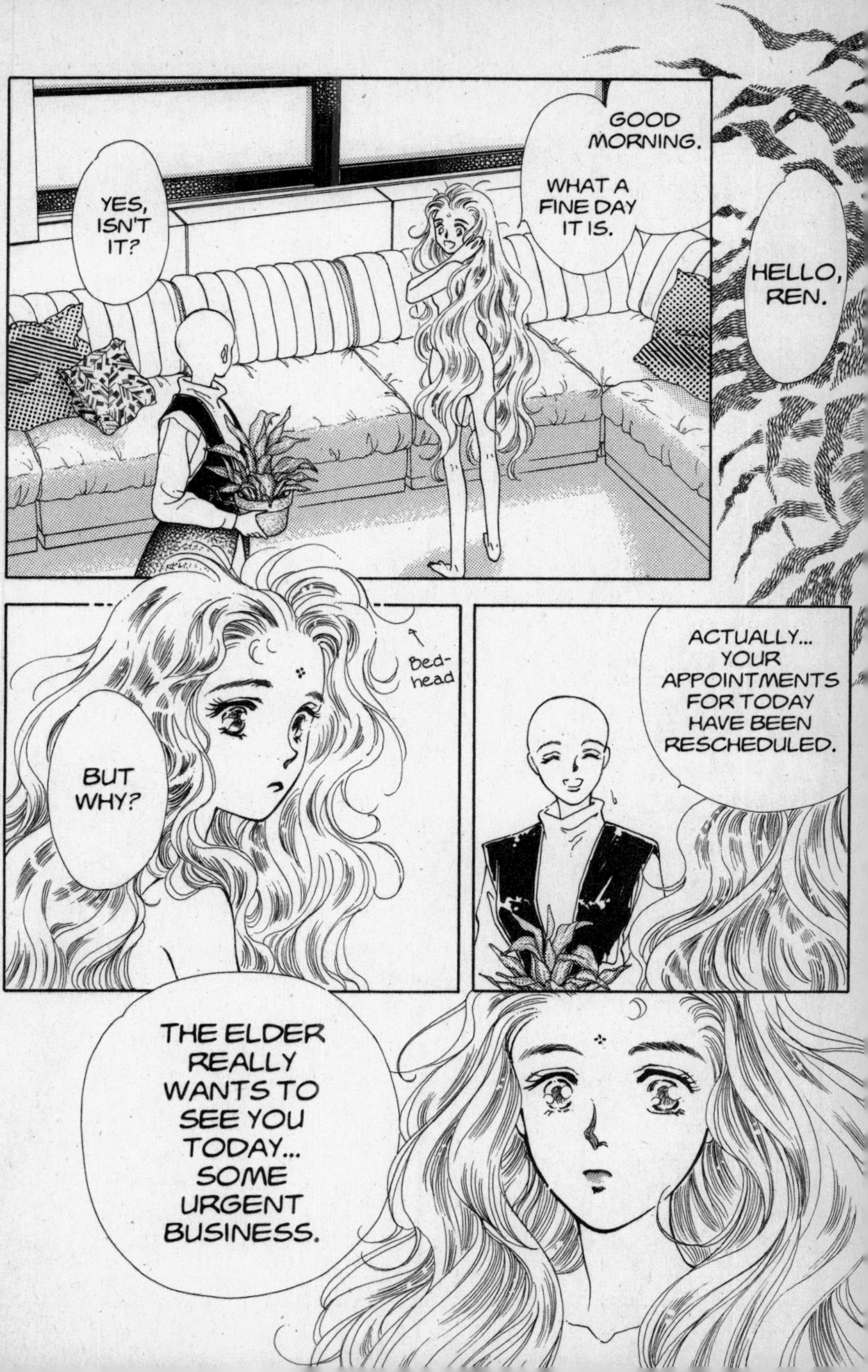
HELLO, REN.
GOOD MORNING.
WHAT A FINE DAY IT IS.
YES, ISN'T IT?
ACTUALLY... YOUR APPOINTMENTS FOR TODAY HAVE BEEN RESCHEDULED.
Bed-head
BUT WHY?
THE ELDER REALLY WANTS TO SEE YOU TODAY... SOME URGENT BUSINESS.

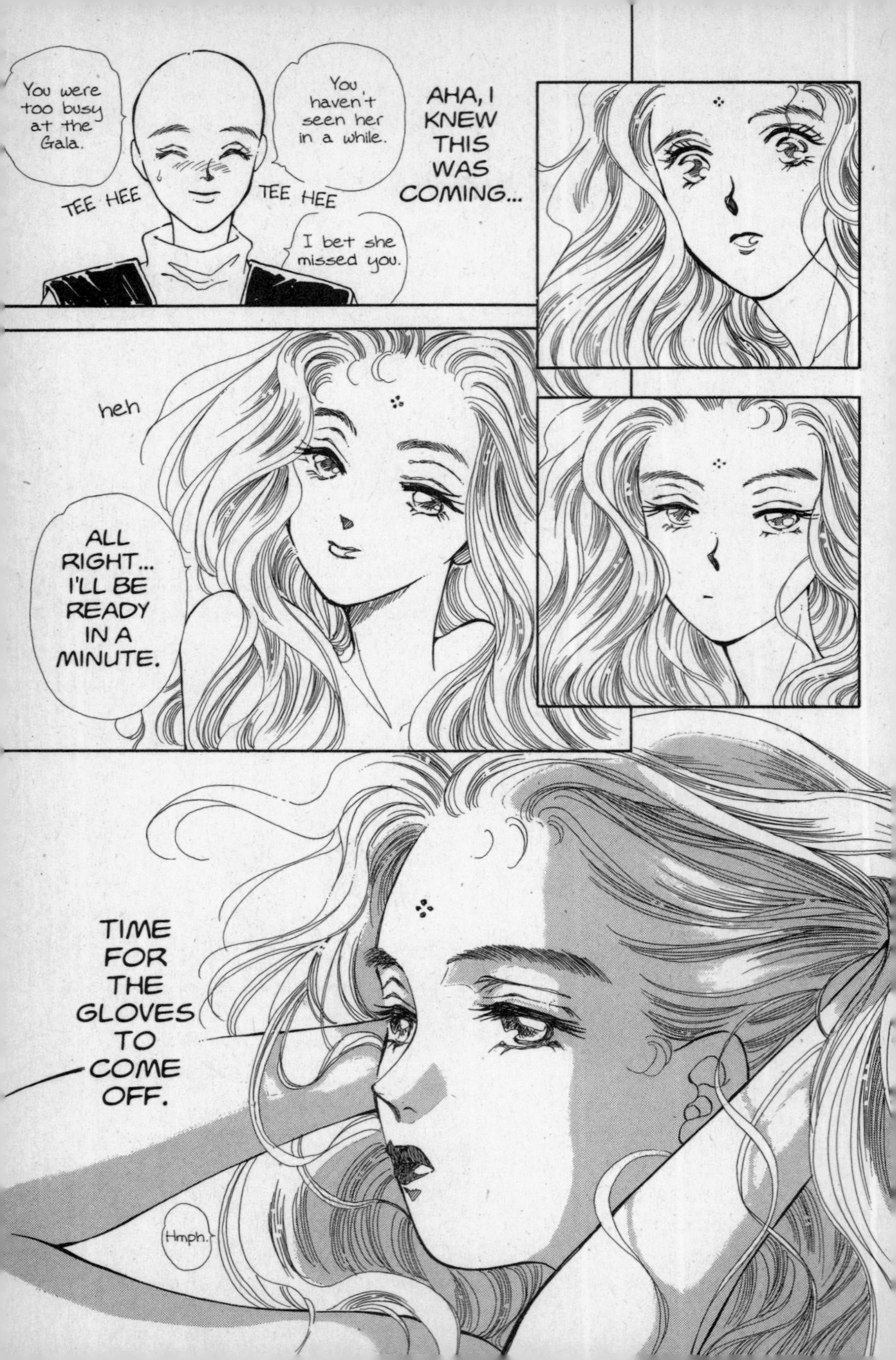
AHA, I KNEW THIS WAS COMING...
You haven't seen her in a while.
You were too busy at the Gala.
TEE HEE
TEE HEE
I bet she missed you.
heh
ALL RIGHT... I'LL BE READY IN A MINUTE.
TIME FOR THE GLOVES TO COME OFF.
Hmph.

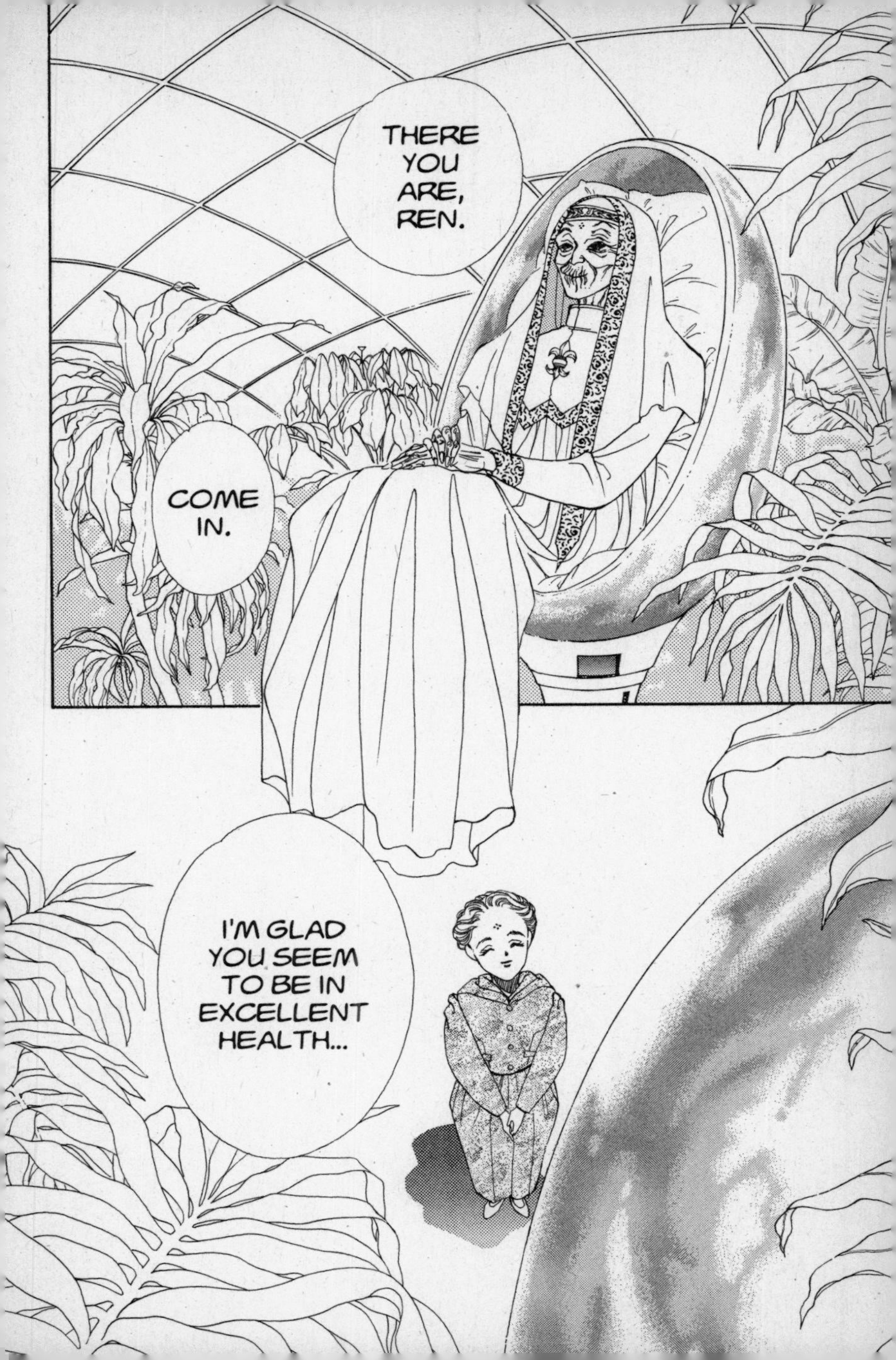
THERE YOU ARE, REN.
COME IN.
I'M GLAD YOU SEEM TO BE IN EXCELLENT HEALTH...

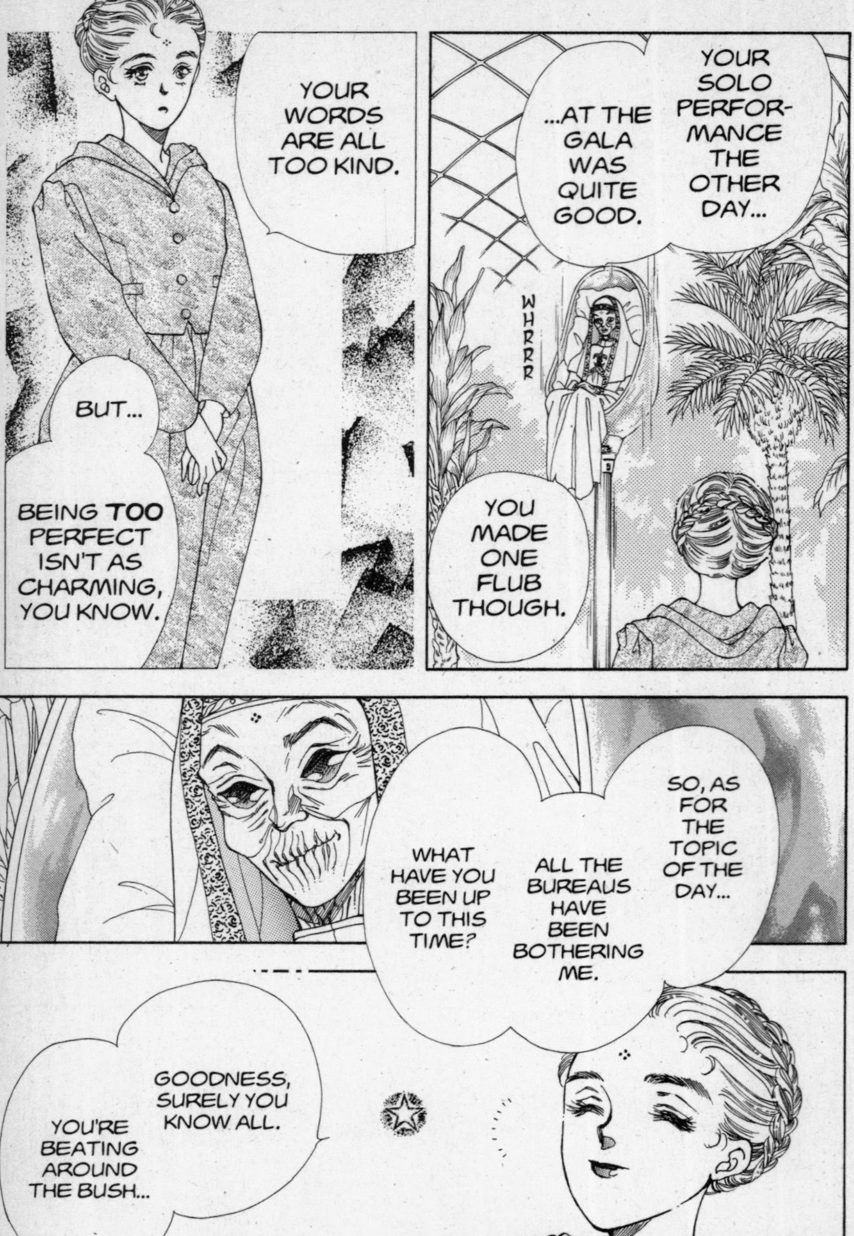
YOUR SOLO PERFORMANCE THE OTHER DAY...
...AT THE GALA WAS QUITE GOOD.
WHRRR
YOU MADE ONE FLUB THOUGH.
YOUR WORDS ARE ALL TOO KIND.
BUT...
BEING TOO PERFECT ISN'T AS CHARMING, YOU KNOW.
SO, AS FOR THE TOPIC OF THE DAY...
ALL THE BUREAUS HAVE BEEN BOTHERING ME.
WHAT HAVE YOU BEEN UP TO THIS TIME?
GOODNESS, SURELY YOU KNOW ALL.
YOU'RE BEATING AROUND THE BUSH...

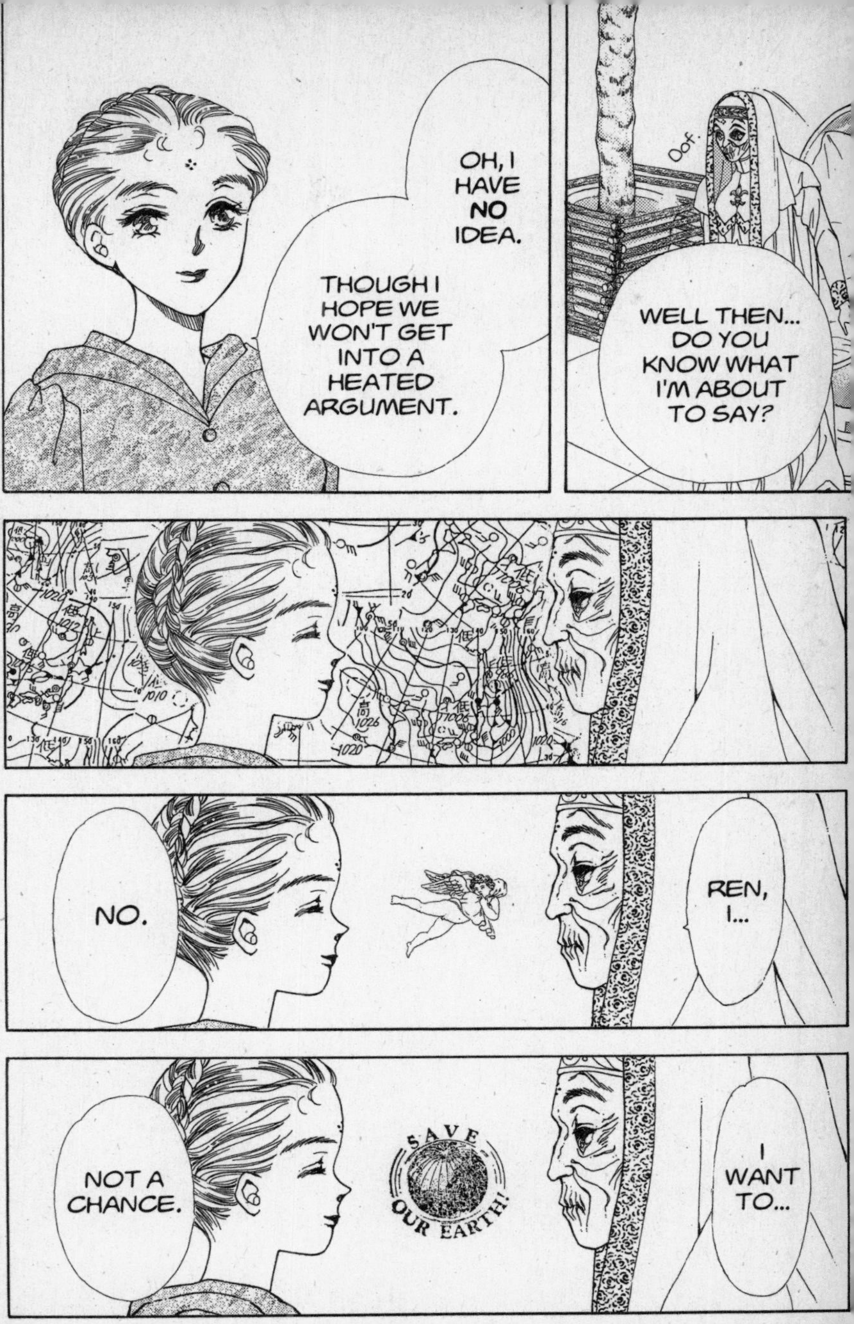
Oof.
WELL THEN... DO YOU KNOW WHAT I'M ABOUT TO SAY?
OH, I HAVE NO IDEA.
THOUGH I HOPE WE WON'T GET INTO A HEATED ARGUMENT.
REN, I...
NO.
I WANT TO...
SAVE OUR EARTH!
NOT A CHANCE.

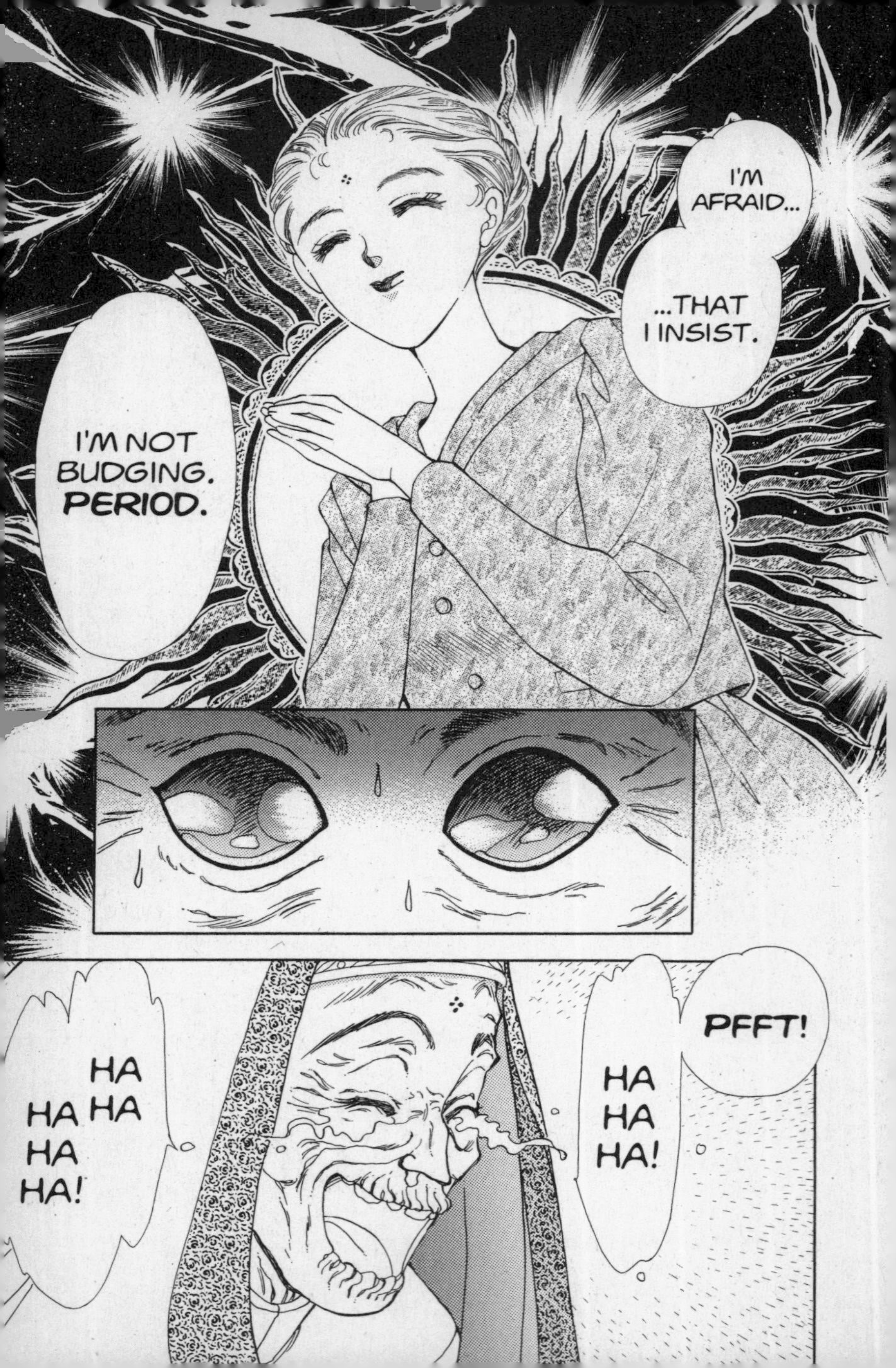
I'M AFRAID...
...THAT I INSIST.
I'M NOT BUDGING. PERIOD.
PFFT!
HA HA HA!
HA HA HA HA HA HA!

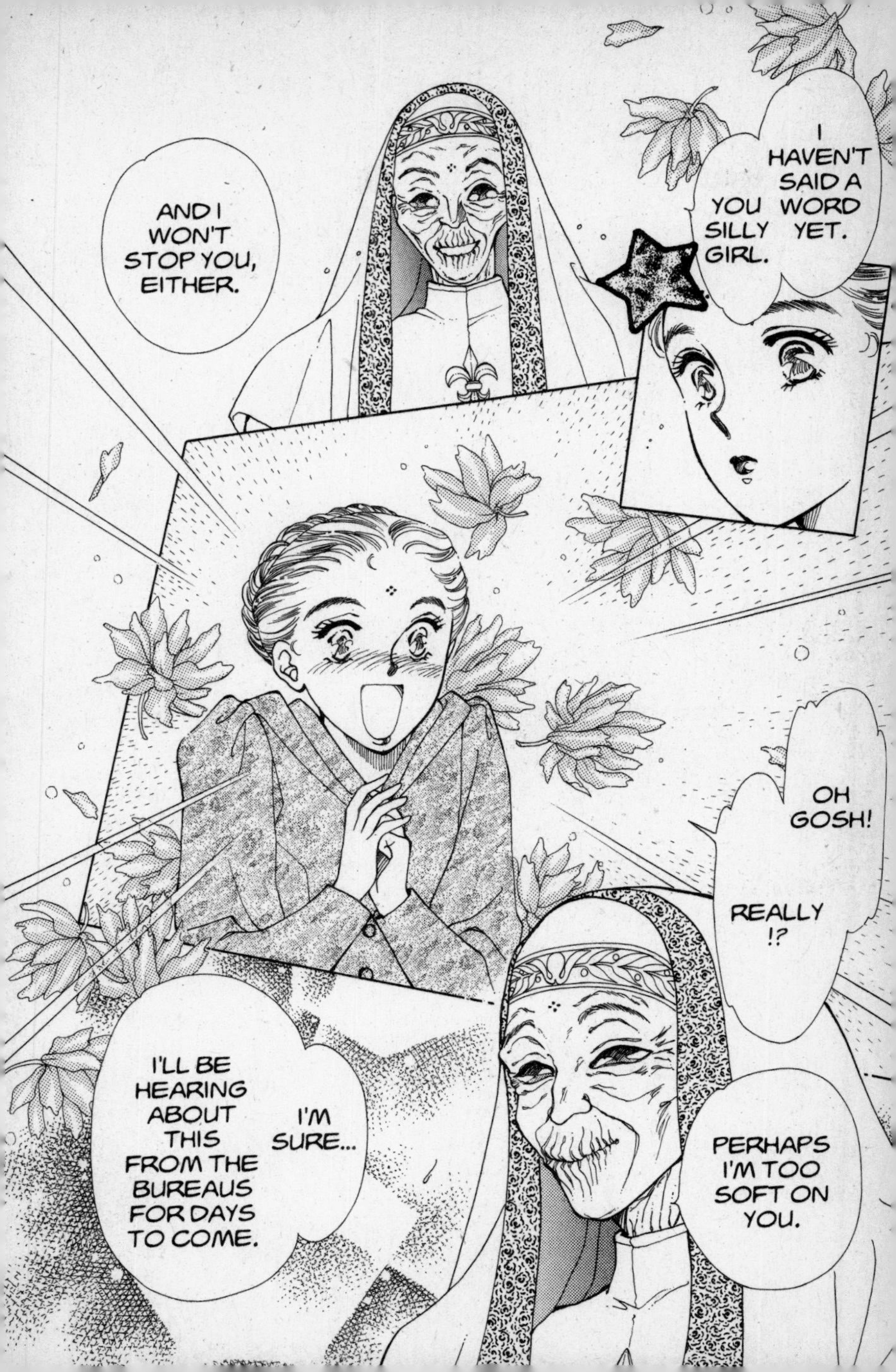
I HAVEN'T SAID A WORD YET.
YOU SILLY GIRL.
AND I WON'T STOP YOU, EITHER.
OH GOSH!
REALLY !?
PERHAPS I'M TOO SOFT ON YOU.
I'M SURE...
I'LL BE HEARING ABOUT THIS FROM THE BUREAUS FOR DAYS TO COME.

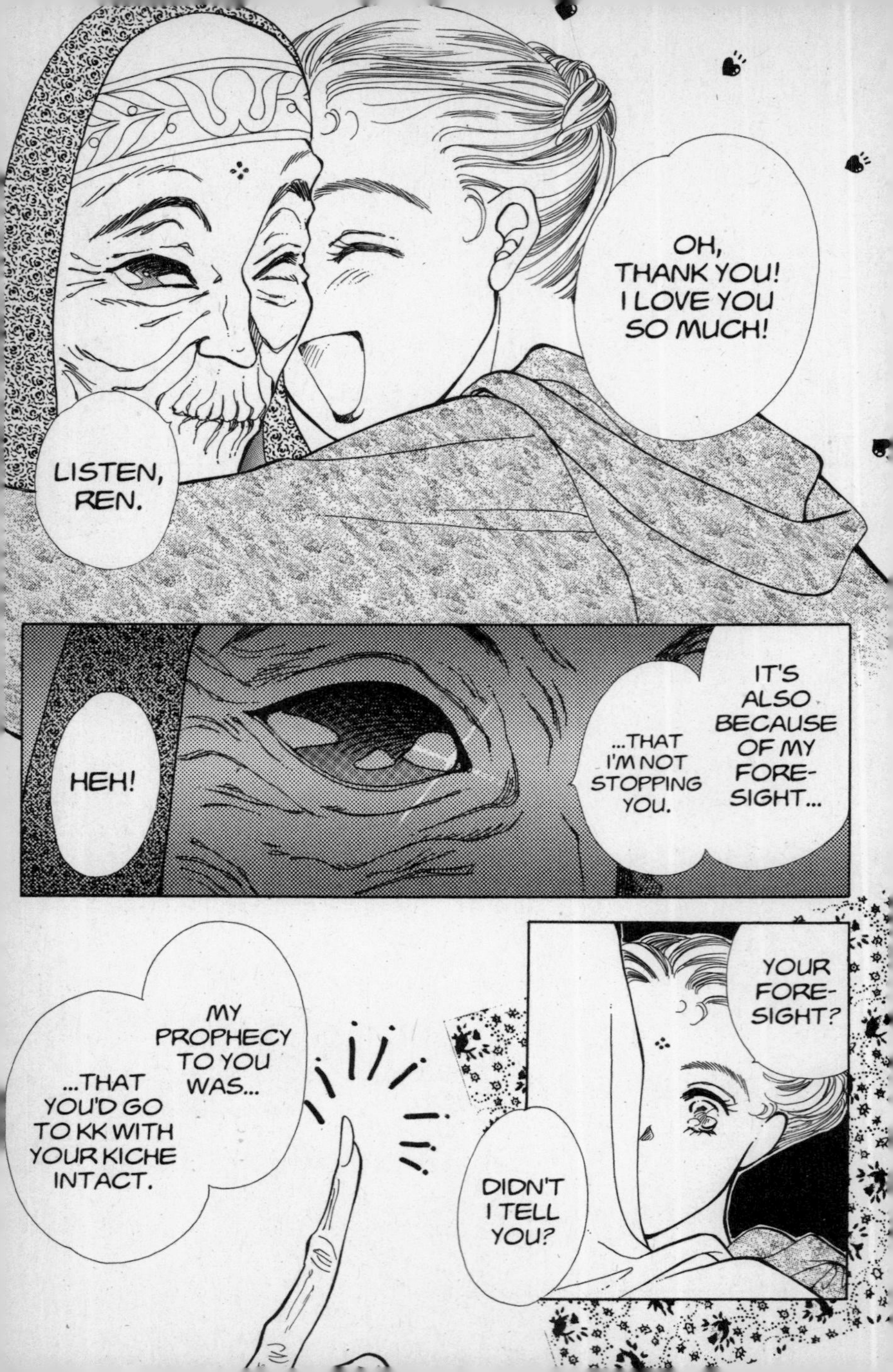
OH, THANK YOU! I LOVE YOU SO MUCH!
LISTEN, REN.
IT'S ALSO BECAUSE OF MY FORE-SIGHT...
...THAT I'M NOT STOPPING YOU.
HEH!
YOUR FORE-SIGHT?
DIDN'T I TELL YOU?
MY PROPHECY TO YOU WAS...
...THAT YOU'D GO TO KK WITH YOUR KICHE INTACT.

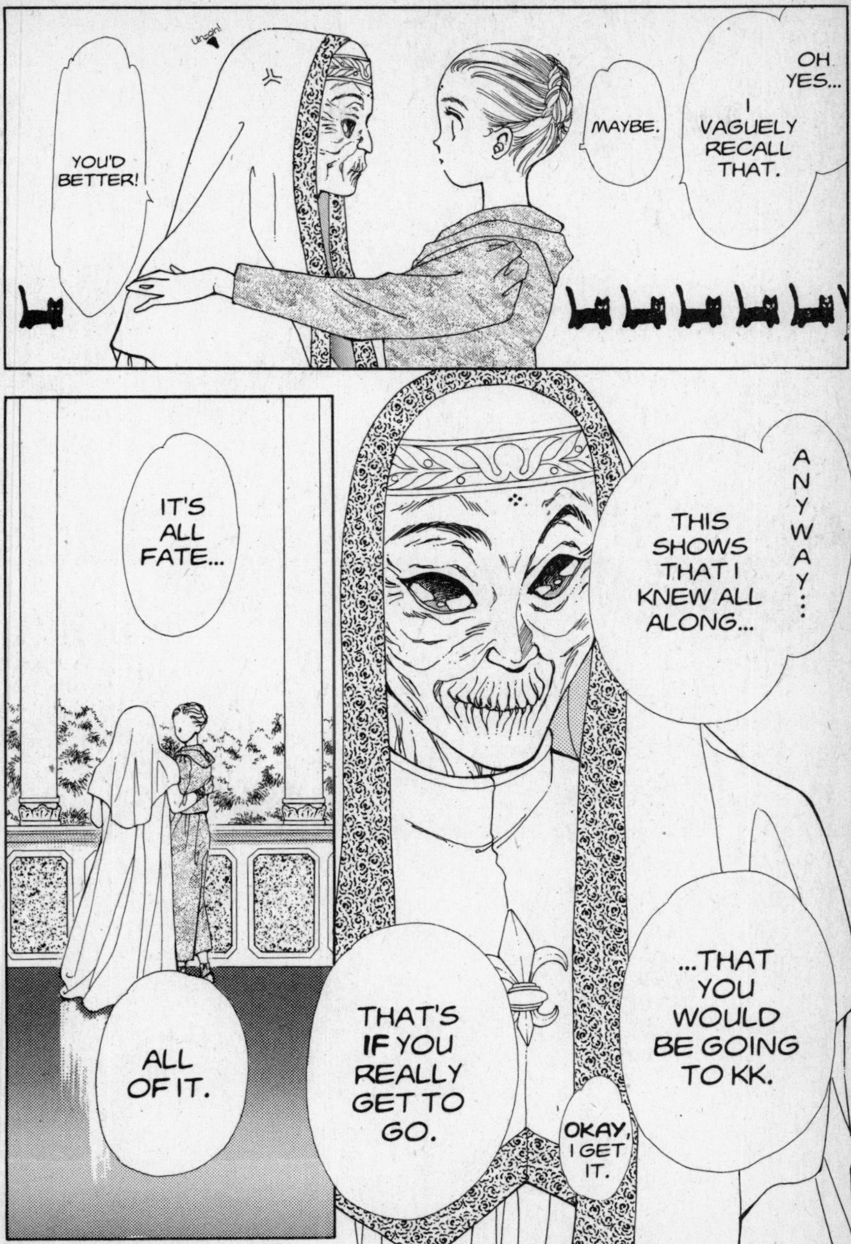
OH YES... I VAGUELY RECALL THAT.
MAYBE.
YOU'D BETTER!
ANYWAY...
THIS SHOWS THAT I KNEW ALL ALONG...
...THAT YOU WOULD BE GOING TO KK.
OKAY, I GET IT.
THAT'S IF YOU REALLY GET TO GO.
IT'S ALL FATE...
ALL OF IT.

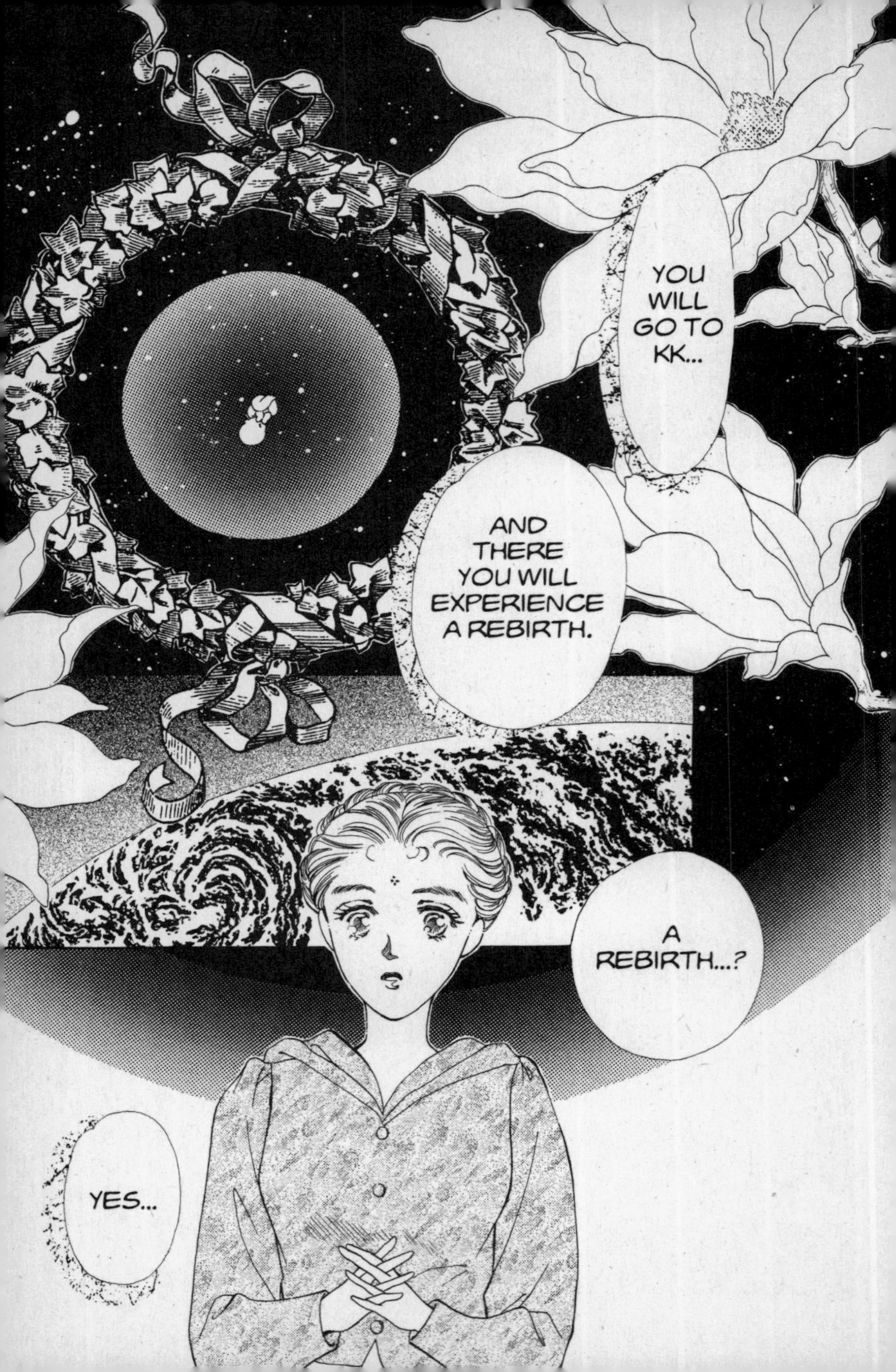
YOU WILL GO TO KK...
AND THERE YOU WILL EXPERIENCE A REBIRTH.
A REBIRTH...?
YES...

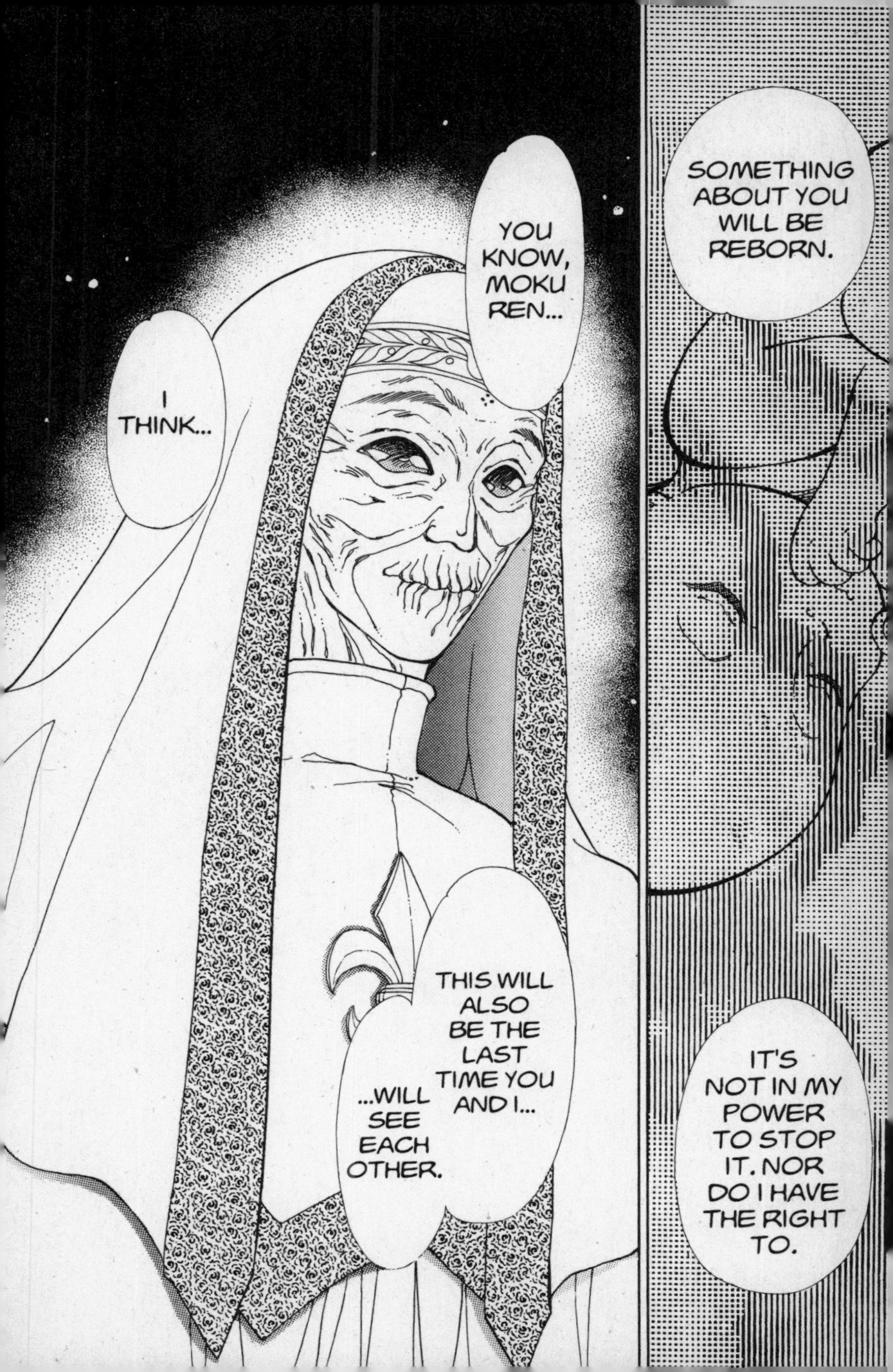
SOMETHING ABOUT YOU WILL BE REBORN.
IT'S NOT IN MY POWER TO STOP IT. NOR DO I HAVE THE RIGHT TO.
YOU KNOW, MOKU REN...
I THINK...
THIS WILL ALSO BE THE LAST TIME YOU AND I...
...WILL SEE EACH OTHER.

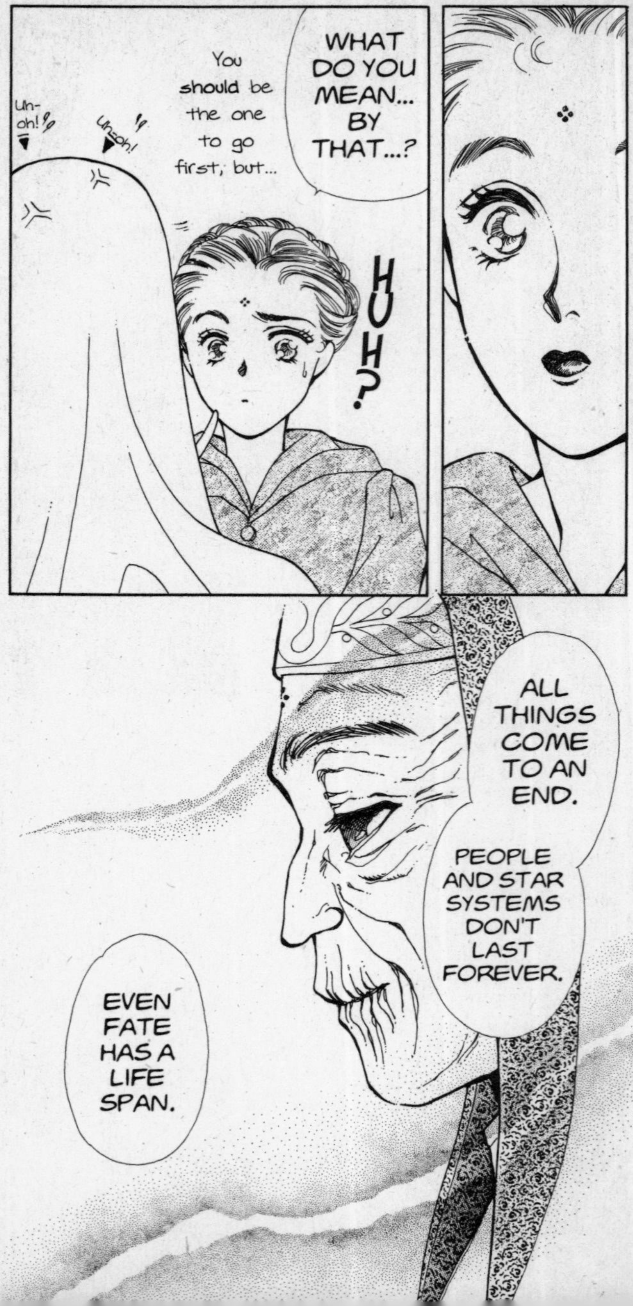
WHAT DO YOU MEAN... BY THAT...?
You should be the one to go first, but...
Uh-oh!
Uh-oh!
HUH?
ALL THINGS COME TO AN END.
PEOPLE AND STAR SYSTEMS DON'T LAST FOREVER.
EVEN FATE HAS A LIFE SPAN.

1/4 COLUMN NONSENSE

PART 4

I may be busy, but if I keep working the entire day, I would get stressed out. So I play video games in the hour before I go to bed. I have a good gaming instinct, if I may say so myself! Tee hee!

I'm pretty good at platform games, too. I'm currently playing "Legend of Zelda." (On the Super Nintendo).

What, I'm way behind the times? Leave me alone! I haven't even gotten a hold of "Dragon Quest V" yet! Hmph.

I have a bit of an emotional attachment for "Dragon Quest" (Dragon Warrior in the U.S. -ed) since I've bought the whole series from the beginning, as they came out.

Continued in part 5.

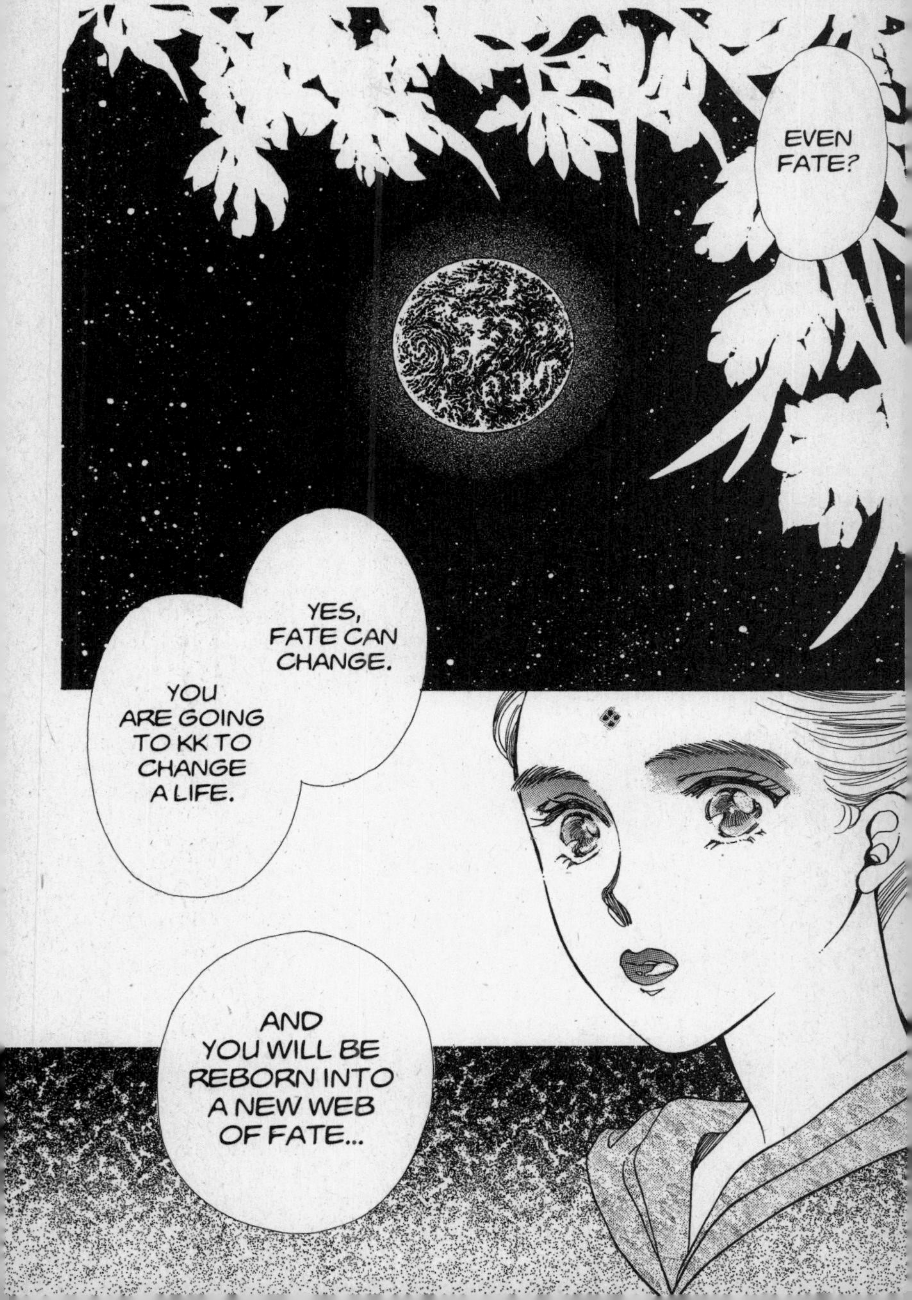
EVEN FATE?
YES, FATE CAN CHANGE.
YOU ARE GOING TO KK TO CHANGE A LIFE.
AND YOU WILL BE REBORN INTO A NEW WEB OF FATE...

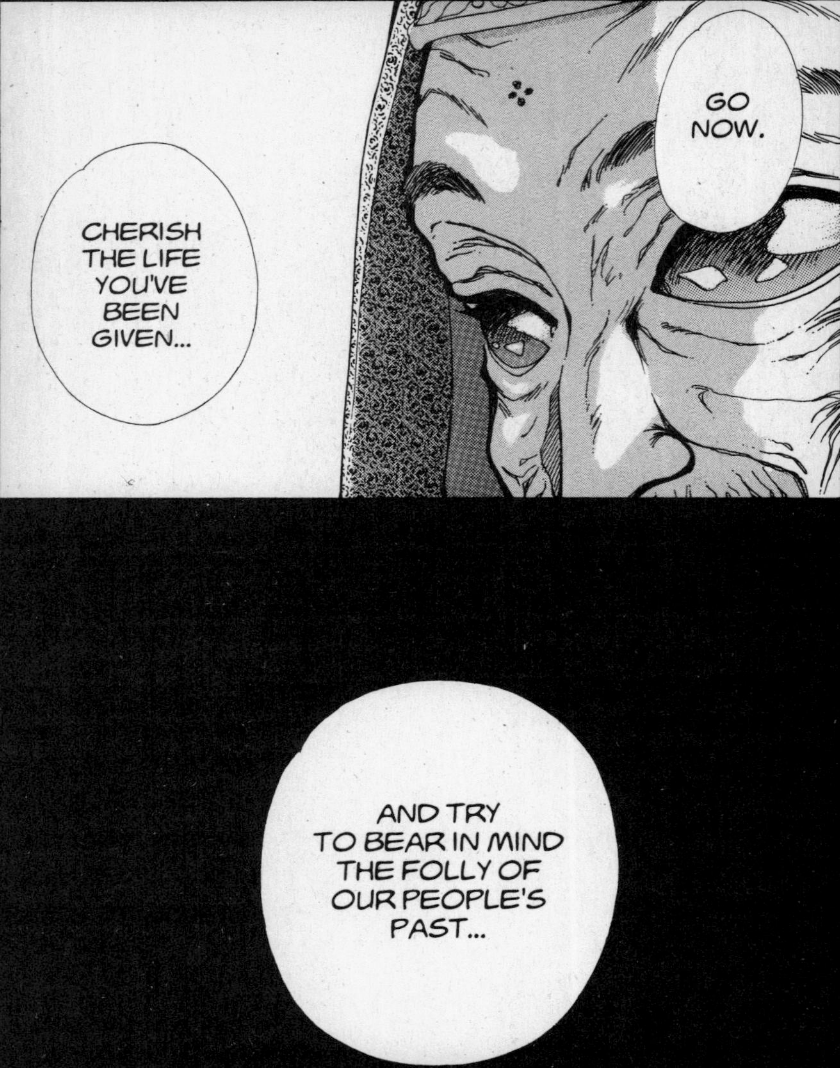
GO NOW.
CHERISH THE LIFE YOU'VE BEEN GIVEN...
AND TRY TO BEAR IN MIND THE FOLLY OF OUR PEOPLE'S PAST...

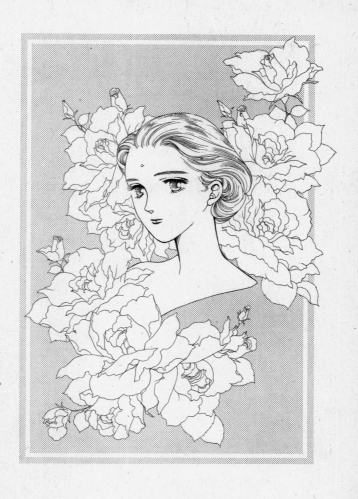

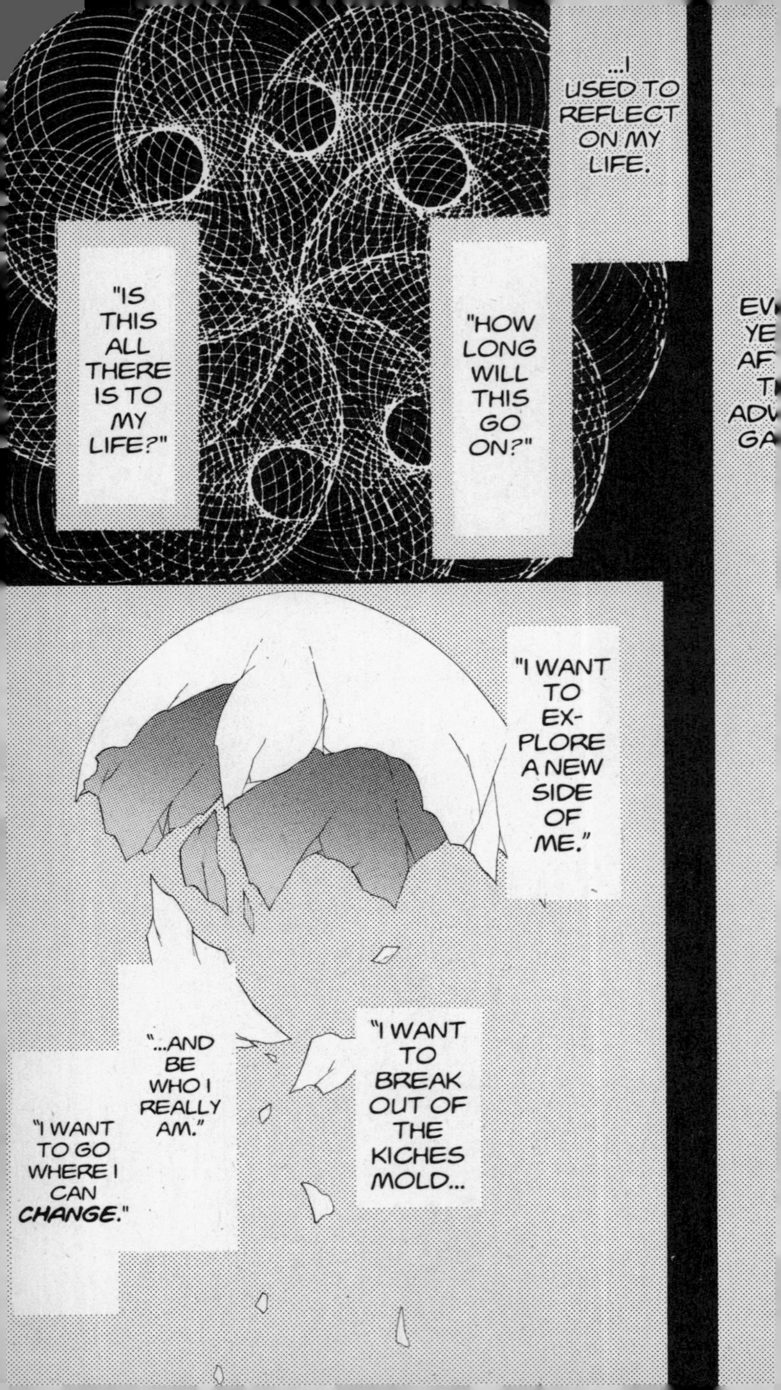
...I USED TO REFLECT ON MY LIFE.
"HOW LONG WILL THIS GO ON?"
"IS THIS ALL THERE IS TO MY LIFE?"
"I WANT TO EX-PLORE A NEW SIDE OF ME."
"I WANT TO BREAK OUT OF THE KICHES MOLD...
"...AND BE WHO I REALLY AM."
"I WANT TO GO WHERE I CAN *CHANGE*."

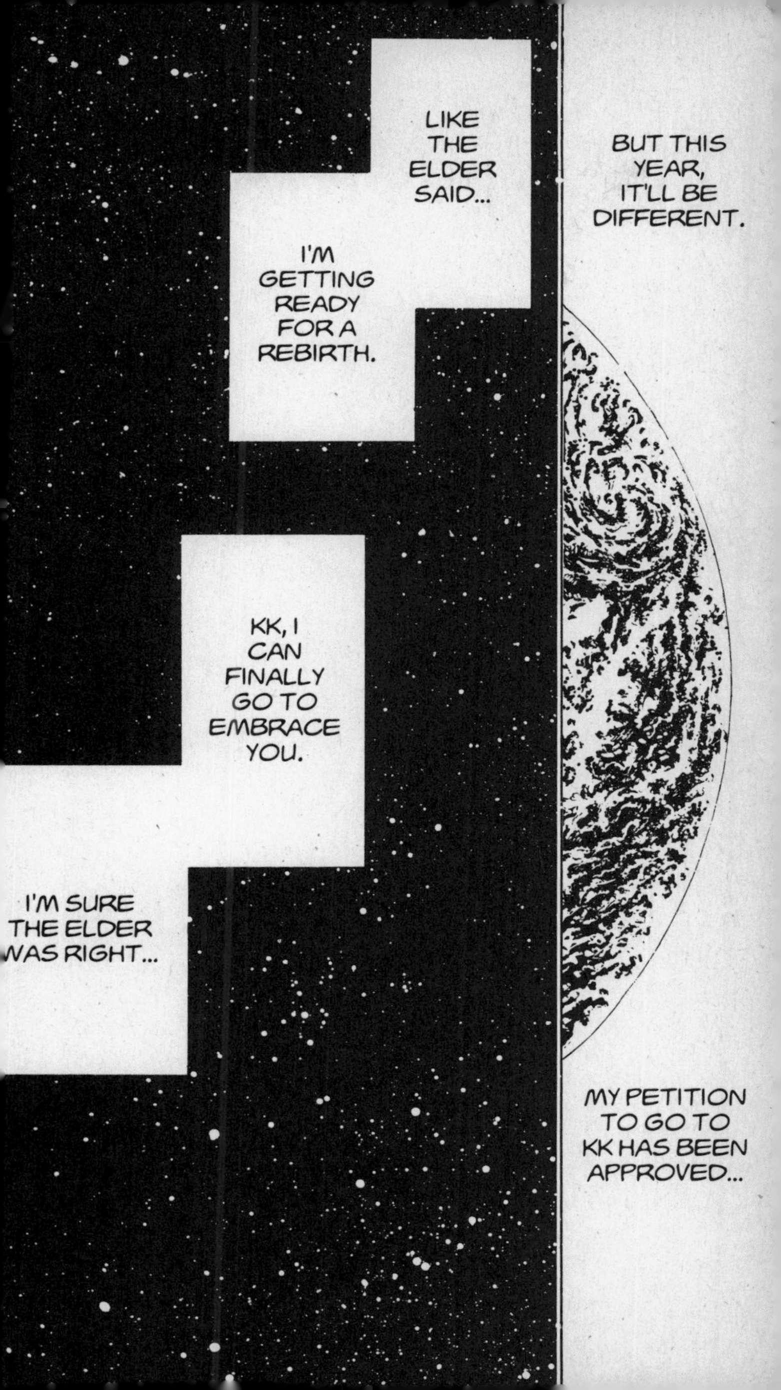
BUT THIS YEAR, IT'LL BE DIFFERENT.
MY PETITION TO GO TO KK HAS BEEN APPROVED...
LIKE THE ELDER SAID...
I'M GETTING READY FOR A REBIRTH.
KK, I CAN FINALLY GO TO EMBRACE YOU.
I'M SURE THE ELDER WAS RIGHT...

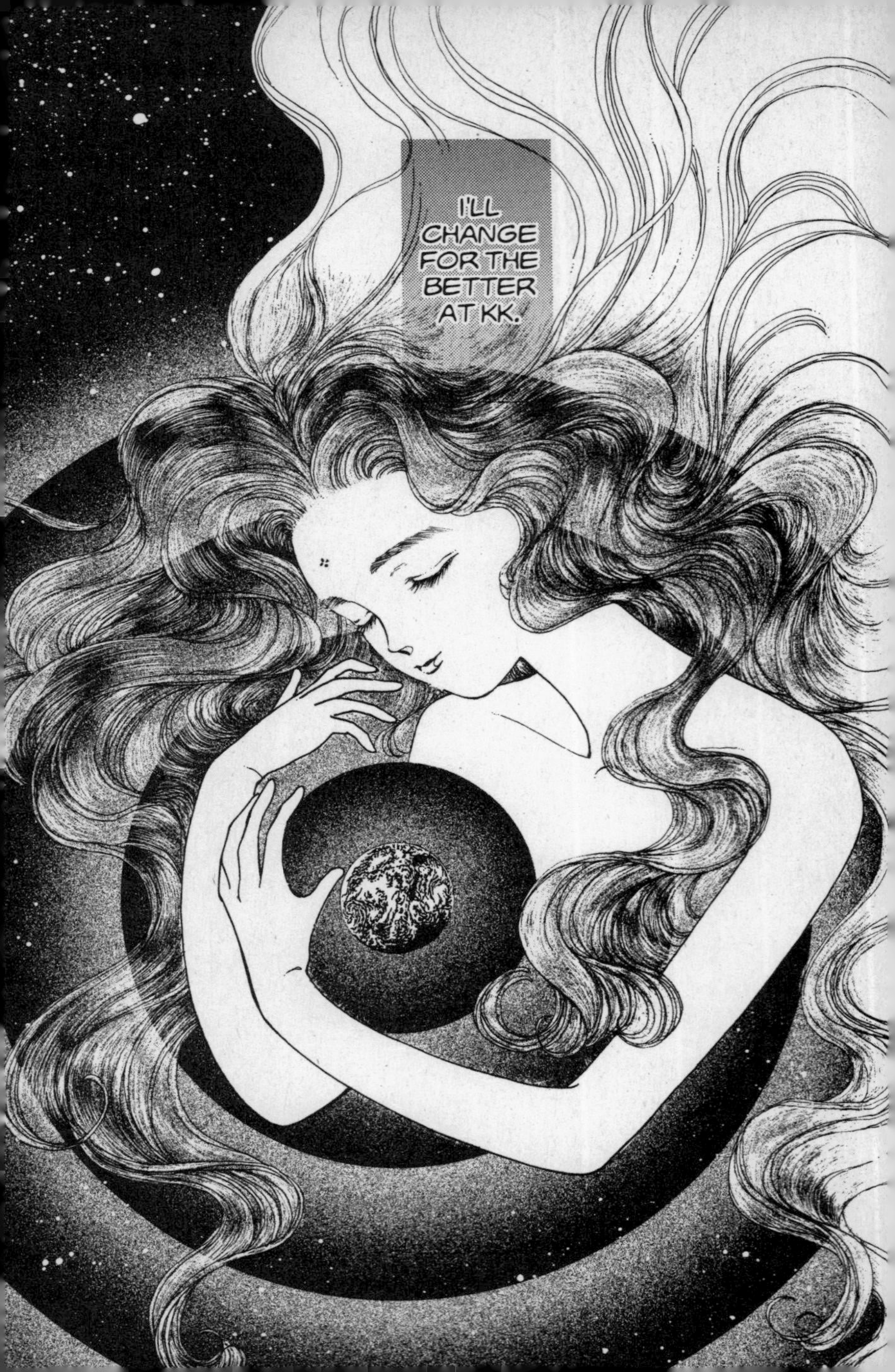
I'LL CHANGE FOR THE BETTER AT KK.

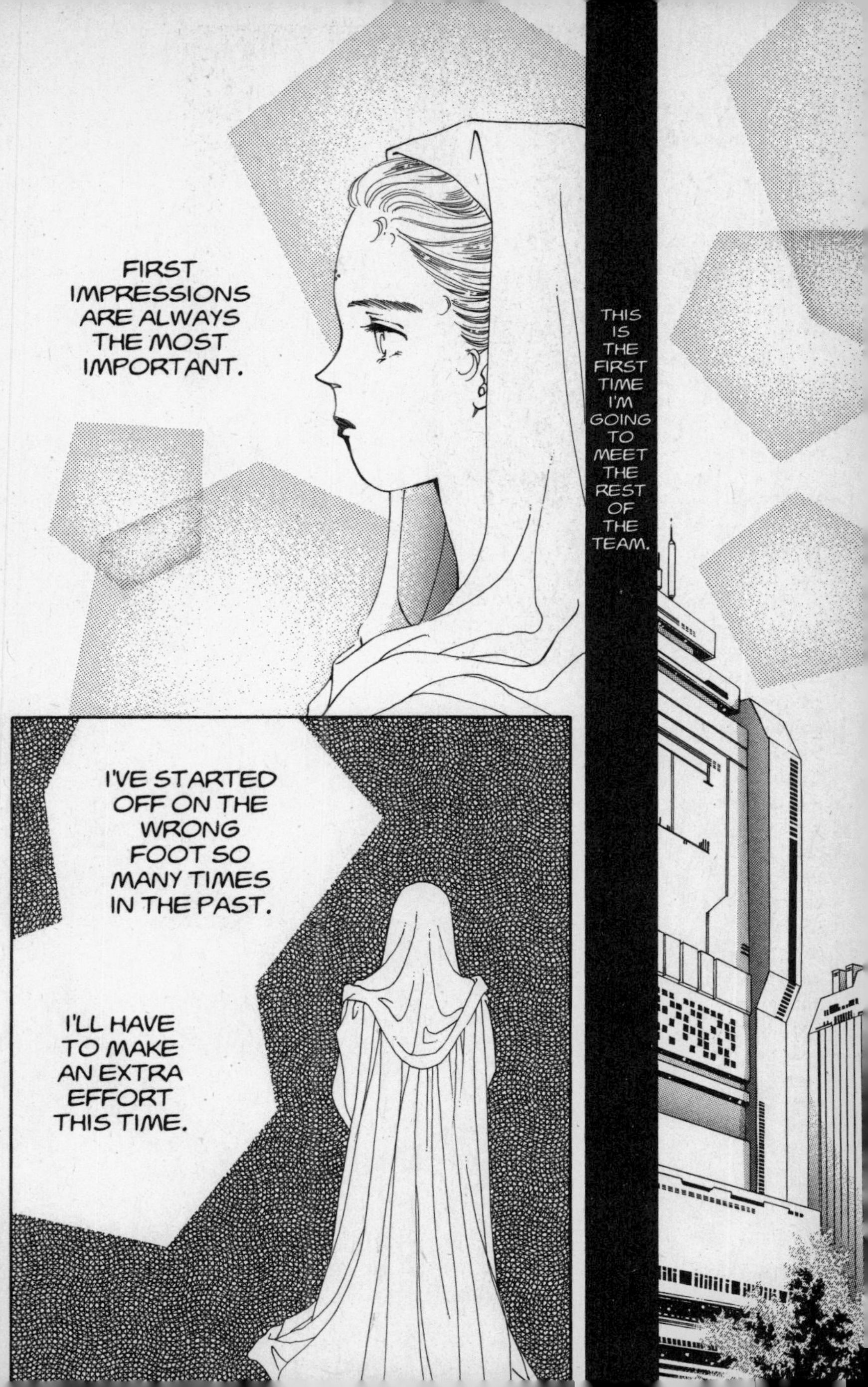
THIS IS THE FIRST TIME I'M GOING TO MEET THE REST OF THE TEAM.
FIRST IMPRESSIONS ARE ALWAYS THE MOST IMPORTANT.
I'VE STARTED OFF ON THE WRONG FOOT SO MANY TIMES IN THE PAST.
I'LL HAVE TO MAKE AN EXTRA EFFORT THIS TIME.

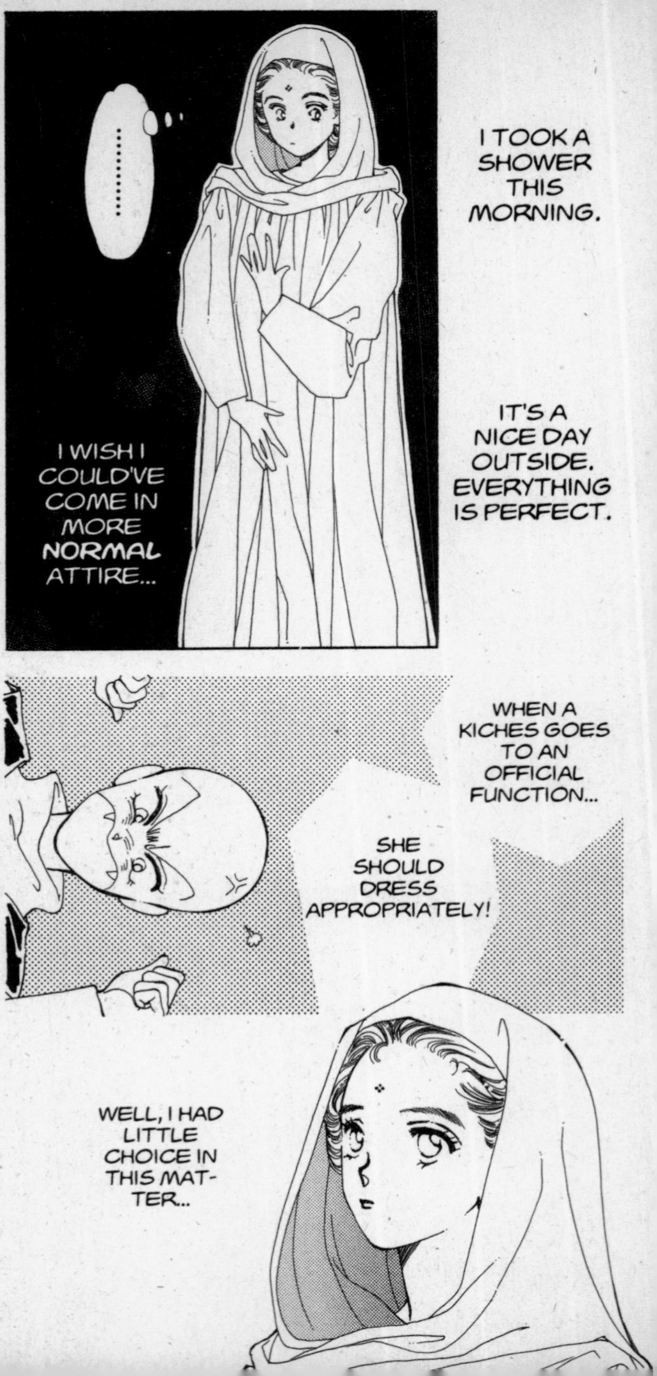
I TOOK A SHOWER THIS MORNING.
IT'S A NICE DAY OUTSIDE. EVERYTHING IS PERFECT.
....
I WISH I COULD'VE COME IN MORE **NORMAL** ATTIRE...
WHEN A KICHES GOES TO AN OFFICIAL FUNCTION...
SHE SHOULD DRESS APPROPRIATELY!
WELL, I HAD LITTLE CHOICE IN THIS MAT-TER...

1/4 COLUMN NONSENSE

PART 5

When I first went to buy my Nintendo console, I happened across a color flier of "Dragon Quest" I by pure coincidence. I had once played an RPG game called "Hydlide" for the PC, so I was curious.

"Hmm, an RPG... Wow, the great Akira Toriyama did the character designs? And oh my gosh, music by Koichi Sugiyama? I love him!"

And so I went to buy it on the day of release with great anticipation...and found that it had been delayed. I tried again two or three more times, and each time I was told that it hadn't come out yet. Come to think of it, "Dragon Quest" has continued to have problems with timely releases.

continued in part 6

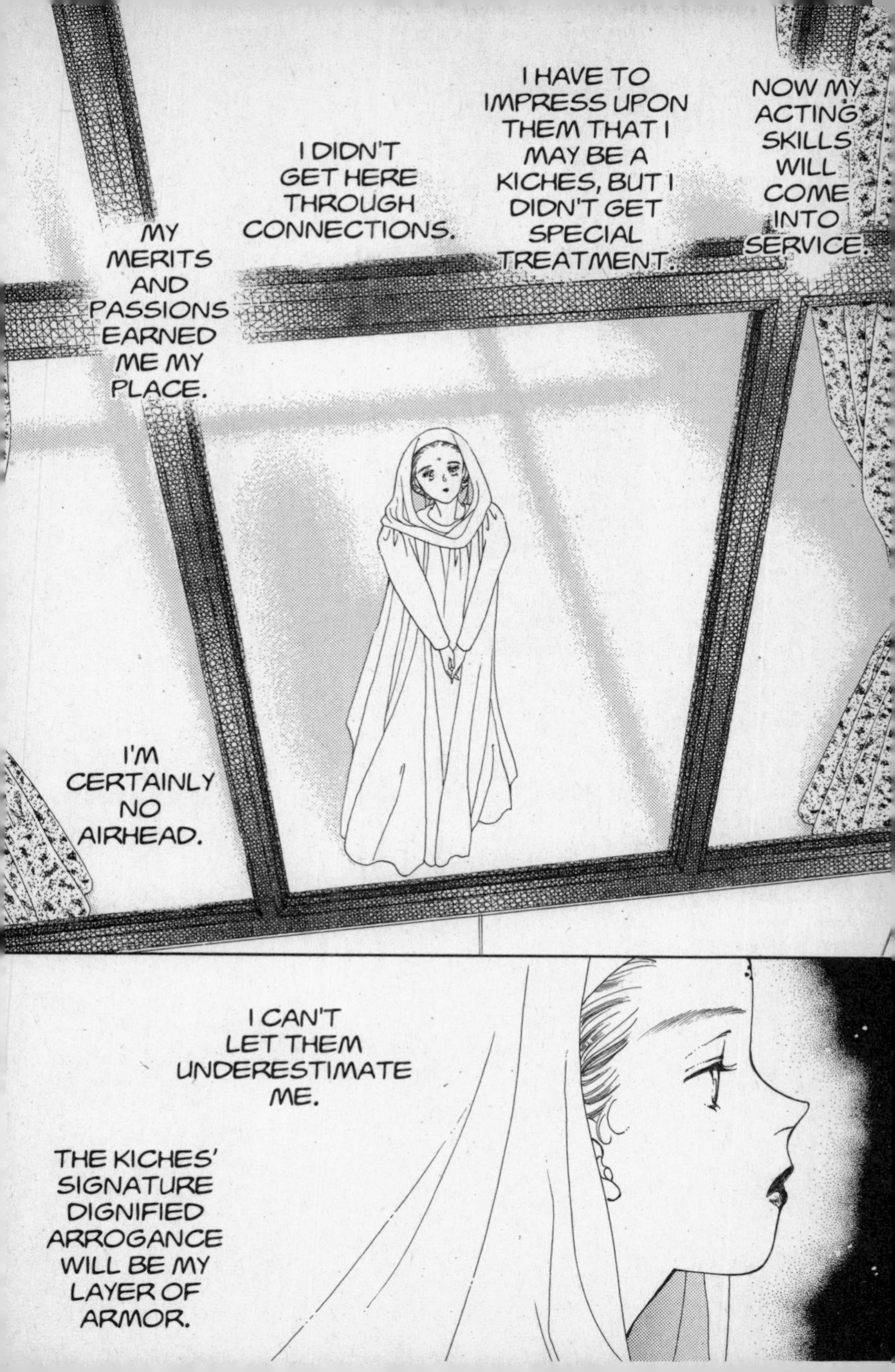
NOW MY ACTING SKILLS WILL COME INTO SERVICE.
I HAVE TO IMPRESS UPON THEM THAT I MAY BE A KICHES, BUT I DIDN'T GET SPECIAL TREATMENT.
I DIDN'T GET HERE THROUGH CONNECTIONS.
MY MERITS AND PASSIONS EARNED ME MY PLACE.
I'M CERTAINLY NO AIRHEAD.
I CAN'T LET THEM UNDERESTIMATE ME.
THE KICHES' SIGNATURE DIGNIFIED ARROGANCE WILL BE MY LAYER OF ARMOR.

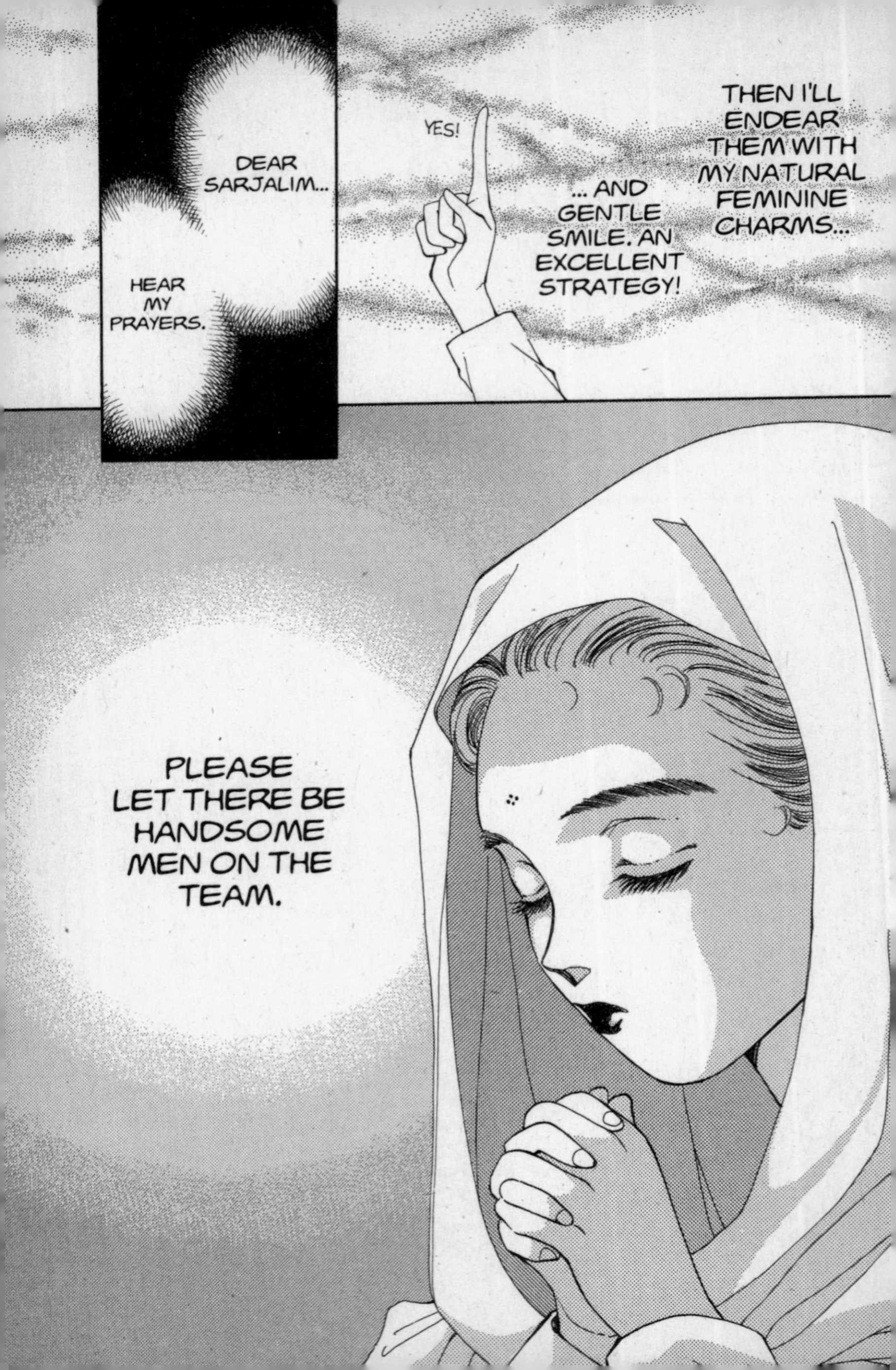
THEN I'LL ENDEAR THEM WITH MY NATURAL FEMININE CHARMS...
... AND GENTLE SMILE. AN EXCELLENT STRATEGY!
YES!
DEAR SARJALIM...
HEAR MY PRAYERS.
PLEASE LET THERE BE HANDSOME MEN ON THE TEAM.

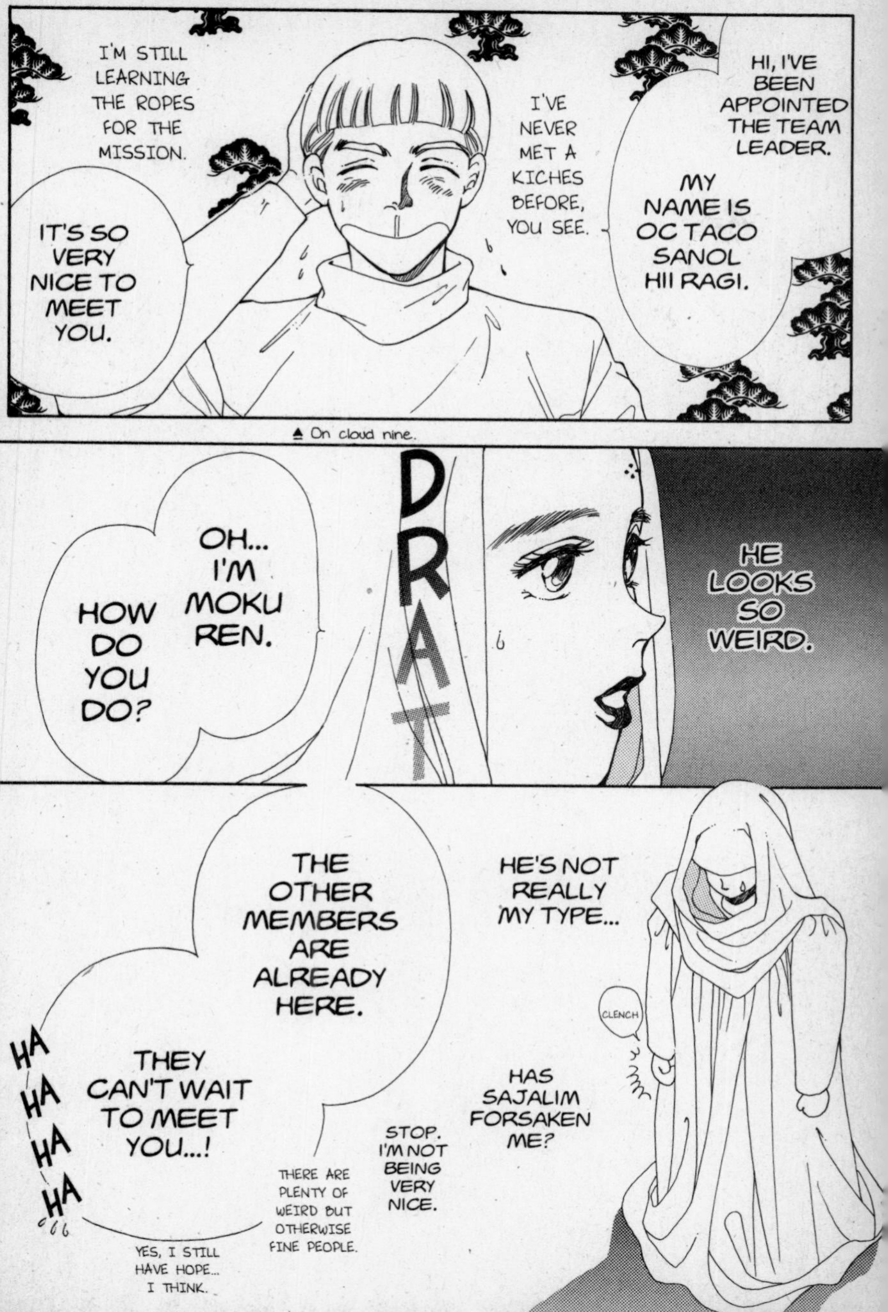
HI, I'VE BEEN APPOINTED THE TEAM LEADER.
MY NAME IS OC TACO SANOL HII RAGI.
I'VE NEVER MET A KICHES BEFORE, YOU SEE.
I'M STILL LEARNING THE ROPES FOR THE MISSION.
IT'S SO VERY NICE TO MEET YOU.
▲ On cloud nine.
HE LOOKS SO WEIRD.
DRAT
OH... I'M MOKU REN.
HOW DO YOU DO?
HE'S NOT REALLY MY TYPE...
CLENCH
HAS SAJALIM FORSAKEN ME?
STOP. I'M NOT BEING VERY NICE.
THERE ARE PLENTY OF WEIRD BUT OTHERWISE FINE PEOPLE.
THE OTHER MEMBERS ARE ALREADY HERE.
THEY CAN'T WAIT TO MEET YOU...!
HA HA HA HA
YES, I STILL HAVE HOPE... I THINK.

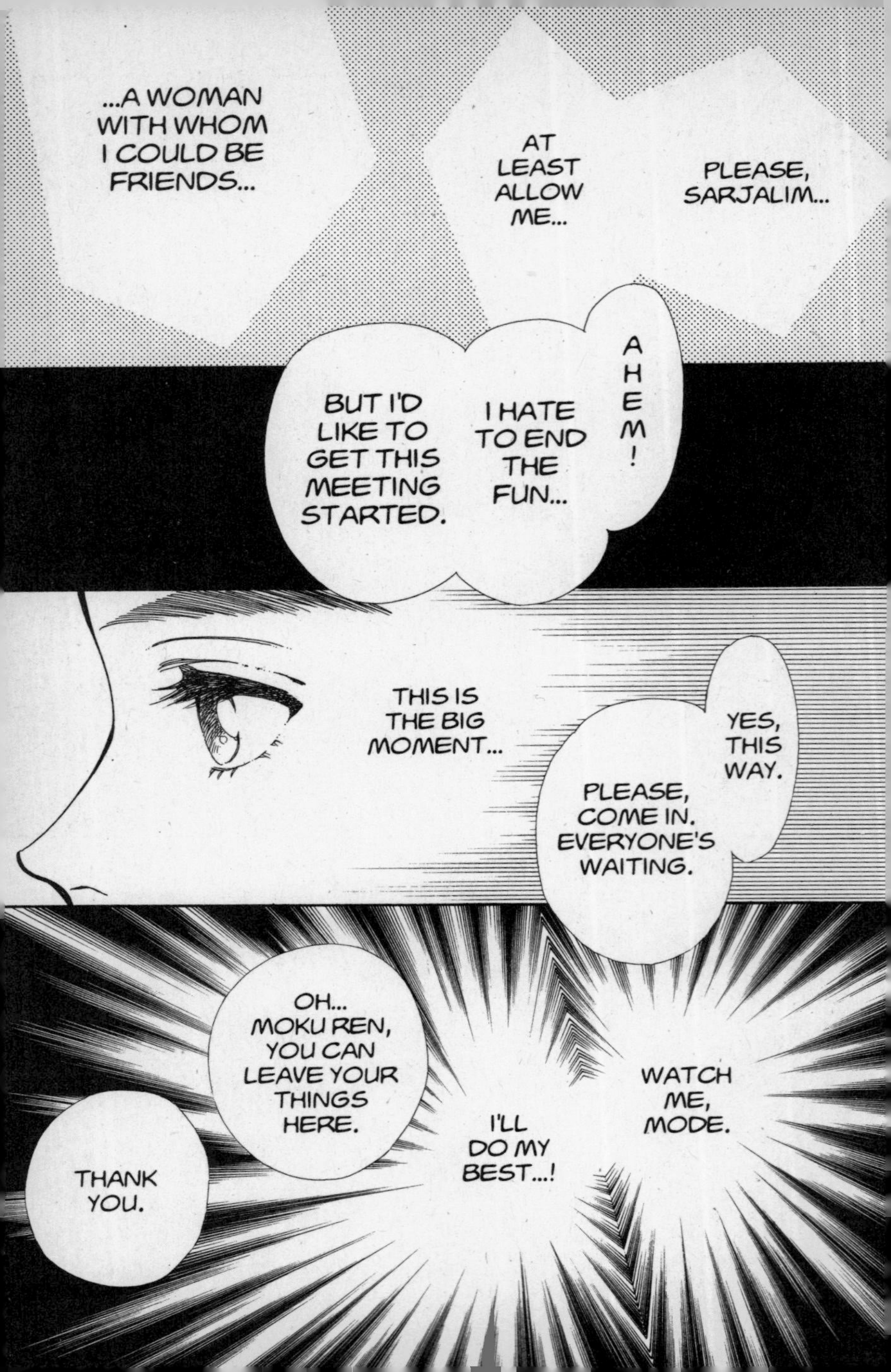
PLEASE, SARJALIM...
AT LEAST ALLOW ME...
...A WOMAN WITH WHOM I COULD BE FRIENDS...
AHEM!
I HATE TO END THE FUN...
BUT I'D LIKE TO GET THIS MEETING STARTED.
YES, THIS WAY.
PLEASE, COME IN. EVERYONE'S WAITING.
THIS IS THE BIG MOMENT...
WATCH ME, MODE.
I'LL DO MY BEST...!
OH... MOKU REN, YOU CAN LEAVE YOUR THINGS HERE.
THANK YOU.

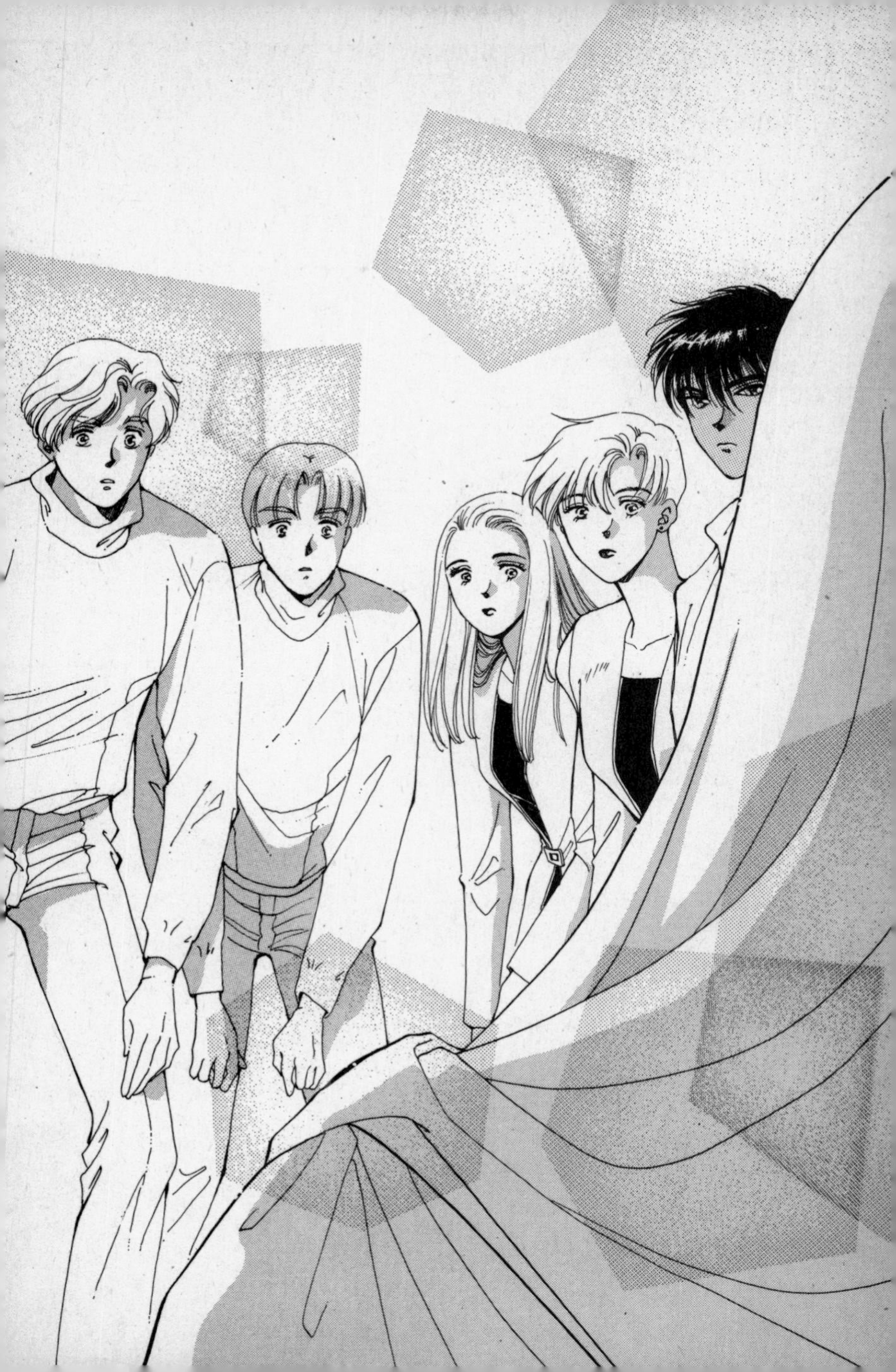

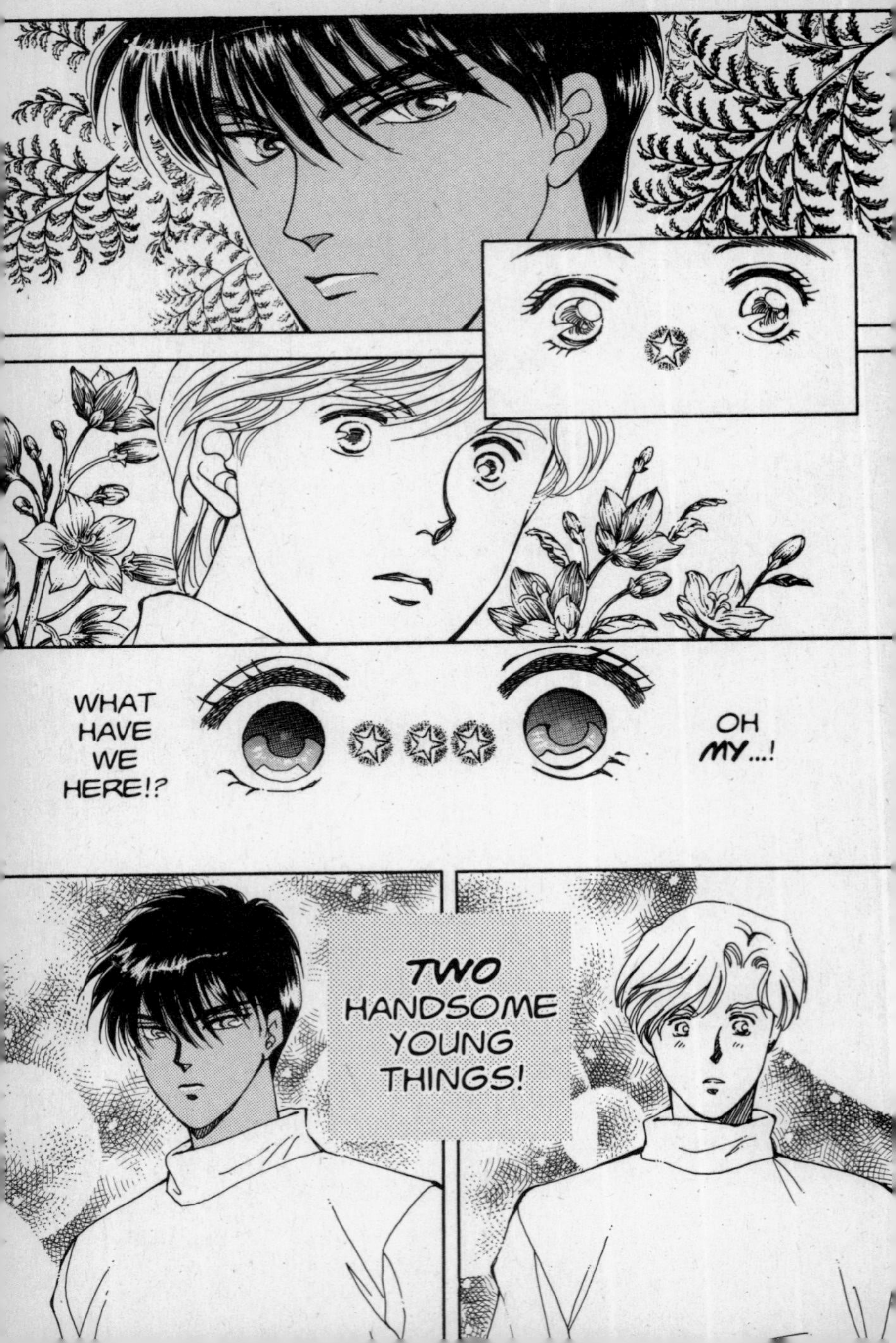
OH MY...!
WHAT HAVE WE HERE!?
TWO HANDSOME YOUNG THINGS!

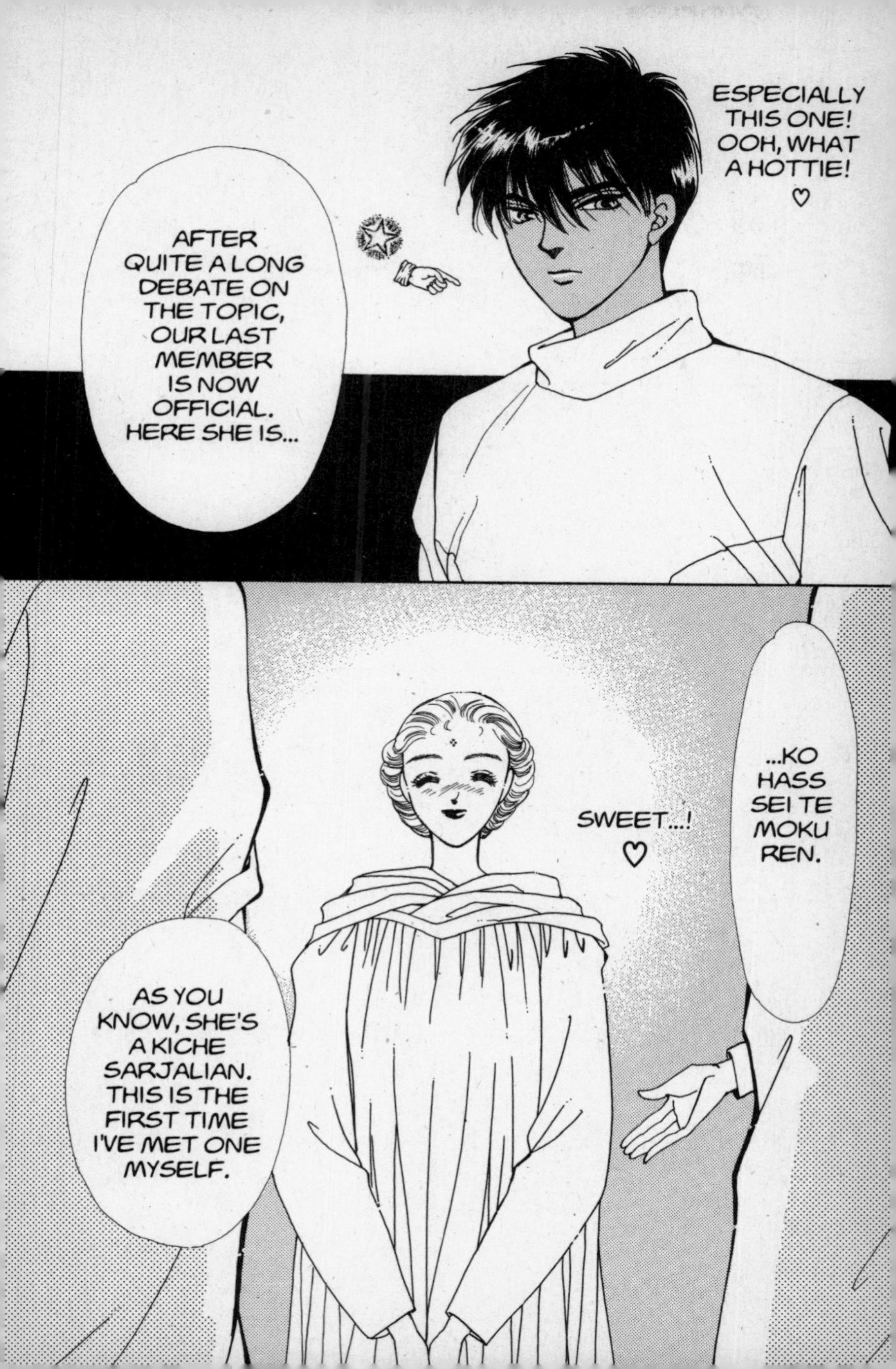

ESPECIALLY THIS ONE! OOH, WHAT A HOTTIE! ♡
AFTER QUITE A LONG DEBATE ON THE TOPIC, OUR LAST MEMBER IS NOW OFFICIAL. HERE SHE IS...
...KO HASS SEI TE MOKU REN.
SWEET...! ♡
AS YOU KNOW, SHE'S A KICHE SARJALIAN. THIS IS THE FIRST TIME I'VE MET ONE MYSELF.

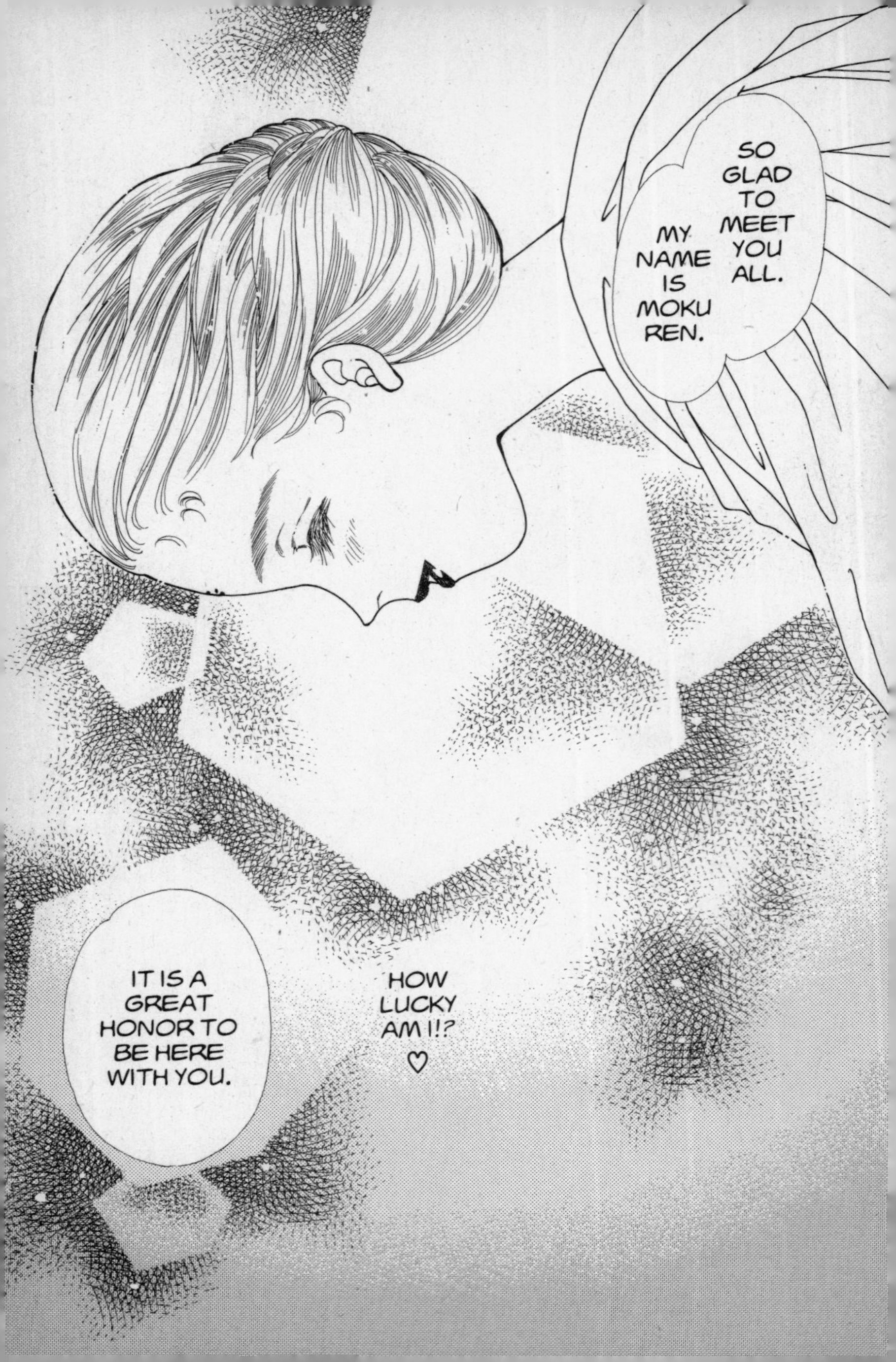
SO GLAD TO MEET YOU ALL.
MY NAME IS MOKU REN.
HOW LUCKY AM I!? ♡
IT IS A GREAT HONOR TO BE HERE WITH YOU.

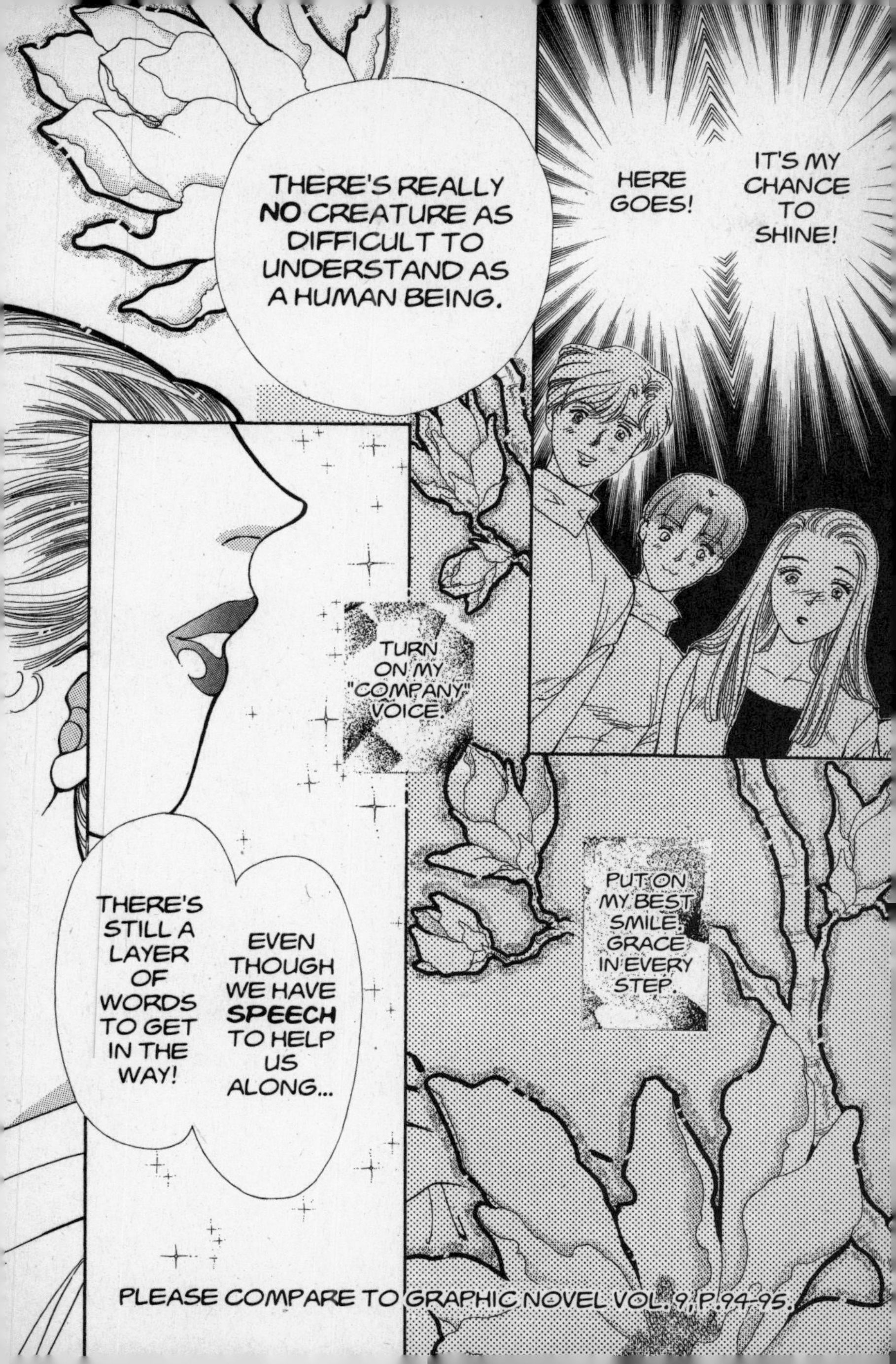
IT'S MY CHANCE TO SHINE!
HERE GOES!
TURN ON MY "COMPANY" VOICE.
PUT ON MY BEST SMILE. GRACE IN EVERY STEP.
THERE'S REALLY **NO** CREATURE AS DIFFICULT TO UNDERSTAND AS A HUMAN BEING.
EVEN THOUGH WE HAVE **SPEECH** TO HELP US ALONG...
THERE'S STILL A LAYER OF WORDS TO GET IN THE WAY!
PLEASE COMPARE TO GRAPHIC NOVEL VOL. 9, P.94-95.

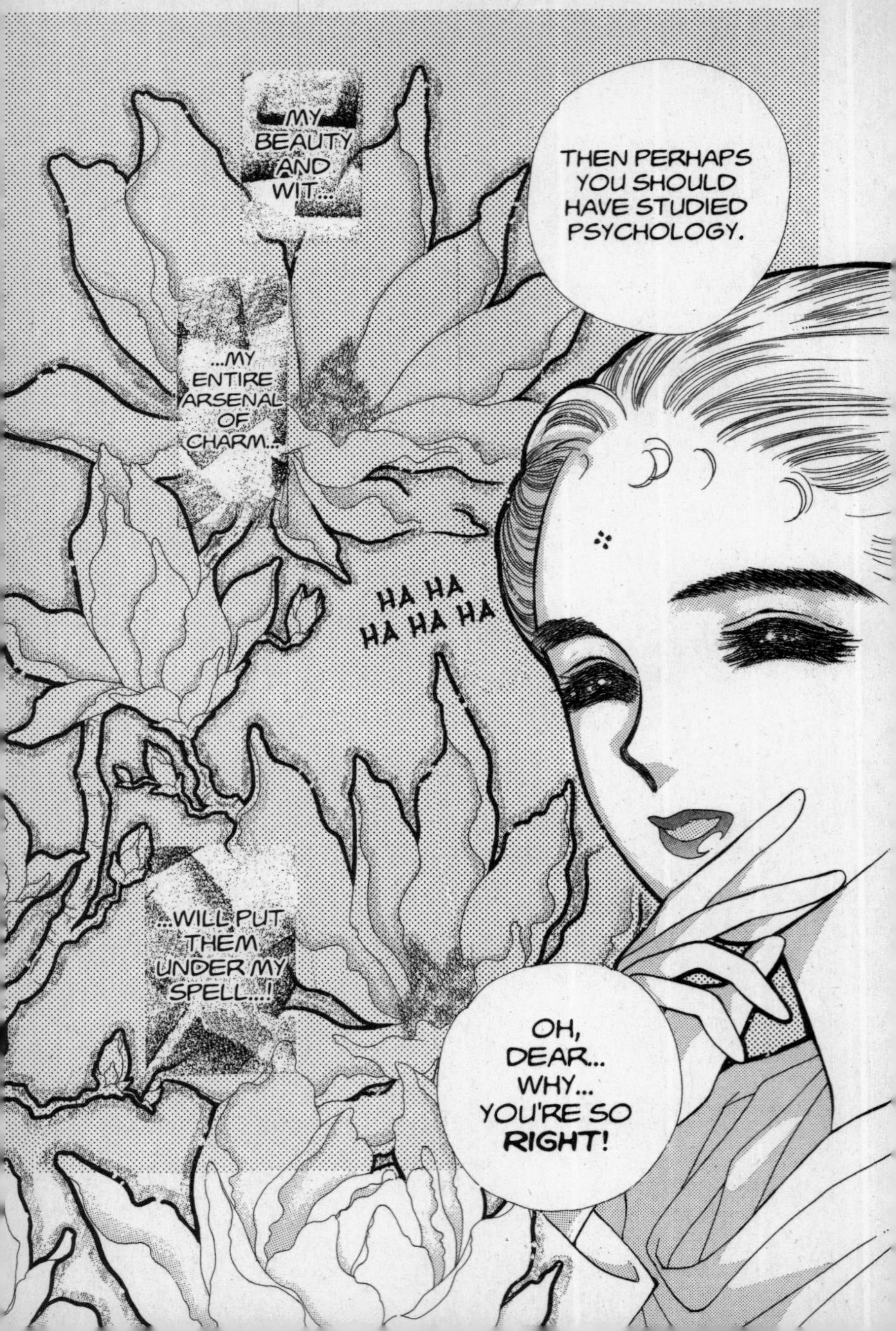
THEN PERHAPS YOU SHOULD HAVE STUDIED PSYCHOLOGY.
OH, DEAR... WHY... YOU'RE SO **RIGHT**!
MY BEAUTY AND WIT...
...MY ENTIRE ARSENAL OF CHARM...
...WILL PUT THEM UNDER MY SPELL...!
HA HA HA HA HA

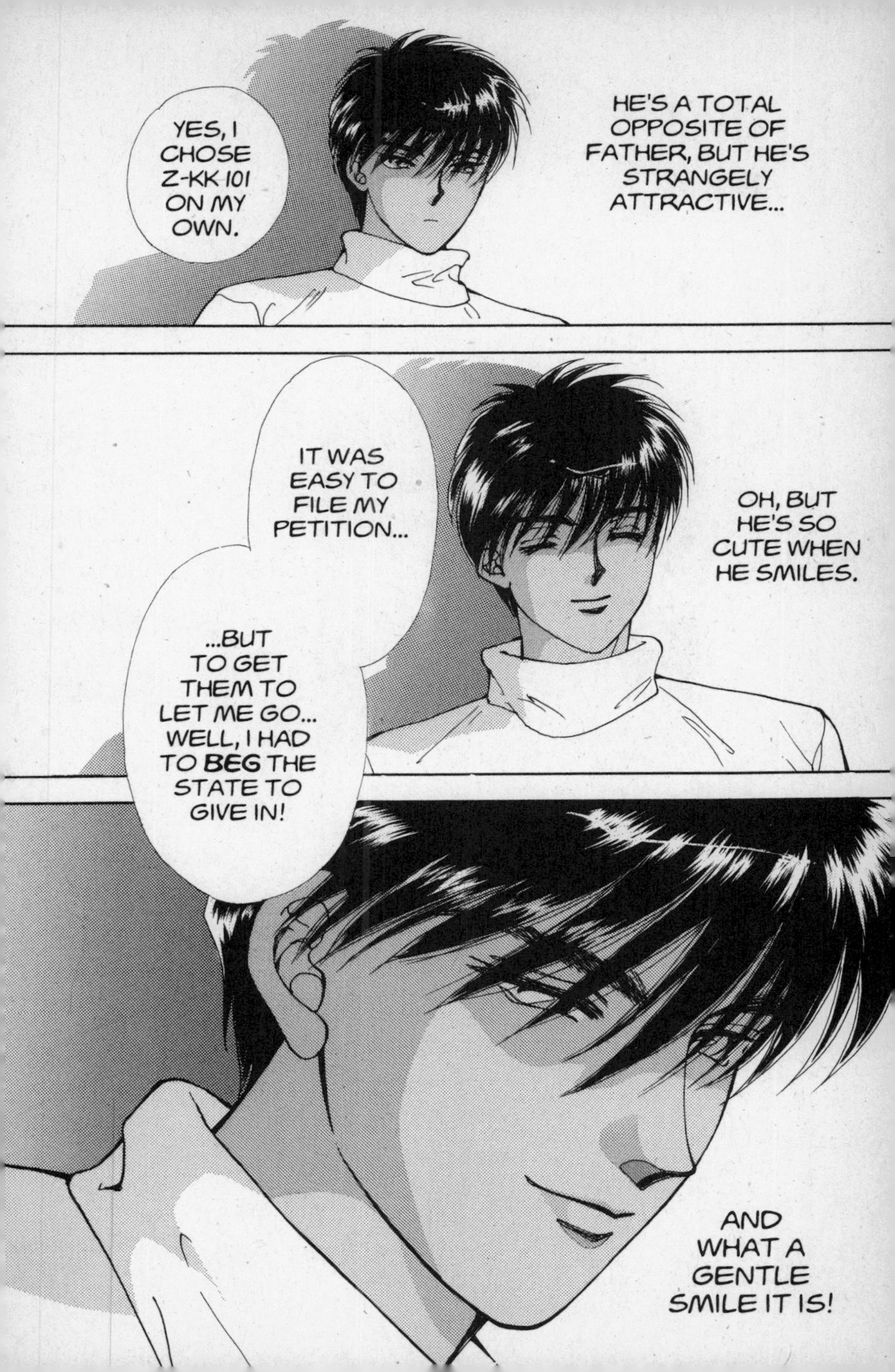

HE'S A TOTAL OPPOSITE OF FATHER, BUT HE'S STRANGELY ATTRACTIVE...
YES, I CHOSE Z-KK 101 ON MY OWN.
OH, BUT HE'S SO CUTE WHEN HE SMILES.
IT WAS EASY TO FILE MY PETITION...
...BUT TO GET THEM TO LET ME GO... WELL, I HAD TO BEG THE STATE TO GIVE IN!
AND WHAT A GENTLE SMILE IT IS!

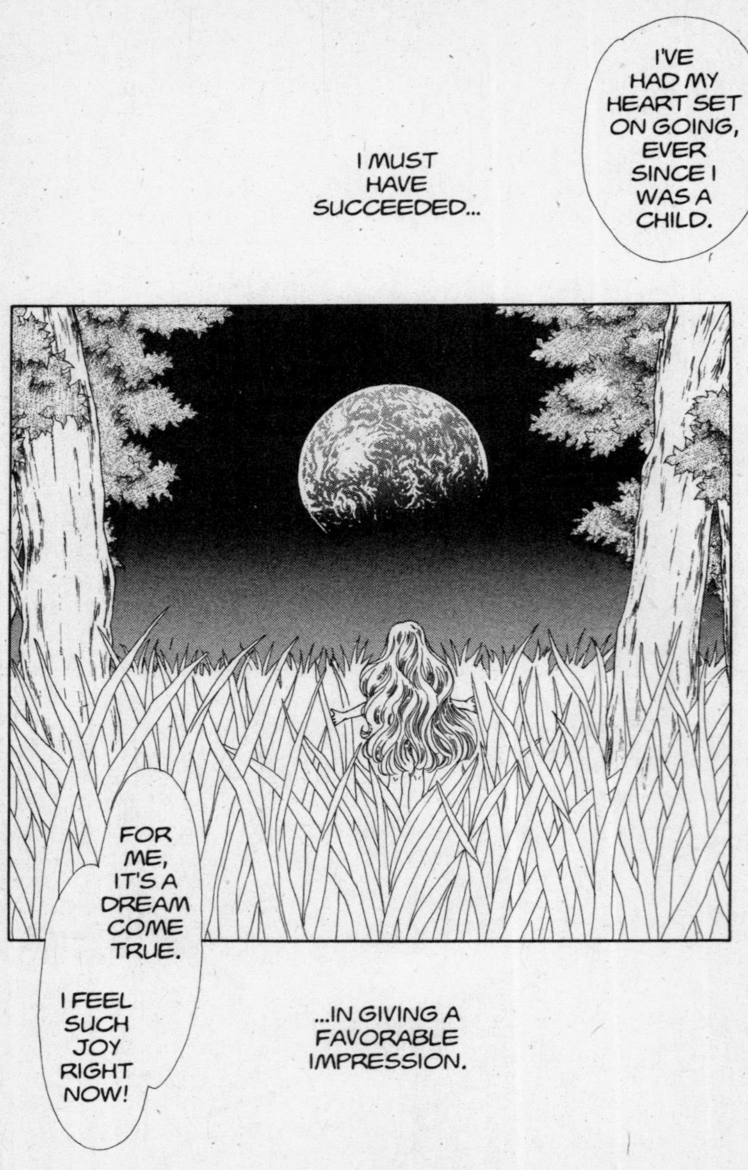
I'VE HAD MY HEART SET ON GOING, EVER SINCE I WAS A CHILD.
I MUST HAVE SUCCEEDED...
...IN GIVING A FAVORABLE IMPRESSION.
FOR ME, IT'S A DREAM COME TRUE.
I FEEL SUCH JOY RIGHT NOW!

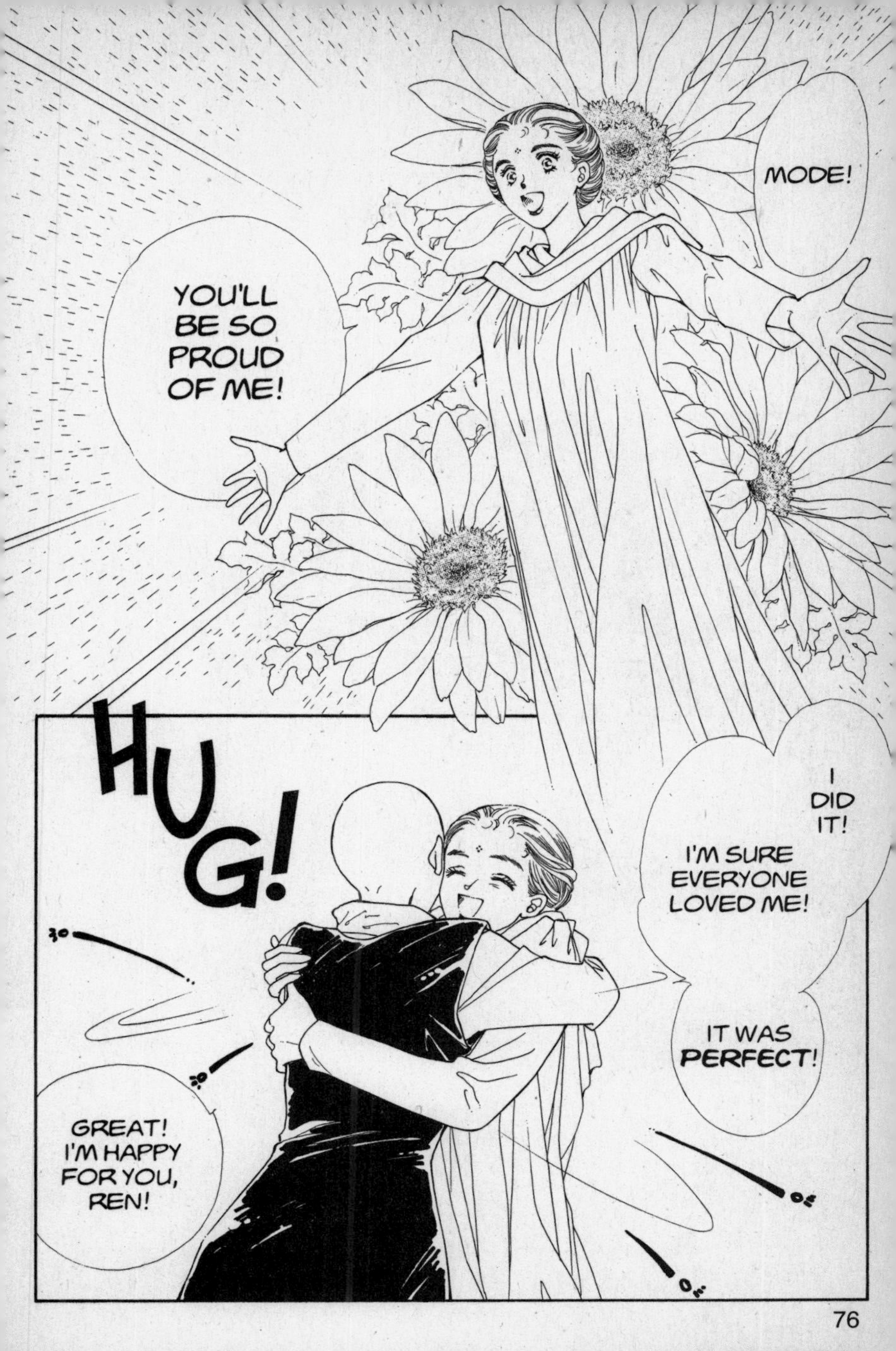
MODE!
YOU'LL BE SO PROUD OF ME!
I DID IT!
I'M SURE EVERYONE LOVED ME!
IT WAS PERFECT!
HUG!
GREAT! I'M HAPPY FOR YOU, REN!

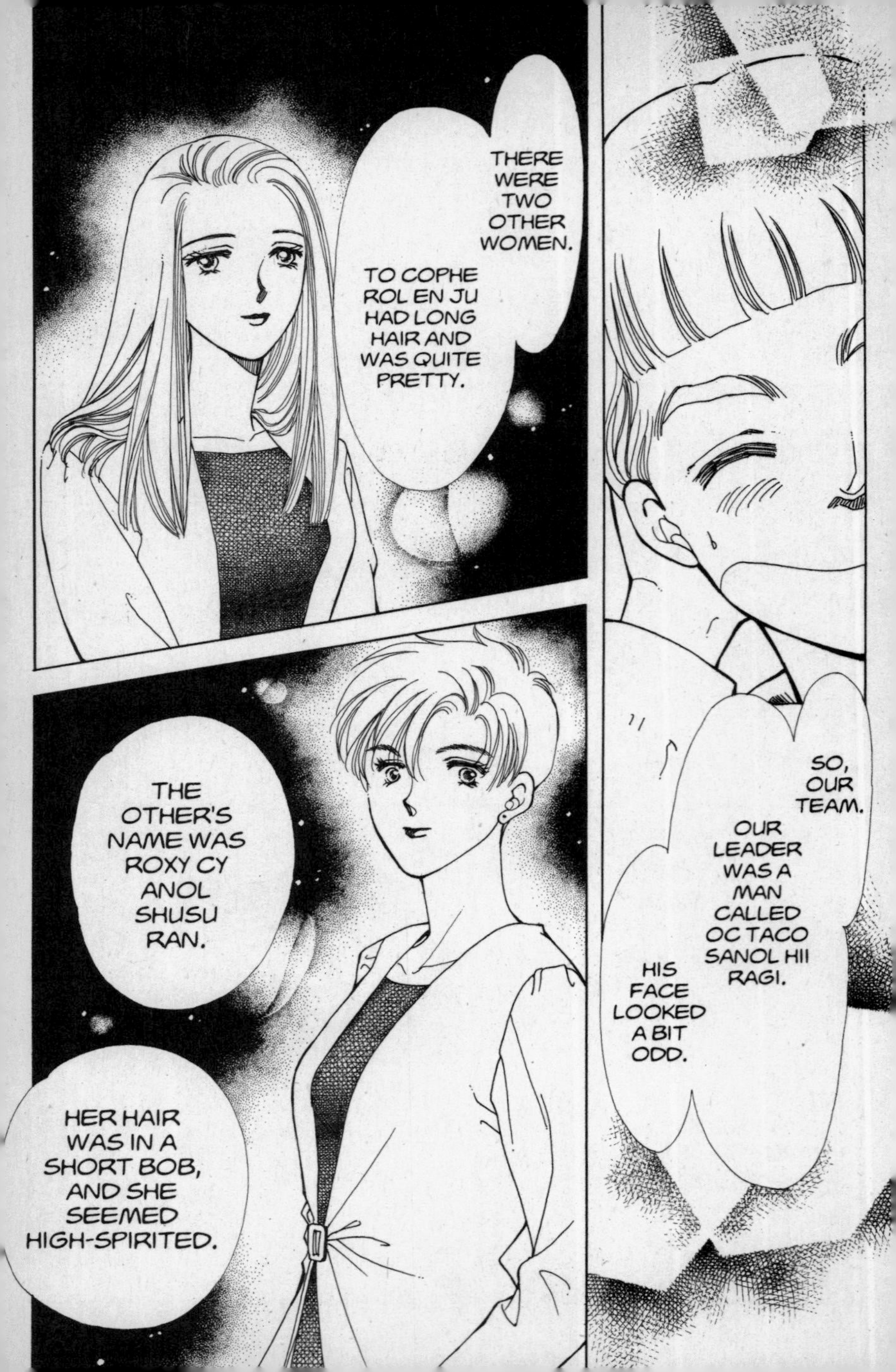
SO, OUR TEAM.
OUR LEADER WAS A MAN CALLED OC TACO SANOL HII RAGI.
HIS FACE LOOKED A BIT ODD.
THERE WERE TWO OTHER WOMEN.
TO COPHE ROL EN JU HAD LONG HAIR AND WAS QUITE PRETTY.
THE OTHER'S NAME WAS ROXY CY ANOL SHUSU RAN.
HER HAIR WAS IN A SHORT BOB, AND SHE SEEMED HIGH-SPIRITED.

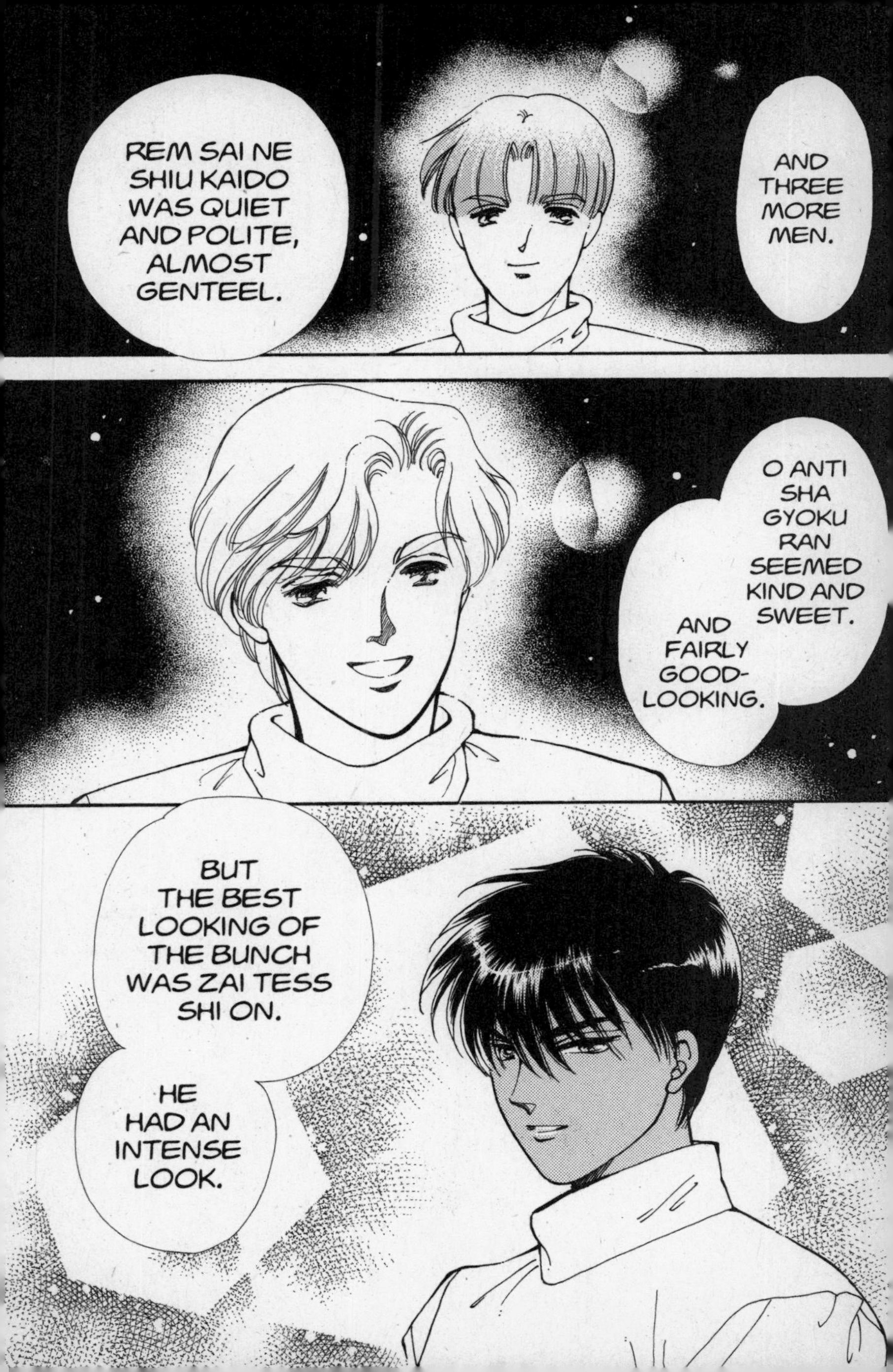
AND THREE MORE MEN.
REM SAI NE SHIU KAIDO WAS QUIET AND POLITE, ALMOST GENTEEL.
O ANTI SHA GYOKU RAN SEEMED KIND AND SWEET.
AND FAIRLY GOOD-LOOKING.
BUT THE BEST LOOKING OF THE BUNCH WAS ZAI TESS SHI ON.
HE HAD AN INTENSE LOOK.

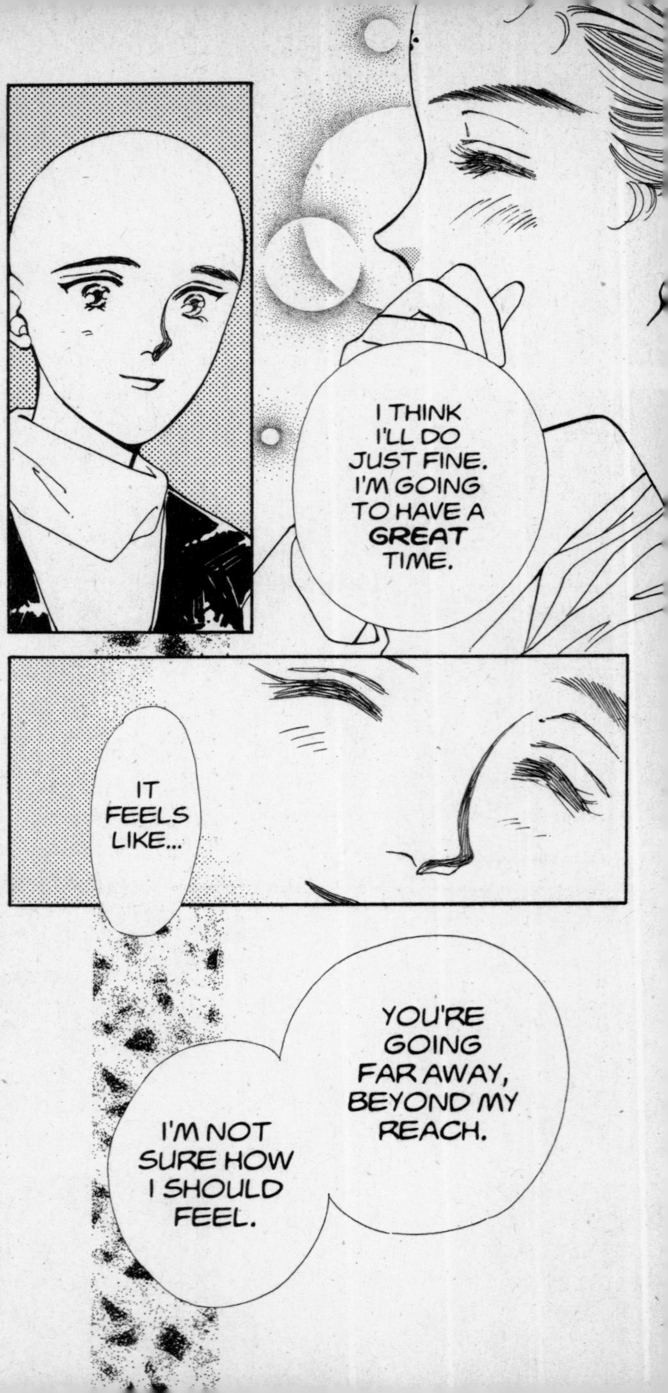
I THINK I'LL DO JUST FINE. I'M GOING TO HAVE A GREAT TIME.
IT FEELS LIKE...
YOU'RE GOING FAR AWAY, BEYOND MY REACH.
I'M NOT SURE HOW I SHOULD FEEL.

1/4 COLUMN NONSENSE

—PART 6—

There's a toy store in my neighborhood called Sun Toys, and I had been able to buy "Dragon Quest I" through IV on the day of release... But V had sold out before I could make my way there. I had been so sure they'd have it, that I'd underestimated its popularity. Sigh. Well, it is on the new console, the Super Nintendo. I bet they sold more copies of it than ever before... I remember that "Dragon Quest IV" was released around the time my cat Tomonori died. I busied myself with the game to keep my mind off my depression. A memorable scene in II was at the end of the game when the wandering souls of the little girl's town went up to Heaven, saying, "Thank you... thank you..." I cried.

continued in part 7

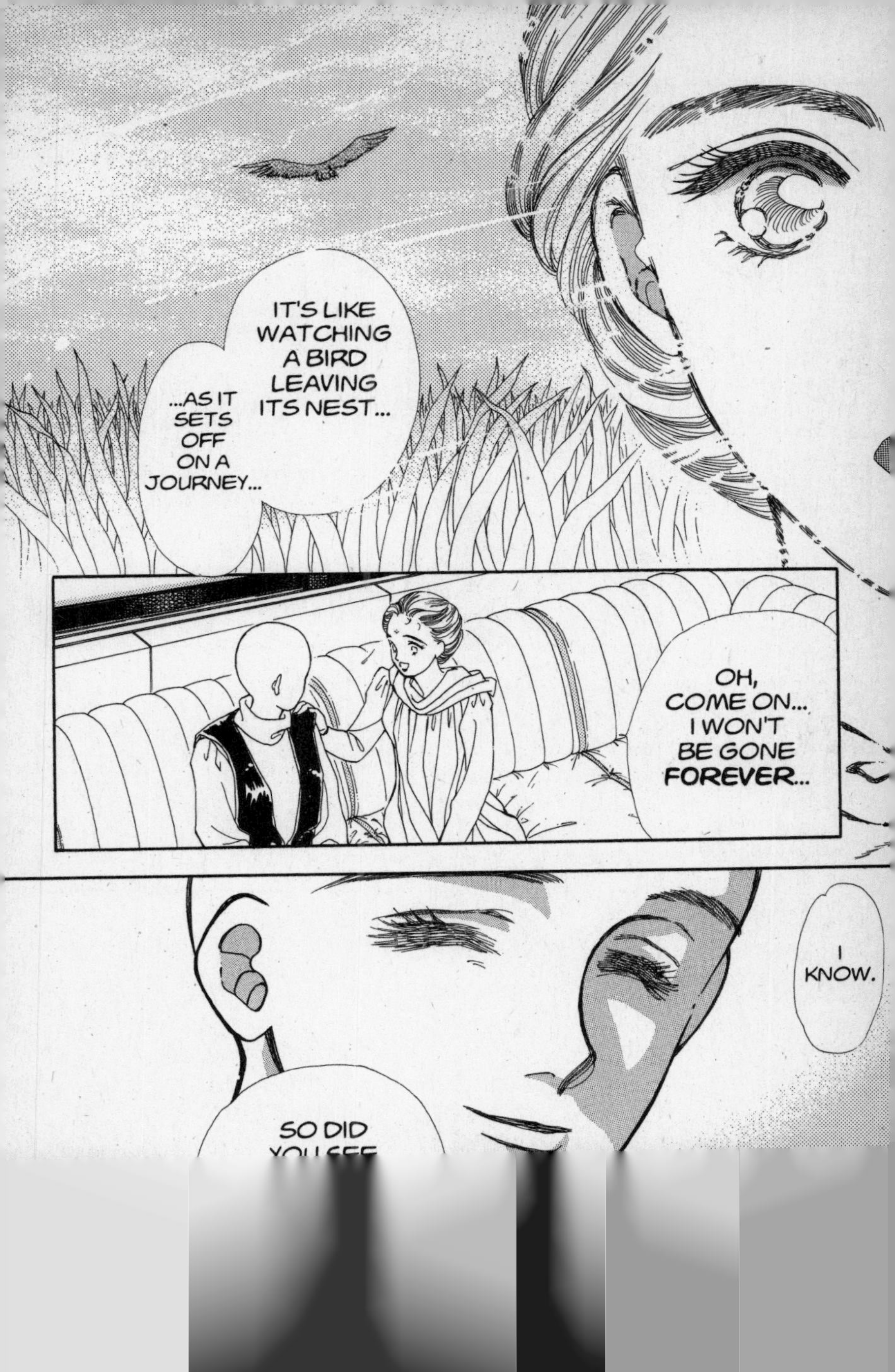
IT'S LIKE WATCHING A BIRD LEAVING ITS NEST...
...AS IT SETS OFF ON A JOURNEY...
OH, COME ON... I WON'T BE GONE FOREVER...
I KNOW.
SO DID

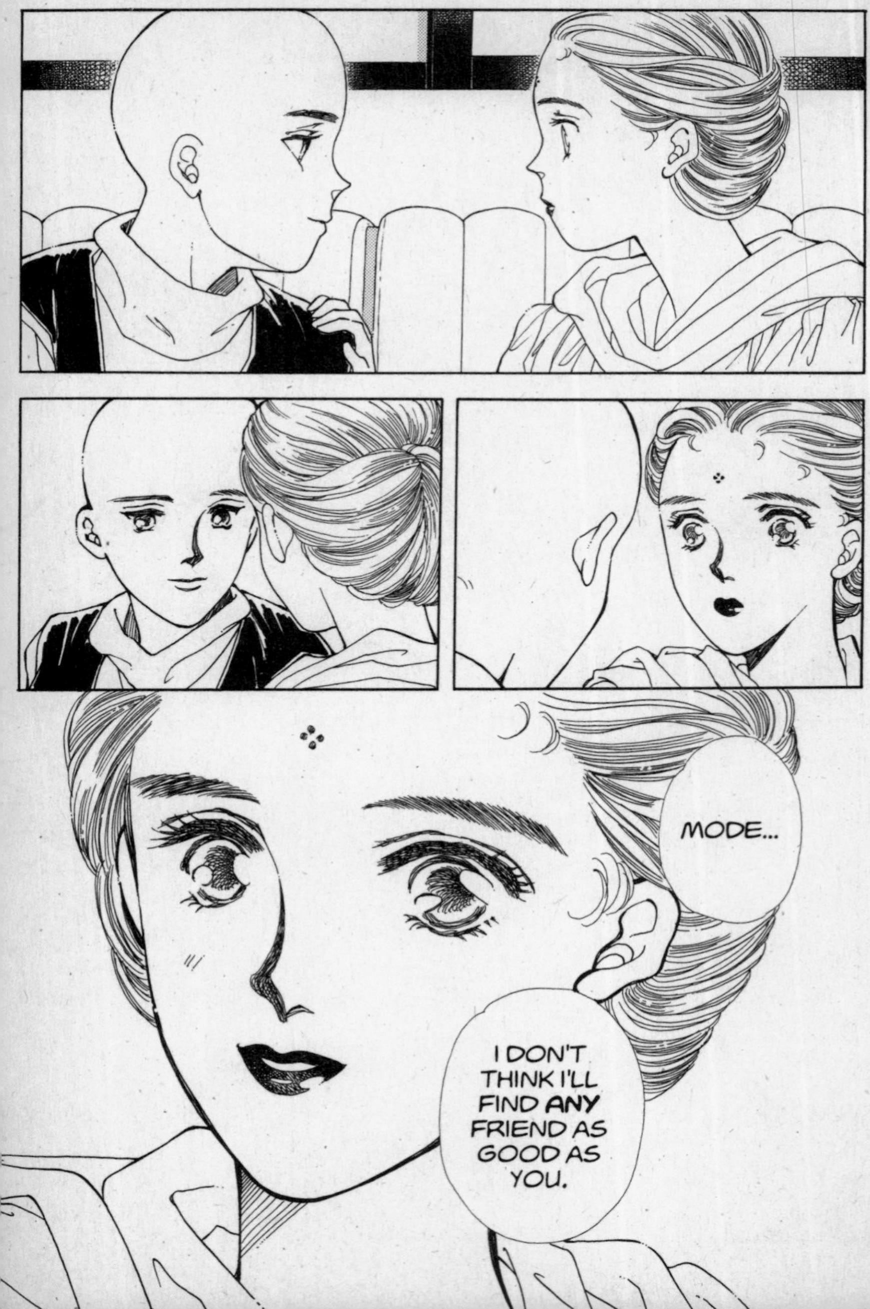
MODE...
I DON'T THINK I'LL FIND ANY FRIEND AS GOOD AS YOU.

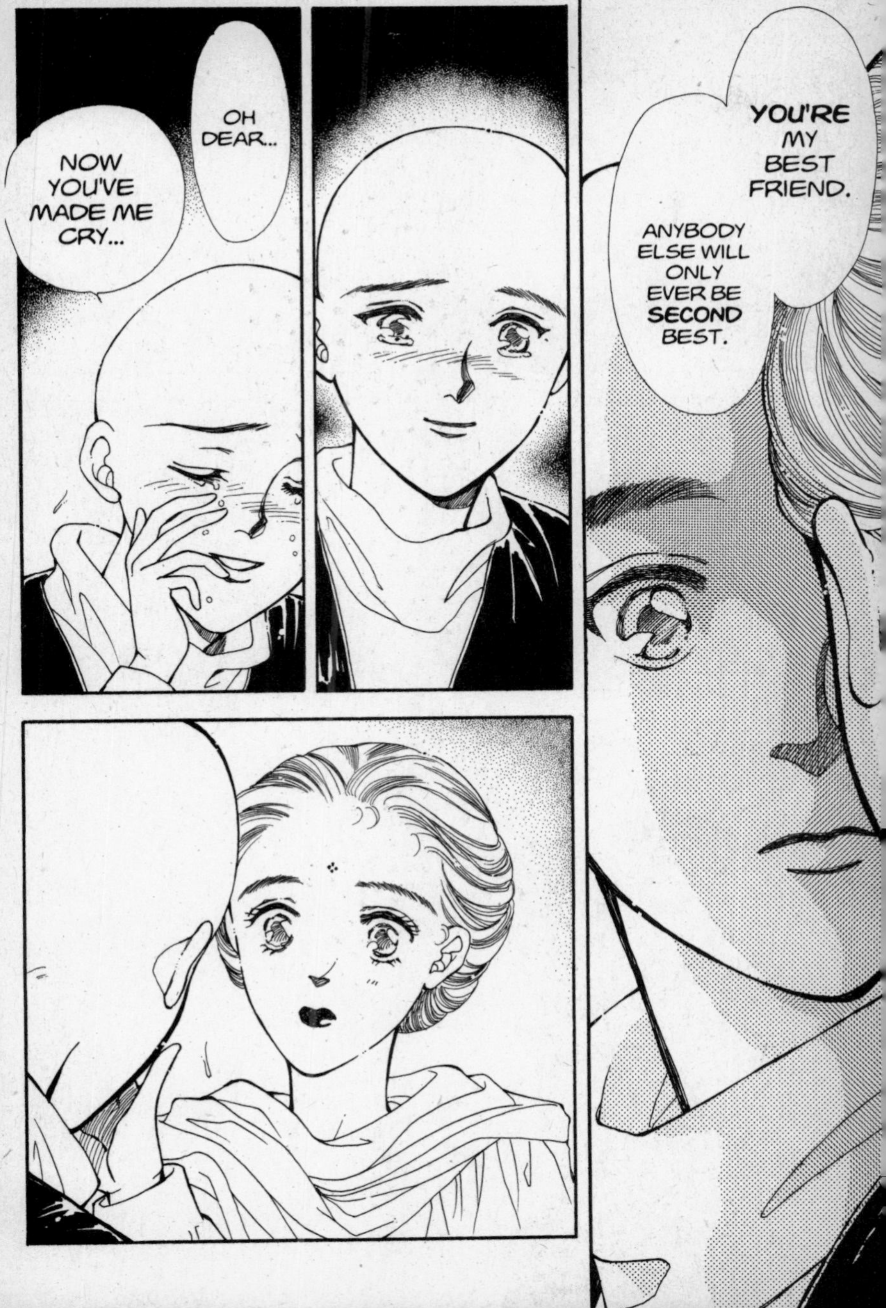
YOU'RE MY BEST FRIEND.
ANYBODY ELSE WILL ONLY EVER BE SECOND BEST.
OH DEAR...
NOW YOU'VE MADE ME CRY...

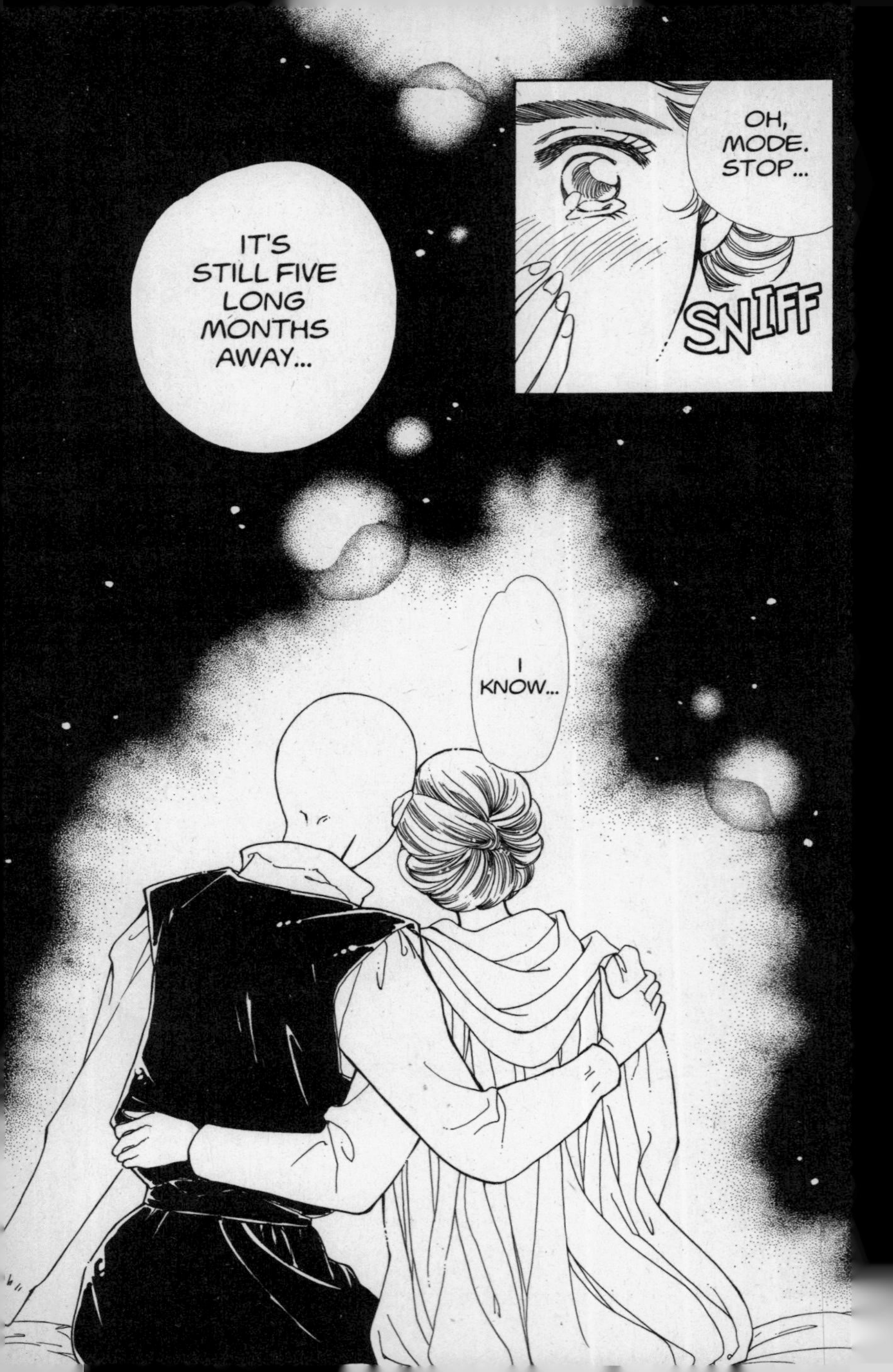
OH, MODE. STOP...
SNIFF
IT'S STILL FIVE LONG MONTHS AWAY...
I KNOW...

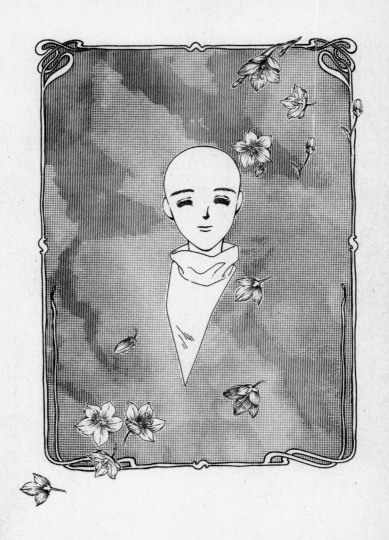

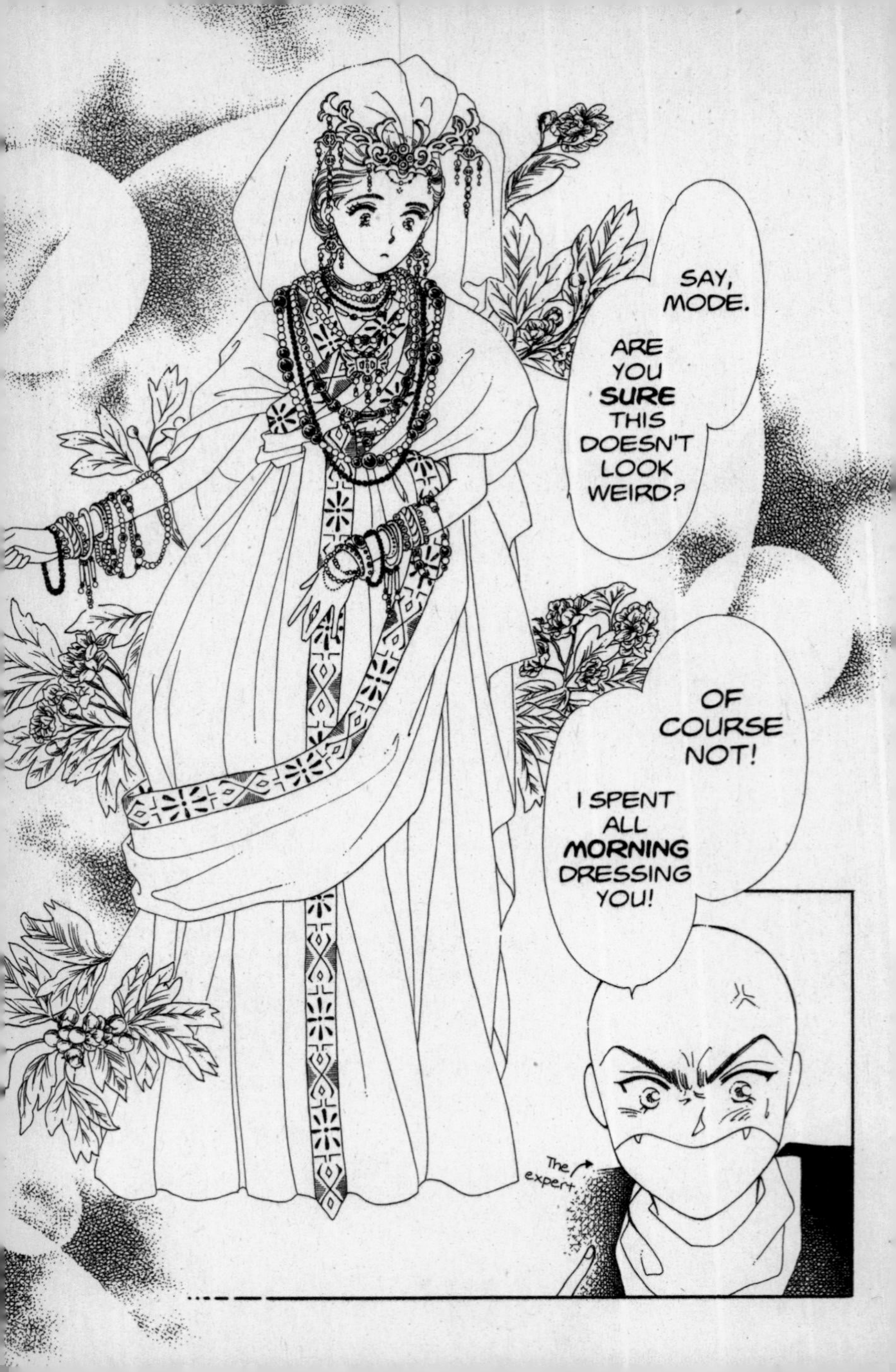
SAY, MODE.
ARE YOU **SURE** THIS DOESN'T LOOK WEIRD?
OF COURSE NOT!
I SPENT ALL **MORNING** DRESSING YOU!
The expert.

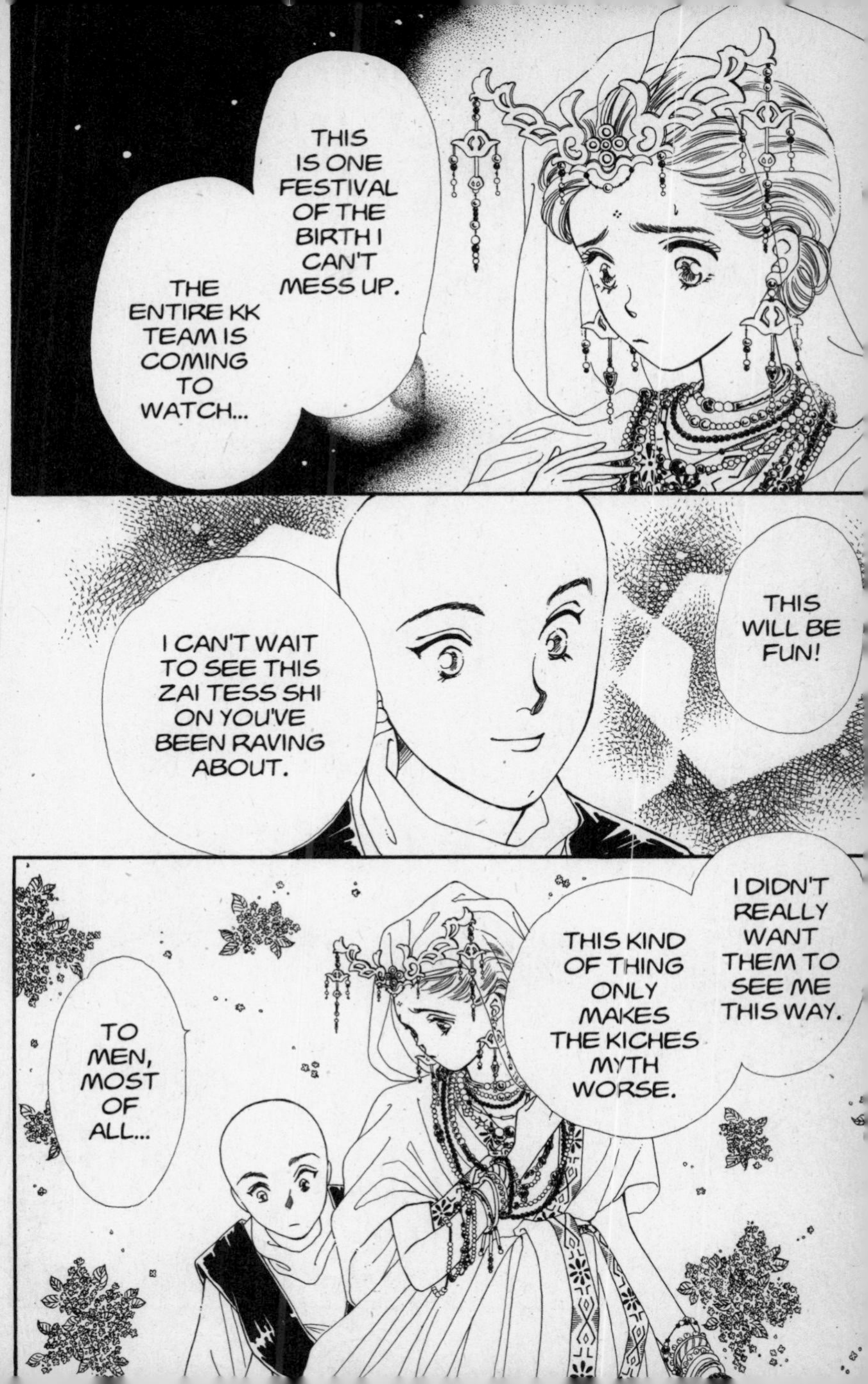
THIS IS ONE FESTIVAL OF THE BIRTH I CAN'T MESS UP.
THE ENTIRE KK TEAM IS COMING TO WATCH...
THIS WILL BE FUN!
I CAN'T WAIT TO SEE THIS ZAI TESS SHI ON YOU'VE BEEN RAVING ABOUT.
I DIDN'T REALLY WANT THEM TO SEE ME THIS WAY.
THIS KIND OF THING ONLY MAKES THE KICHES MYTH WORSE.
TO MEN, MOST OF ALL...

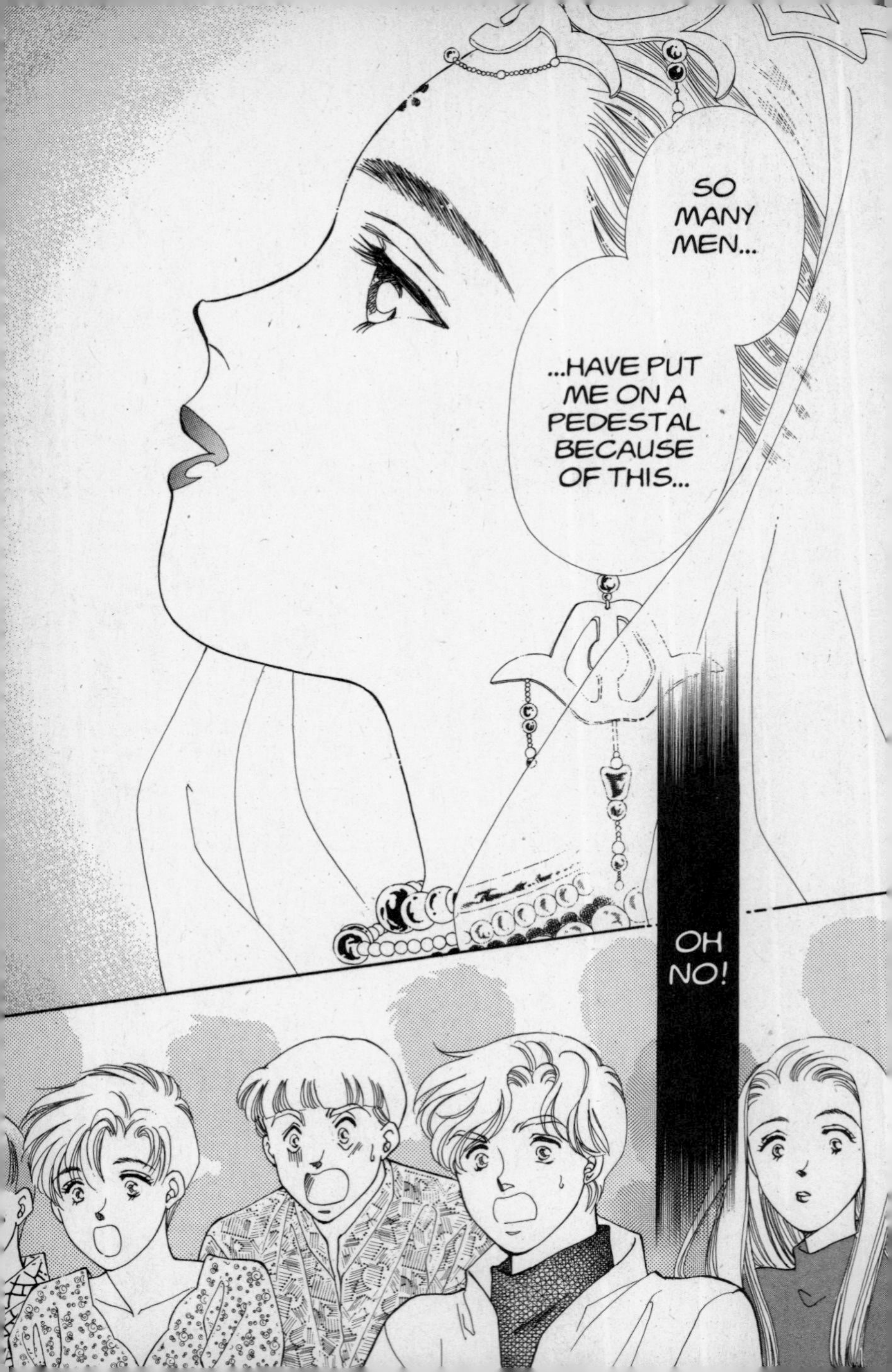
SO MANY MEN...
...HAVE PUT ME ON A PEDESTAL BECAUSE OF THIS...
OH NO!

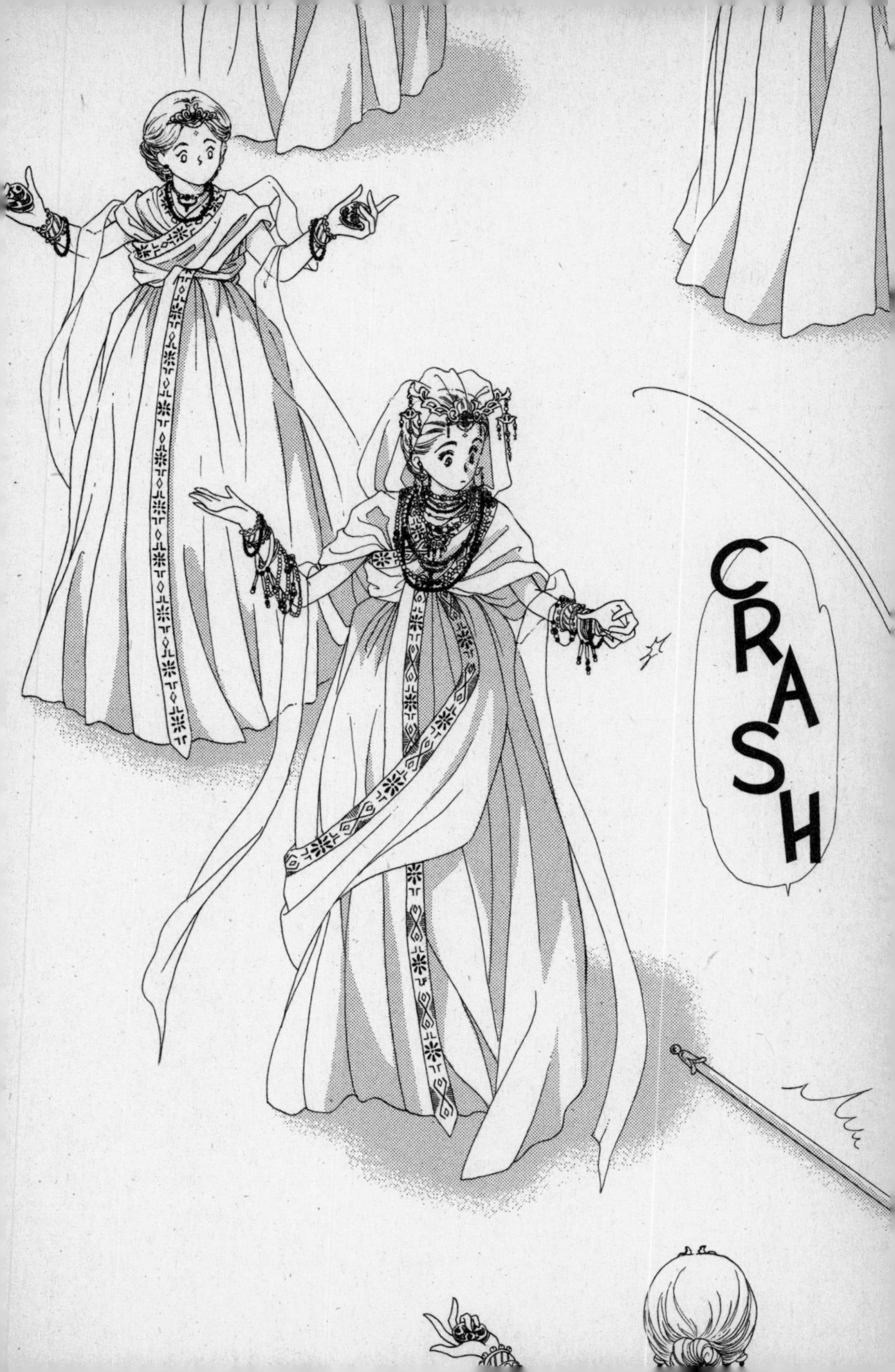
CRASH

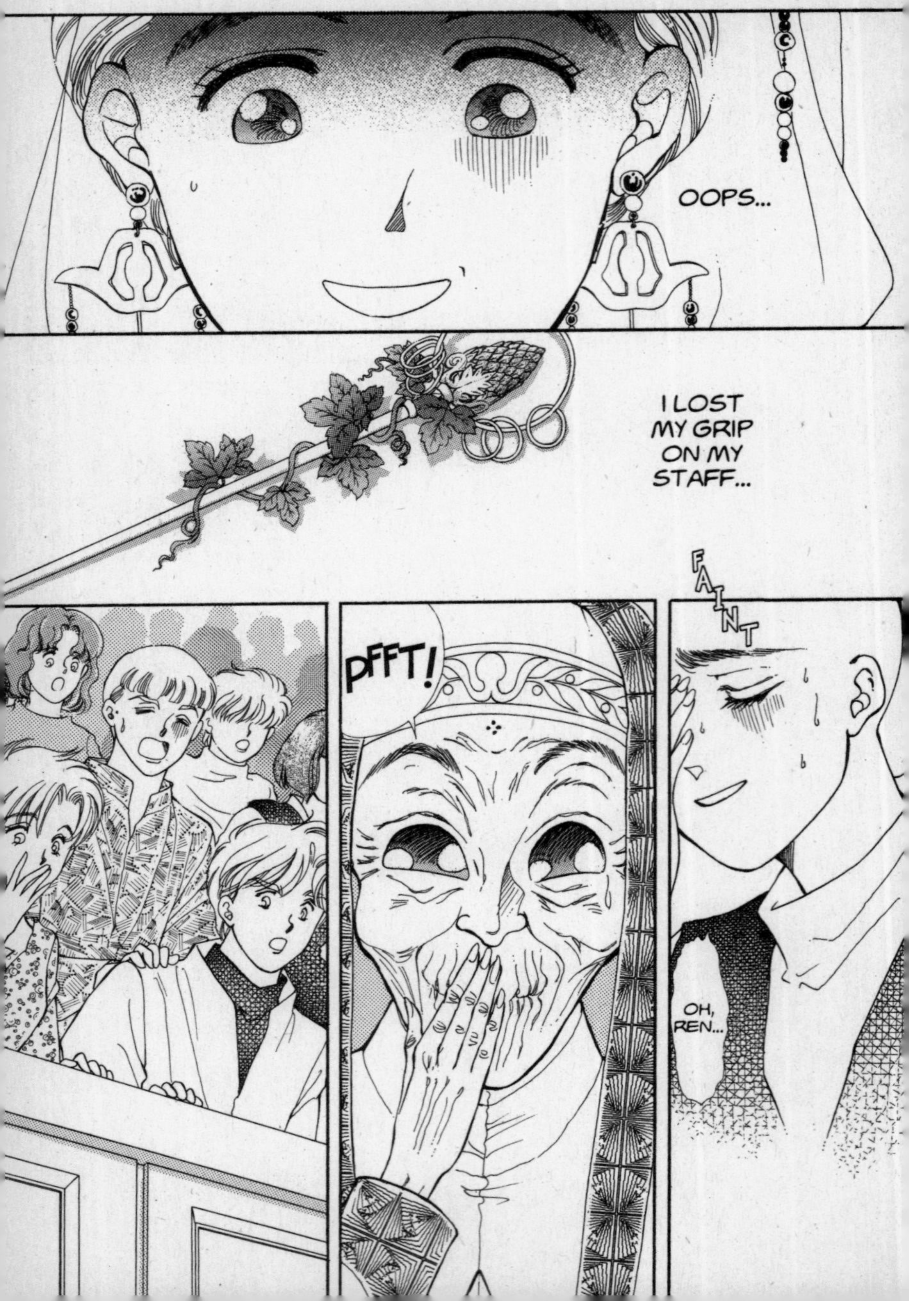
OOPS...
I LOST MY GRIP ON MY STAFF...
FAINT
OH, REN...
PFFT!

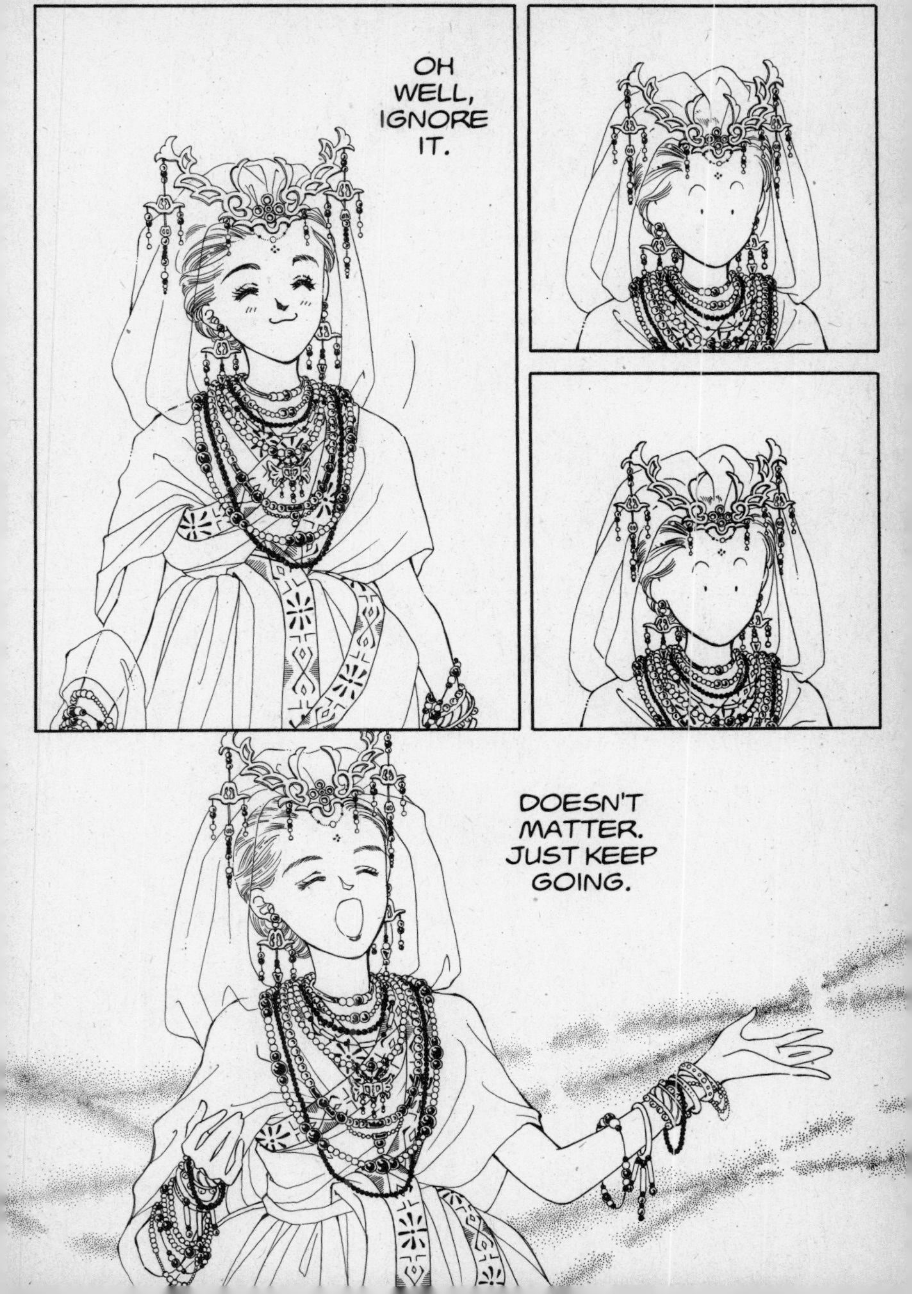
OH WELL, IGNORE IT.
DOESN'T MATTER. JUST KEEP GOING.

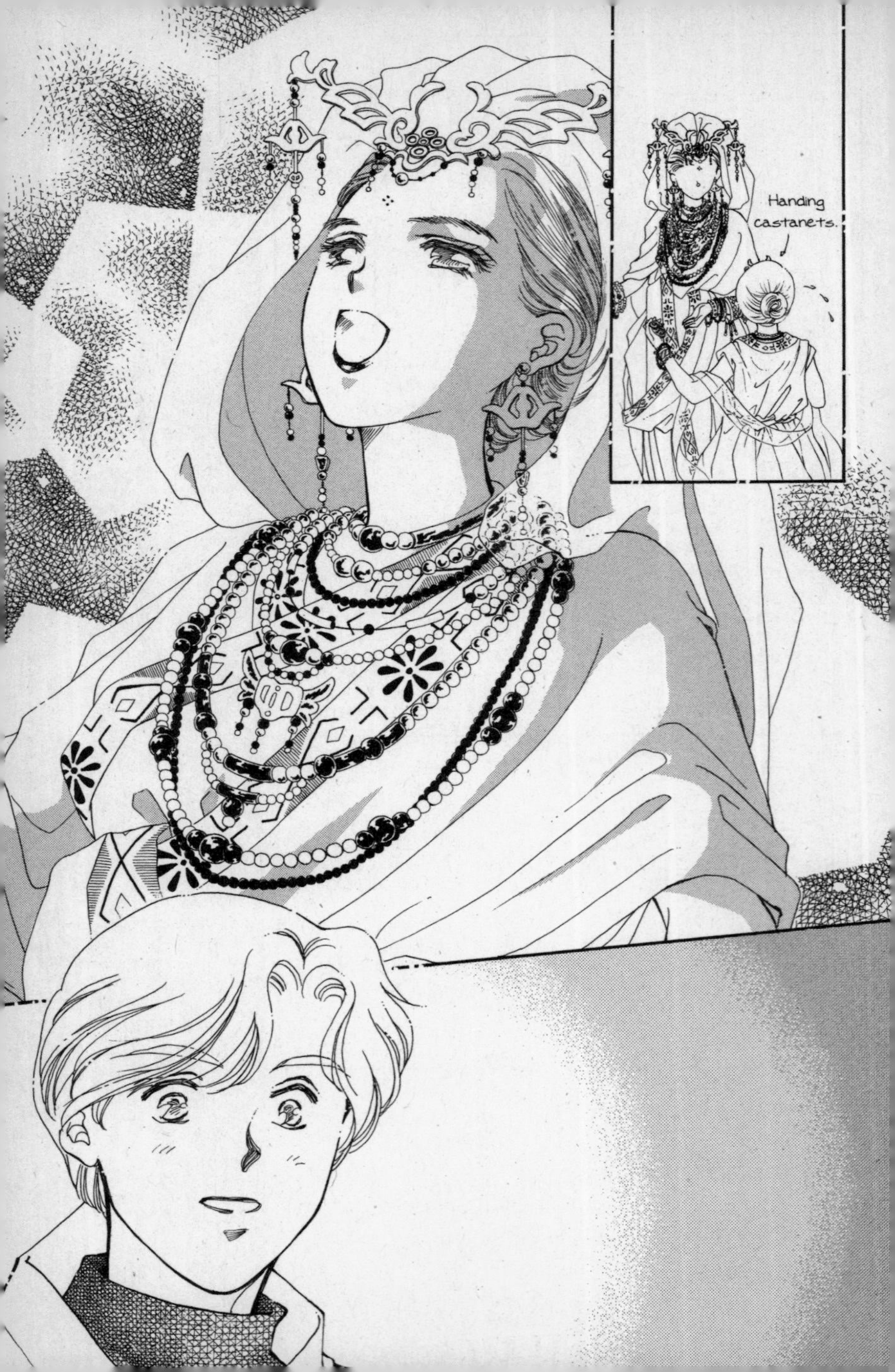
Handing castanets.

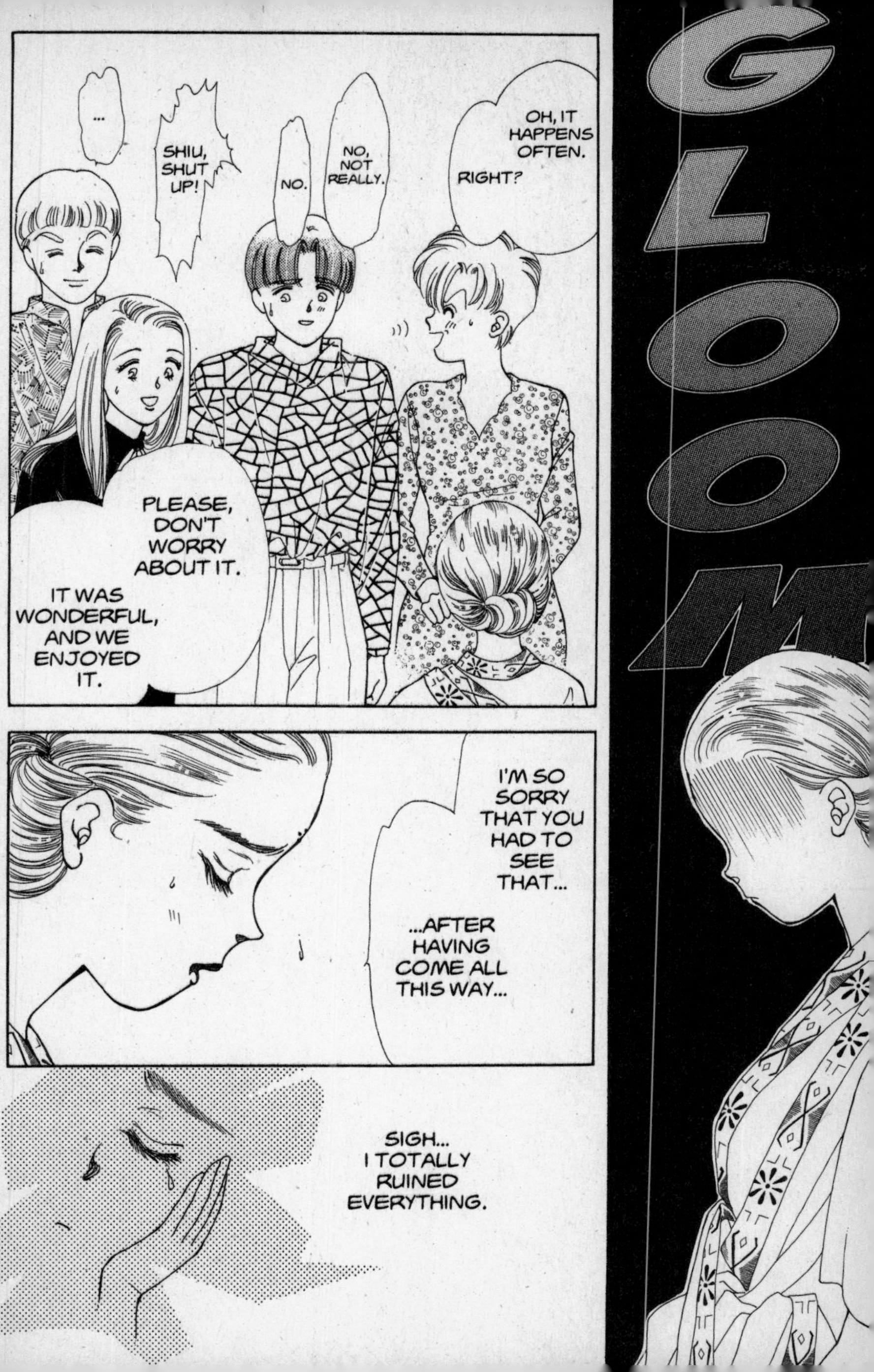
GLOOM
OH, IT HAPPENS OFTEN.
RIGHT?
NO, NOT REALLY.
NO.
SHIU, SHUT UP!
...
PLEASE, DON'T WORRY ABOUT IT.
IT WAS WONDERFUL, AND WE ENJOYED IT.
I'M SO SORRY THAT YOU HAD TO SEE THAT...
...AFTER HAVING COME ALL THIS WAY...
SIGH... I TOTALLY RUINED EVERYTHING.

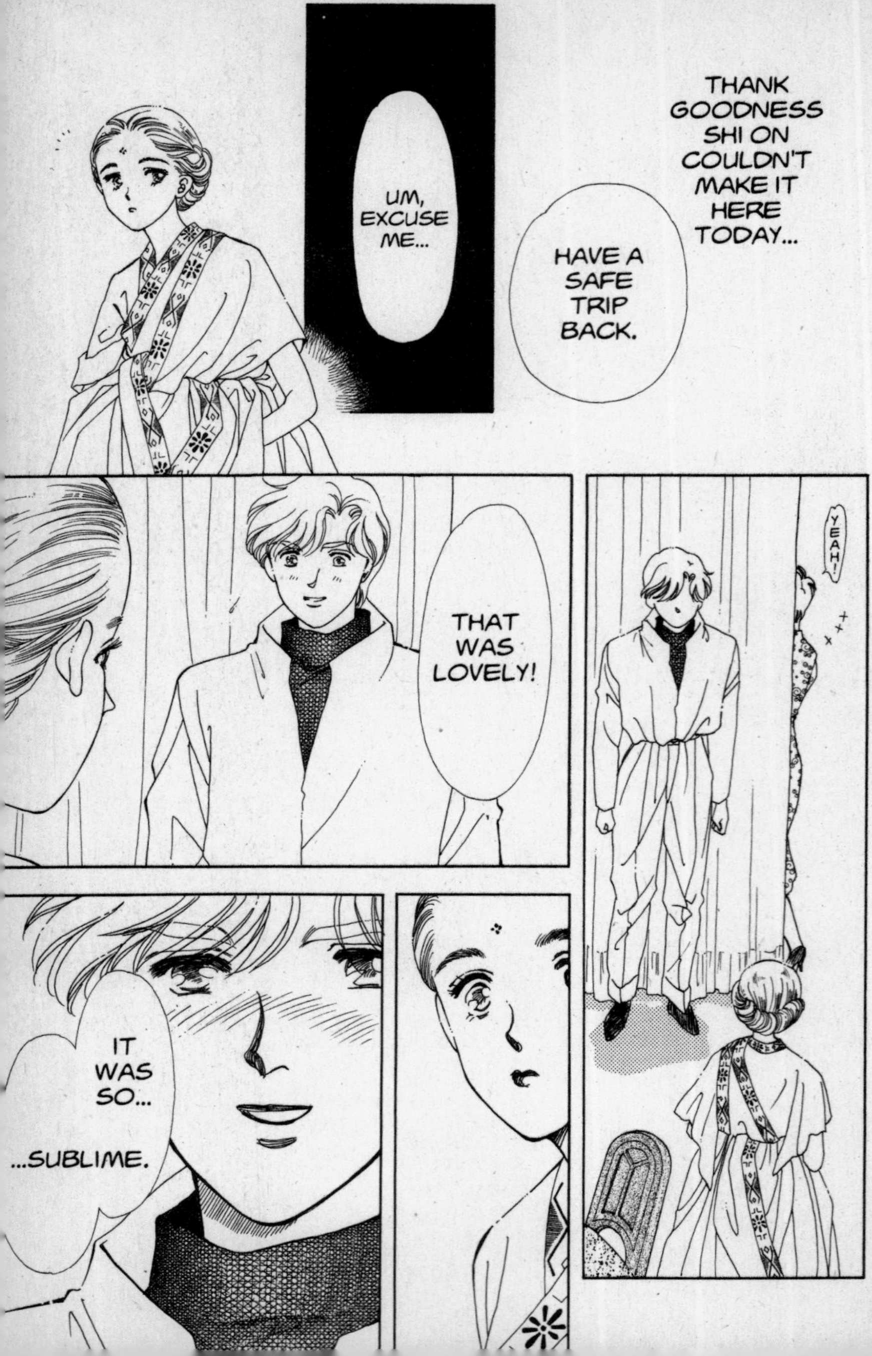
THANK GOODNESS SHI ON COULDN'T MAKE IT HERE TODAY...
HAVE A SAFE TRIP BACK.
UM, EXCUSE ME...
YEAH!
THAT WAS LOVELY!
IT WAS SO...
...SUBLIME.

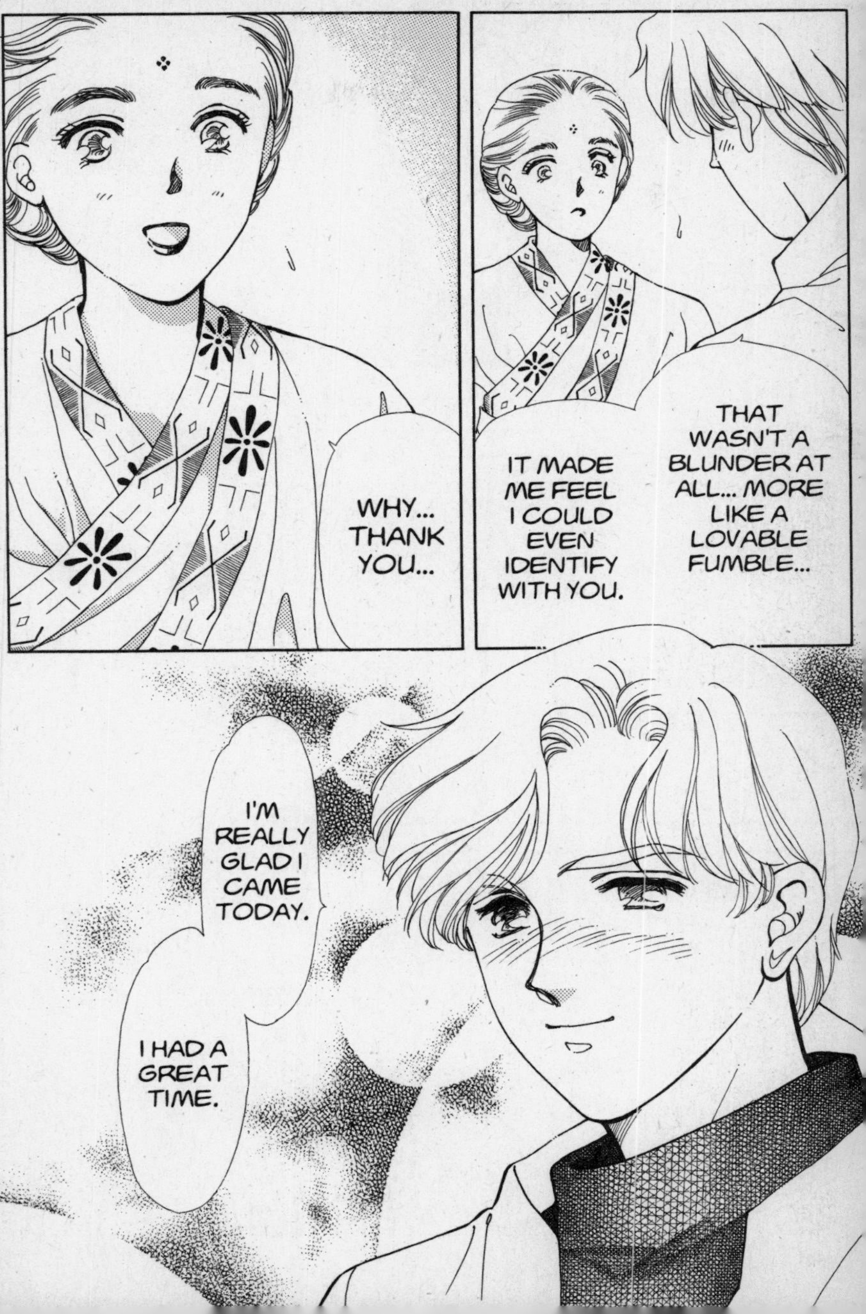
THAT WASN'T A BLUNDER AT ALL... MORE LIKE A LOVABLE FUMBLE...
IT MADE ME FEEL I COULD EVEN IDENTIFY WITH YOU.
WHY... THANK YOU...
I'M REALLY GLAD I CAME TODAY.
I HAD A GREAT TIME.

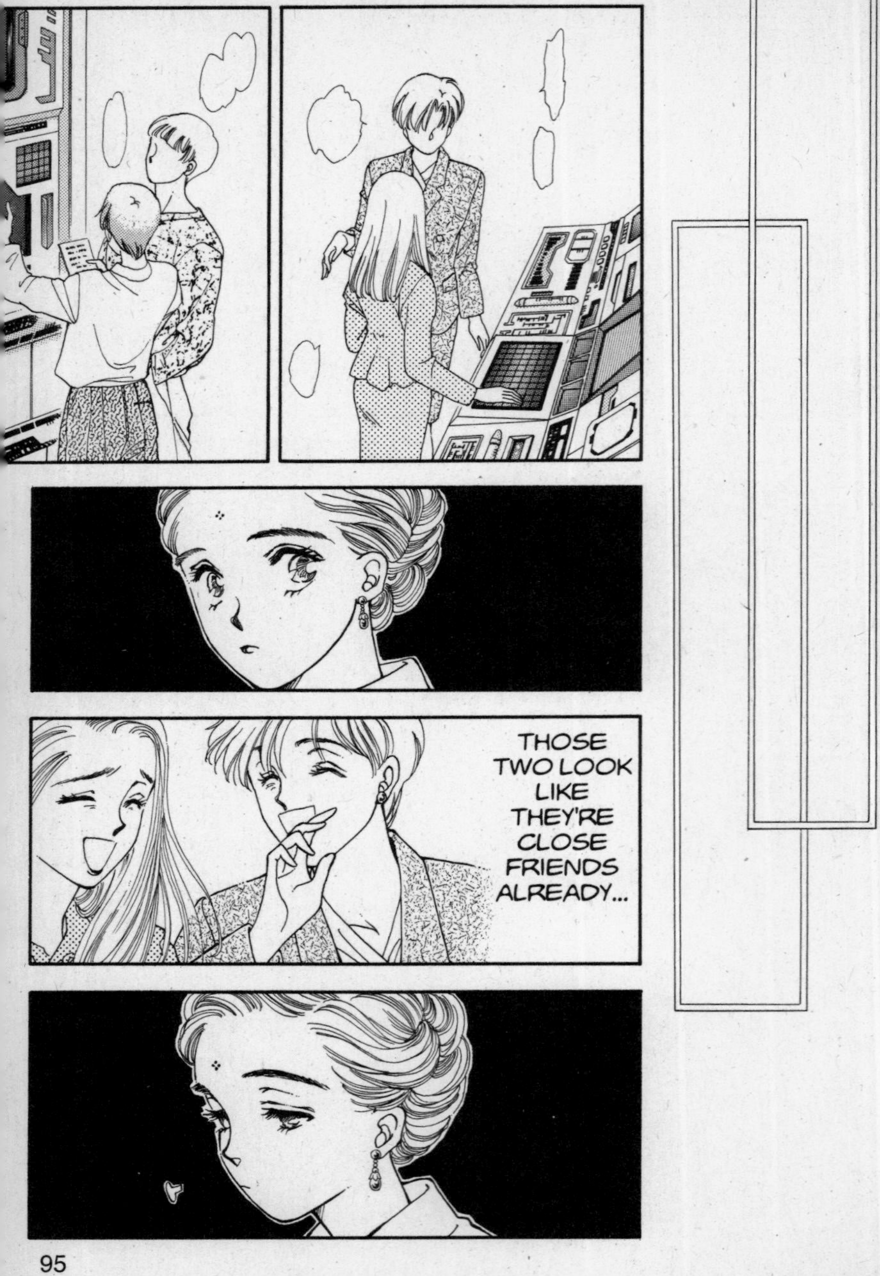
THOSE TWO LOOK LIKE THEY'RE CLOSE FRIENDS ALREADY...

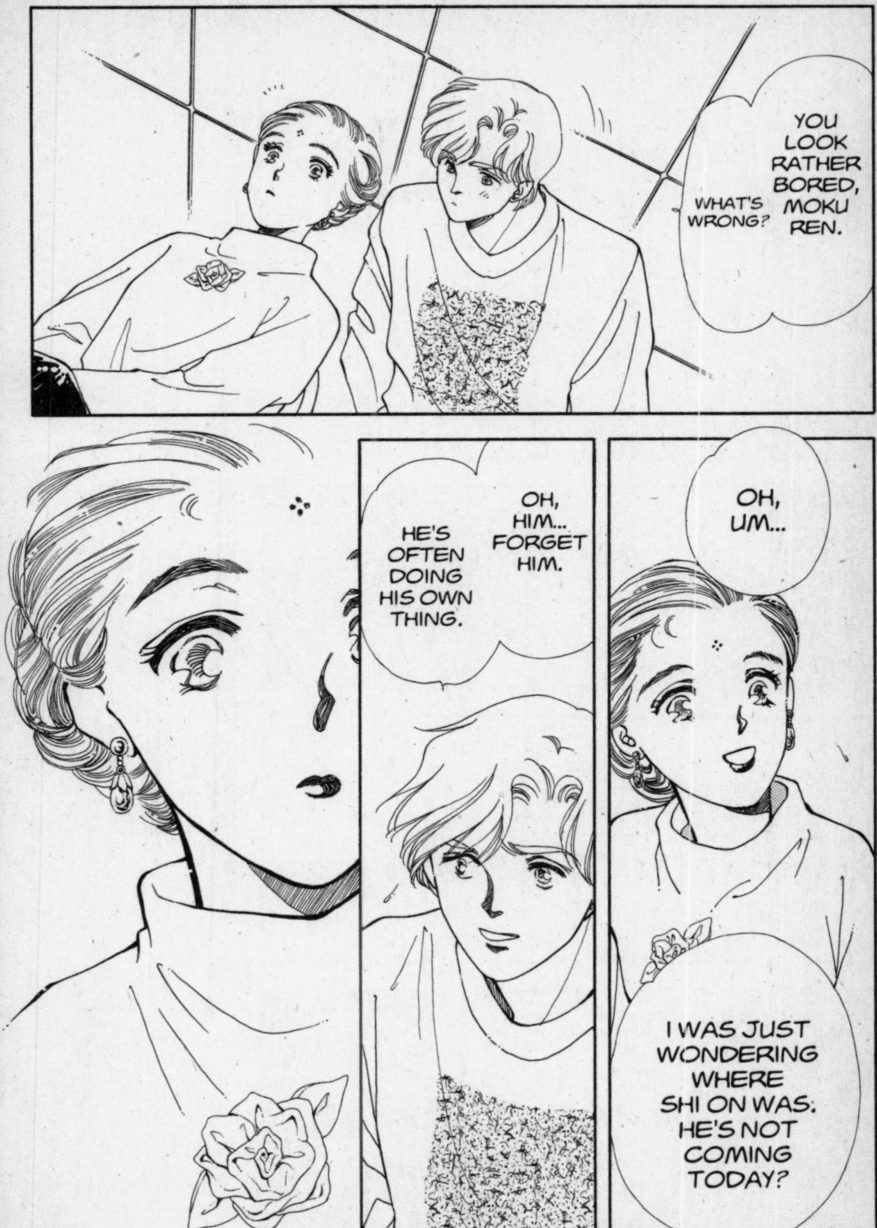
YOU LOOK RATHER BORED, MOKU REN.
WHAT'S WRONG?
OH, UM...
I WAS JUST WONDERING WHERE SHI ON WAS: HE'S NOT COMING TODAY?
OH, HIM... FORGET HIM.
HE'S OFTEN DOING HIS OWN THING.

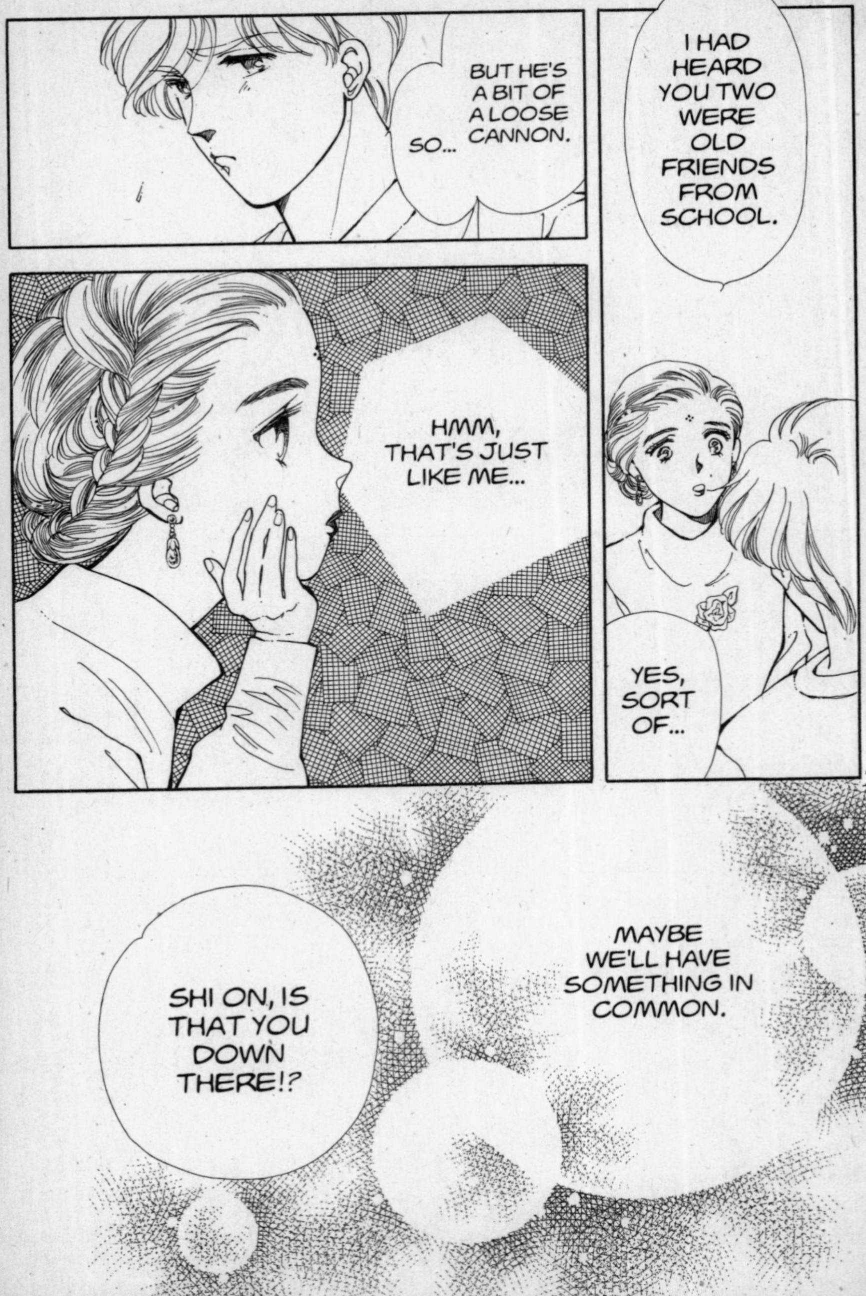
I HAD HEARD YOU TWO WERE OLD FRIENDS FROM SCHOOL.
YES, SORT OF...
BUT HE'S A BIT OF A LOOSE CANNON.
SO...
HMM, THAT'S JUST LIKE ME...
MAYBE WE'LL HAVE SOMETHING IN COMMON.
SHI ON, IS THAT YOU DOWN THERE!?

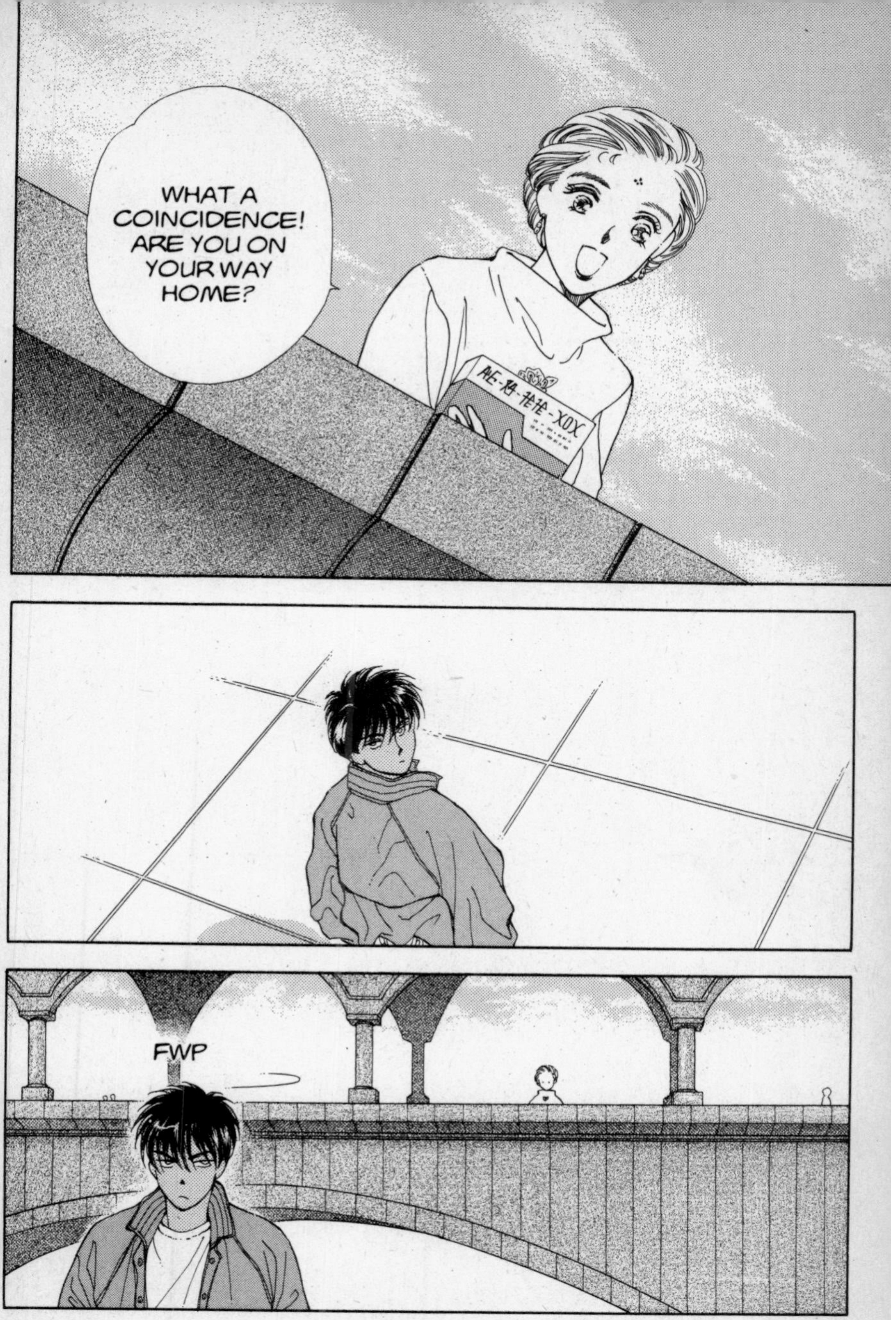
WHAT A COINCIDENCE! ARE YOU ON YOUR WAY HOME?
FWP

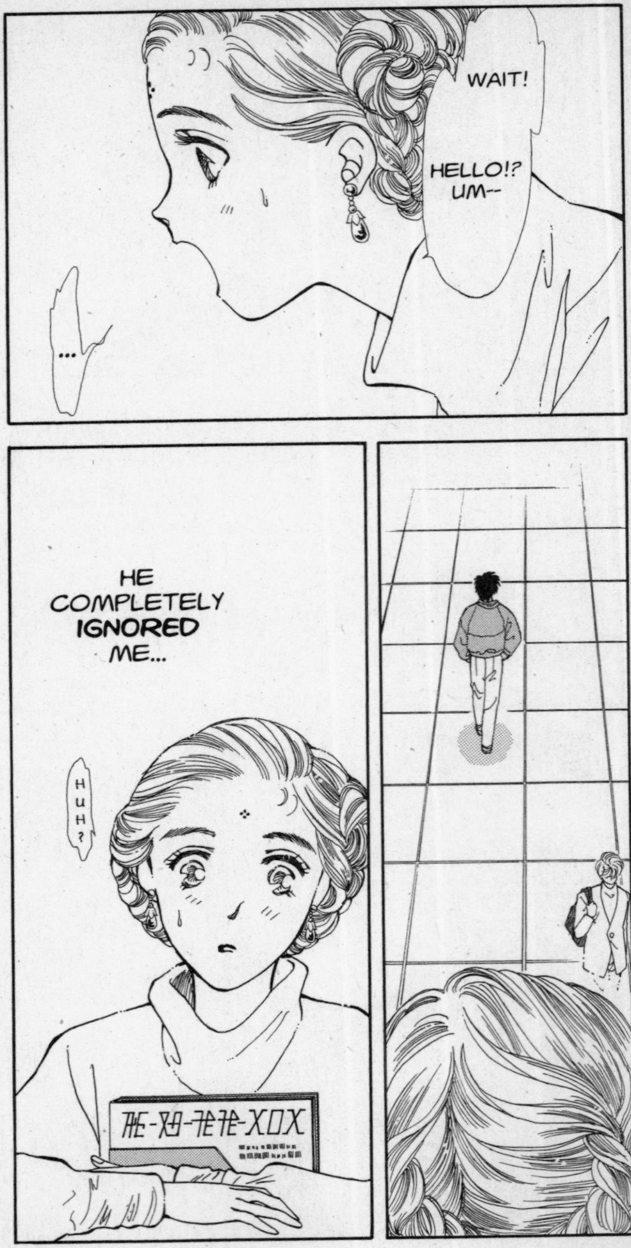
WAIT!
HELLO!? UM--
...
HE COMPLETELY IGNORED ME...
HUH?

1/4 COLUMN NONSENSE

PART 7

More about "DQ IV". Do you remember the whole side plot about the love story between Necrosaro and Rosa? That made me feel so sorry for poor Necrosaro when I was forced to fight him in the final boss battle... And poor Rosa... I remember wanting to get the battle over with, to put Necrosaro out of his misery.

In an RPG with a story like this, players become emotionally invested in the characters. Countless people play the same game, but it's interesting how we all end up having different adventures. I always name my protagonist Tomonori, by the way.

continued in part 8

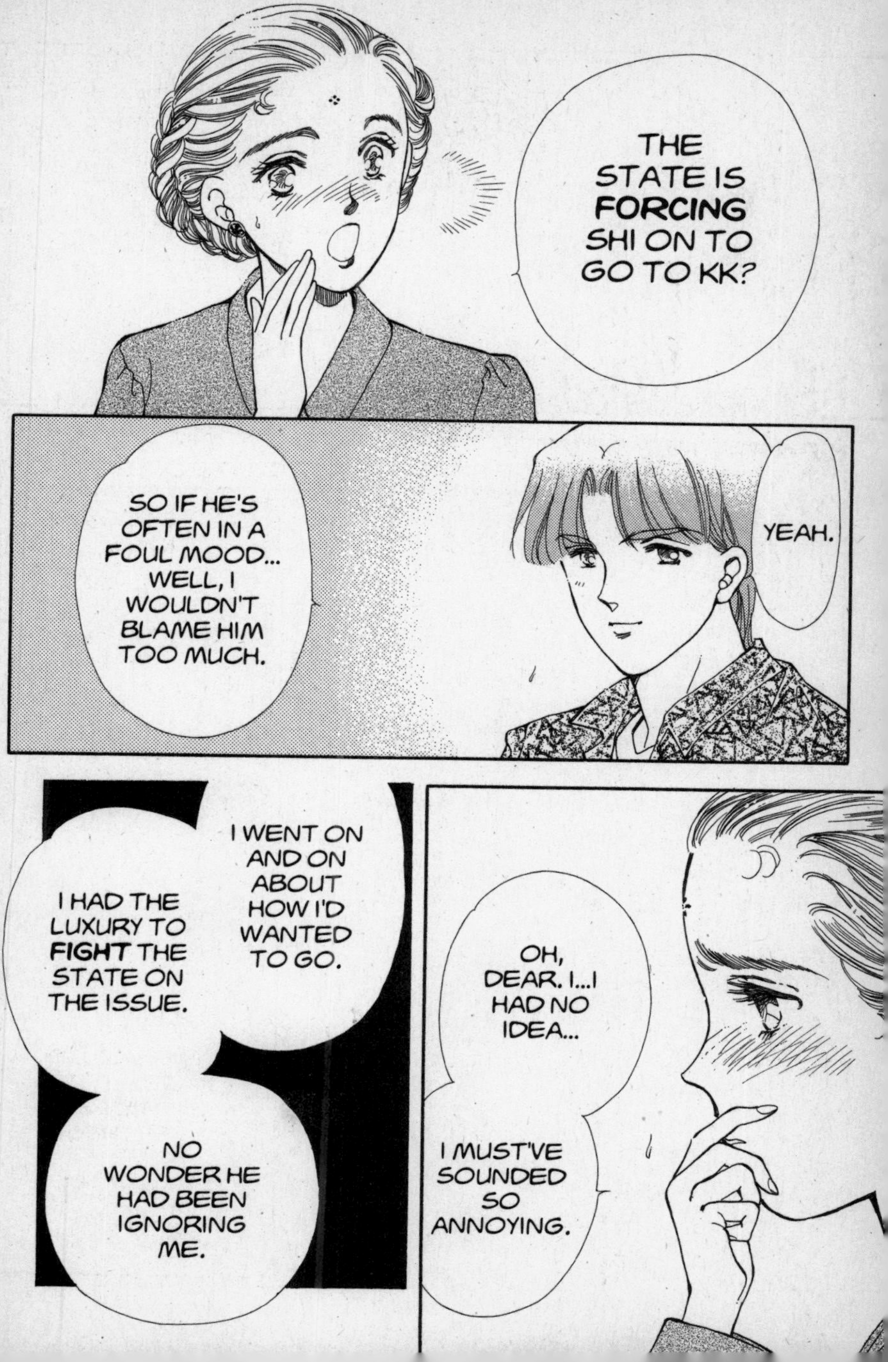
THE STATE IS **FORCING** SHI ON TO GO TO KK?
YEAH.
SO IF HE'S OFTEN IN A FOUL MOOD... WELL, I WOULDN'T BLAME HIM TOO MUCH.
OH, DEAR. I...I HAD NO IDEA...
I MUST'VE SOUNDED SO ANNOYING.
I WENT ON AND ON ABOUT HOW I'D WANTED TO GO.
I HAD THE LUXURY TO **FIGHT** THE STATE ON THE ISSUE.
NO WONDER HE HAD BEEN IGNORING ME.

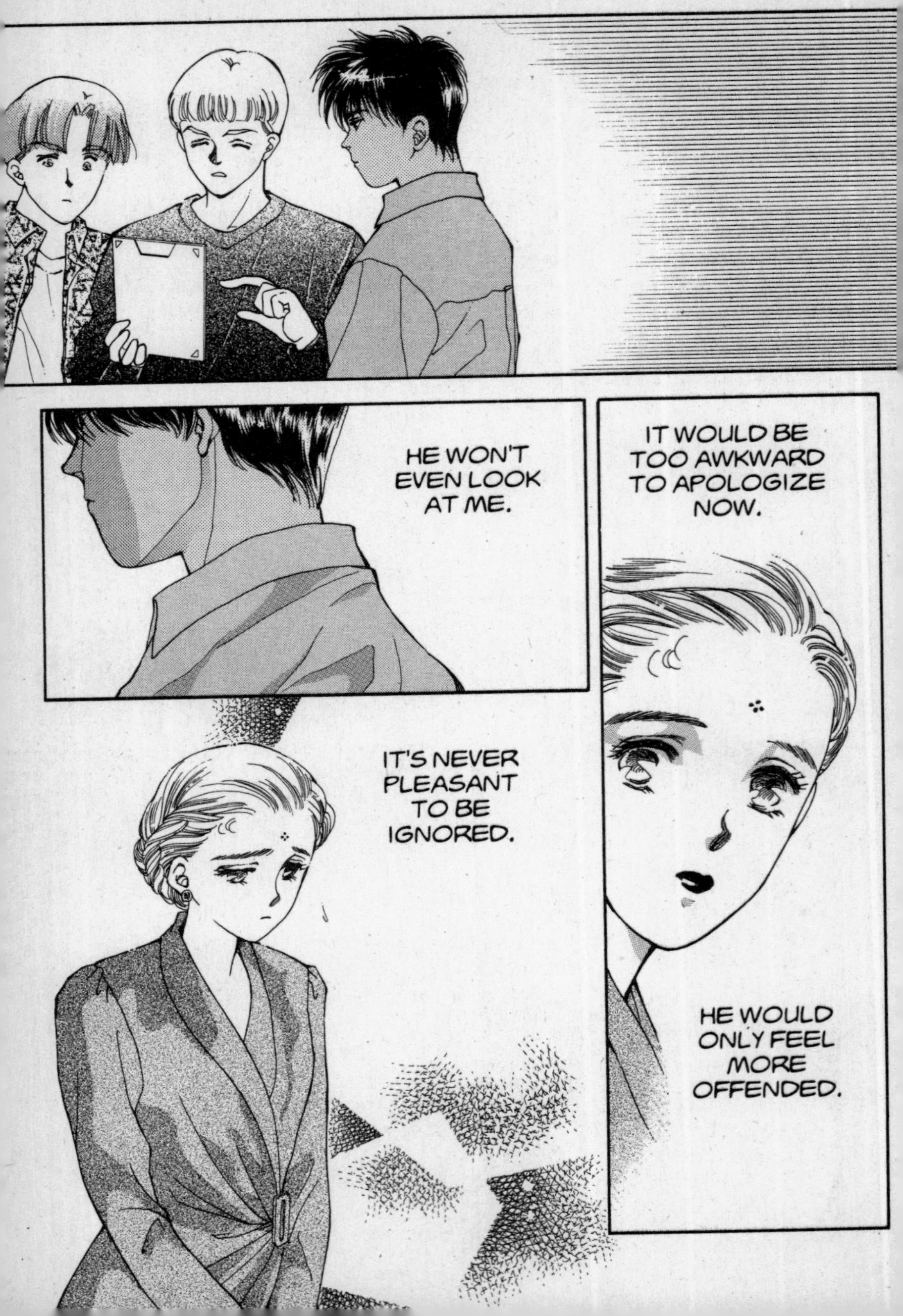
IT WOULD BE TOO AWKWARD TO APOLOGIZE NOW.
HE WOULD ONLY FEEL MORE OFFENDED.
HE WON'T EVEN LOOK AT ME.
IT'S NEVER PLEASANT TO BE IGNORED.

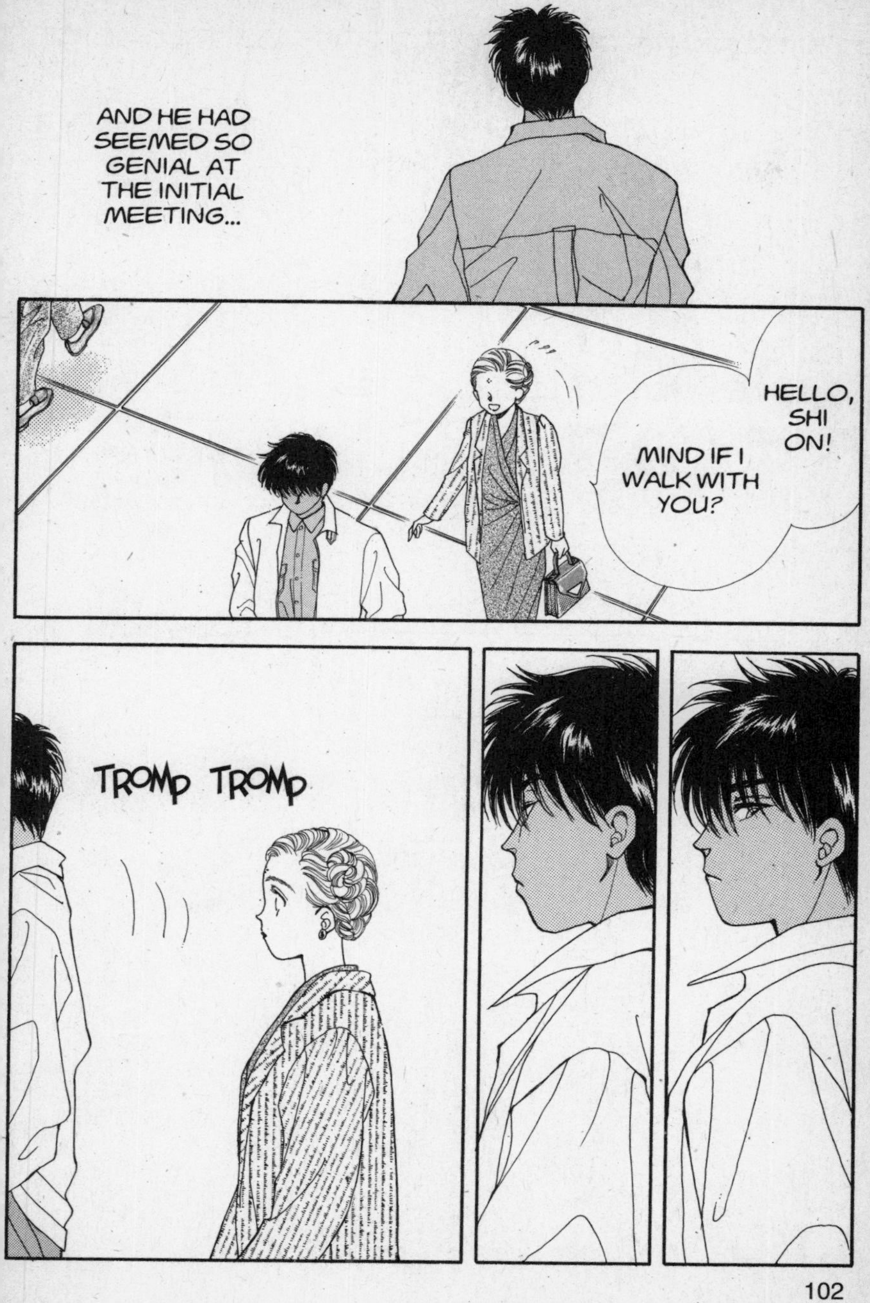
AND HE HAD SEEMED SO GENIAL AT THE INITIAL MEETING...
HELLO, SHI ON!
MIND IF I WALK WITH YOU?
TROMP TROMP

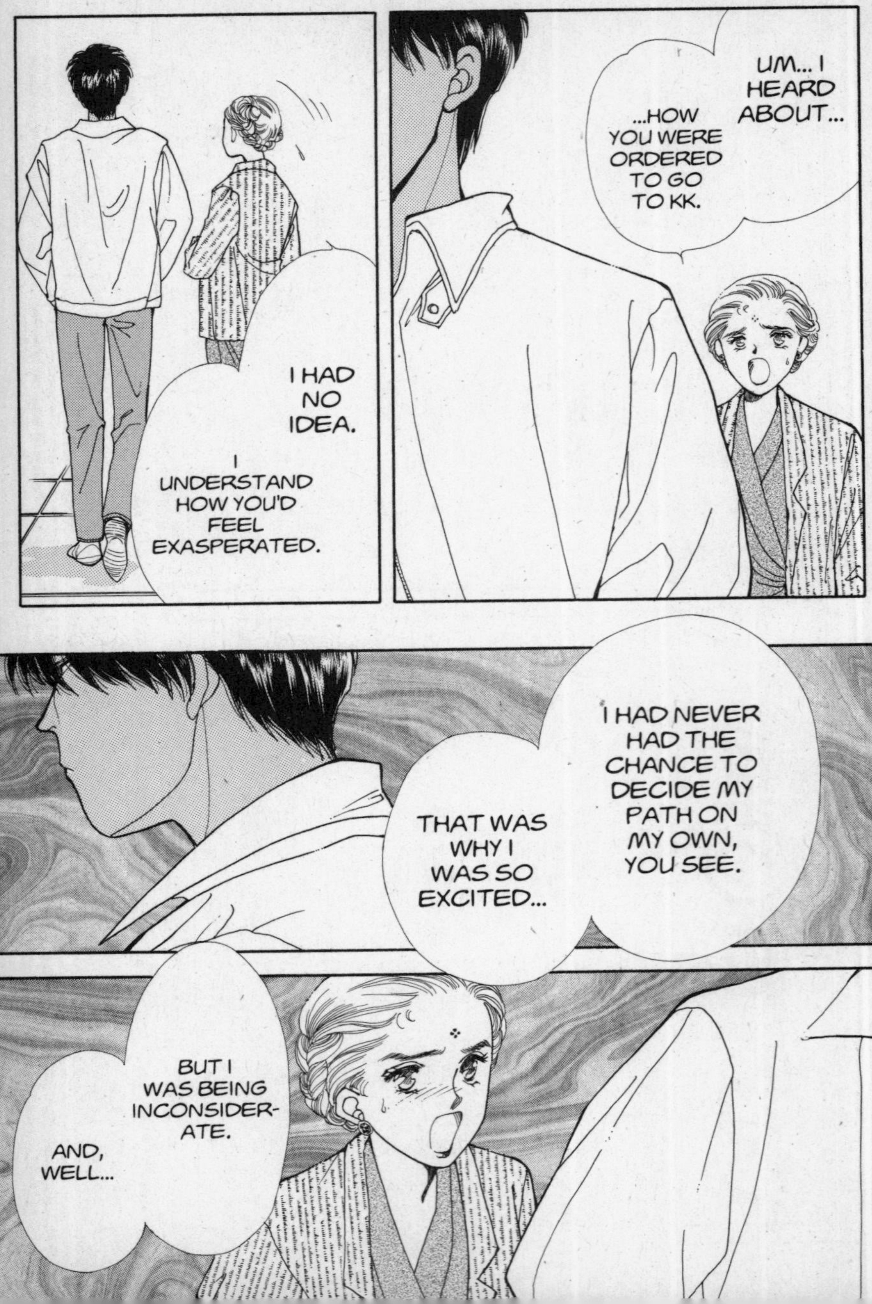
UM... I HEARD ABOUT...
...HOW YOU WERE ORDERED TO GO TO KK.
I HAD NO IDEA.
I UNDERSTAND HOW YOU'D FEEL EXASPERATED.
I HAD NEVER HAD THE CHANCE TO DECIDE MY PATH ON MY OWN, YOU SEE.
THAT WAS WHY I WAS SO EXCITED...
BUT I WAS BEING INCONSIDER-ATE.
AND, WELL...

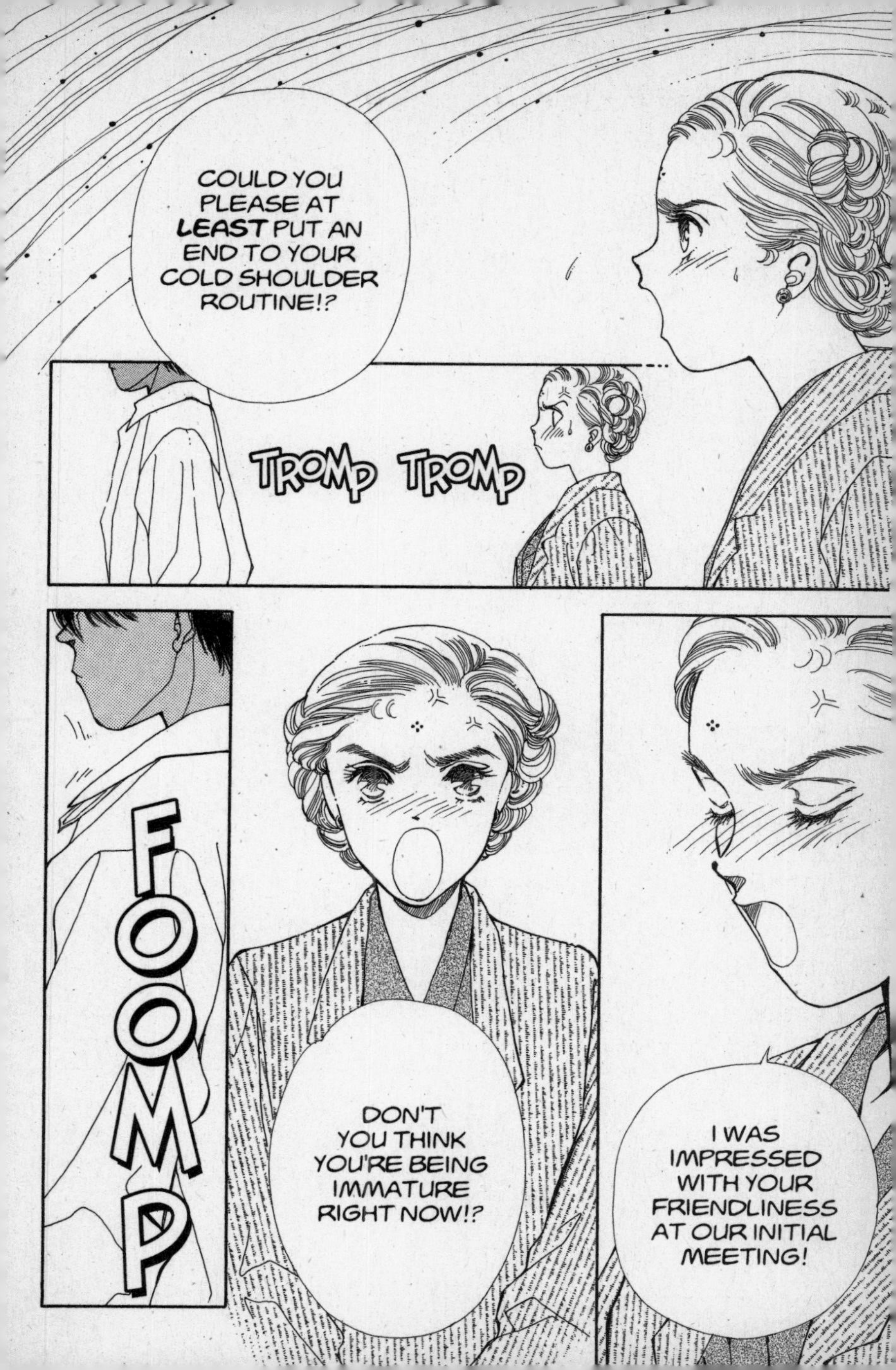
COULD YOU PLEASE AT **LEAST** PUT AN END TO YOUR COLD SHOULDER ROUTINE!?
TROMP TROMP
I WAS IMPRESSED WITH YOUR FRIENDLINESS AT OUR INITIAL MEETING!
DON'T YOU THINK YOU'RE BEING IMMATURE RIGHT NOW!?
FOOMP

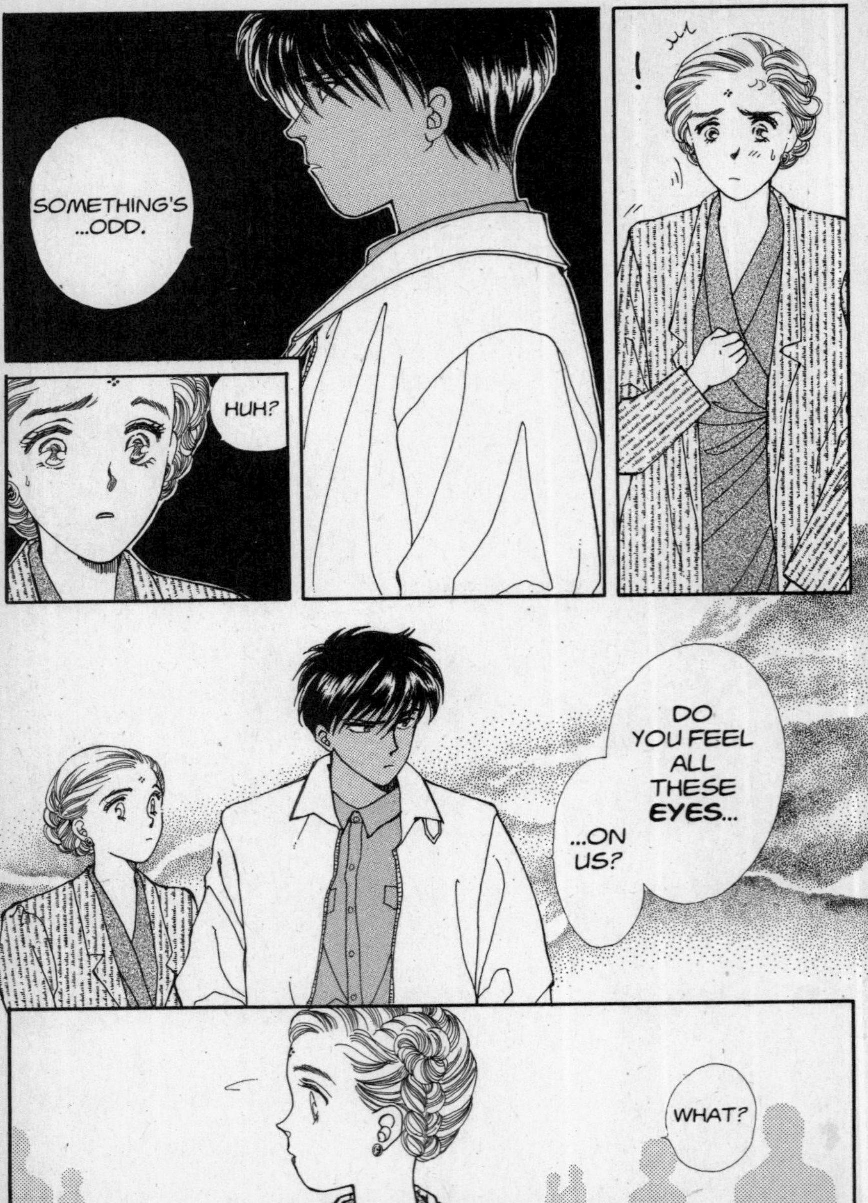
!
SOMETHING'S ...ODD.
HUH?
DO YOU FEEL ALL THESE EYES...
...ON US?
WHAT?

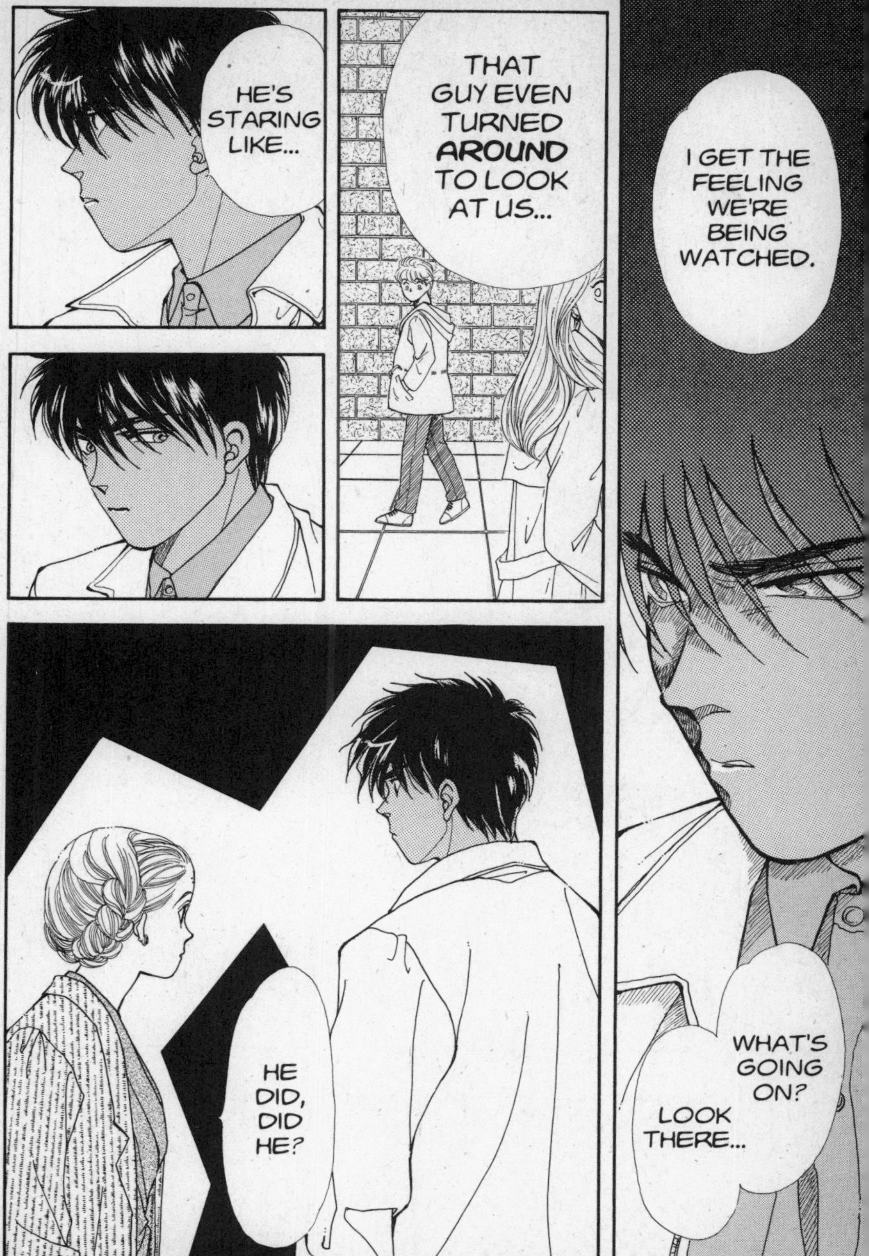
I GET THE FEELING WE'RE BEING WATCHED.
WHAT'S GOING ON?
LOOK THERE...
THAT GUY EVEN TURNED **AROUND** TO LOOK AT US...
HE'S STARING LIKE...
HE DID, DID HE?

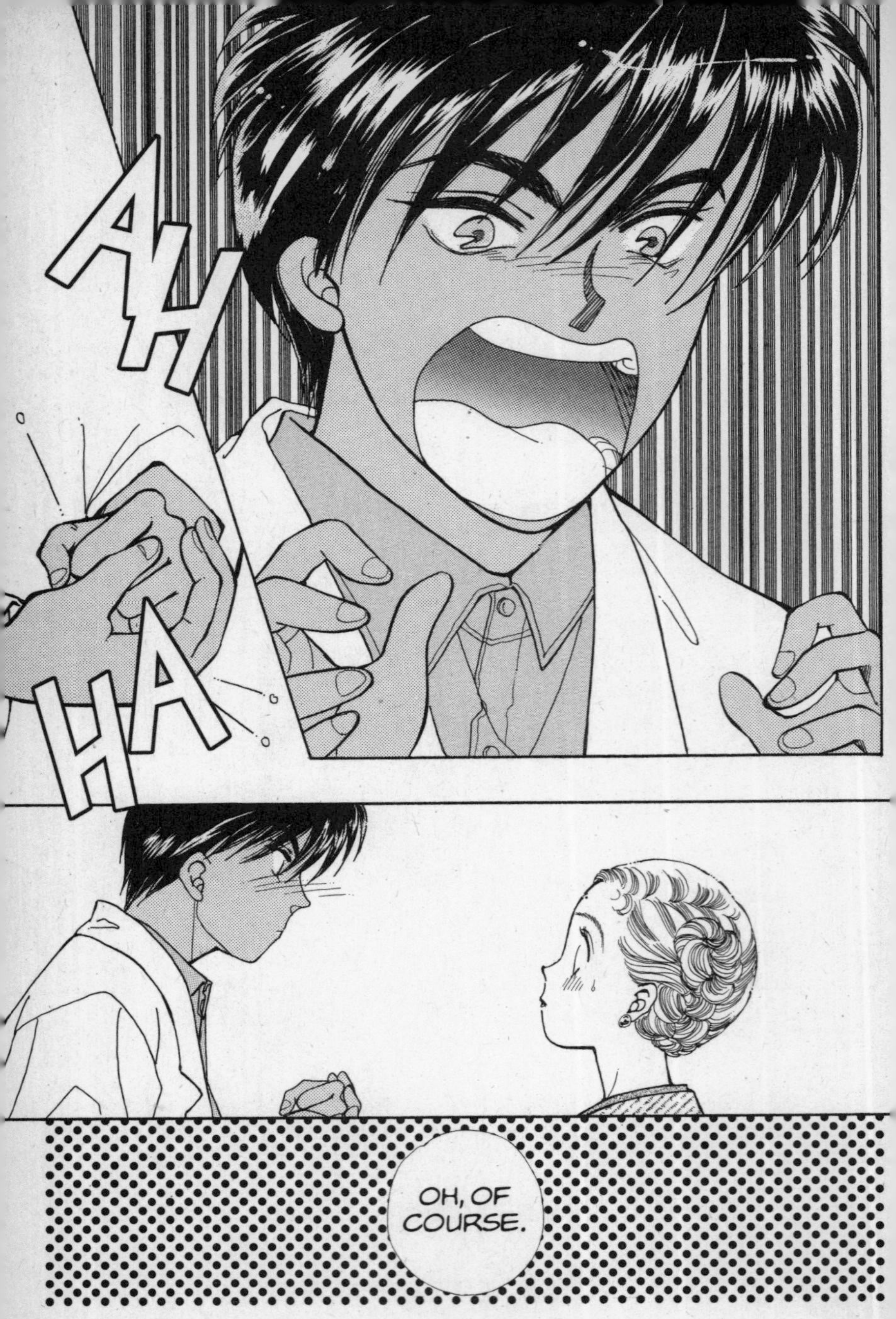
AH HA HA
OH, OF COURSE.

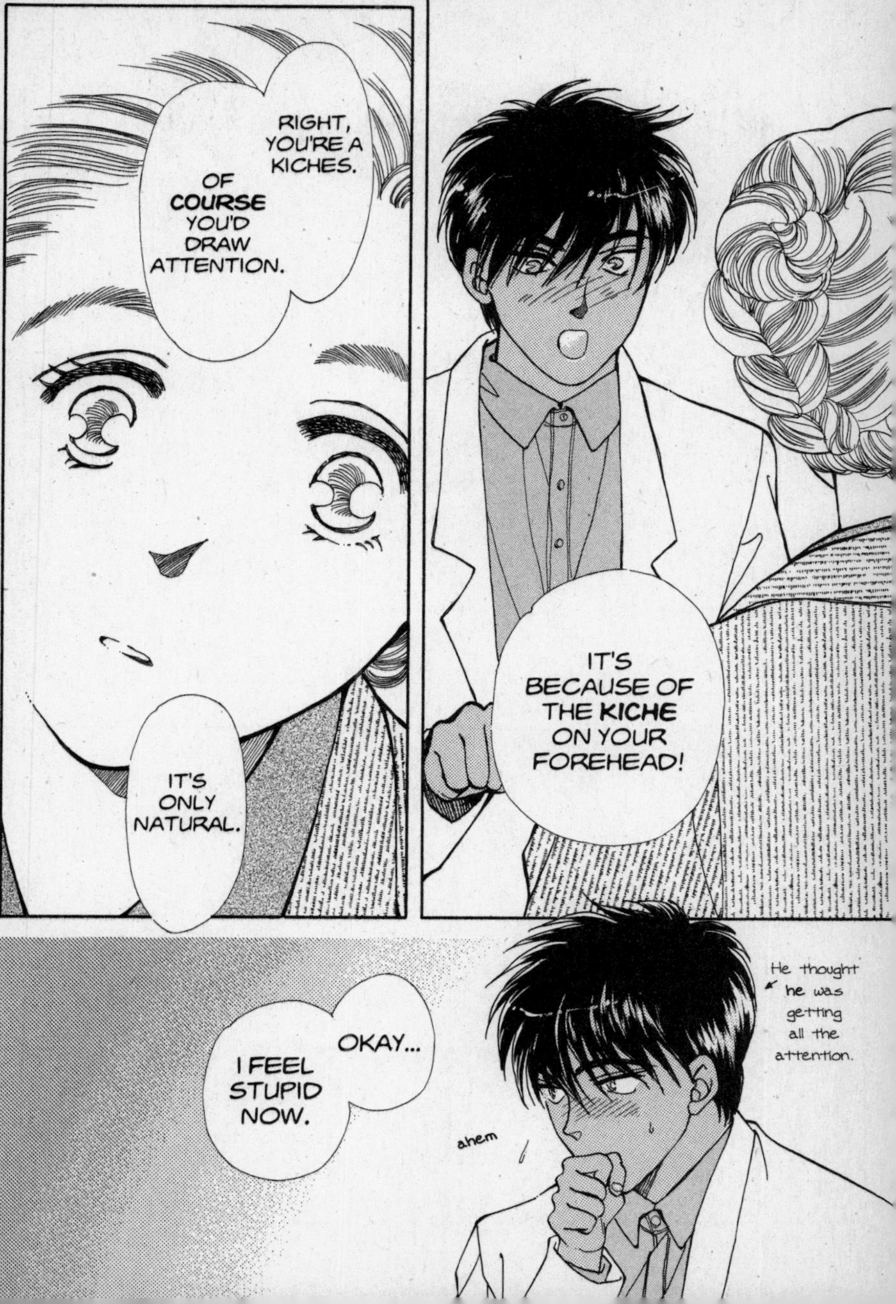
IT'S BECAUSE OF THE KICHE ON YOUR FOREHEAD!
RIGHT, YOU'RE A KICHES.
OF COURSE YOU'D DRAW ATTENTION.
IT'S ONLY NATURAL.
He thought he was getting all the attention.
OKAY... I FEEL STUPID NOW.
ahem

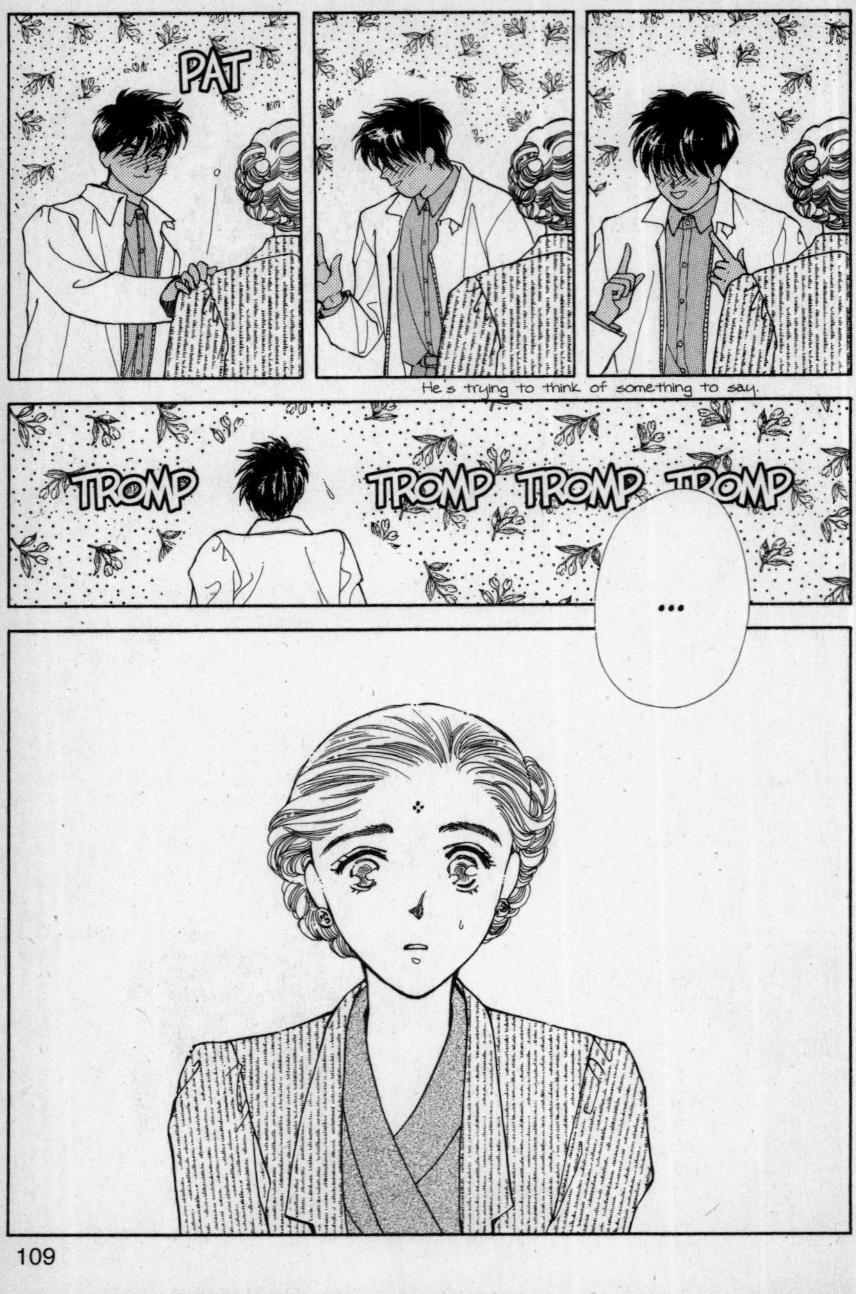
PAT
He's trying to think of something to say.
TROMP TROMP TROMP TROMP
...

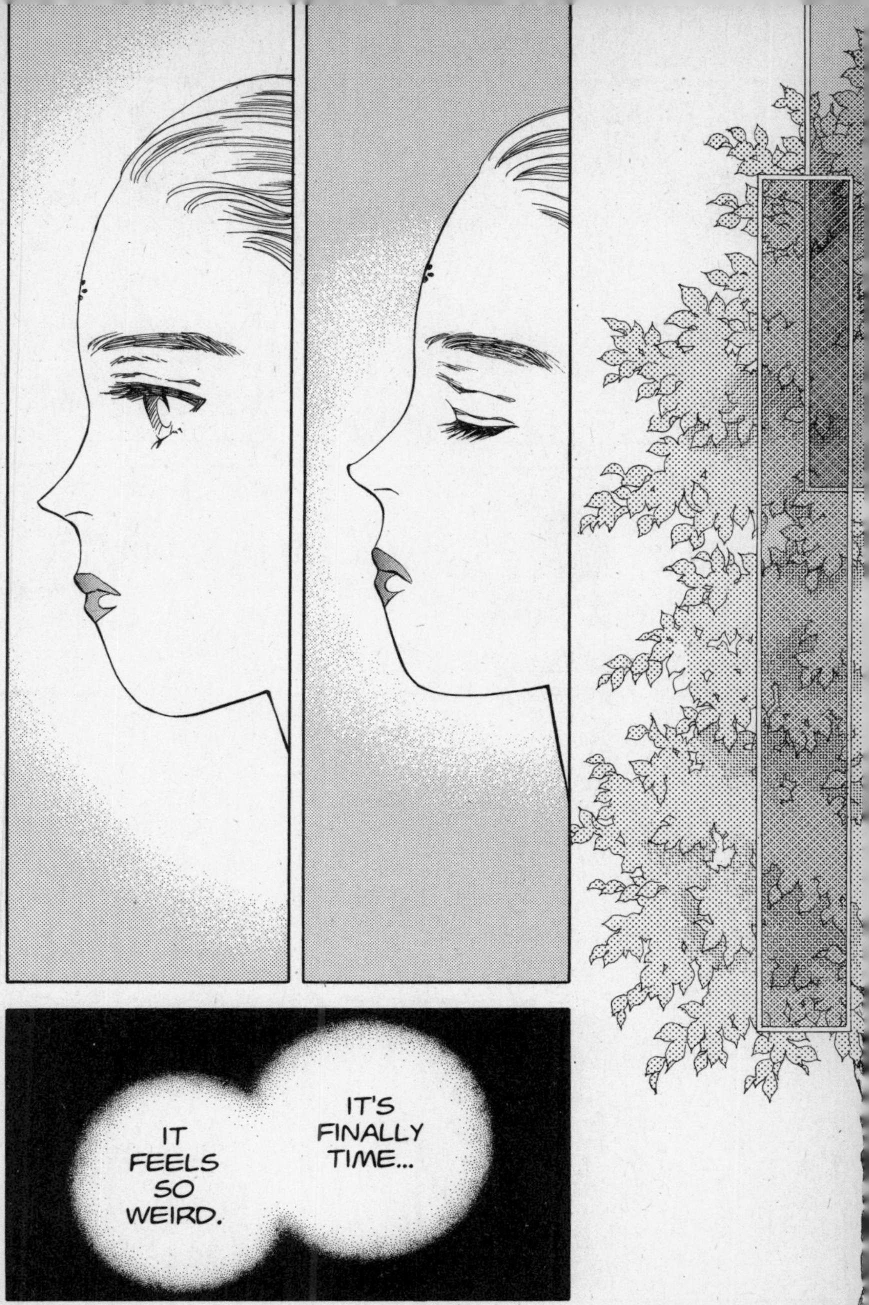
IT'S FINALLY TIME...
IT FEELS SO WEIRD.

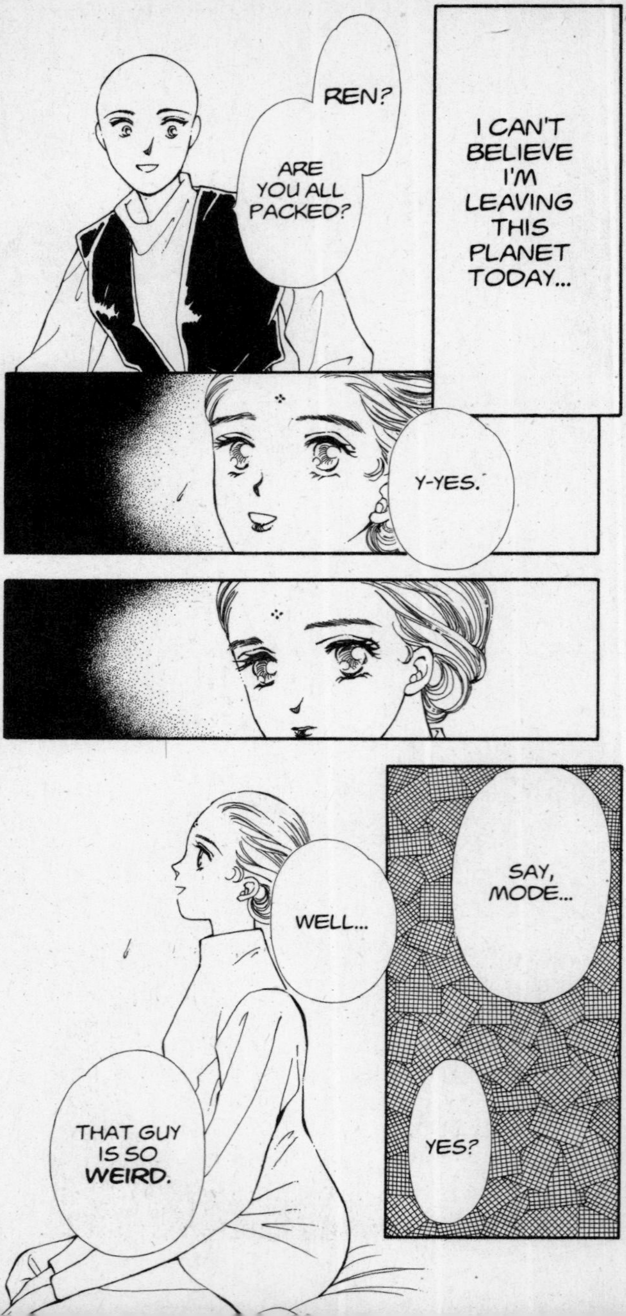
I CAN'T BELIEVE I'M LEAVING THIS PLANET TODAY...
REN?
ARE YOU ALL PACKED?
Y-YES.
SAY, MODE...
YES?
WELL...
THAT GUY IS SO WEIRD.

1/4 COLUMN NONSENSE

PART 8

I've never played any of the "Final Fantasy" series, but now that I've played "Romancing SaGa", which is from the same company, it's suddenly piqued my interest. A number of my readers write about "FF" in their fan letters, and they say that the story of "FF IV," particularly, had a nuance very similar to PSME. They say it's very amusing when you play it with PSME character names...

I've gotten quite a few letters like that, so I'm getting intrigued.

Oh, but "Mother II" (EarthBound in the U.S. -ed) will be coming out soon, too... ♪ I really liked the first "Mother" (EarthBound 0 in the U.S. -ed). I cried at the last battle. Shigesato Itoi, its creator, is awesome!

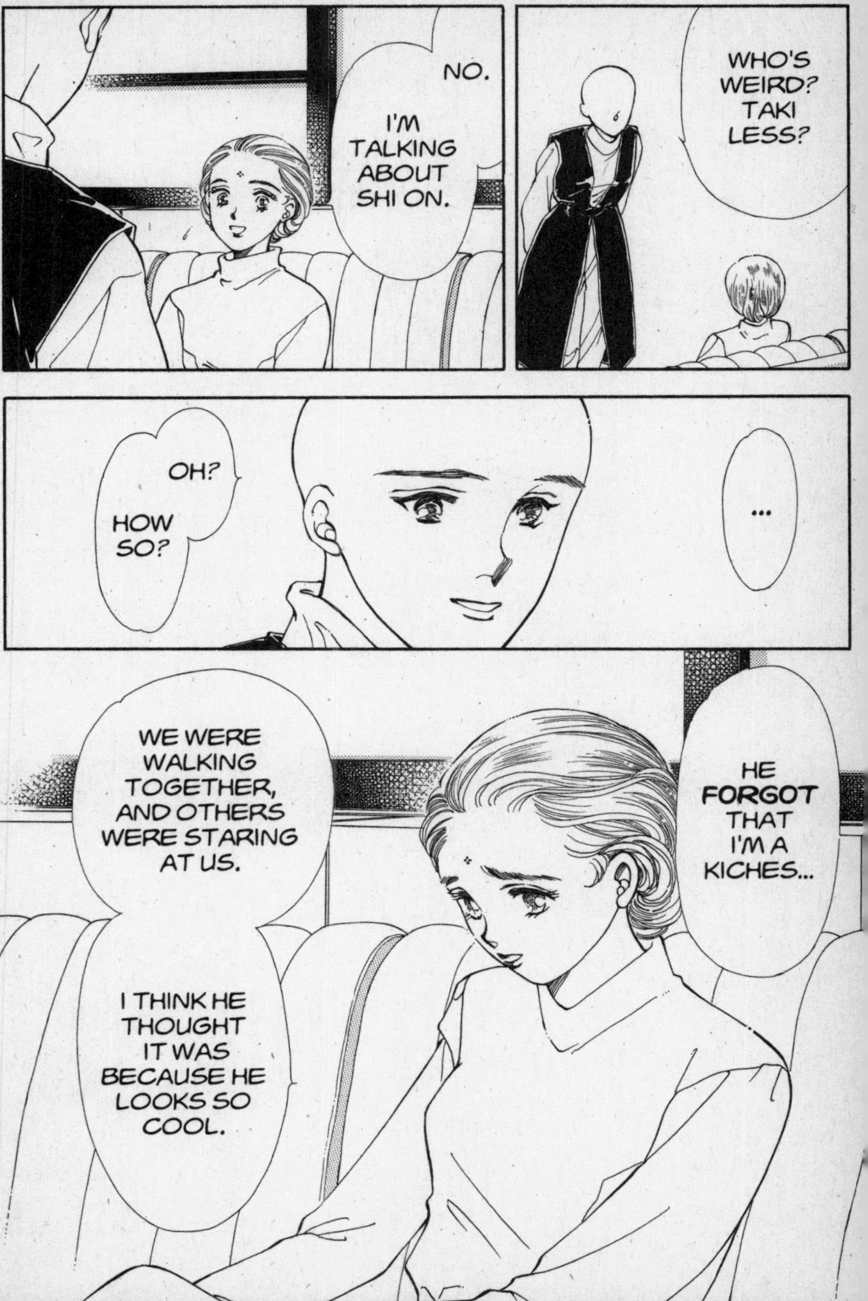
WHO'S WEIRD? TAKI LESS?
NO.
I'M TALKING ABOUT SHI ON.
...
OH? HOW SO?
HE FORGOT THAT I'M A KICHES...
WE WERE WALKING TOGETHER, AND OTHERS WERE STARING AT US.
I THINK HE THOUGHT IT WAS BECAUSE HE LOOKS SO COOL.

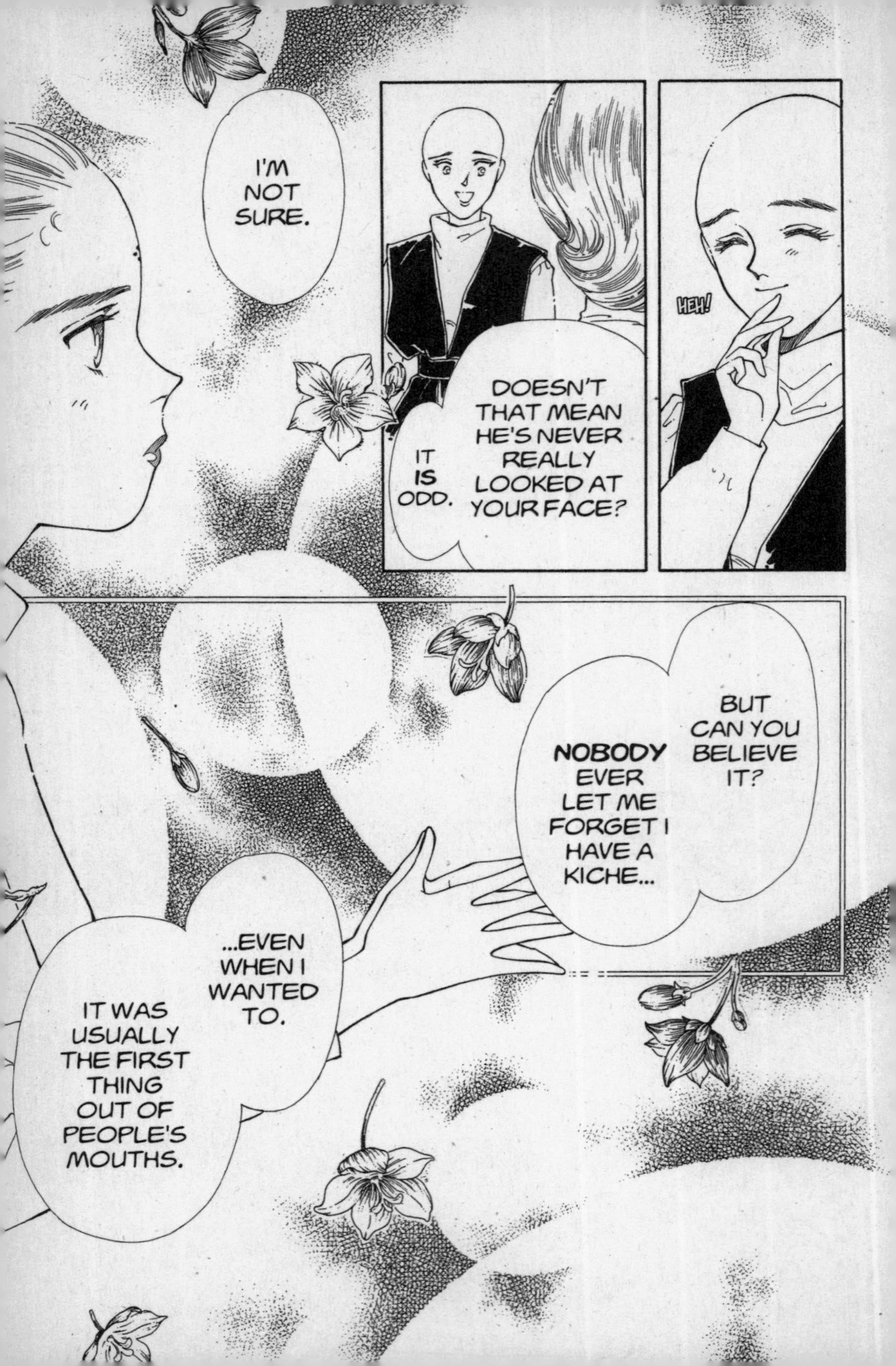
HEH!
IT IS ODD.
DOESN'T THAT MEAN HE'S NEVER REALLY LOOKED AT YOUR FACE?
I'M NOT SURE.
BUT CAN YOU BELIEVE IT?
NOBODY EVER LET ME FORGET I HAVE A KICHE...
...EVEN WHEN I WANTED TO.
IT WAS USUALLY THE FIRST THING OUT OF PEOPLE'S MOUTHS.

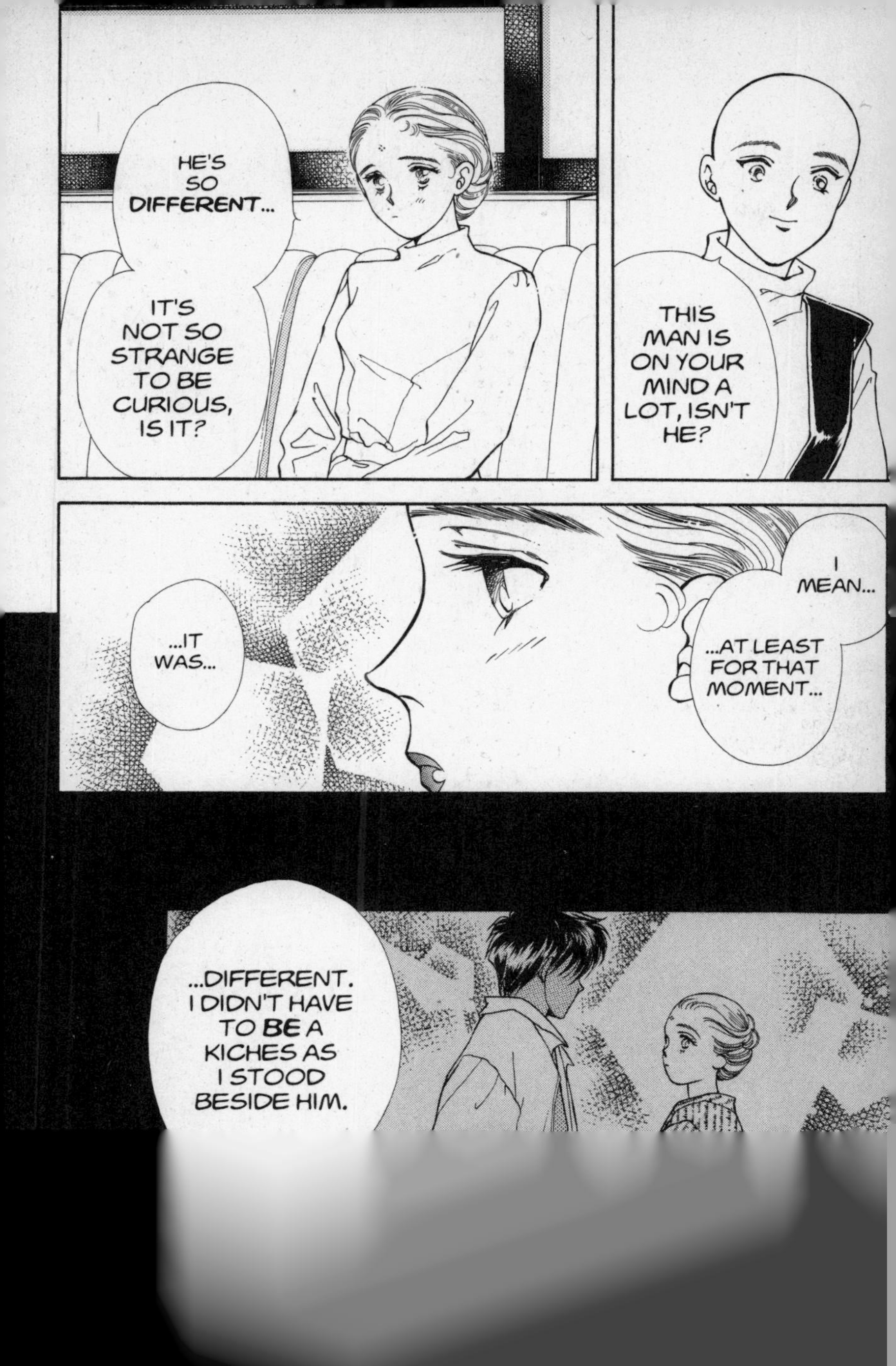
THIS MAN IS ON YOUR MIND A LOT, ISN'T HE?
HE'S SO DIFFERENT...
IT'S NOT SO STRANGE TO BE CURIOUS, IS IT?
I MEAN...
...AT LEAST FOR THAT MOMENT...
...IT WAS...
...DIFFERENT. I DIDN'T HAVE TO BE A KICHES AS I STOOD BESIDE HIM.

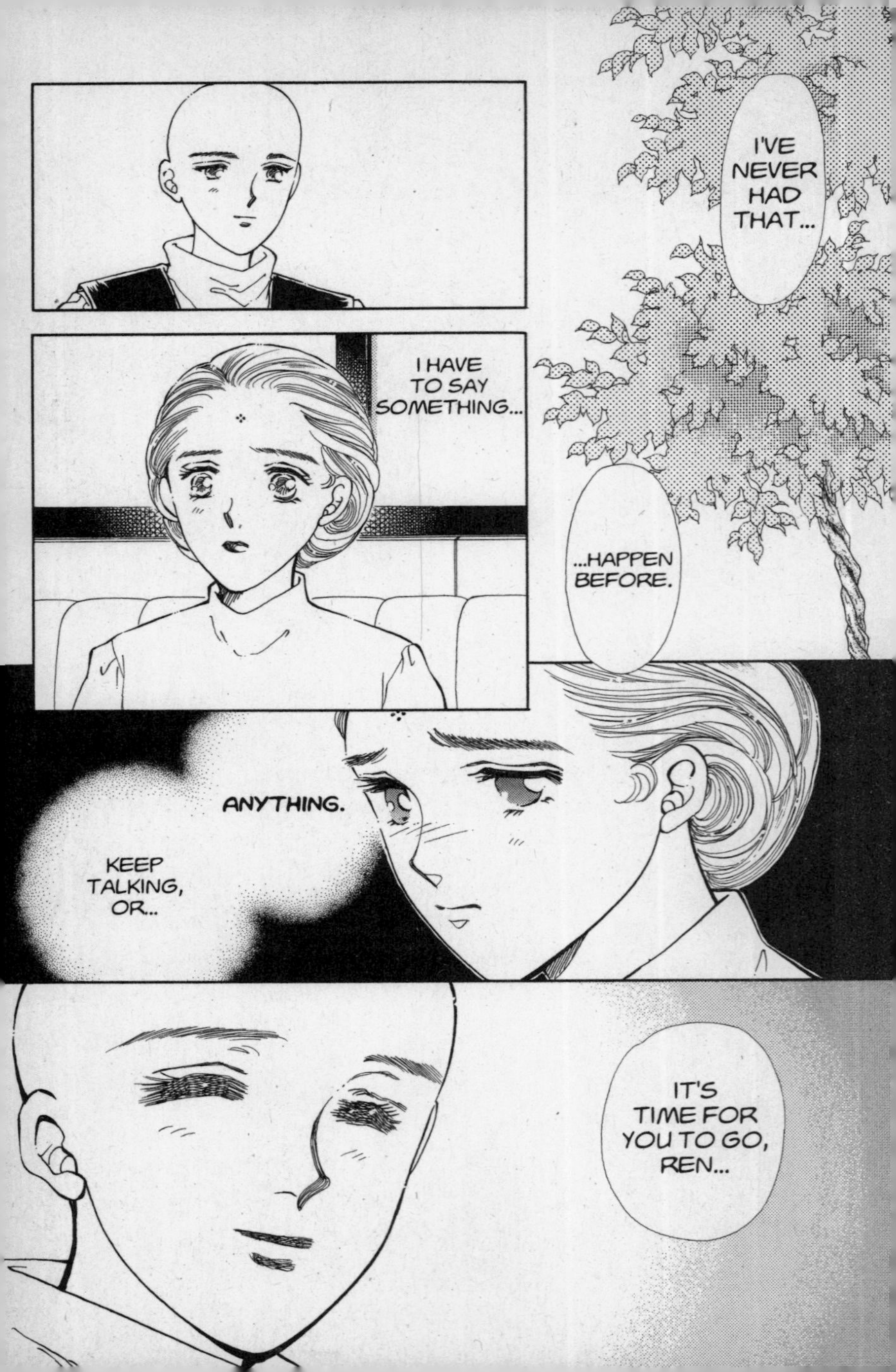
I'VE NEVER HAD THAT...
...HAPPEN BEFORE.
I HAVE TO SAY SOMETHING...
ANYTHING.
KEEP TALKING, OR...
IT'S TIME FOR YOU TO GO, REN...

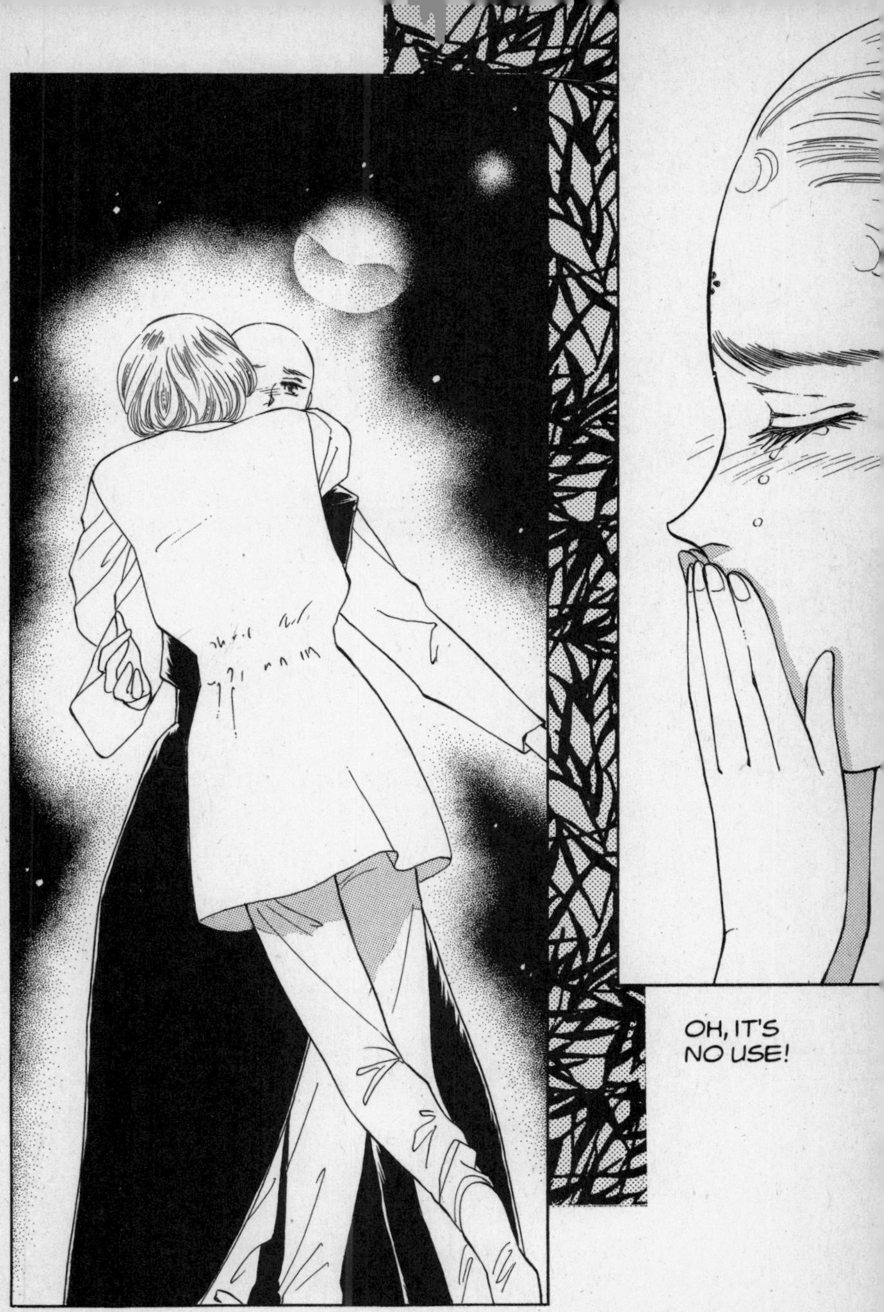
OH, IT'S
NO USE!

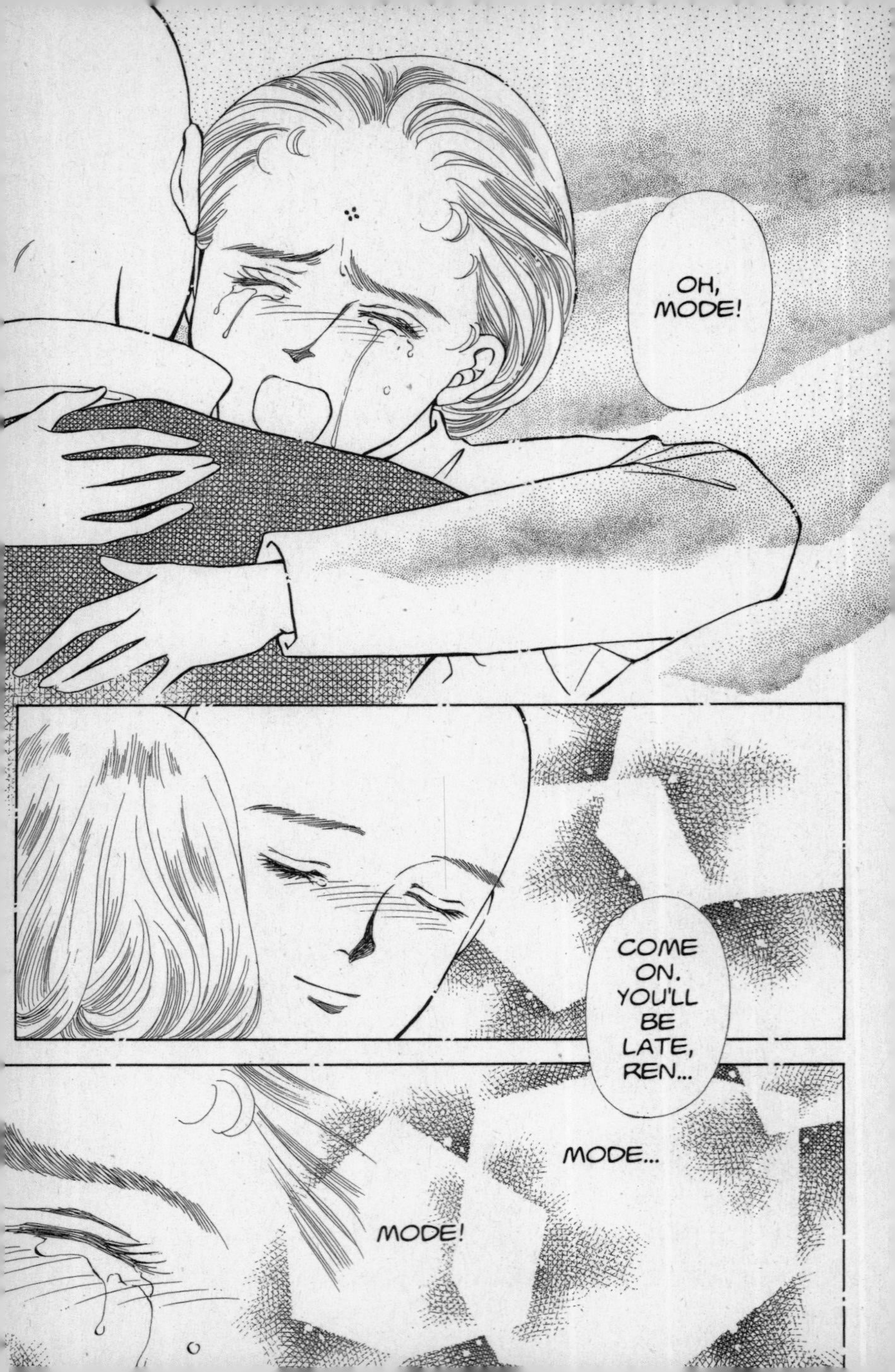
OH, MODE!
COME ON. YOU'LL BE LATE, REN...
MODE...
MODE!

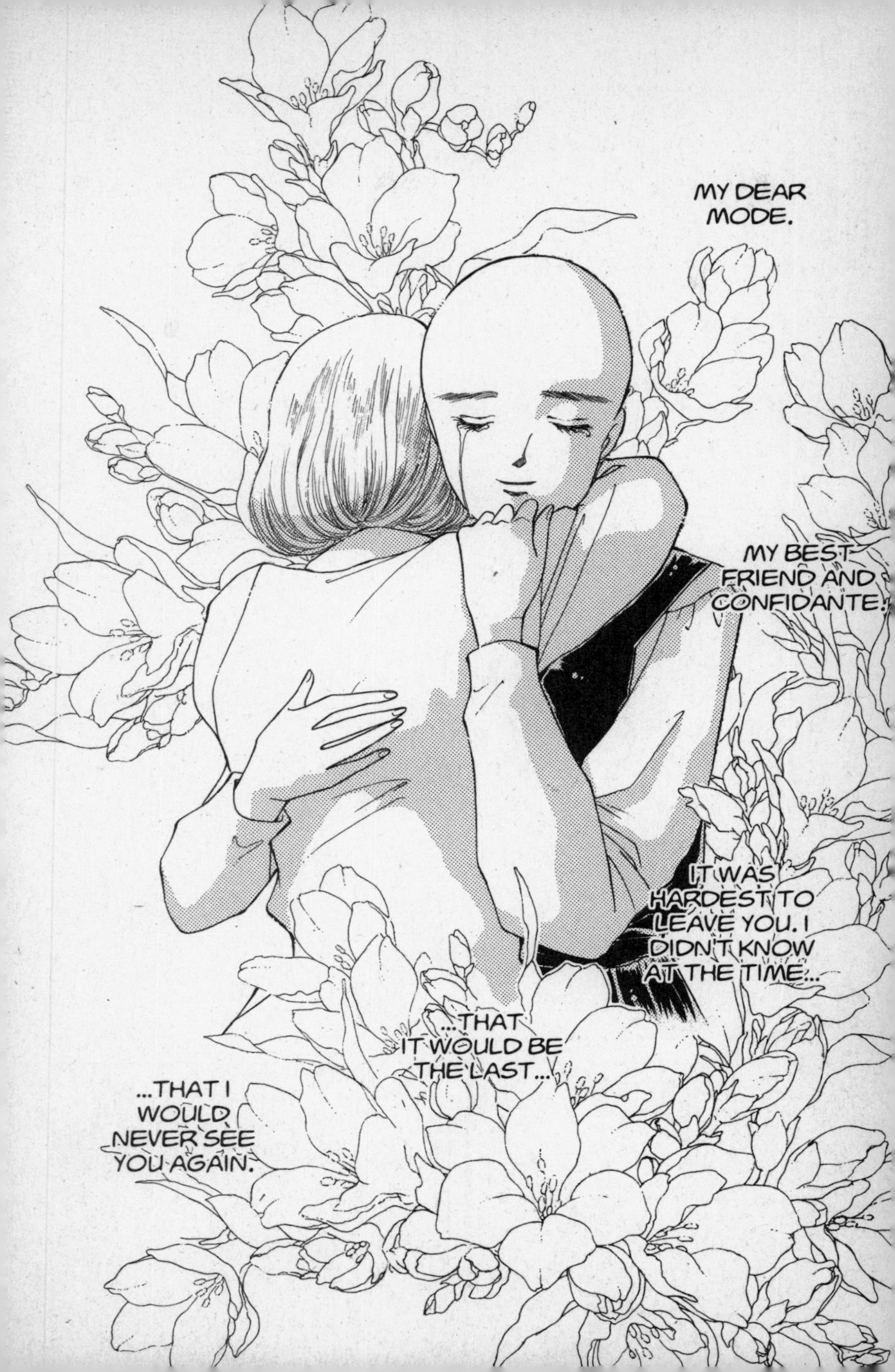
MY DEAR MODE.
MY BEST FRIEND AND CONFIDANTE.
IT WAS HARDEST TO LEAVE YOU. I DIDN'T KNOW AT THE TIME...
...THAT IT WOULD BE THE LAST...
...THAT I WOULD NEVER SEE YOU AGAIN.

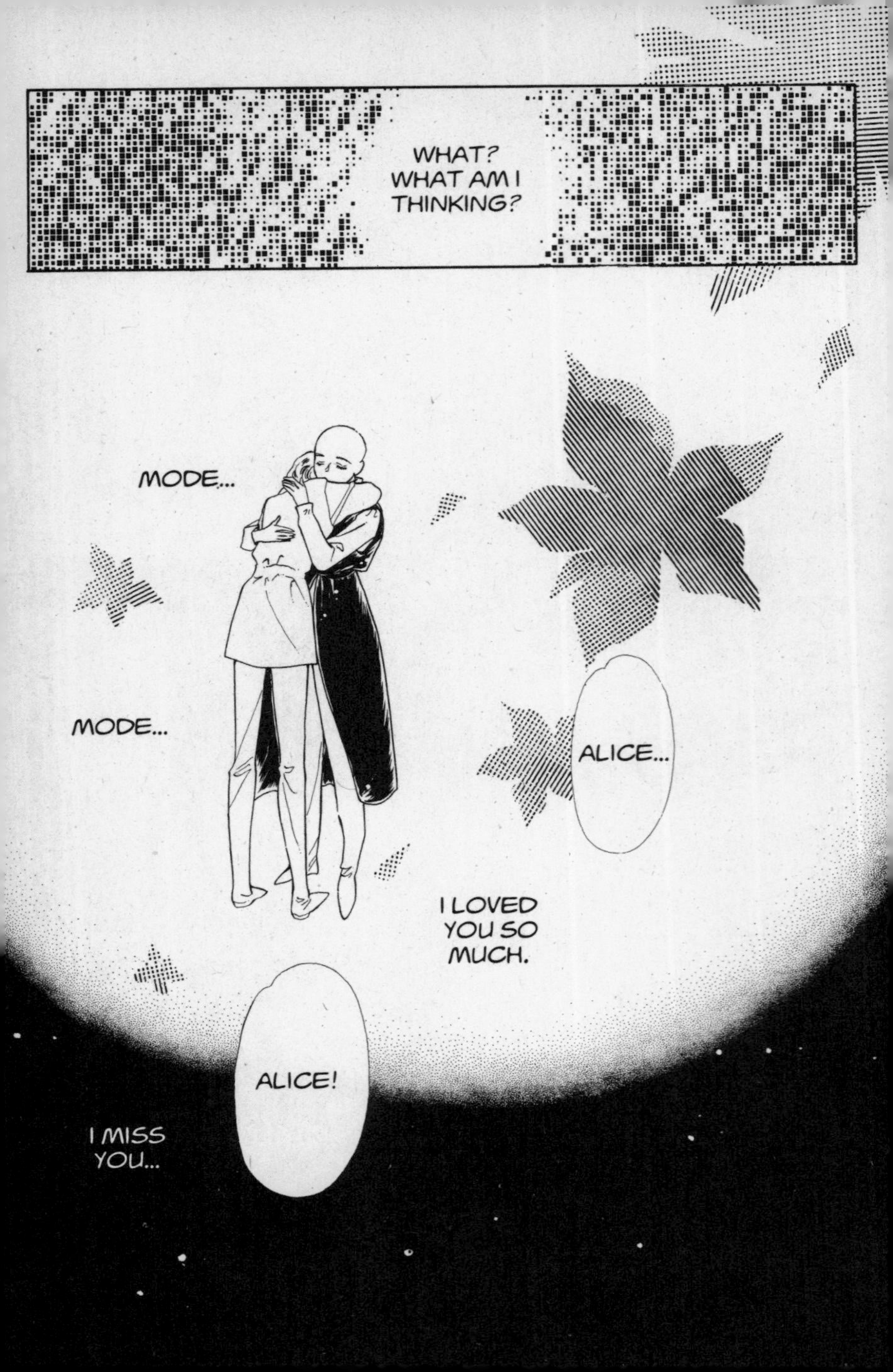
WHAT? WHAT AM I THINKING?
MODE...
MODE...
ALICE...
I LOVED YOU SO MUCH.
ALICE!
I MISS YOU...

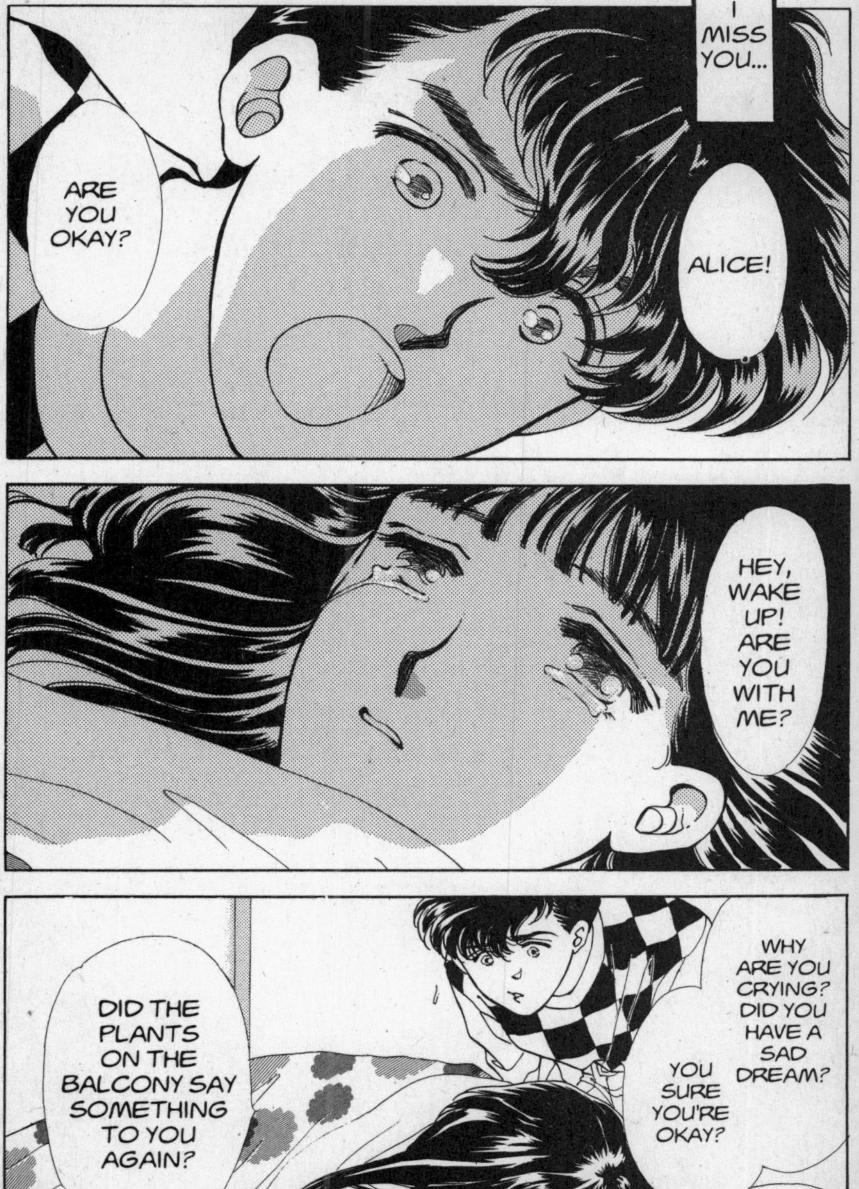
I MISS YOU...
ALICE!
ARE YOU OKAY?
HEY, WAKE UP! ARE YOU WITH ME?
WHY ARE YOU CRYING? DID YOU HAVE A SAD DREAM?
YOU SURE YOU'RE OKAY?
DID THE PLANTS ON THE BALCONY SAY SOMETHING TO YOU AGAIN?

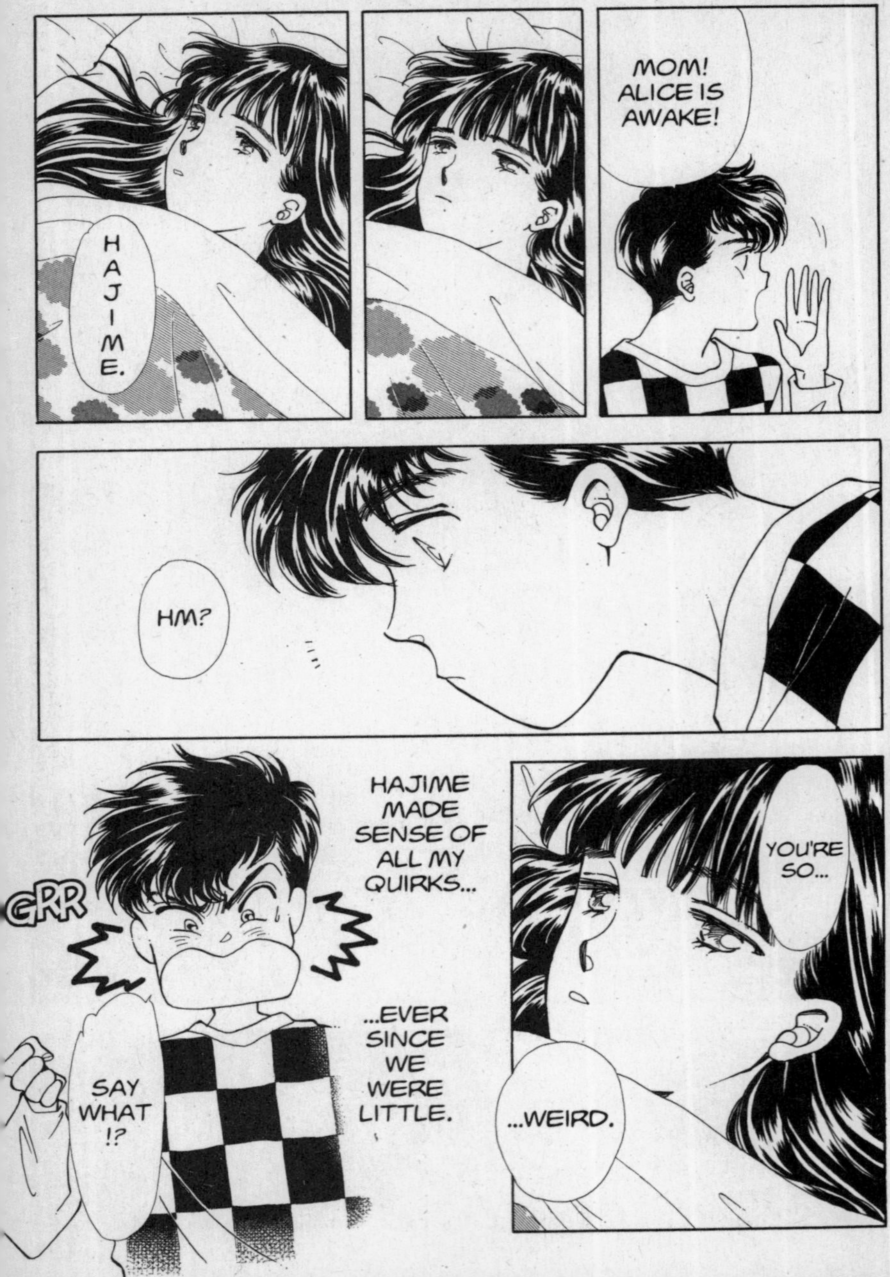
MOM! ALICE IS AWAKE!
HAJIME.
HM?
YOU'RE SO...
...WEIRD.
HAJIME MADE SENSE OF ALL MY QUIRKS...
GRR
...EVER SINCE WE WERE LITTLE.
SAY WHAT!?

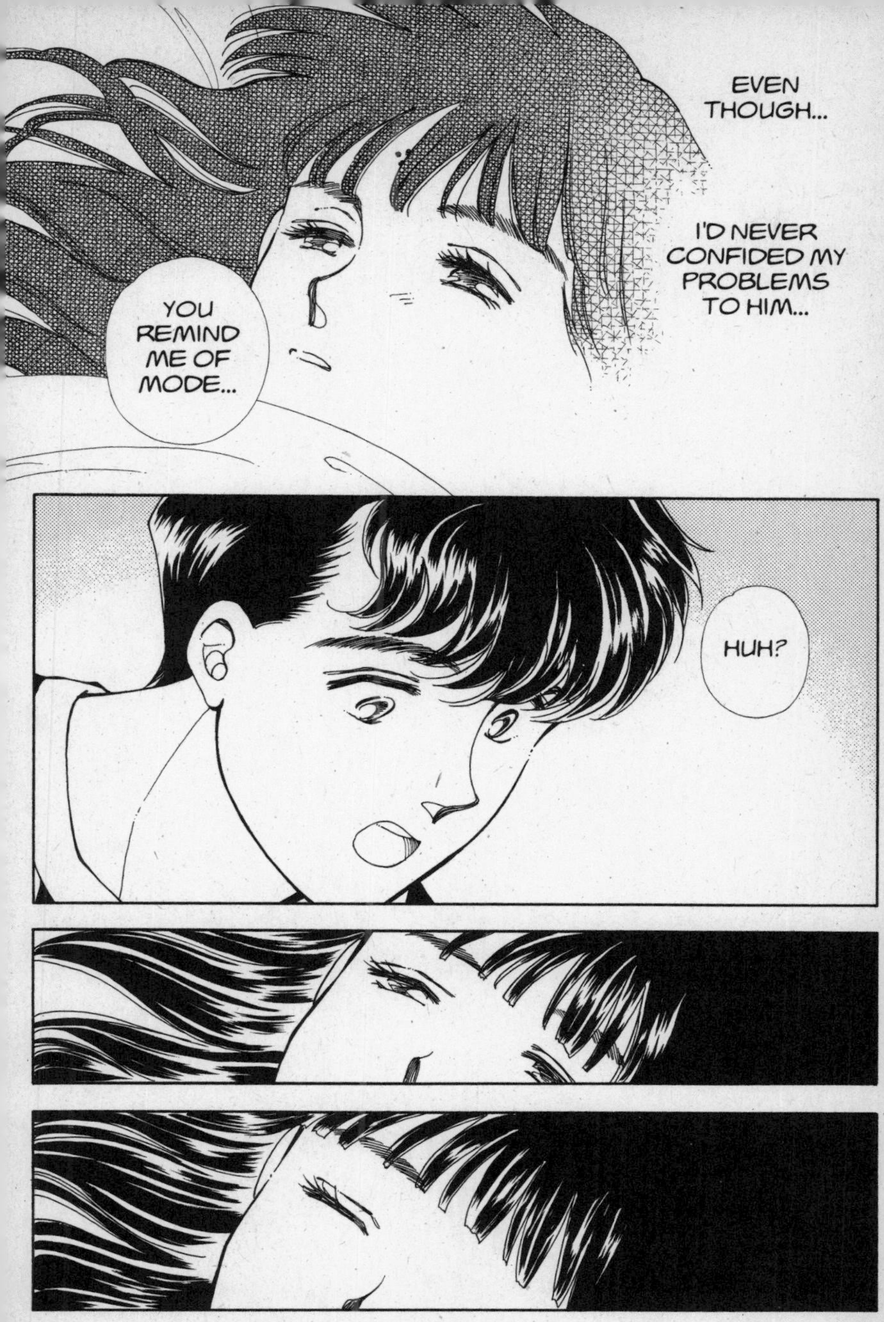
EVEN THOUGH...
I'D NEVER CONFIDED MY PROBLEMS TO HIM...
YOU REMIND ME OF MODE...
HUH?

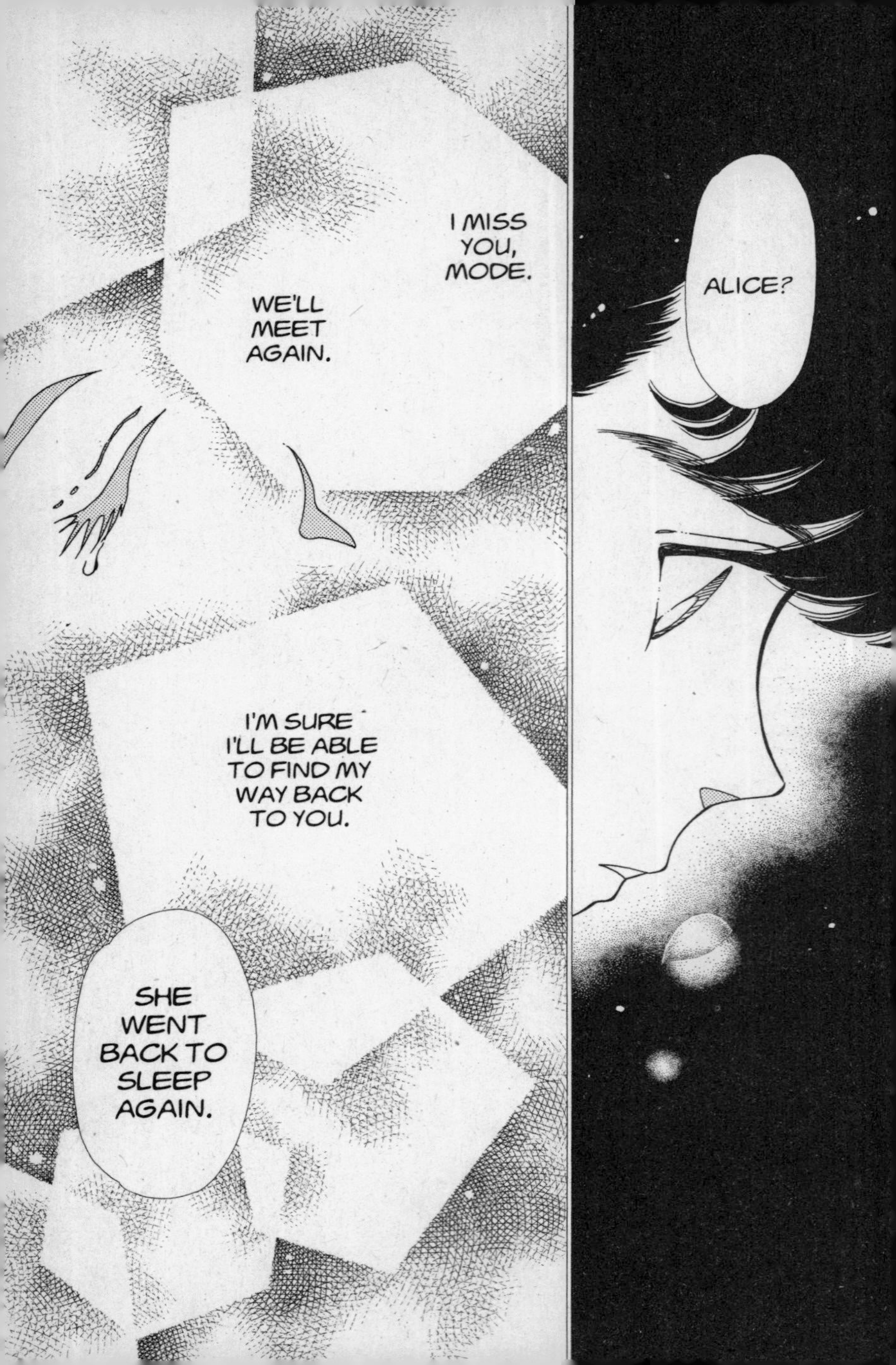
ALICE?
I MISS YOU, MODE.
WE'LL MEET AGAIN.
I'M SURE I'LL BE ABLE TO FIND MY WAY BACK TO YOU.
SHE WENT BACK TO SLEEP AGAIN.

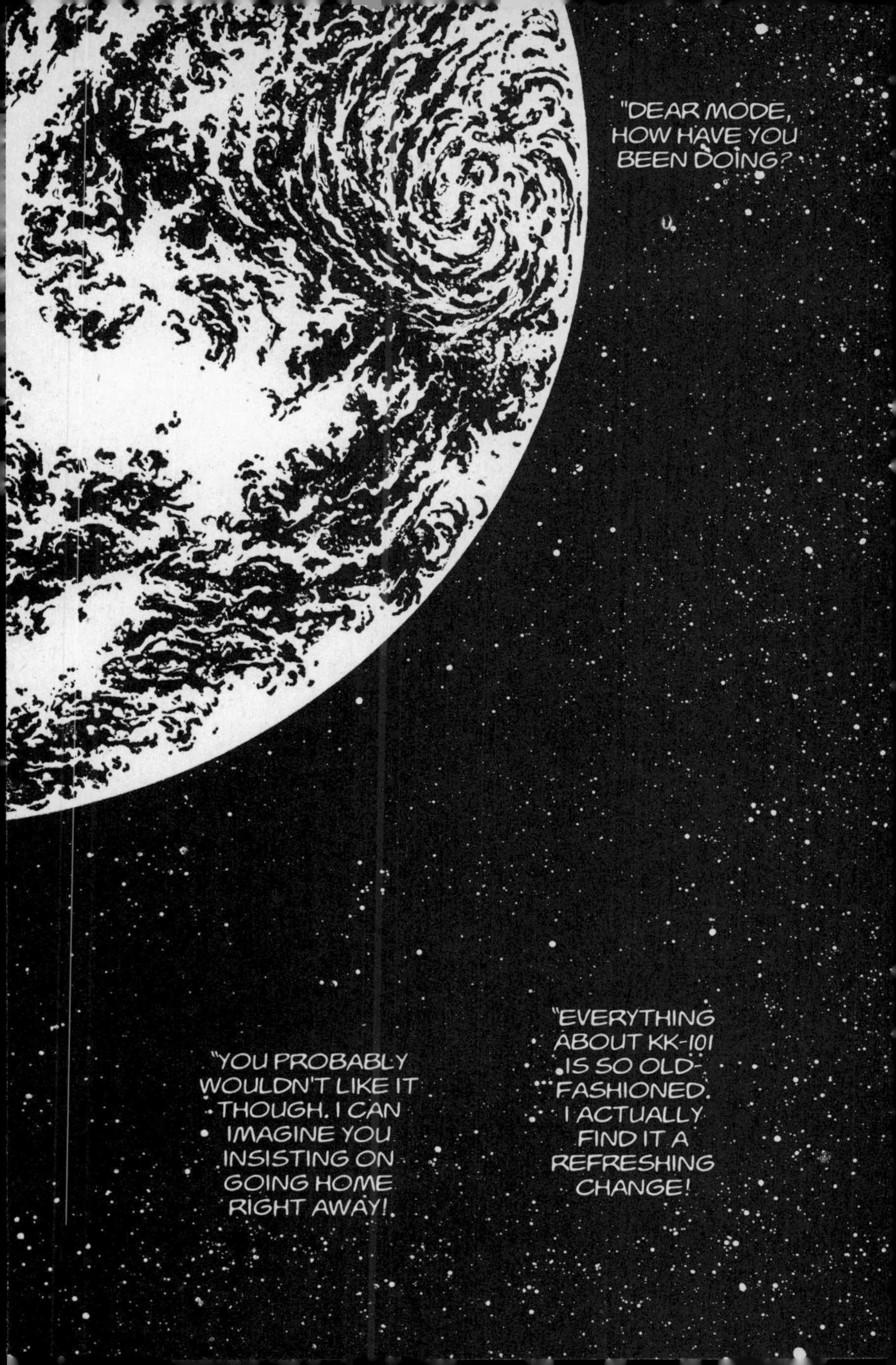
"DEAR MODE, HOW HAVE YOU BEEN DOING?
"EVERYTHING ABOUT KK-101 IS SO OLD-FASHIONED. I ACTUALLY FIND IT A REFRESHING CHANGE!
"YOU PROBABLY WOULDN'T LIKE IT THOUGH. I CAN IMAGINE YOU INSISTING ON GOING HOME RIGHT AWAY!

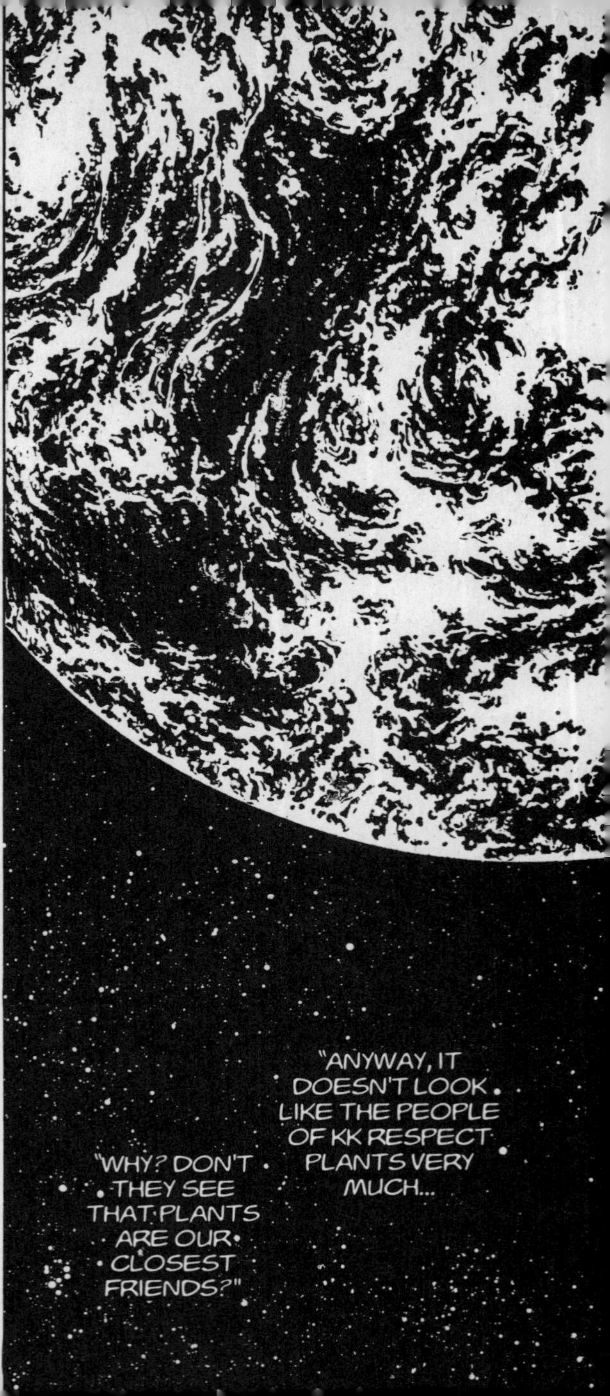
"ANYWAY, IT DOESN'T LOOK LIKE THE PEOPLE OF KK RESPECT PLANTS VERY MUCH...
"WHY? DON'T THEY SEE THAT PLANTS ARE OUR CLOSEST FRIENDS?"

1/4 COLUMN NONSENSE

PART 9

Changing the subject... I'd like to talk about cats. Actually, I recently took in a stray. ♪ So now I have a total of three cats at my place: Tsuki, Futa, and the new one.

This newcomer is only two and a half months old right now, and she's a calico kitty. You see, there's a stray in my neighborhood who gets pregnant often. As usual, she had another litter of five kittens this summer. The calico was one of them. And...the mother cat made the entryway to my house her base of operations.

Continued in Part 10.

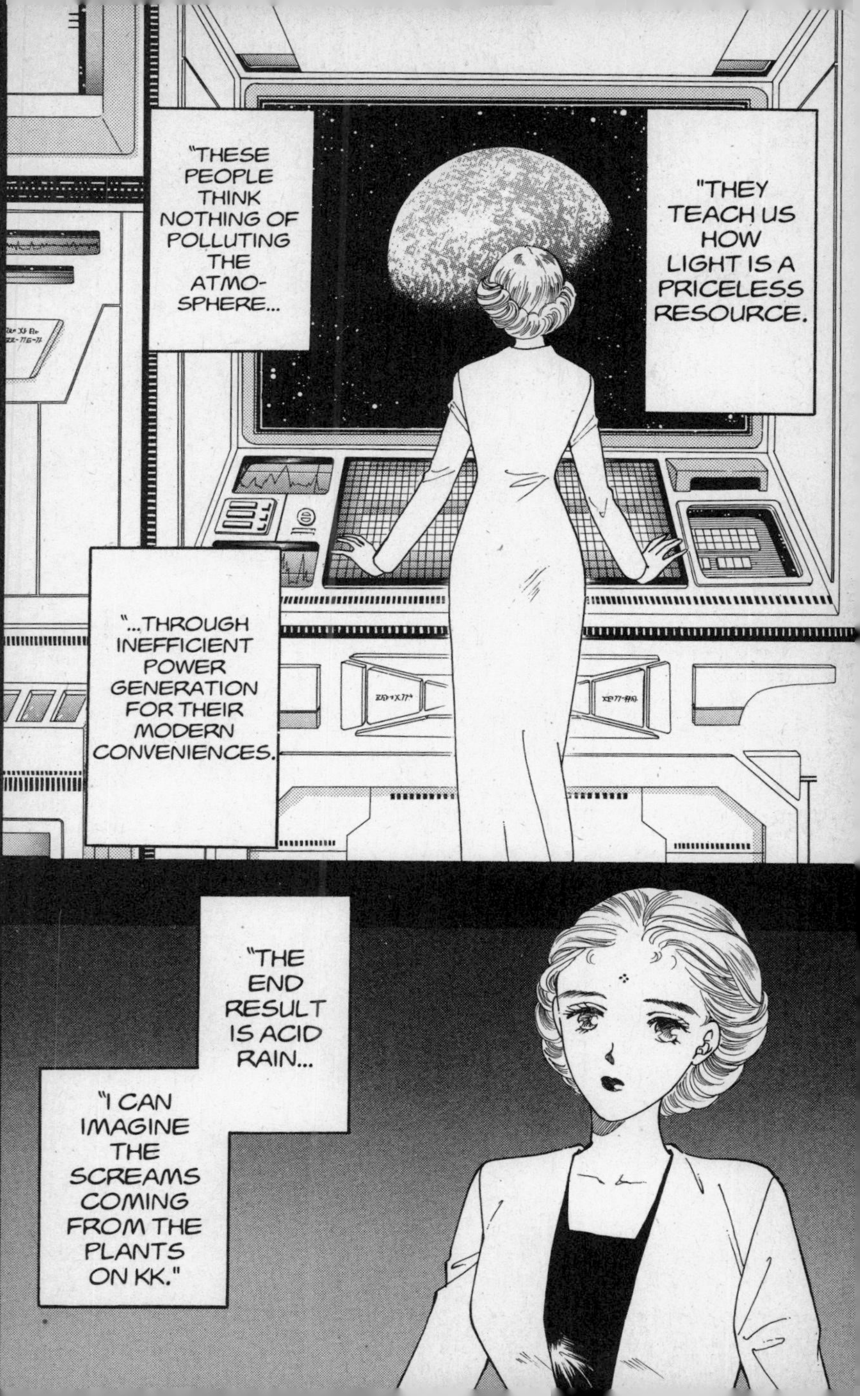
"THEY TEACH US HOW LIGHT IS A PRICELESS RESOURCE.
"THESE PEOPLE THINK NOTHING OF POLLUTING THE ATMO-SPHERE...
"...THROUGH INEFFICIENT POWER GENERATION FOR THEIR MODERN CONVENIENCES.
"THE END RESULT IS ACID RAIN...
"I CAN IMAGINE THE SCREAMS COMING FROM THE PLANTS ON KK."

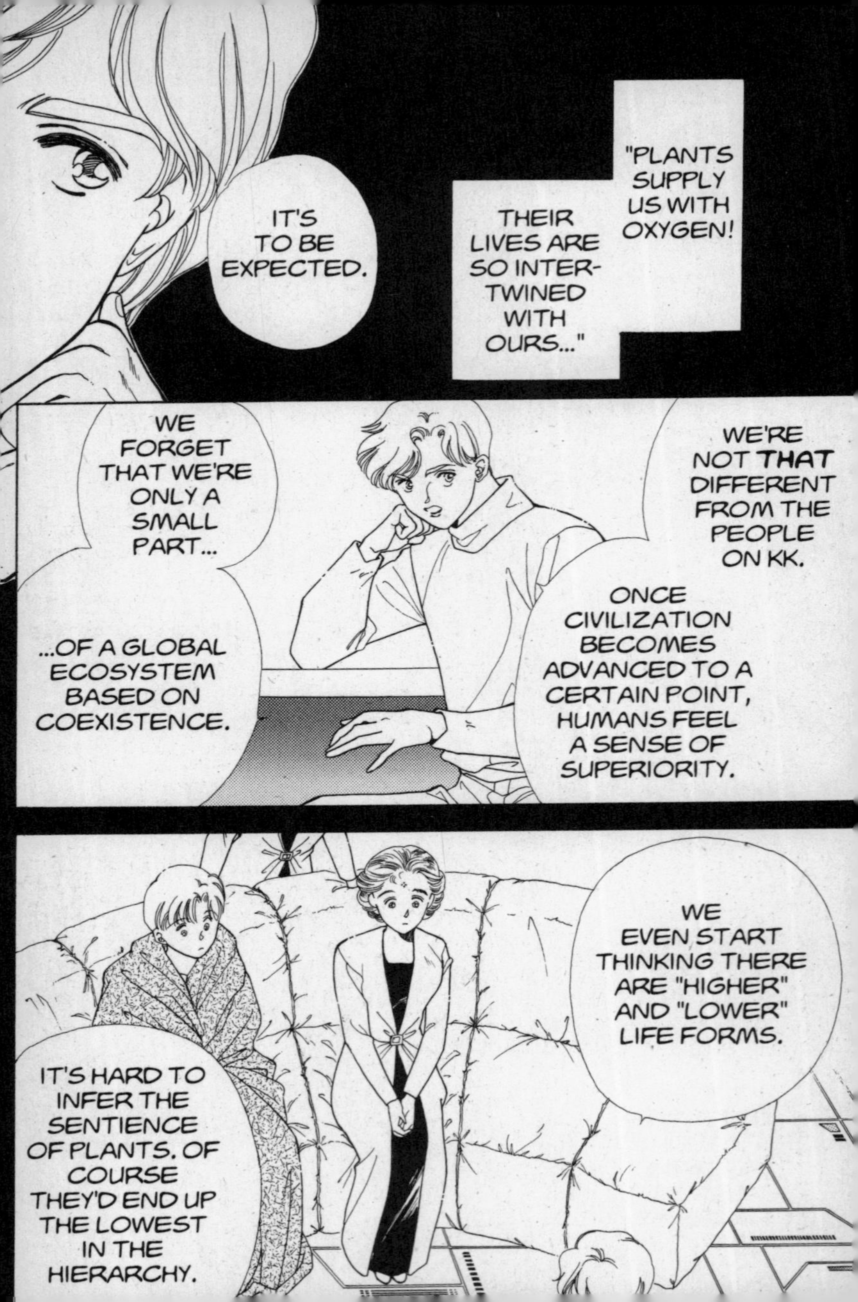
"PLANTS SUPPLY US WITH OXYGEN!
THEIR LIVES ARE SO INTER-TWINED WITH OURS..."
IT'S TO BE EXPECTED.
WE'RE NOT **THAT** DIFFERENT FROM THE PEOPLE ON KK.
ONCE CIVILIZATION BECOMES ADVANCED TO A CERTAIN POINT, HUMANS FEEL A SENSE OF SUPERIORITY.
WE FORGET THAT WE'RE ONLY A SMALL PART...
...OF A GLOBAL ECOSYSTEM BASED ON COEXISTENCE.
WE EVEN START THINKING THERE ARE "HIGHER" AND "LOWER" LIFE FORMS.
IT'S HARD TO INFER THE SENTIENCE OF PLANTS. OF COURSE THEY'D END UP THE LOWEST IN THE HIERARCHY.

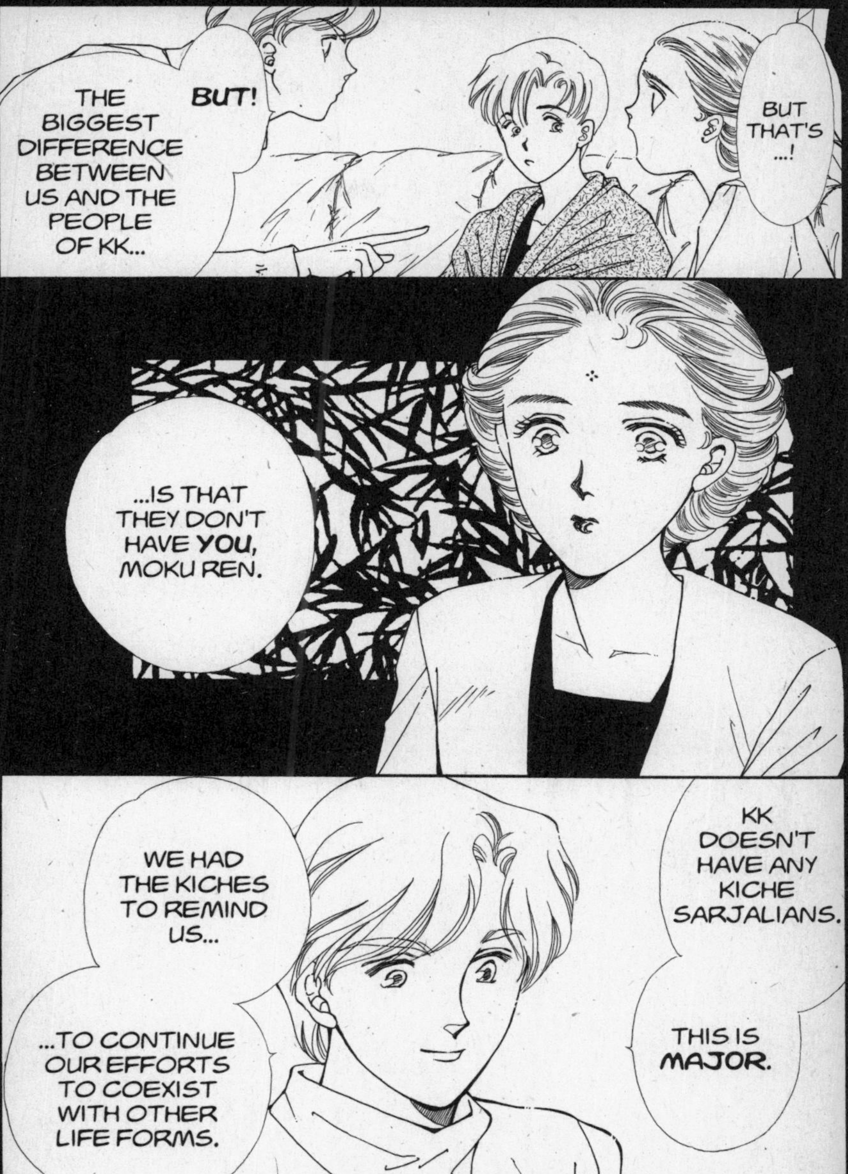
BUT THAT'S ...!
BUT!
THE BIGGEST DIFFERENCE BETWEEN US AND THE PEOPLE OF KK...
...IS THAT THEY DON'T HAVE YOU, MOKU REN.
KK DOESN'T HAVE ANY KICHE SARJALIANS.
THIS IS MAJOR.
WE HAD THE KICHES TO REMIND US...
...TO CONTINUE OUR EFFORTS TO COEXIST WITH OTHER LIFE FORMS.

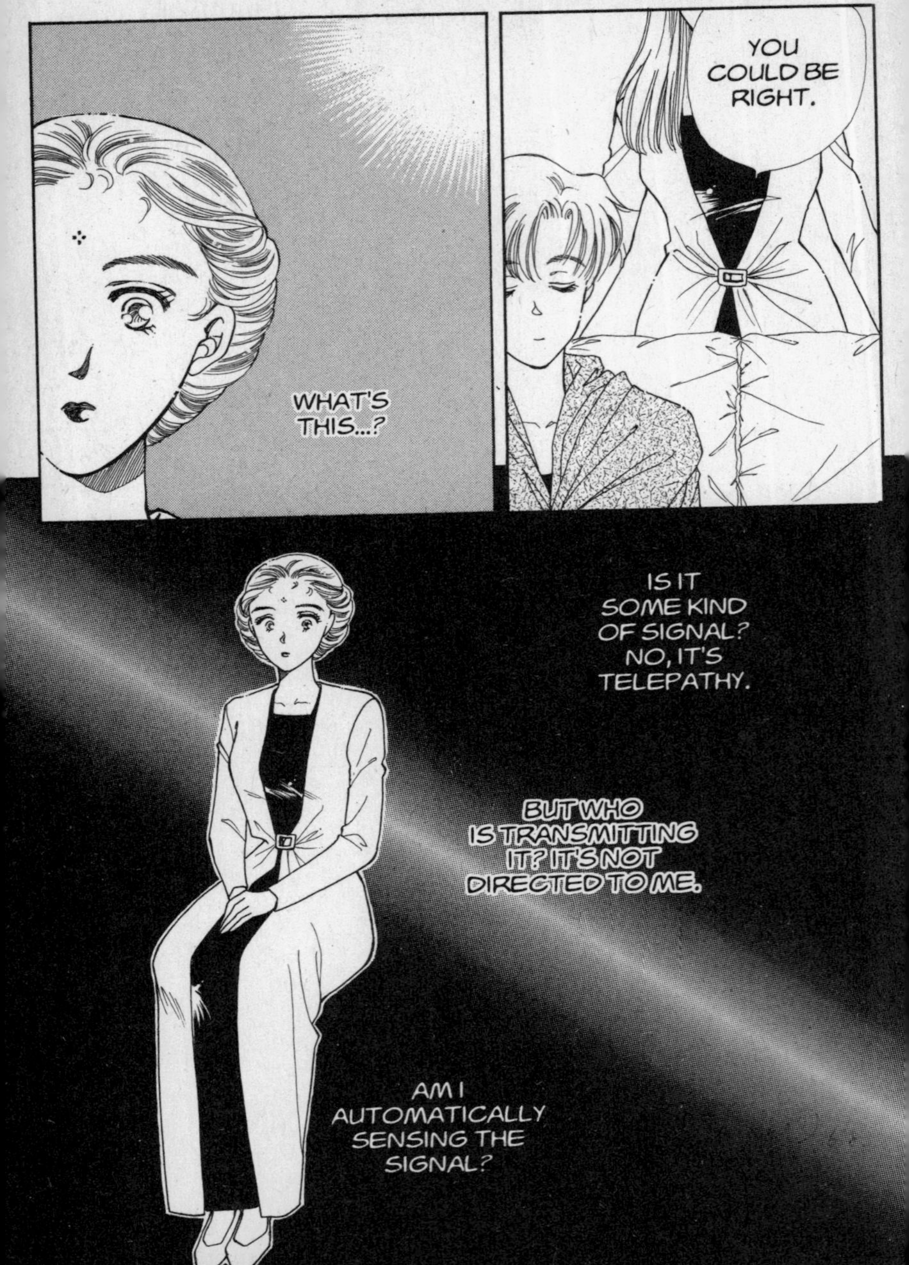
YOU COULD BE RIGHT.
WHAT'S THIS...?
IS IT SOME KIND OF SIGNAL? NO, IT'S TELEPATHY.
BUT WHO IS TRANSMITTING IT? IT'S NOT DIRECTED TO ME.
AM I AUTOMATICALLY SENSING THE SIGNAL?

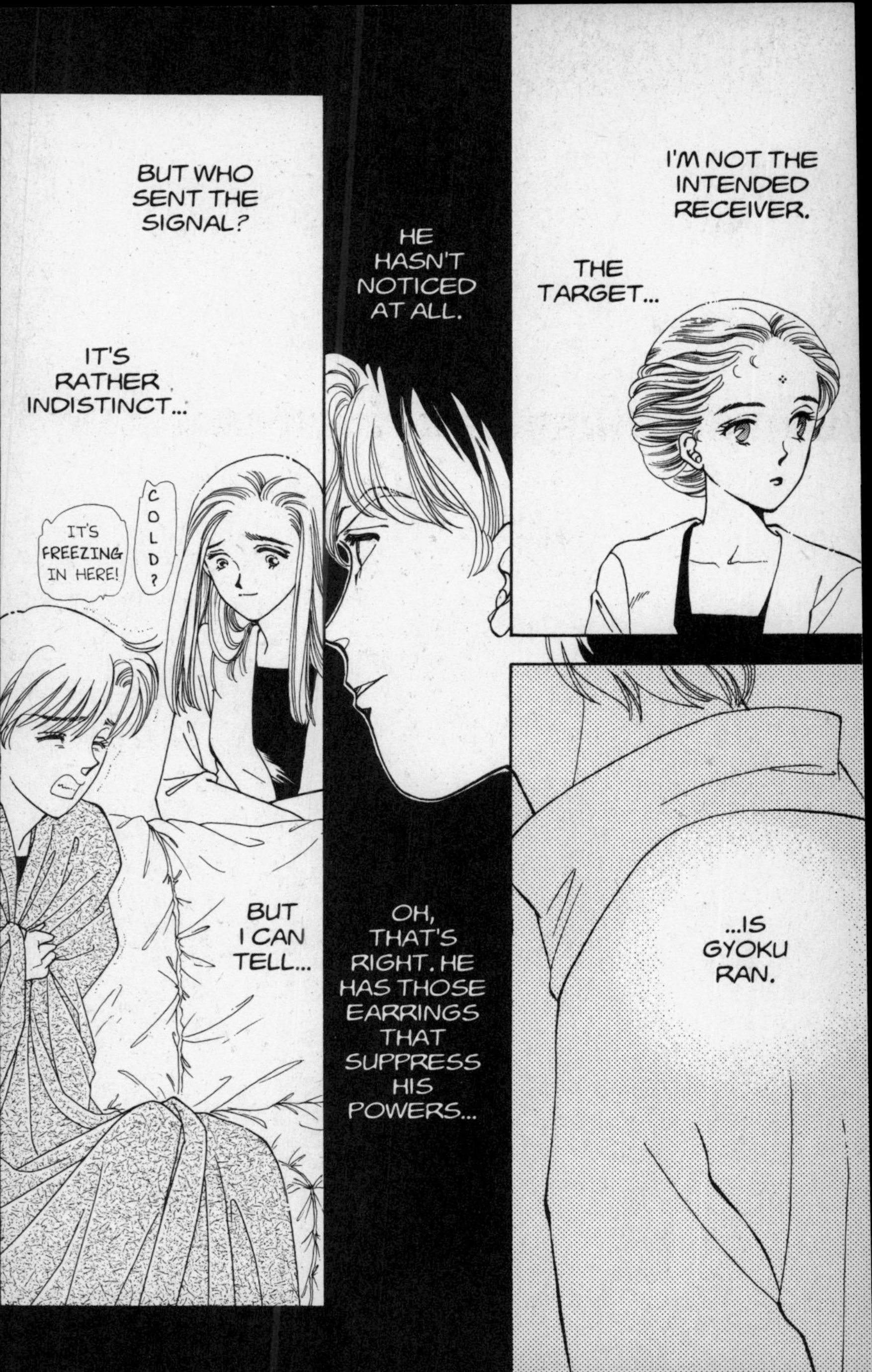

I'M NOT THE INTENDED RECEIVER.
THE TARGET...
...IS GYOKU RAN.
HE HASN'T NOTICED AT ALL.
OH, THAT'S RIGHT. HE HAS THOSE EARRINGS THAT SUPPRESS HIS POWERS...
BUT WHO SENT THE SIGNAL?
IT'S RATHER INDISTINCT...
COLD?
IT'S FREEZING IN HERE!
BUT I CAN TELL...

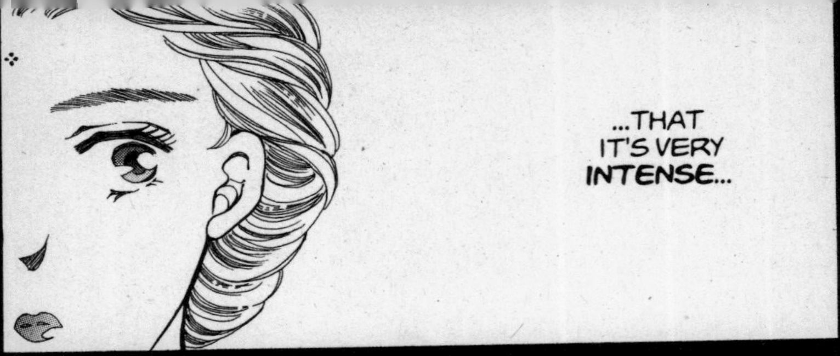
...THAT IT'S VERY INTENSE...

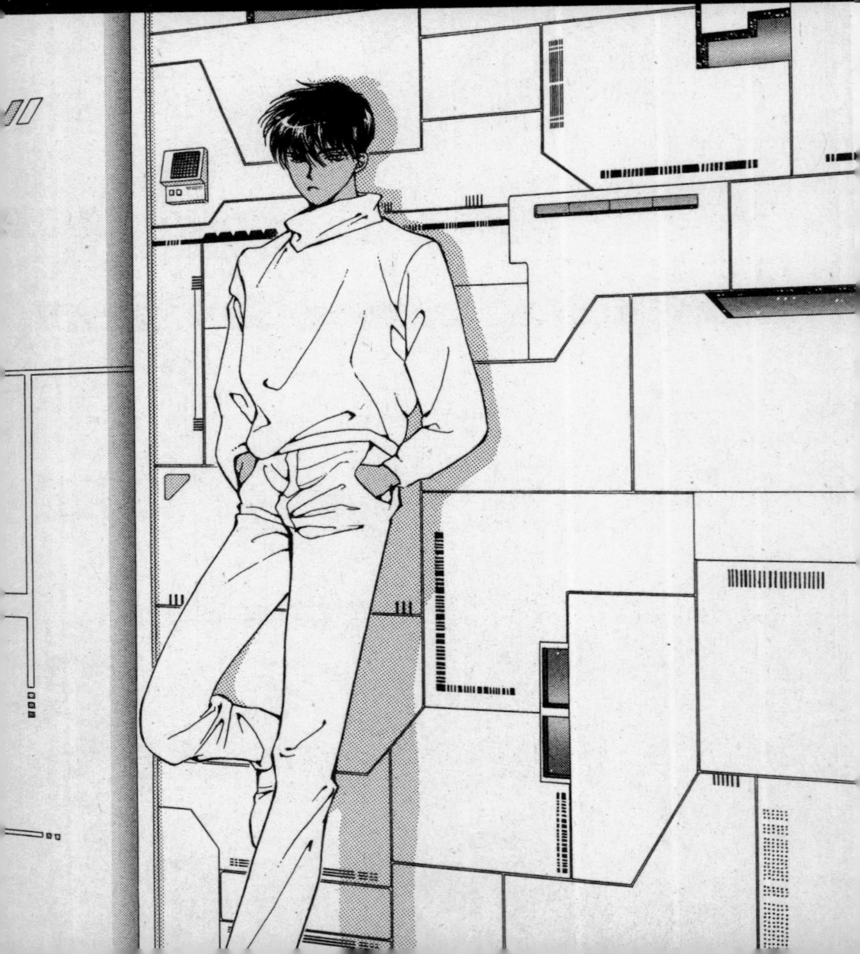

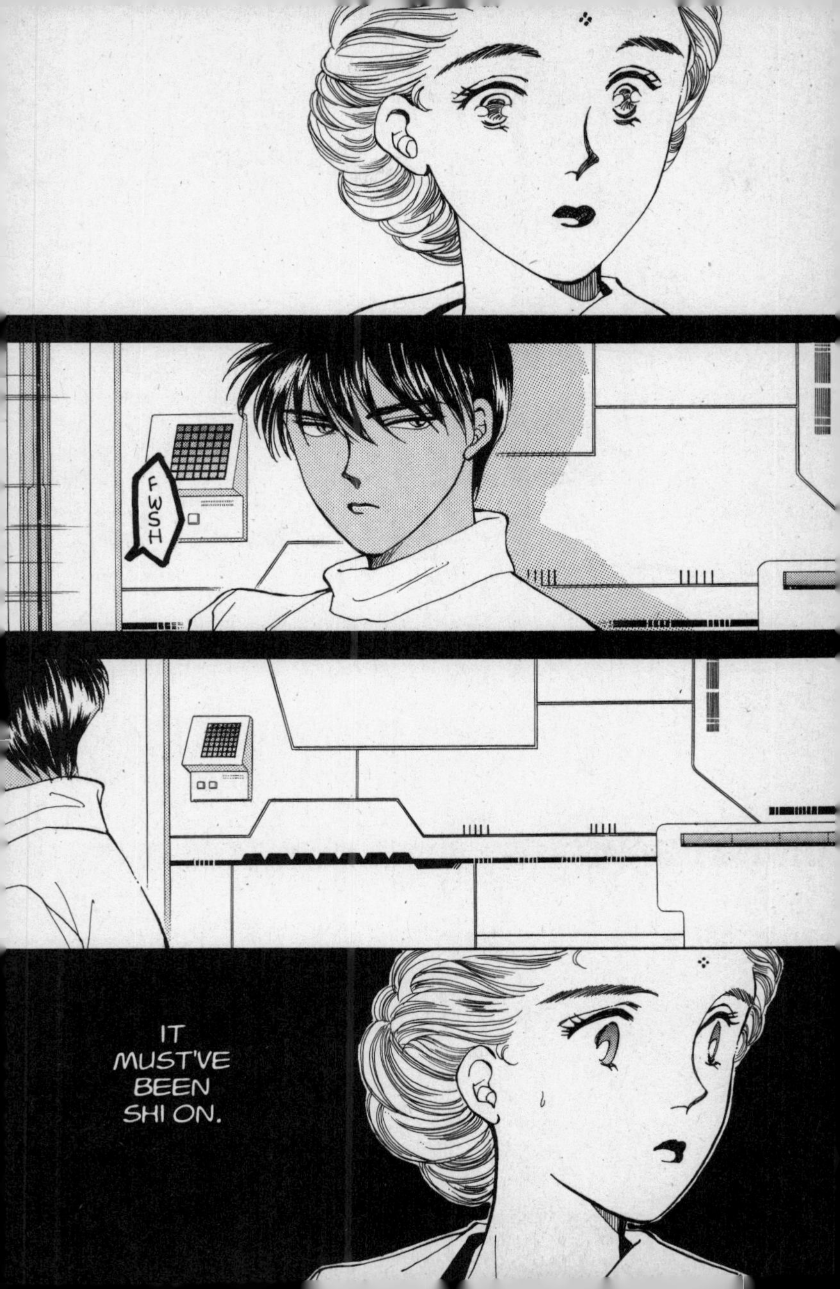
FWSH
IT MUST'VE BEEN SHI ON.

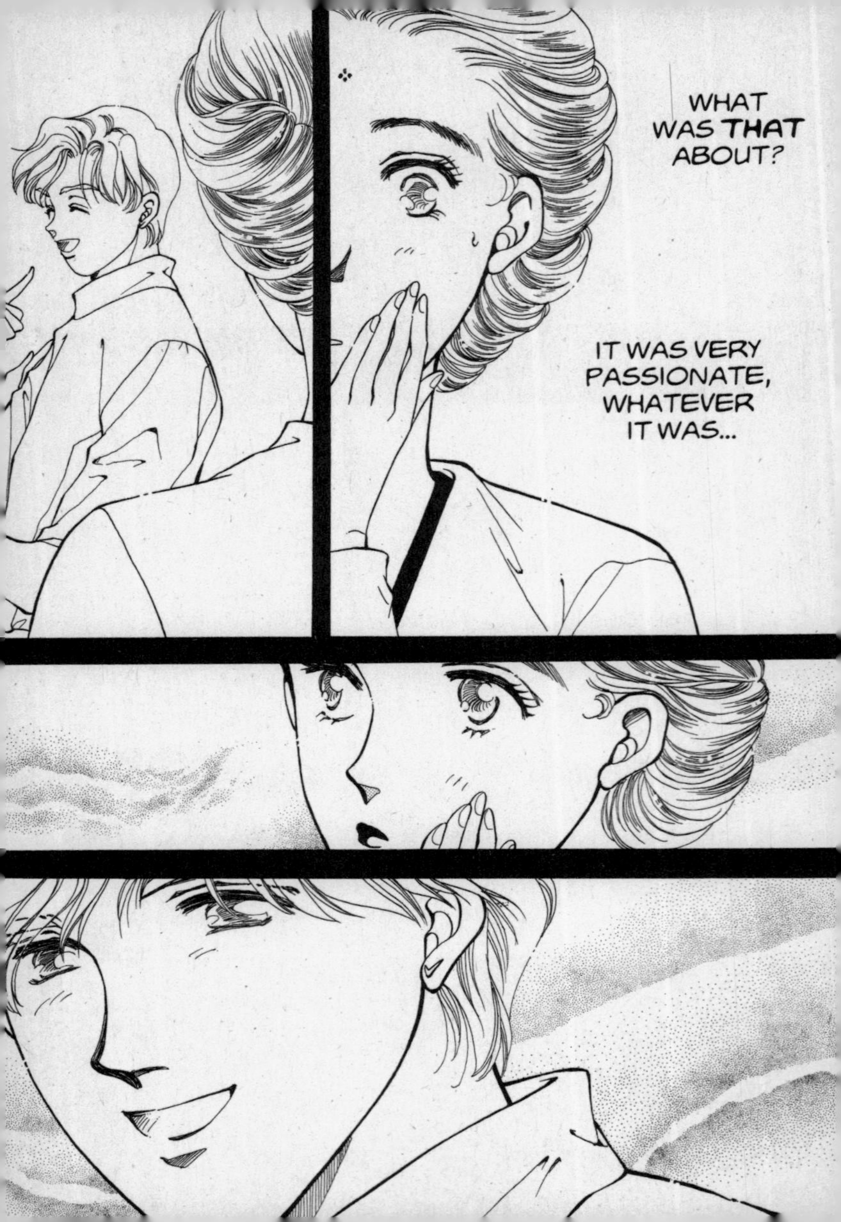
WHAT WAS THAT ABOUT?
IT WAS VERY PASSIONATE, WHATEVER IT WAS...

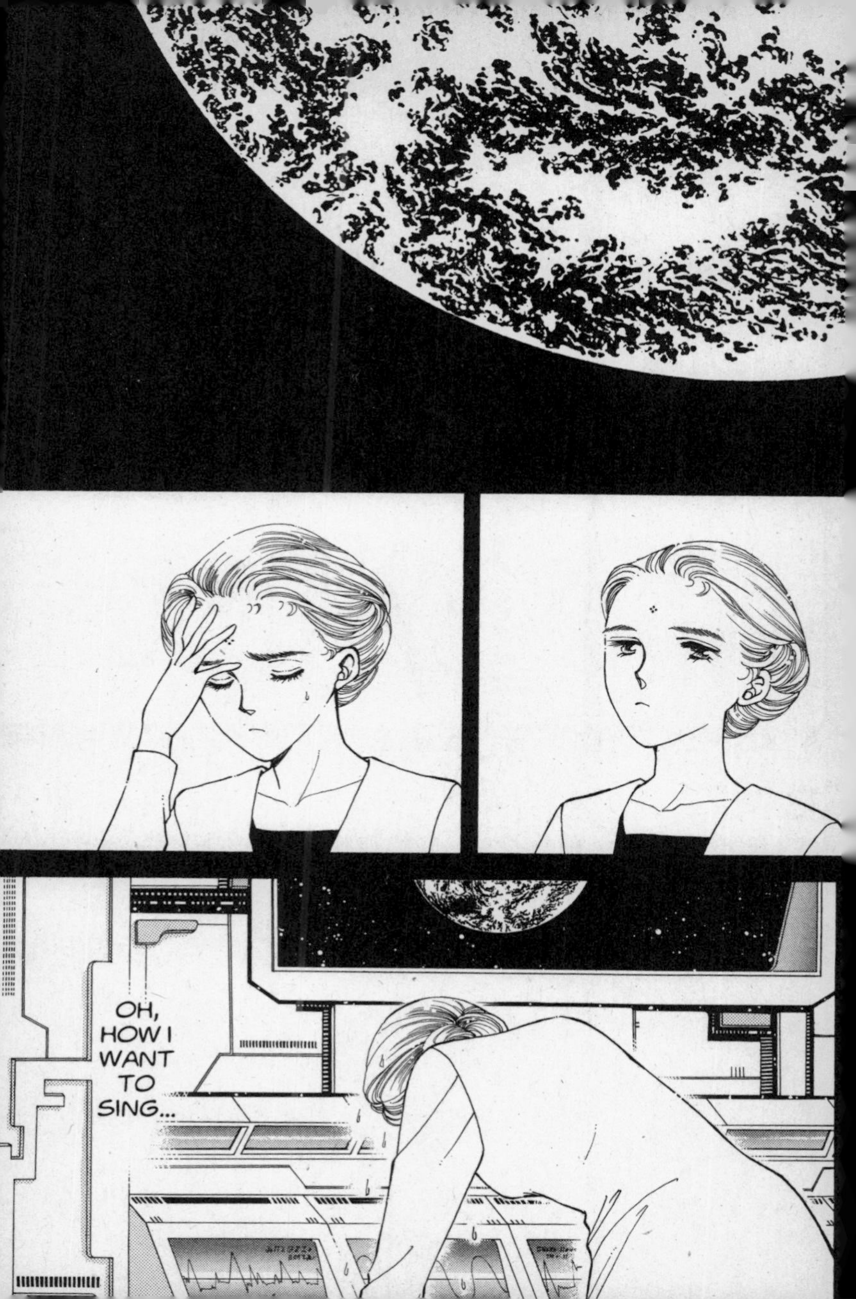
OH, HOW I WANT TO SING...

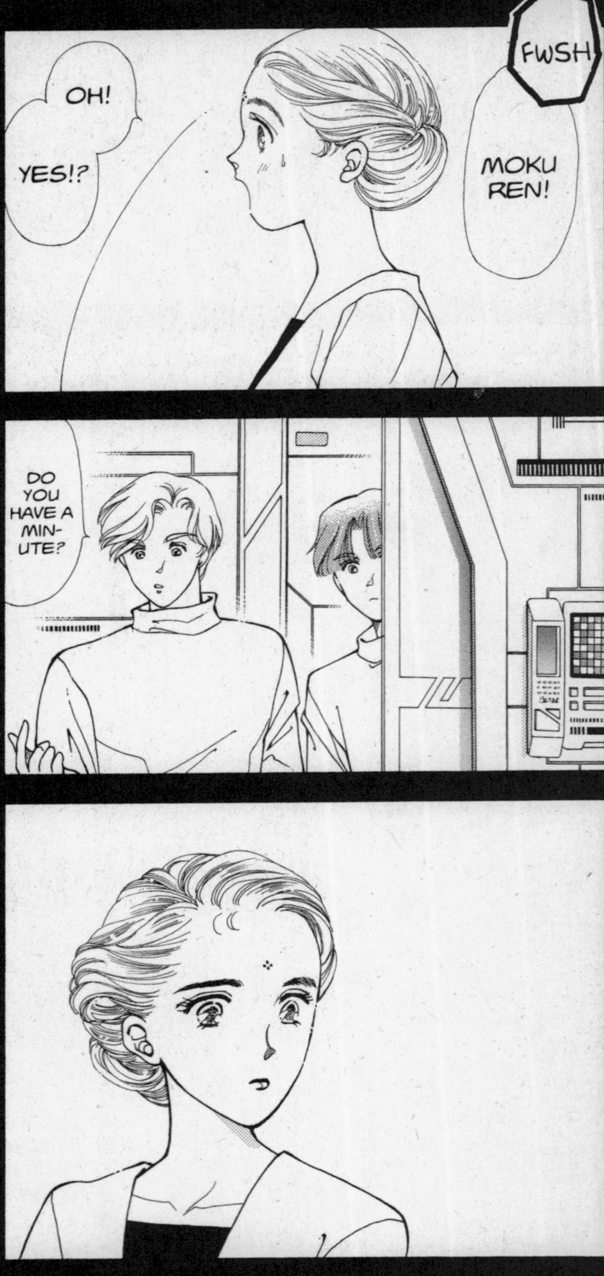
FWSH
MOKU REN!
OH!
YES!?
DO YOU HAVE A MINUTE?

1/4 COLUMN NONSENSE

—PART 10—

The boy across the street told me two of the kittens scampered into the street, and got hit by a car. He buried them in the park... The other three huddled in my entryway... But one day, the calico went missing... I wondered what had happened and was a bit worried, but a day later, I found she had returned. However, she was barely alive... She dragged one leg behind her, and her breathing was labored. She wouldn't even drink any milk I offered her, so I figured she was in big trouble, and rushed her to the vet. She was covered in fleas. The vet said she was severely anemic, and had a hernia and a broken pelvis.

continued in part 11

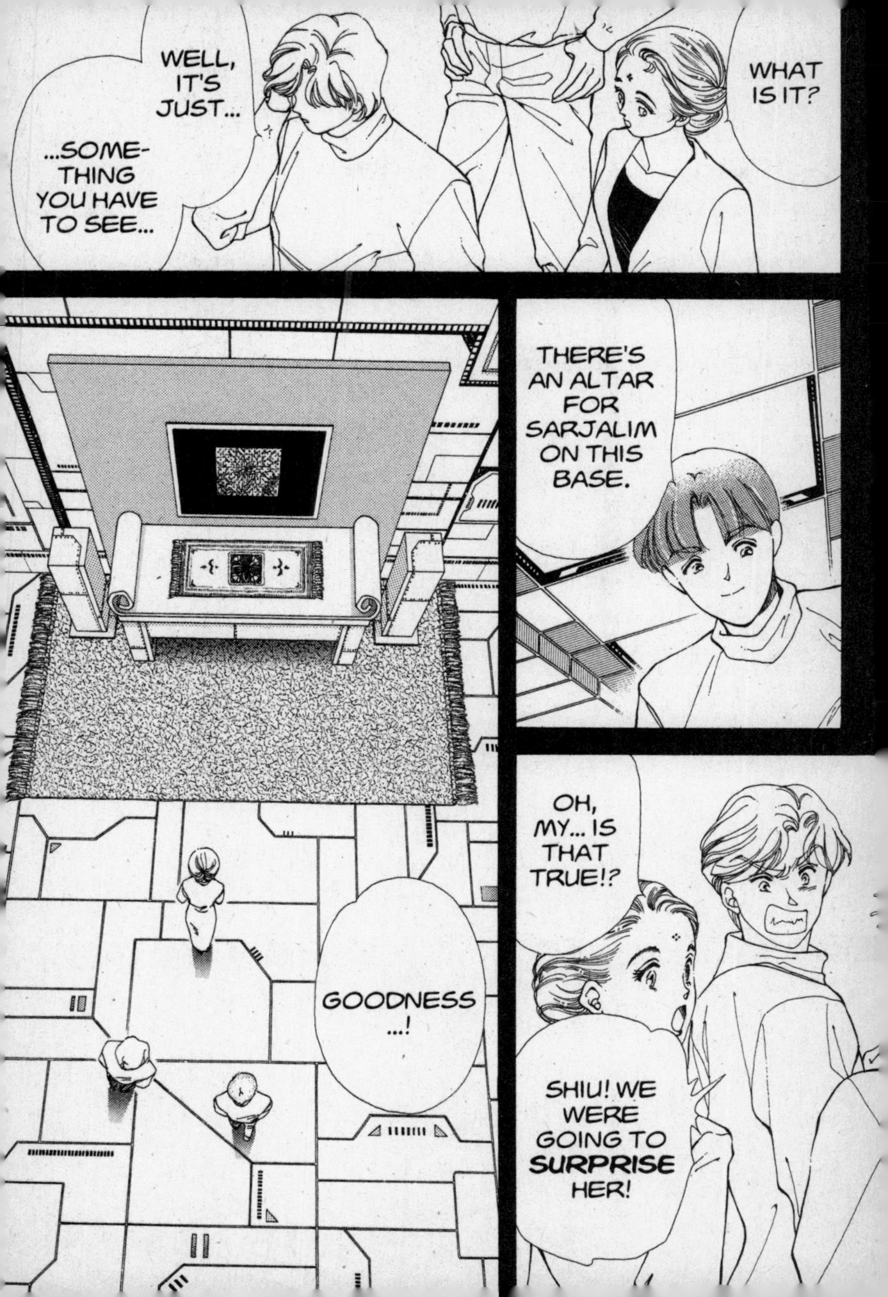
WHAT IS IT?
WELL, IT'S JUST...
...SOME-THING YOU HAVE TO SEE...
THERE'S AN ALTAR FOR SARJALIM ON THIS BASE.
OH, MY... IS THAT TRUE!?
SHIU! WE WERE GOING TO **SURPRISE** HER!
GOODNESS ...!

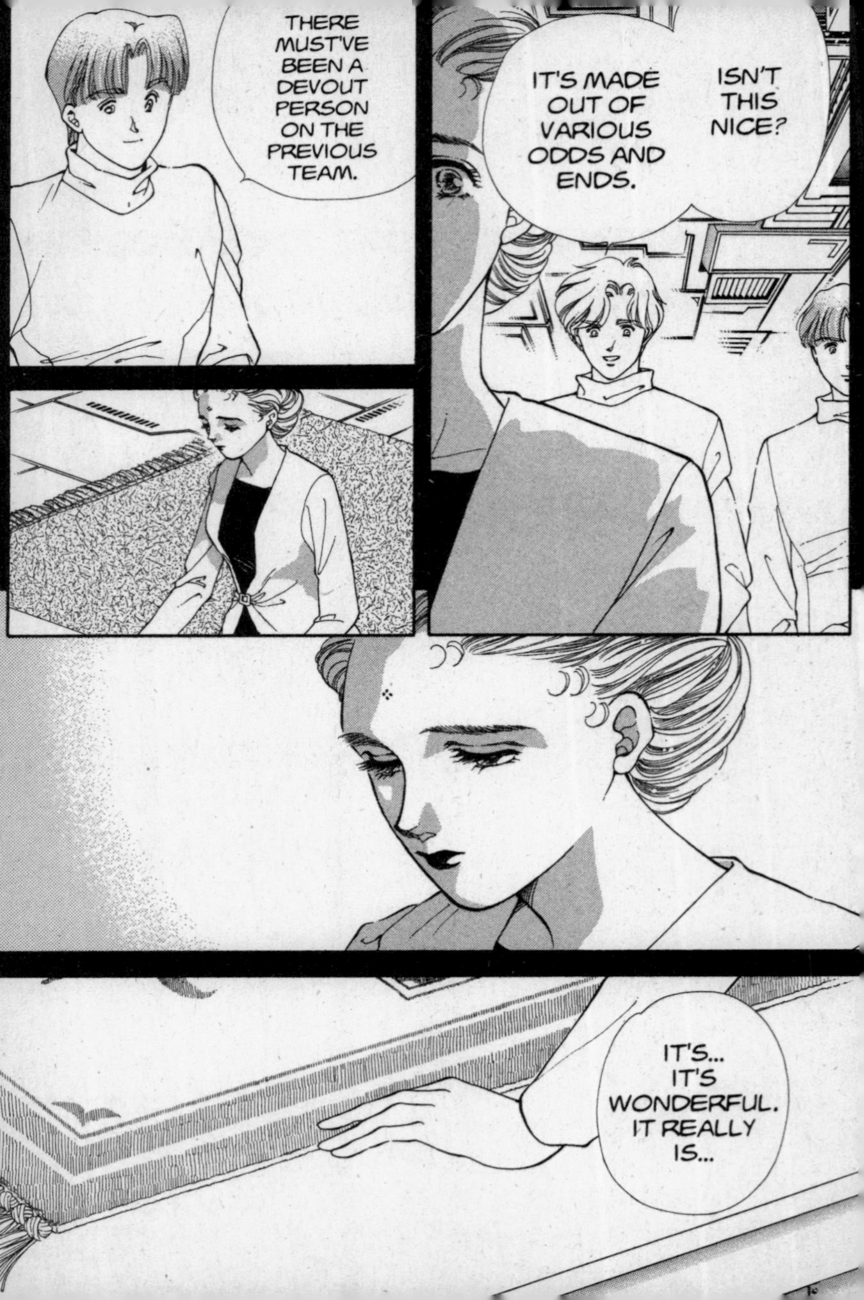
ISN'T THIS NICE?
IT'S MADE OUT OF VARIOUS ODDS AND ENDS.
THERE MUST'VE BEEN A DEVOUT PERSON ON THE PREVIOUS TEAM.
IT'S... IT'S WONDERFUL. IT REALLY IS...

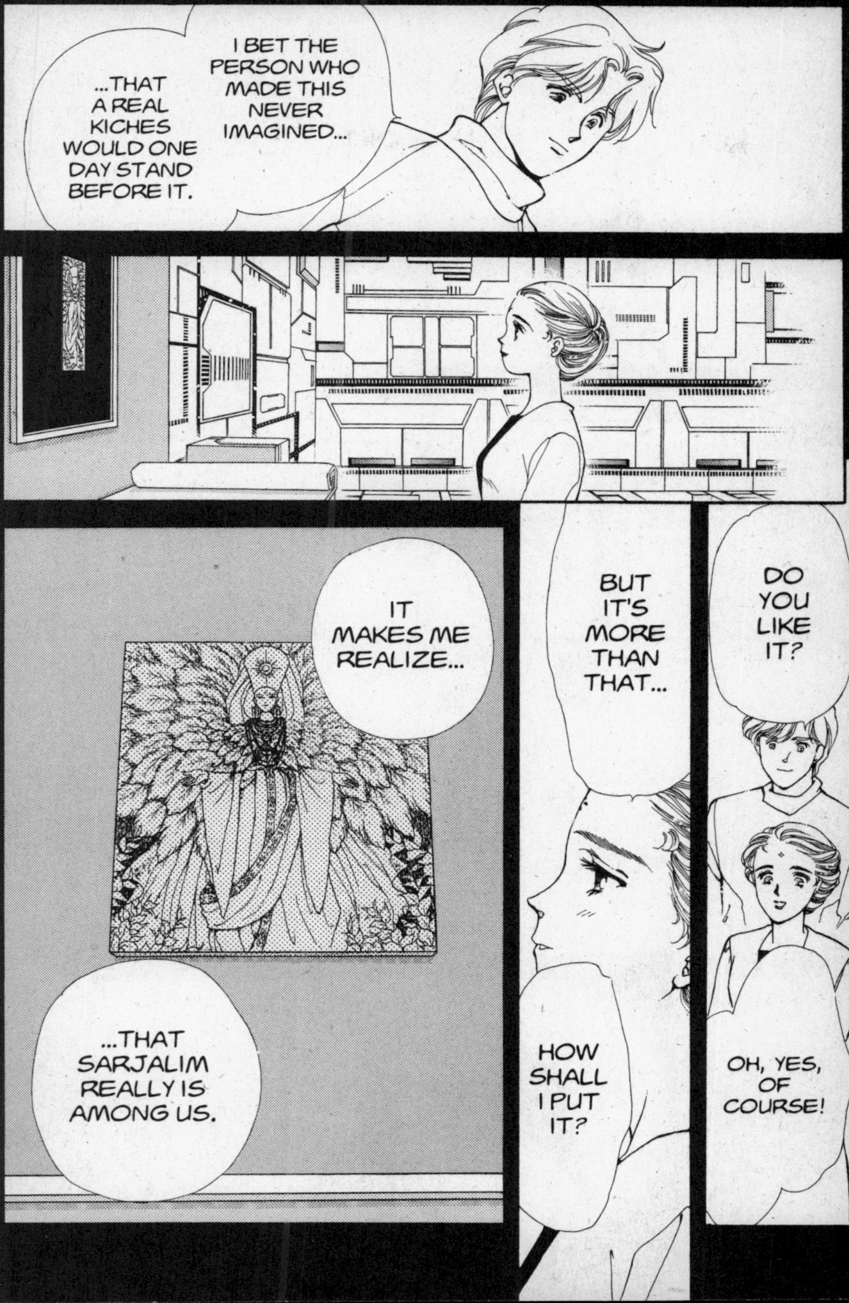
I BET THE PERSON WHO MADE THIS NEVER IMAGINED...
...THAT A REAL KICHES WOULD ONE DAY STAND BEFORE IT.
DO YOU LIKE IT?
OH, YES, OF COURSE!
BUT IT'S MORE THAN THAT...
HOW SHALL I PUT IT?
IT MAKES ME REALIZE...
...THAT SARJALIM REALLY IS AMONG US.

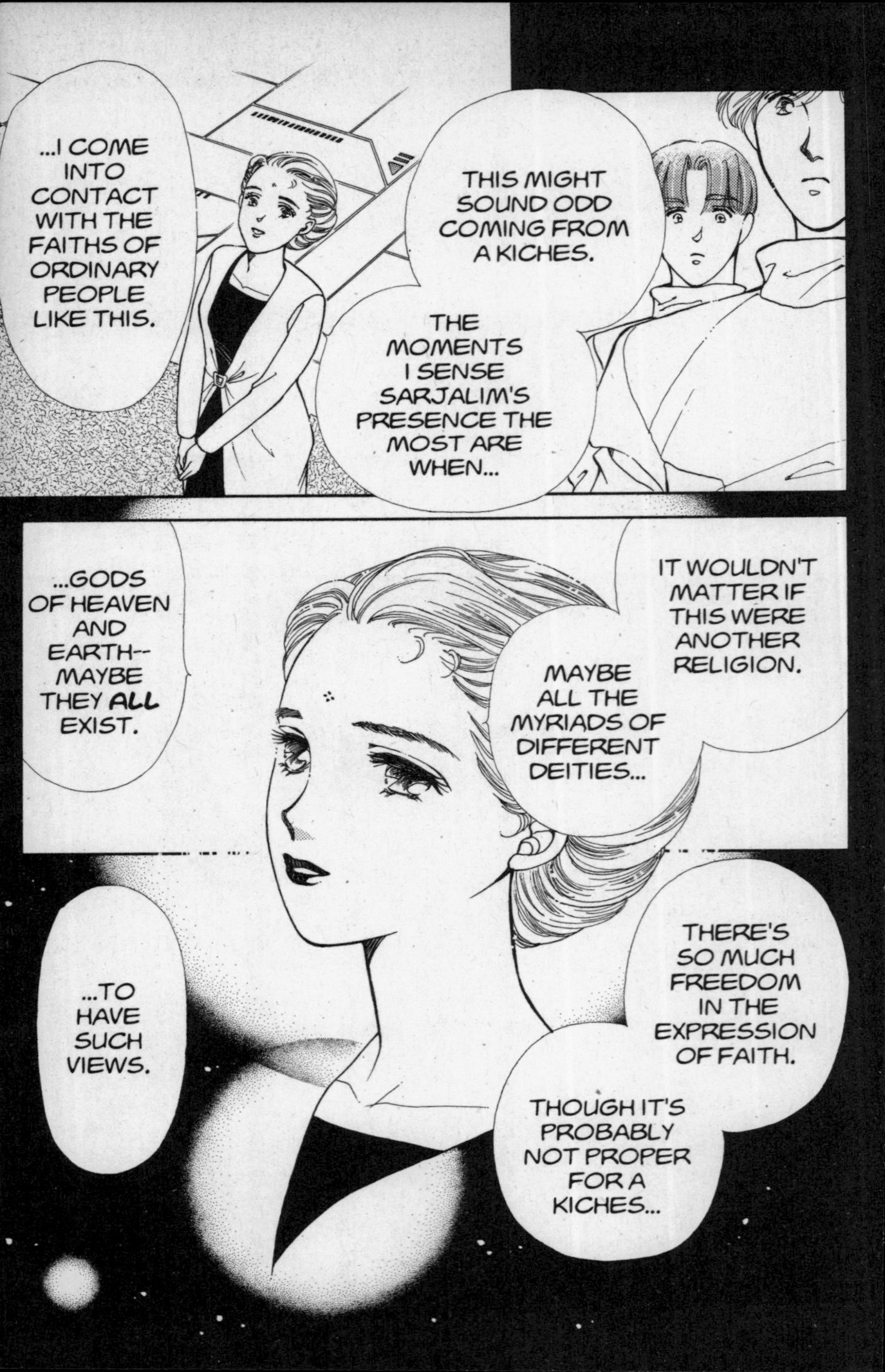
THIS MIGHT SOUND ODD COMING FROM A KICHES.
THE MOMENTS I SENSE SARJALIM'S PRESENCE THE MOST ARE WHEN...
...I COME INTO CONTACT WITH THE FAITHS OF ORDINARY PEOPLE LIKE THIS.
IT WOULDN'T MATTER IF THIS WERE ANOTHER RELIGION.
MAYBE ALL THE MYRIADS OF DIFFERENT DEITIES...
...GODS OF HEAVEN AND EARTH-- MAYBE THEY **ALL** EXIST.
THERE'S SO MUCH FREEDOM IN THE EXPRESSION OF FAITH.
THOUGH IT'S PROBABLY NOT PROPER FOR A KICHES...
...TO HAVE SUCH VIEWS.

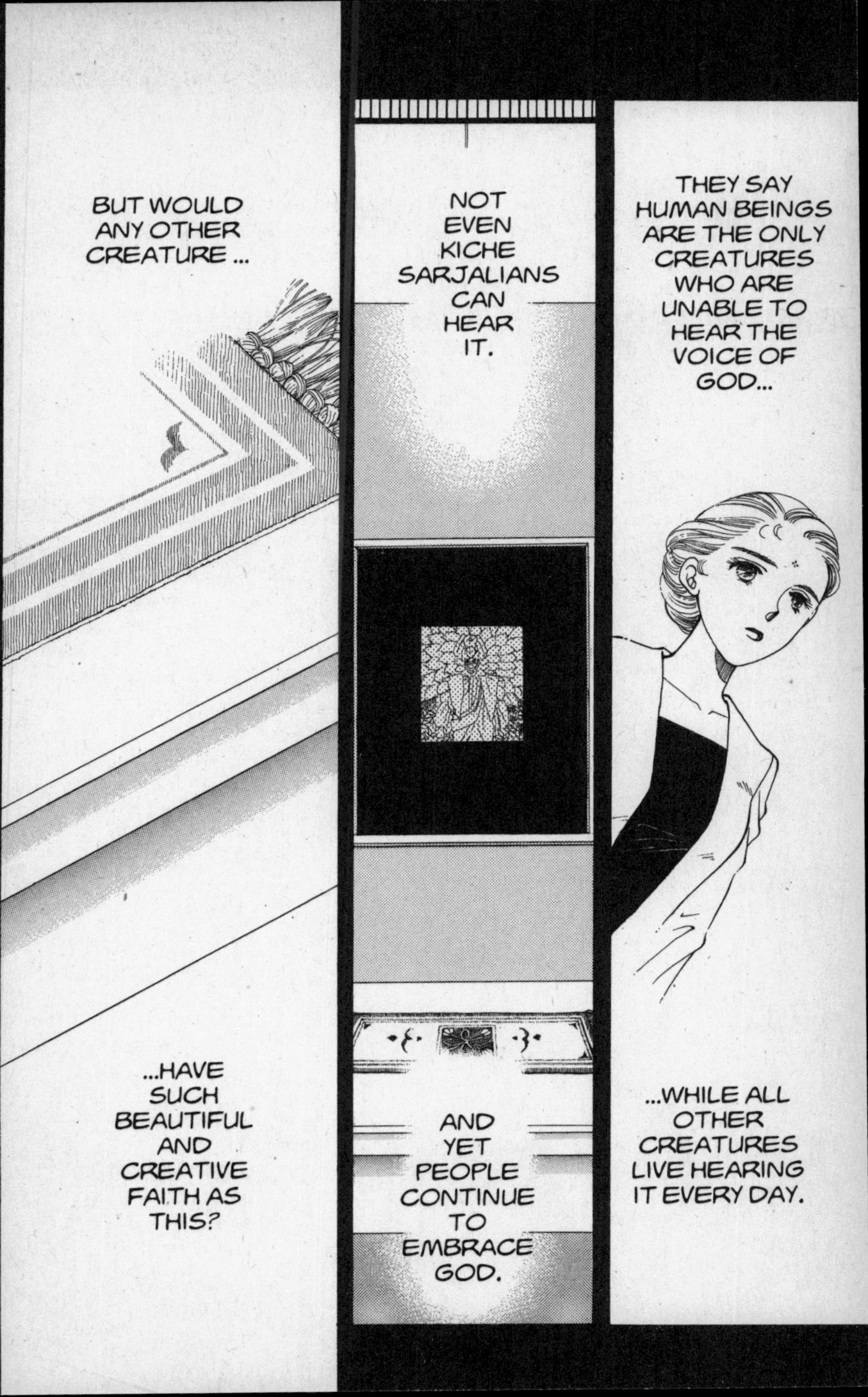
THEY SAY HUMAN BEINGS ARE THE ONLY CREATURES WHO ARE UNABLE TO HEAR THE VOICE OF GOD...
...WHILE ALL OTHER CREATURES LIVE HEARING IT EVERY DAY.
NOT EVEN KICHE SARJALIANS CAN HEAR IT.
AND YET PEOPLE CONTINUE TO EMBRACE GOD.
BUT WOULD ANY OTHER CREATURE ...
...HAVE SUCH BEAUTIFUL AND CREATIVE FAITH AS THIS?

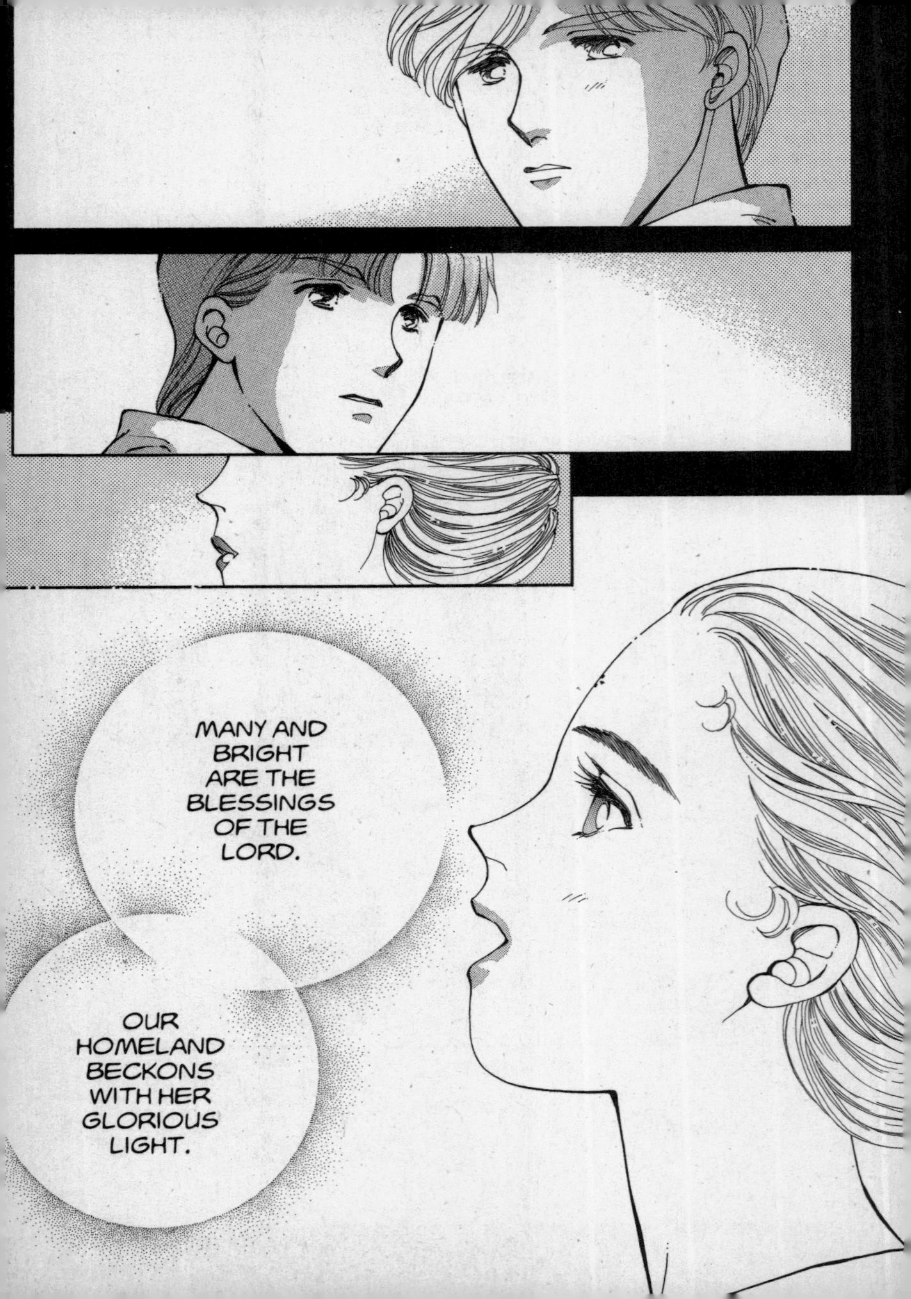
MANY AND BRIGHT ARE THE BLESSINGS OF THE LORD.
OUR HOMELAND BECKONS WITH HER GLORIOUS LIGHT.

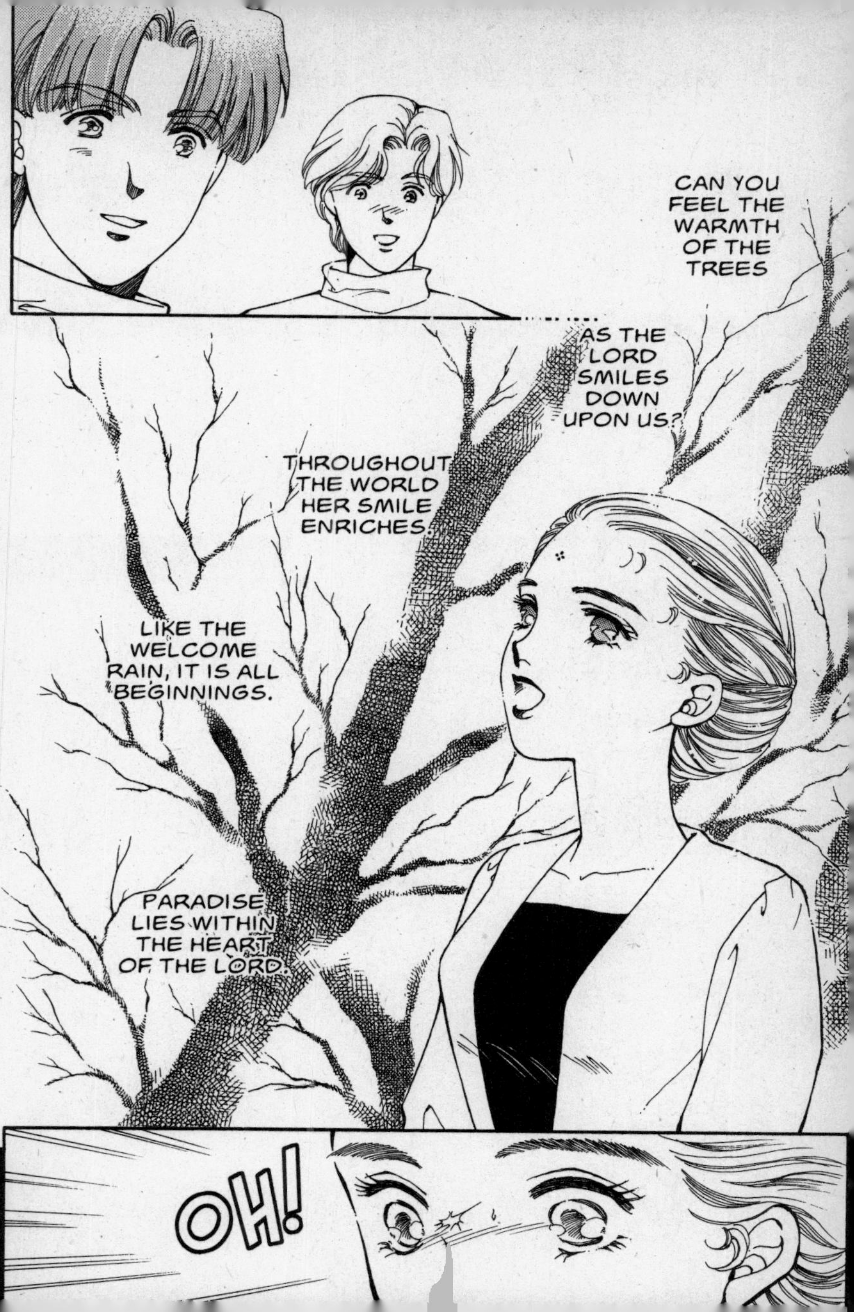
CAN YOU FEEL THE WARMTH OF THE TREES
AS THE LORD SMILES DOWN UPON US?
THROUGHOUT THE WORLD HER SMILE ENRICHES.
LIKE THE WELCOME RAIN, IT IS ALL BEGINNINGS.
PARADISE LIES WITHIN THE HEART OF THE LORD.
OH!

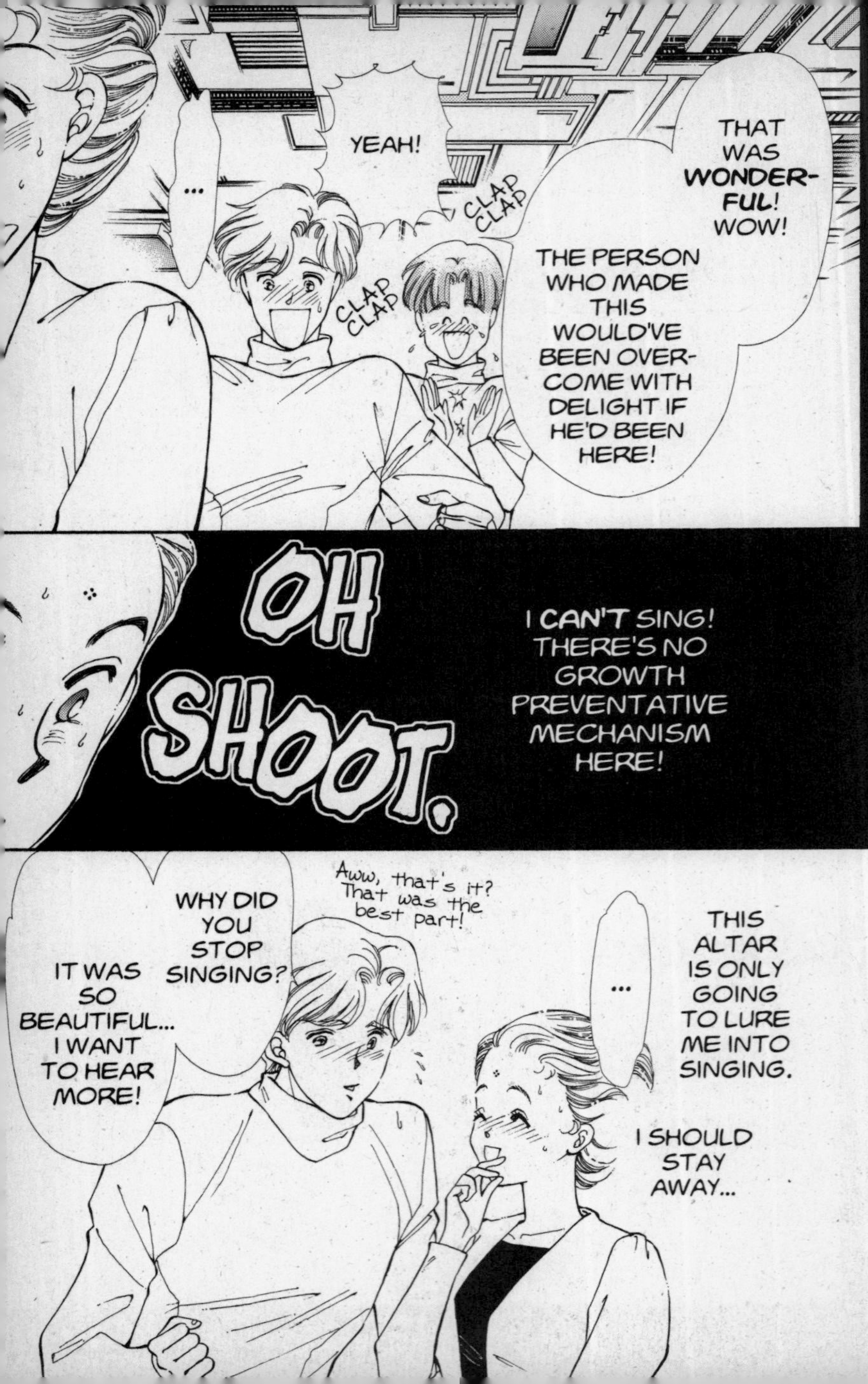
THAT WAS WONDERFUL! WOW!
THE PERSON WHO MADE THIS WOULD'VE BEEN OVERCOME WITH DELIGHT IF HE'D BEEN HERE!
CLAP CLAP
YEAH!
CLAP CLAP
...
I CAN'T SING! THERE'S NO GROWTH PREVENTATIVE MECHANISM HERE!
OH SHOOT.
THIS ALTAR IS ONLY GOING TO LURE ME INTO SINGING.
...
I SHOULD STAY AWAY...
Aww, that's it? That was the best part!
WHY DID YOU STOP SINGING?
IT WAS SO BEAUTIFUL... I WANT TO HEAR MORE!

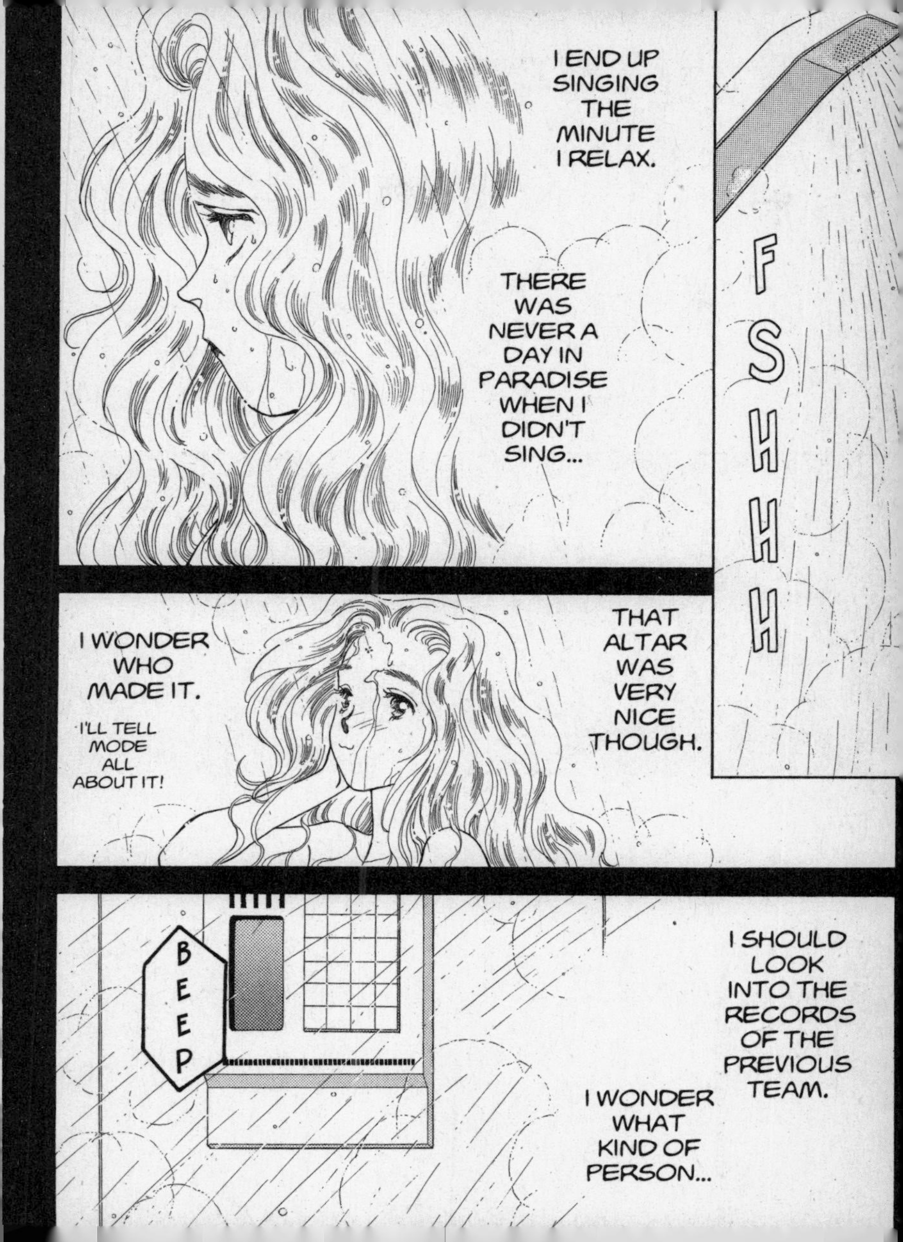
FSHHH
I END UP SINGING THE MINUTE I RELAX.
THERE WAS NEVER A DAY IN PARADISE WHEN I DIDN'T SING...
THAT ALTAR WAS VERY NICE THOUGH.
I WONDER WHO MADE IT.
I'LL TELL MODE ALL ABOUT IT!
I SHOULD LOOK INTO THE RECORDS OF THE PREVIOUS TEAM.
I WONDER WHAT KIND OF PERSON...
BEEP

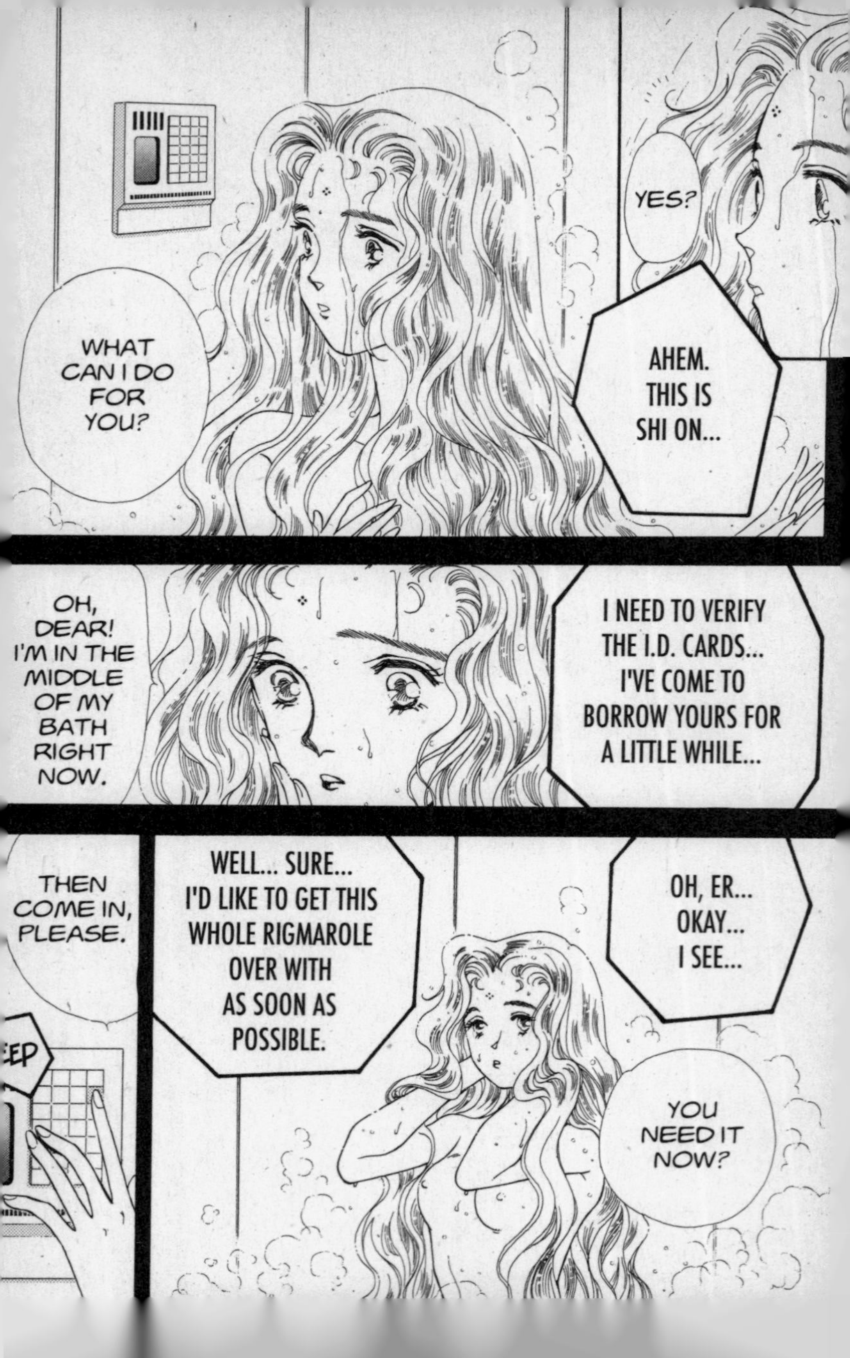
YES?
AHEM. THIS IS SHI ON...
WHAT CAN I DO FOR YOU?
I NEED TO VERIFY THE I.D. CARDS... I'VE COME TO BORROW YOURS FOR A LITTLE WHILE...
OH, DEAR! I'M IN THE MIDDLE OF MY BATH RIGHT NOW.
OH, ER... OKAY... I SEE...
YOU NEED IT NOW?
WELL... SURE... I'D LIKE TO GET THIS WHOLE RIGMAROLE OVER WITH AS SOON AS POSSIBLE.
THEN COME IN, PLEASE.

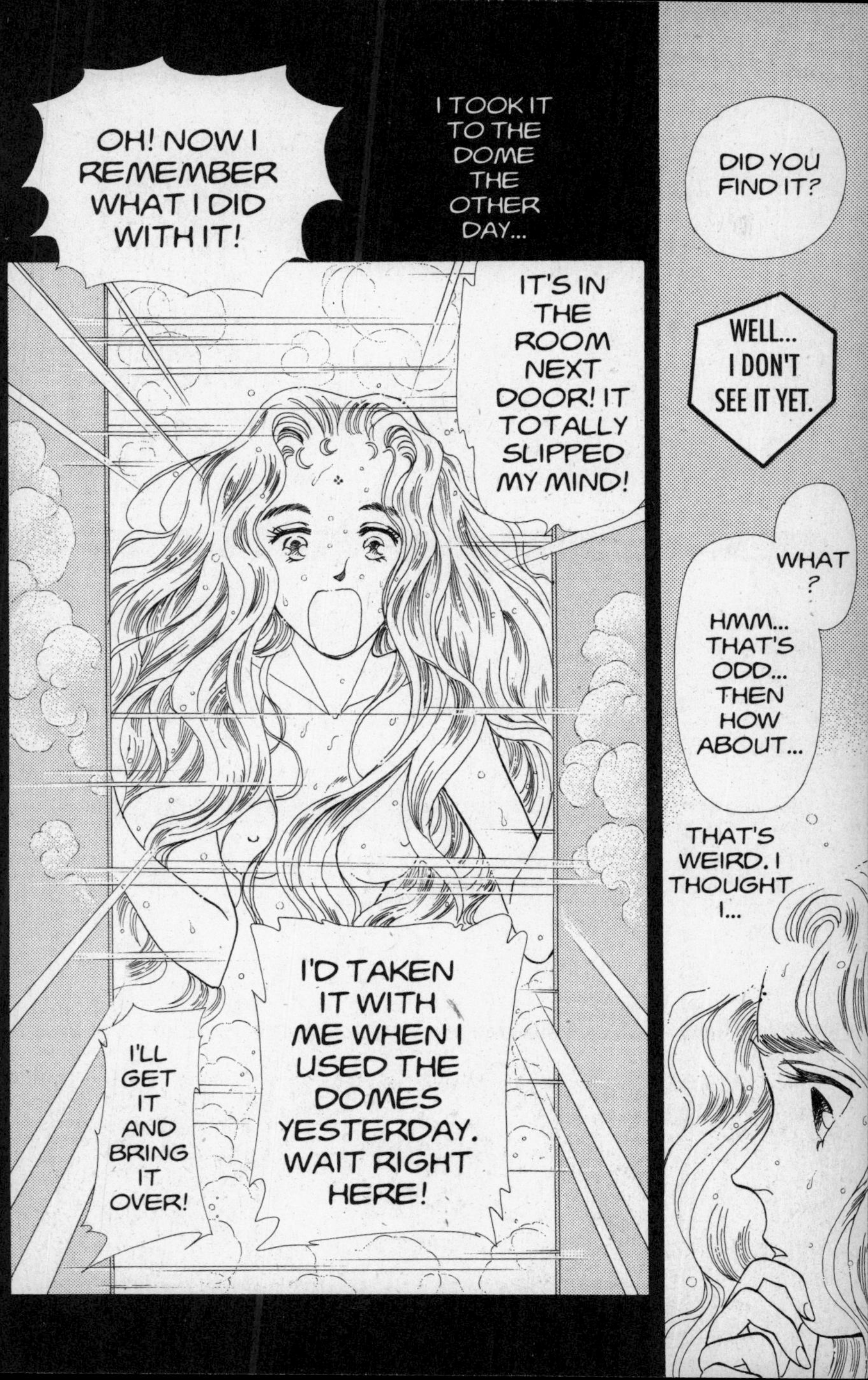
DID YOU FIND IT?
WELL... I DON'T SEE IT YET.
WHAT ?
HMM... THAT'S ODD... THEN HOW ABOUT...
THAT'S WEIRD. I THOUGHT I...
I TOOK IT TO THE DOME THE OTHER DAY...
OH! NOW I REMEMBER WHAT I DID WITH IT!
IT'S IN THE ROOM NEXT DOOR! IT TOTALLY SLIPPED MY MIND!
I'D TAKEN IT WITH ME WHEN I USED THE DOMES YESTERDAY. WAIT RIGHT HERE!
I'LL GET IT AND BRING IT OVER!

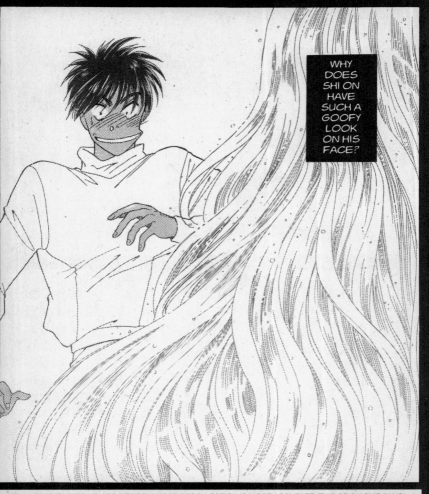

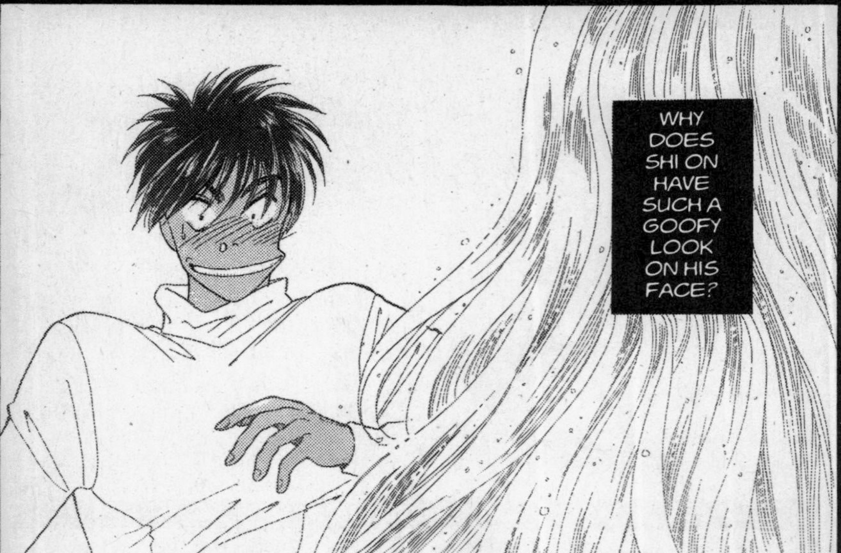
WHY DOES SHI ON HAVE SUCH A GOOFY LOOK ON HIS FACE?

*WE'LL LEAVE IT UP TO YOU TO DECIDE WHOSE RECOLLECTION IS MORE ACCURATE, THIS OR SHION'S IN VOL. 9.

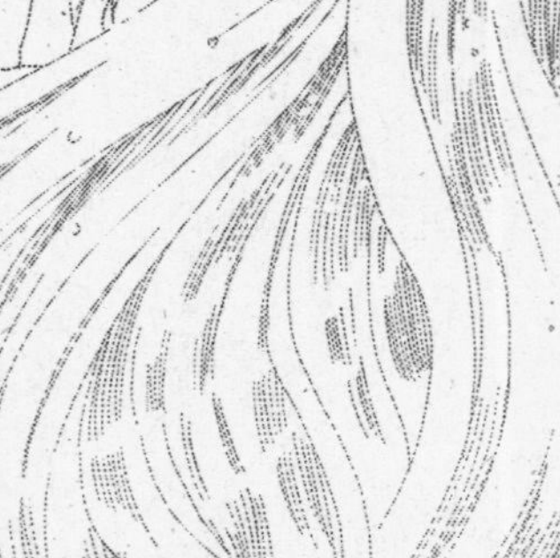
REN, HOW ARE YOU DOING?

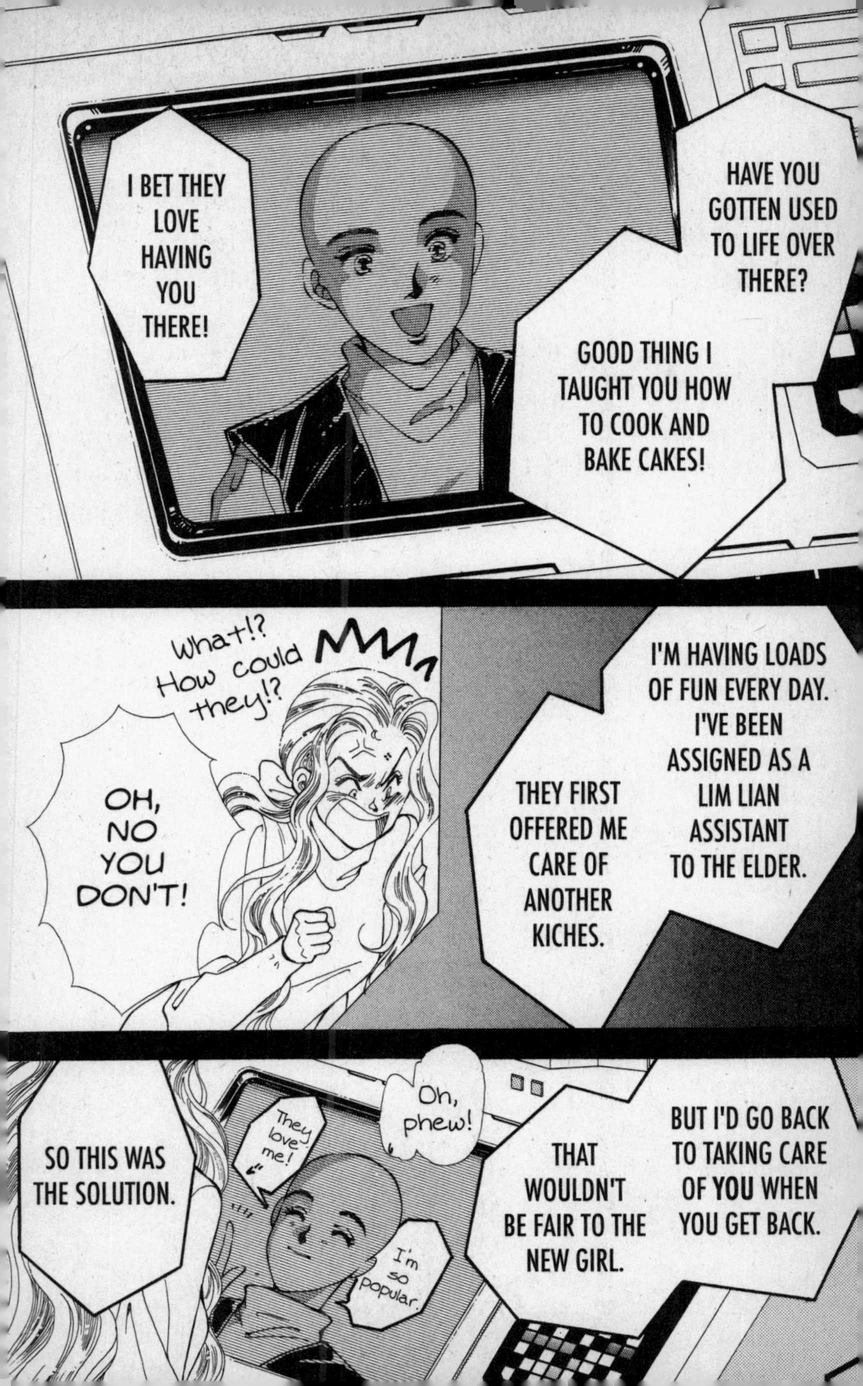
HAVE YOU GOTTEN USED TO LIFE OVER THERE?
GOOD THING I TAUGHT YOU HOW TO COOK AND BAKE CAKES!
I BET THEY LOVE HAVING YOU THERE!
I'M HAVING LOADS OF FUN EVERY DAY. I'VE BEEN ASSIGNED AS A LIM LIAN ASSISTANT TO THE ELDER.
THEY FIRST OFFERED ME CARE OF ANOTHER KICHES.
What!? How could they!?
OH, NO YOU DON'T!
BUT I'D GO BACK TO TAKING CARE OF YOU WHEN YOU GET BACK.
THAT WOULDN'T BE FAIR TO THE NEW GIRL.
Oh, phew!
They love me!
I'm so popular.
SO THIS WAS THE SOLUTION.

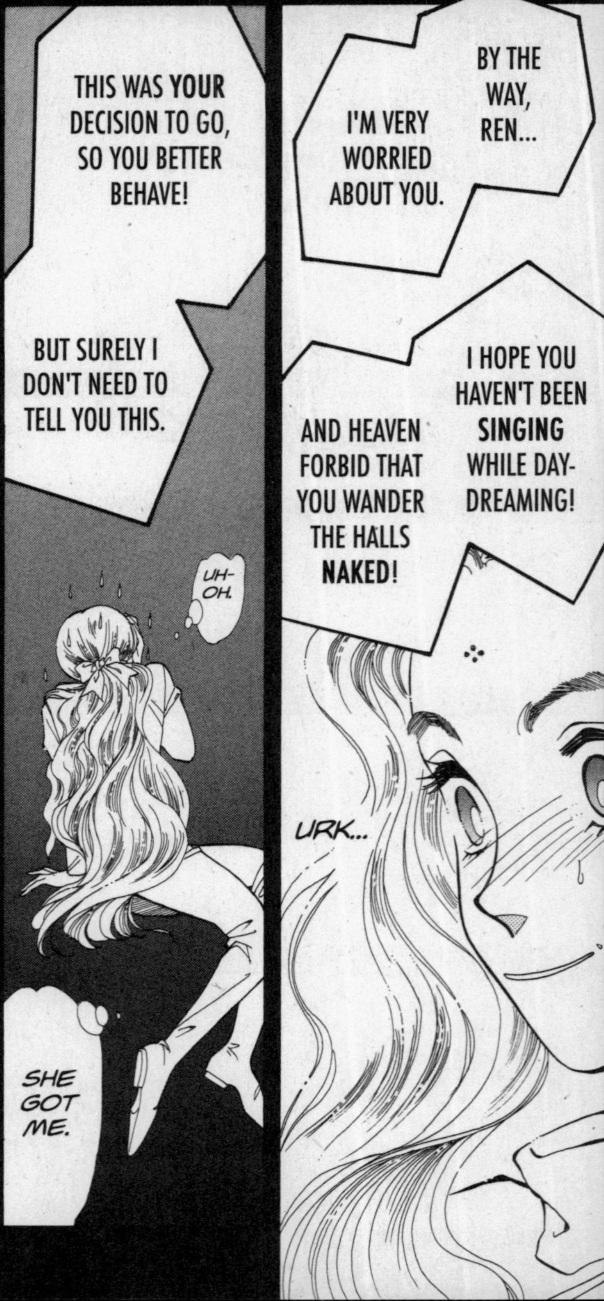
BY THE WAY, REN...
I'M VERY WORRIED ABOUT YOU.
I HOPE YOU HAVEN'T BEEN SINGING WHILE DAY-DREAMING!
AND HEAVEN FORBID THAT YOU WANDER THE HALLS NAKED!
URK...
THIS WAS YOUR DECISION TO GO, SO YOU BETTER BEHAVE!
BUT SURELY I DON'T NEED TO TELL YOU THIS.
UH-OH.
SHE GOT ME.

1/4 COLUMN NONSENSE

PART 11

I had the vet operate on her, and he told me afterwards that it looked like somebody had kicked her in the stomach. When he opened her up, the peritoneum was ripped, and her internal organs were a mess. The muscle on her right leg was torn, so he had been forced to pull over a muscle from someplace else and attach it instead... As a result, after the surgery, her back looked very stiff and unnatural.

She had dragged herself back home through such horrible pain. I felt sick to my stomach.

continued in part 12

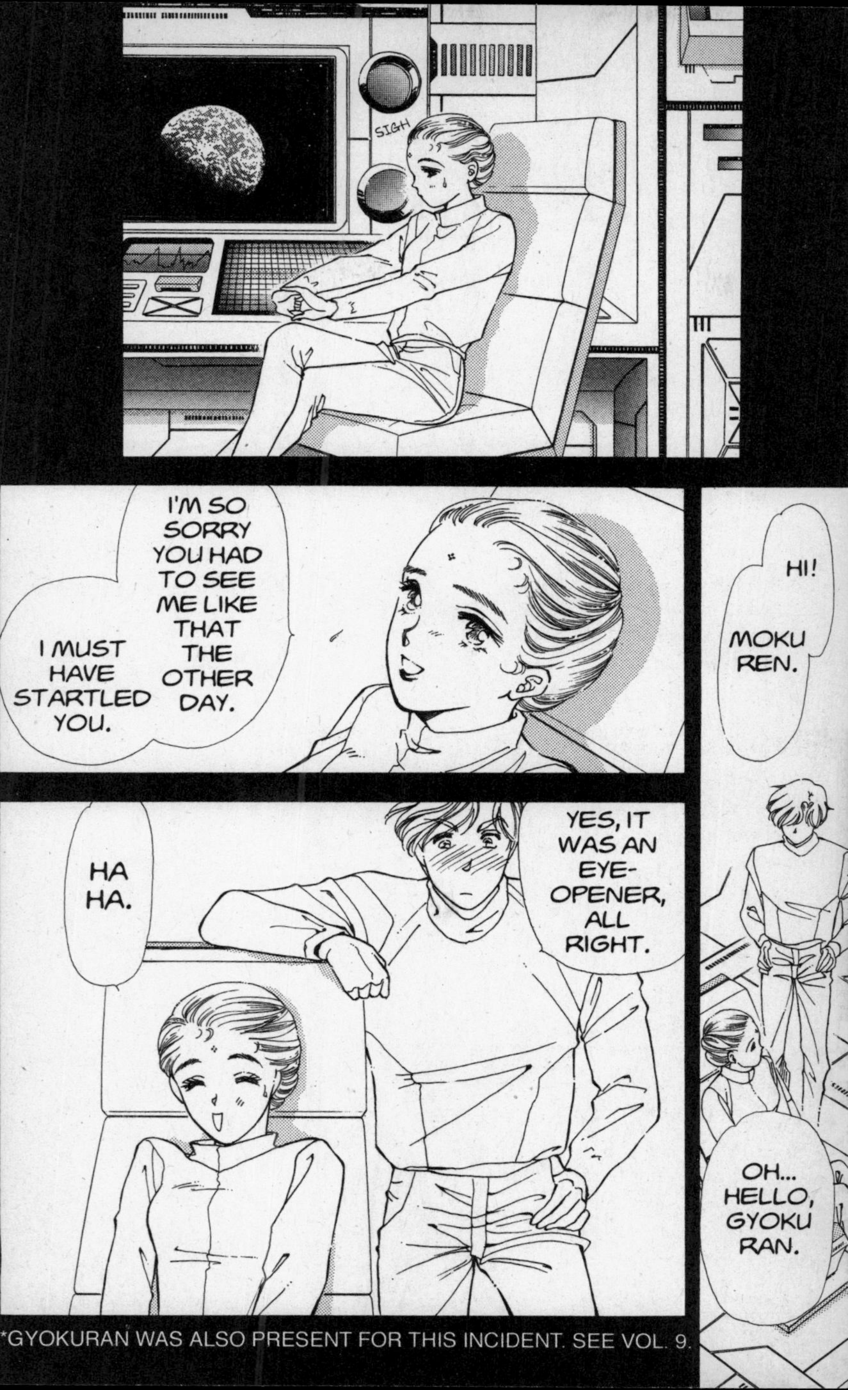
SIGH
HI!
MOKU REN.
OH... HELLO, GYOKU RAN.
I'M SO SORRY YOU HAD TO SEE ME LIKE THAT THE OTHER DAY.
I MUST HAVE STARTLED YOU.
YES, IT WAS AN EYE-OPENER, ALL RIGHT.
HA HA.

*GYOKURAN WAS ALSO PRESENT FOR THIS INCIDENT. SEE VOL. 9.

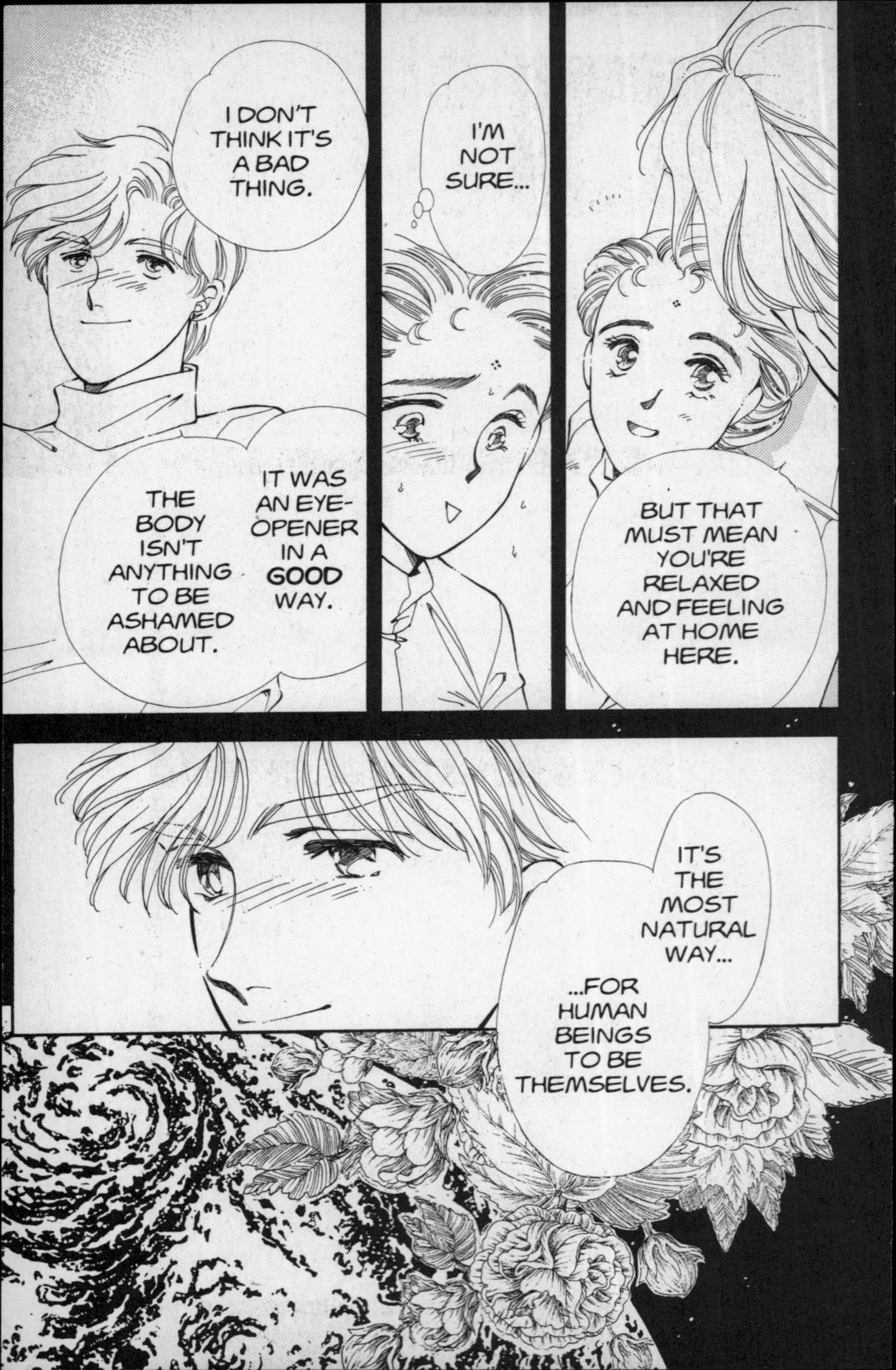
BUT THAT MUST MEAN YOU'RE RELAXED AND FEELING AT HOME HERE.
I'M NOT SURE...
I DON'T THINK IT'S A BAD THING.
IT WAS AN EYE-OPENER IN A GOOD WAY.
THE BODY ISN'T ANYTHING TO BE ASHAMED ABOUT.
IT'S THE MOST NATURAL WAY...
...FOR HUMAN BEINGS TO BE THEMSELVES.

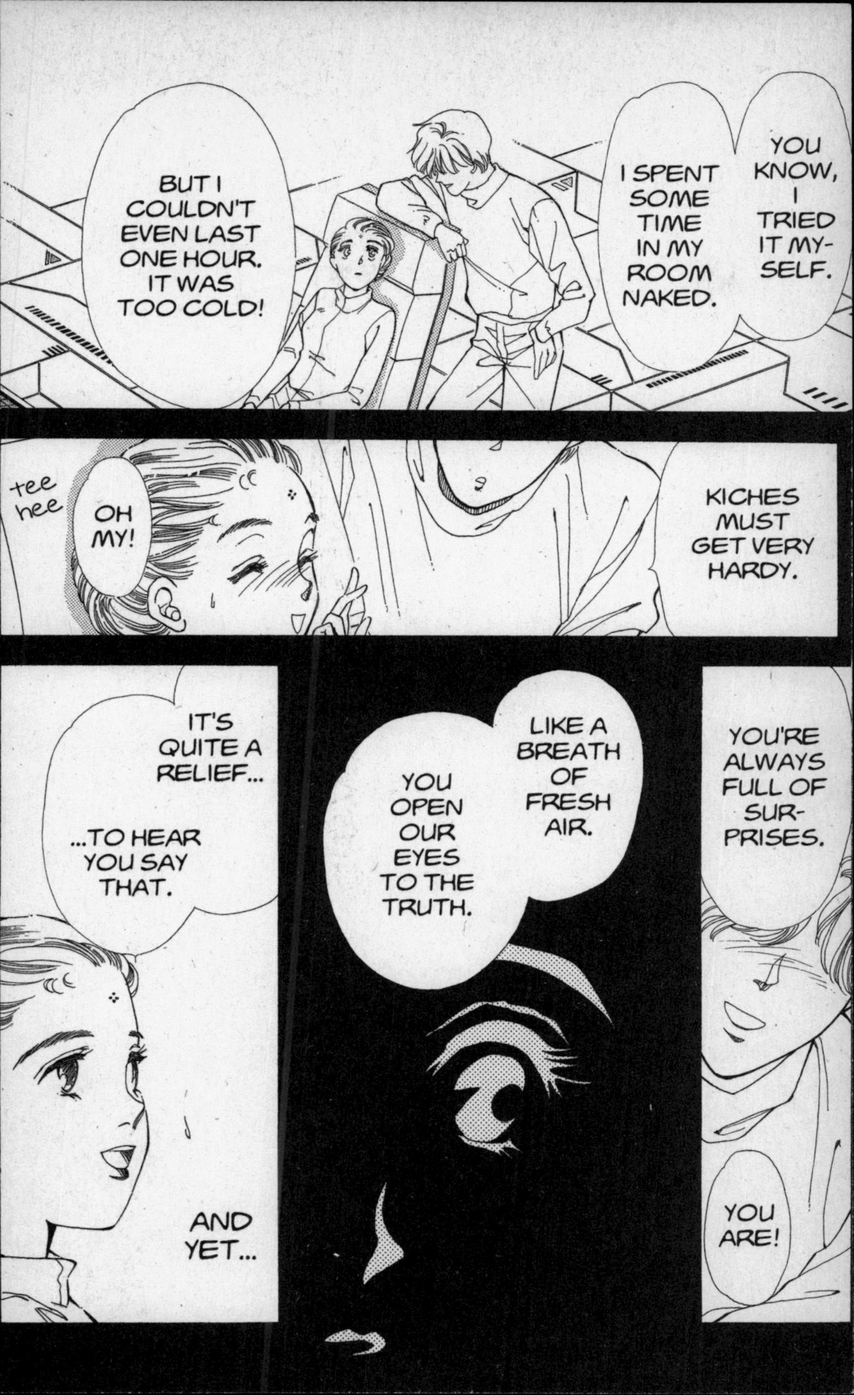
YOU KNOW, I TRIED IT MY-SELF.
I SPENT SOME TIME IN MY ROOM NAKED.
BUT I COULDN'T EVEN LAST ONE HOUR. IT WAS TOO COLD!
KICHES MUST GET VERY HARDY.
OH MY!
tee hee
YOU'RE ALWAYS FULL OF SUR-PRISES.
YOU ARE!
LIKE A BREATH OF FRESH AIR.
YOU OPEN OUR EYES TO THE TRUTH.
IT'S QUITE A RELIEF...
...TO HEAR YOU SAY THAT.
AND YET...

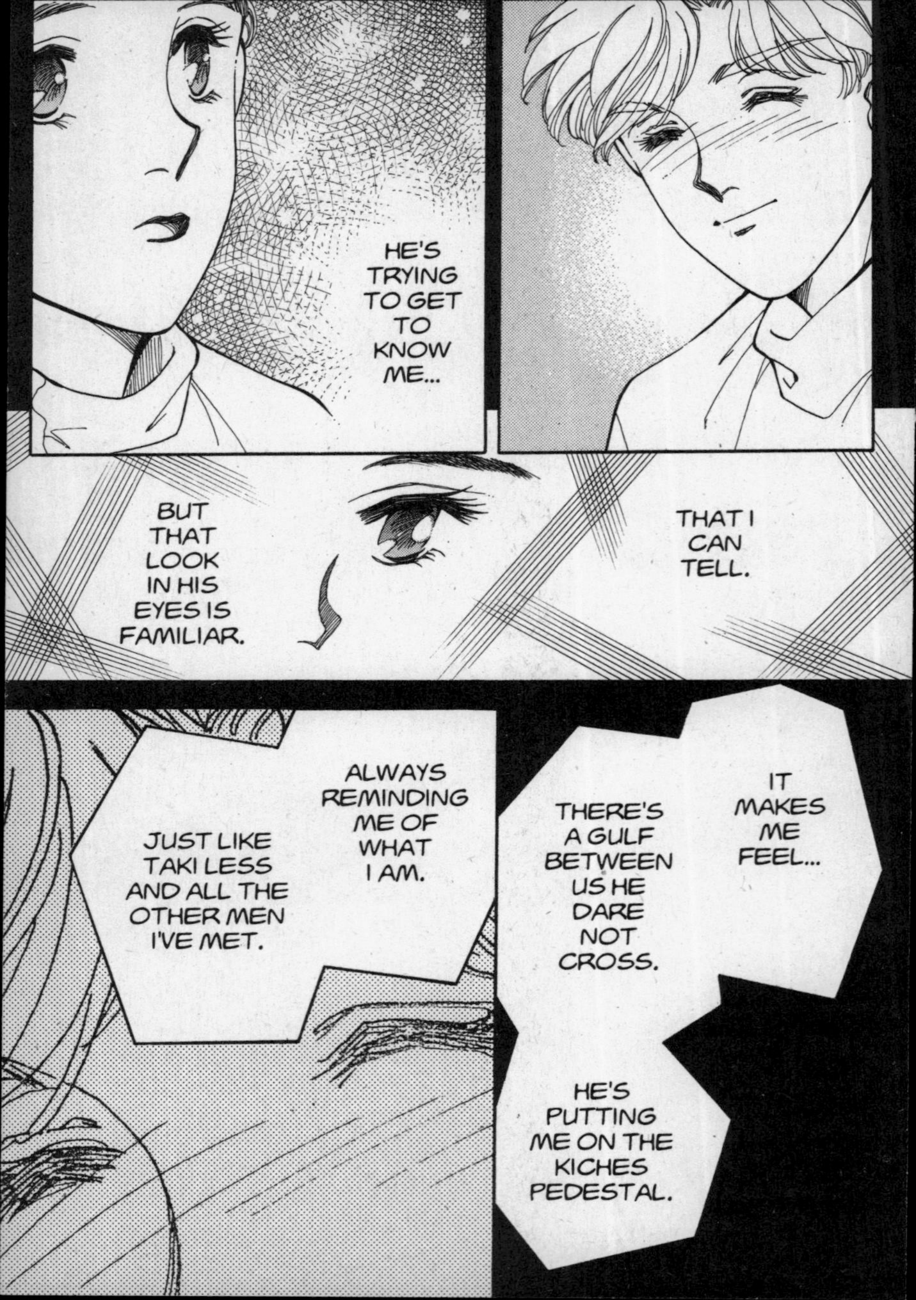
HE'S TRYING TO GET TO KNOW ME...
THAT I CAN TELL.
BUT THAT LOOK IN HIS EYES IS FAMILIAR.
IT MAKES ME FEEL...
THERE'S A GULF BETWEEN US HE DARE NOT CROSS.
HE'S PUTTING ME ON THE KICHES PEDESTAL.
ALWAYS REMINDING ME OF WHAT I AM.
JUST LIKE TAKI LESS AND ALL THE OTHER MEN I'VE MET.

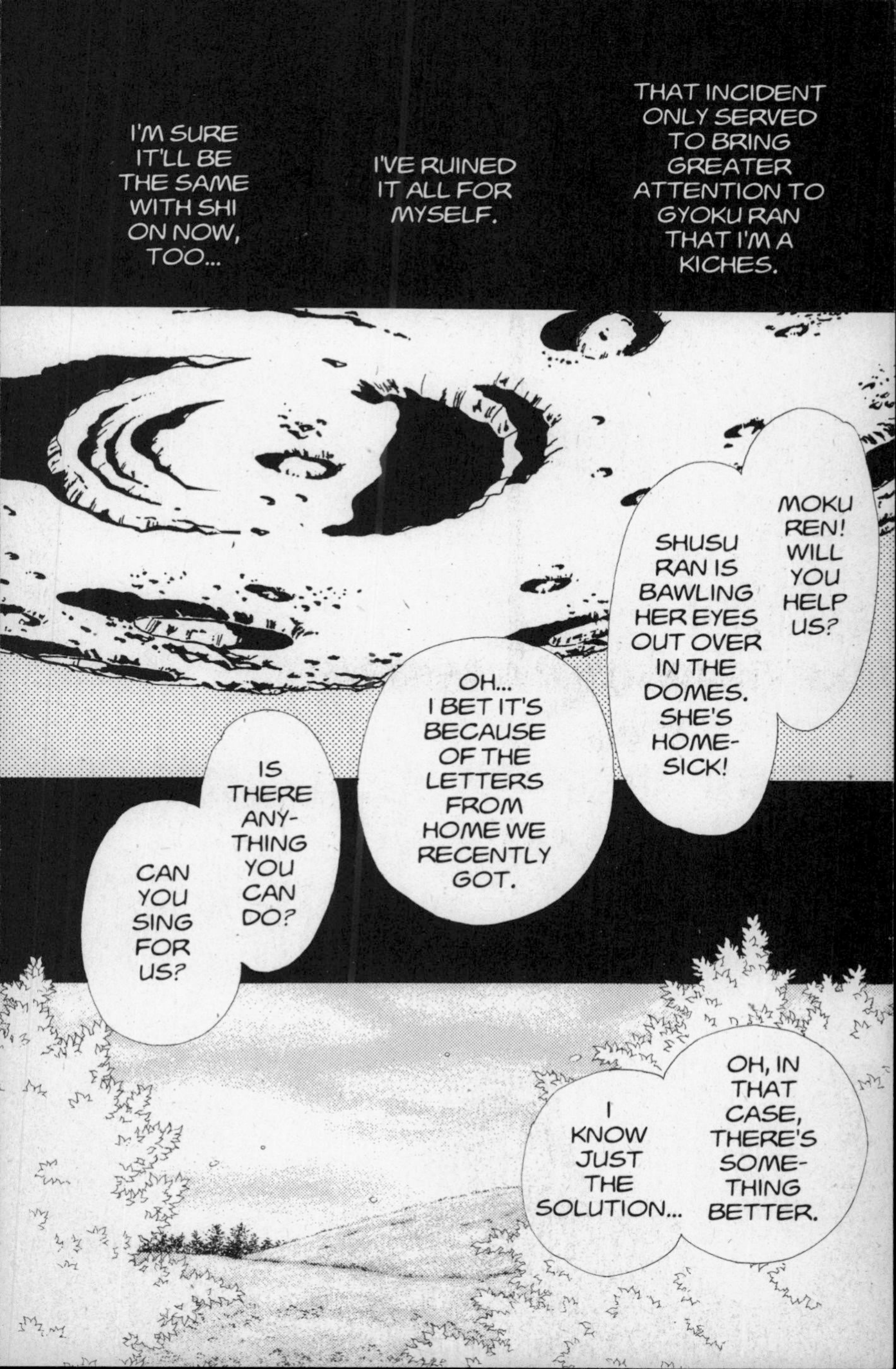
THAT INCIDENT ONLY SERVED TO BRING GREATER ATTENTION TO GYOKU RAN THAT I'M A KICHES.
I'VE RUINED IT ALL FOR MYSELF.
I'M SURE IT'LL BE THE SAME WITH SHI ON NOW, TOO...
MOKU REN! WILL YOU HELP US?
SHUSU RAN IS BAWLING HER EYES OUT OVER IN THE DOMES. SHE'S HOME-SICK!
OH... I BET IT'S BECAUSE OF THE LETTERS FROM HOME WE RECENTLY GOT.
IS THERE ANY-THING YOU CAN DO?
CAN YOU SING FOR US?
OH, IN THAT CASE, THERE'S SOME-THING BETTER.
I KNOW JUST THE SOLUTION...

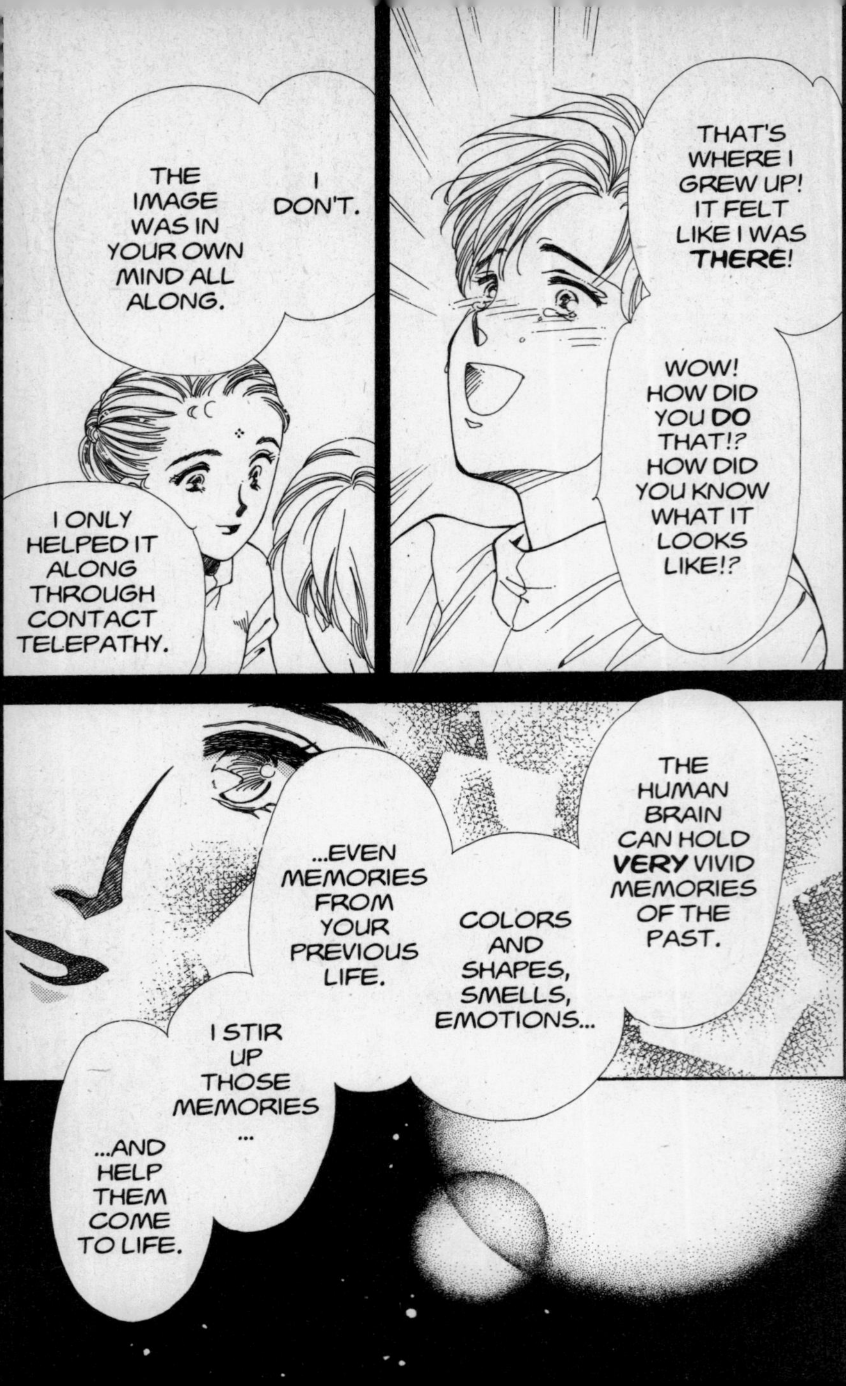
THAT'S WHERE I GREW UP! IT FELT LIKE I WAS **THERE**!
WOW! HOW DID YOU **DO** THAT!? HOW DID YOU KNOW WHAT IT LOOKS LIKE!?
I DON'T.
THE IMAGE WAS IN YOUR OWN MIND ALL ALONG.
I ONLY HELPED IT ALONG THROUGH CONTACT TELEPATHY.
THE HUMAN BRAIN CAN HOLD **VERY** VIVID MEMORIES OF THE PAST.
COLORS AND SHAPES, SMELLS, EMOTIONS...
...EVEN MEMORIES FROM YOUR PREVIOUS LIFE.
I STIR UP THOSE MEMORIES ...
...AND HELP THEM COME TO LIFE.

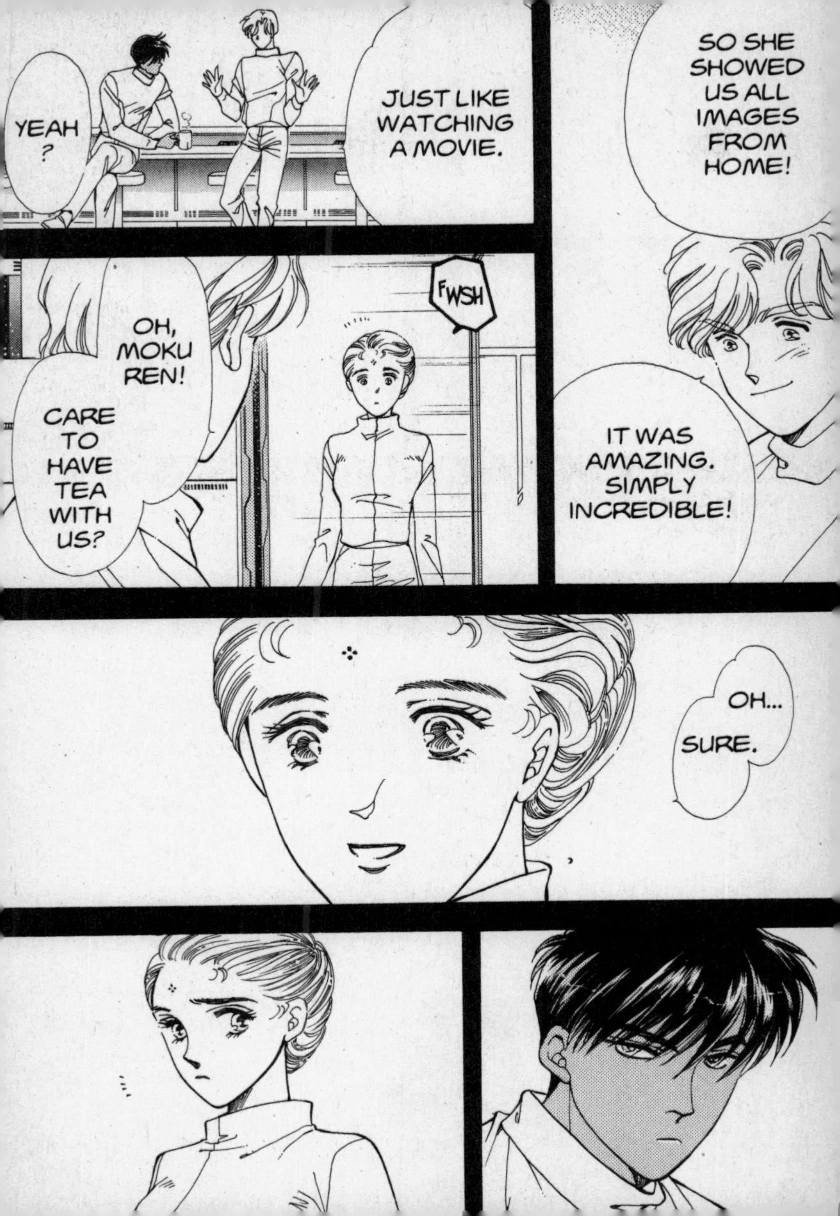
SO SHE SHOWED US ALL IMAGES FROM HOME!
IT WAS AMAZING. SIMPLY INCREDIBLE!
JUST LIKE WATCHING A MOVIE.
YEAH?
FWSH
OH, MOKU REN!
CARE TO HAVE TEA WITH US?
OH... SURE.

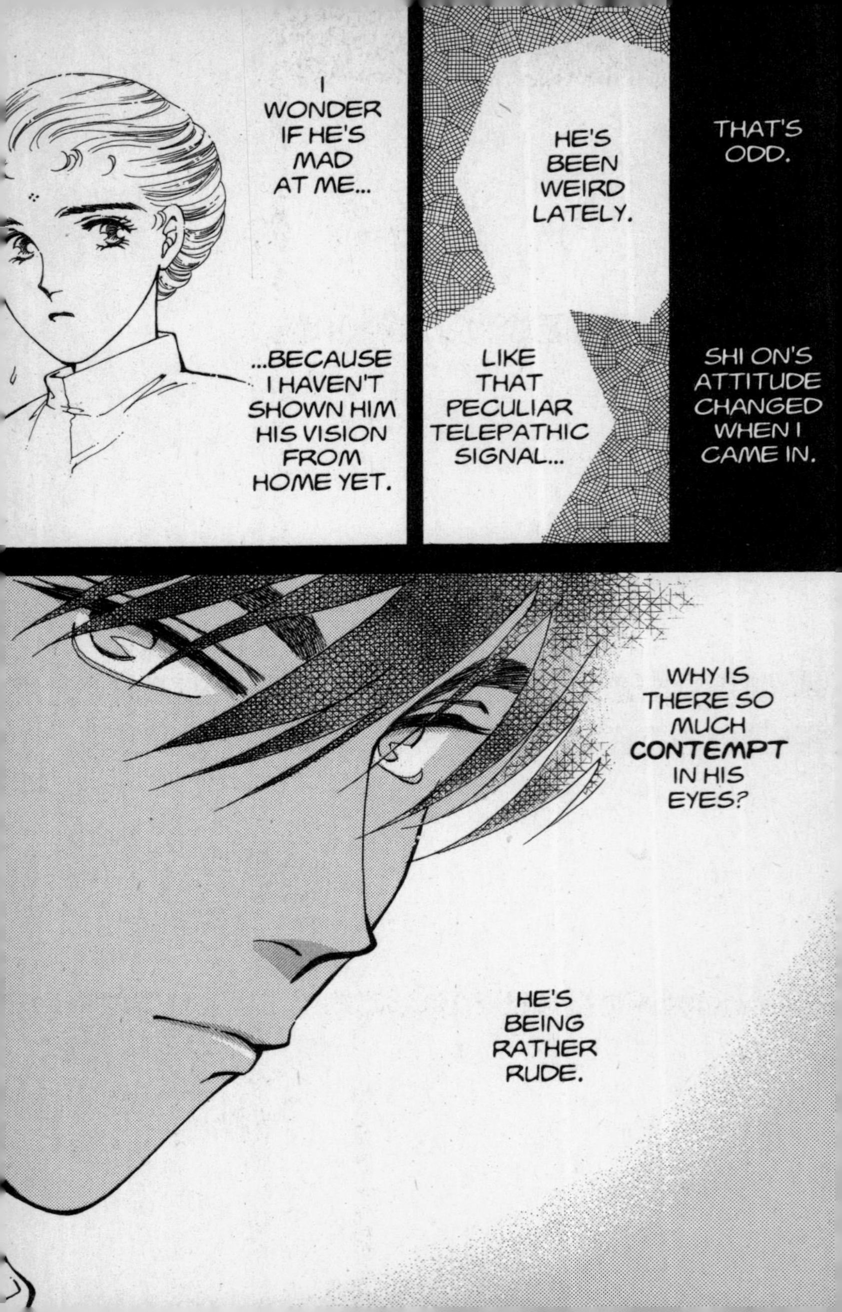
THAT'S ODD.
SHI ON'S ATTITUDE CHANGED WHEN I CAME IN.
HE'S BEEN WEIRD LATELY.
LIKE THAT PECULIAR TELEPATHIC SIGNAL...
I WONDER IF HE'S MAD AT ME...
...BECAUSE I HAVEN'T SHOWN HIM HIS VISION FROM HOME YET.
WHY IS THERE SO MUCH CONTEMPT IN HIS EYES?
HE'S BEING RATHER RUDE.

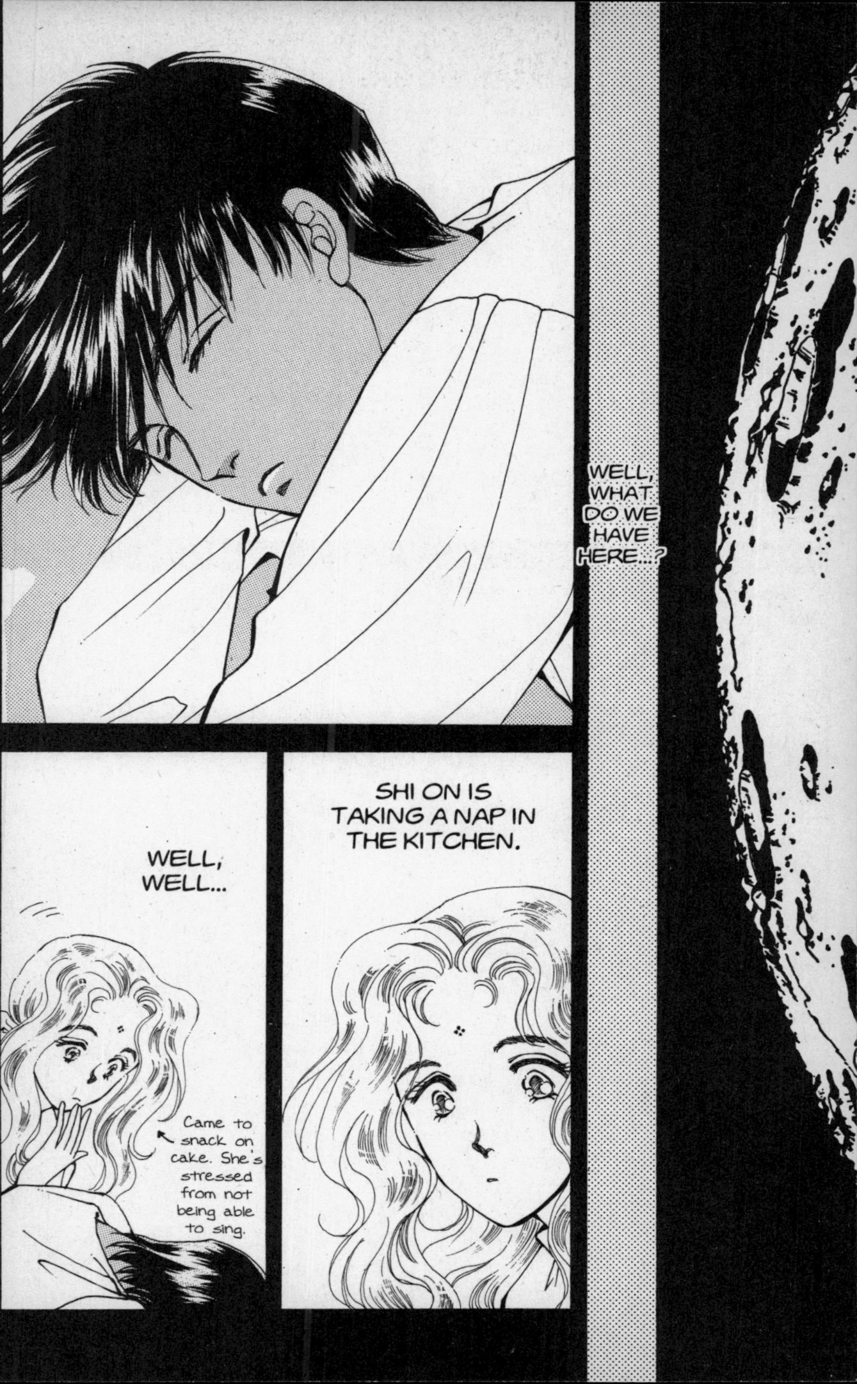
WELL, WHAT DO WE HAVE HERE...?
SHI ON IS TAKING A NAP IN THE KITCHEN.
WELL, WELL...
Came to snack on cake. She's stressed from not being able to sing.

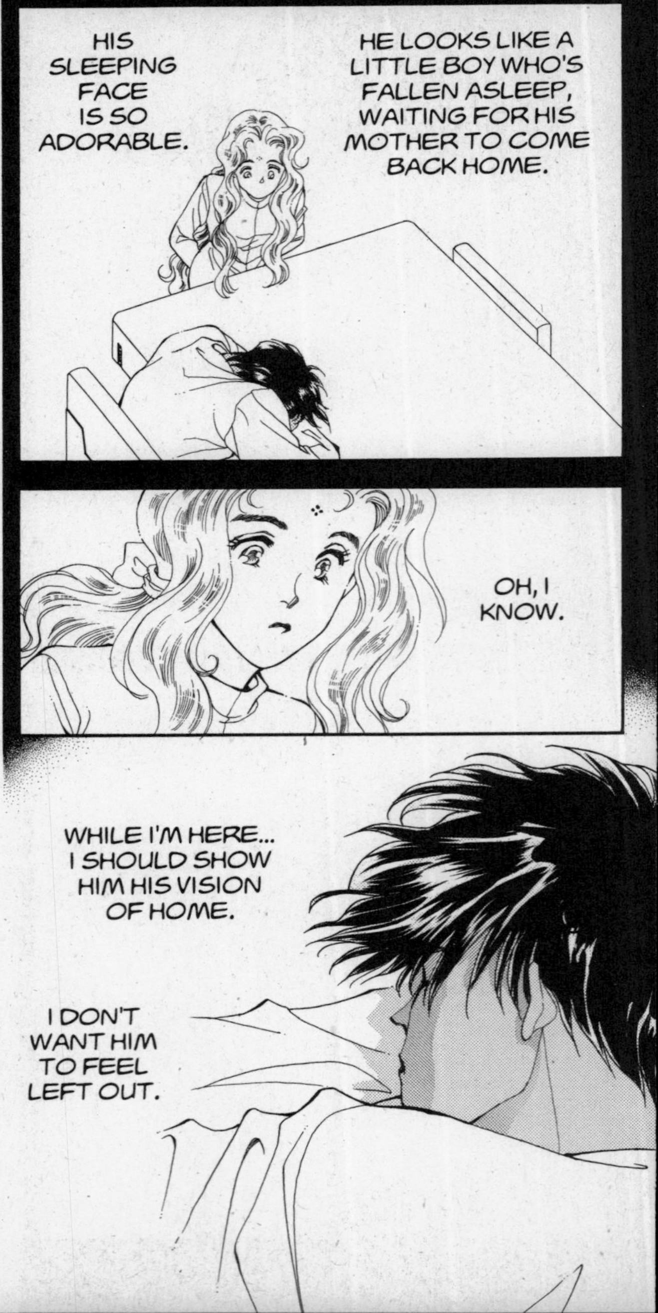

HE LOOKS LIKE A LITTLE BOY WHO'S FALLEN ASLEEP, WAITING FOR HIS MOTHER TO COME BACK HOME.
HIS SLEEPING FACE IS SO ADORABLE.
OH, I KNOW.
WHILE I'M HERE... I SHOULD SHOW HIM HIS VISION OF HOME.
I DON'T WANT HIM TO FEEL LEFT OUT.

1/4 COLUMN NONSENSE

PART 12

This poor, helpless kitten had her bones broken and muscles ripped because of an act of human cruelty. I have no way of knowing who did it, but I felt so overwhelmingly sick and guilty... And so I decided to adopt her. She's home now, after her long stay at the hospital, but she still has to be confined in a cage for another month because of her extensive injuries.

It's all so despicable. The vet bills certainly weren't cheap, either. I felt so angry and wretched that I had to right the wrongs that this stranger committed. I bet the person doesn't even remember doing it.

Continued in part 13

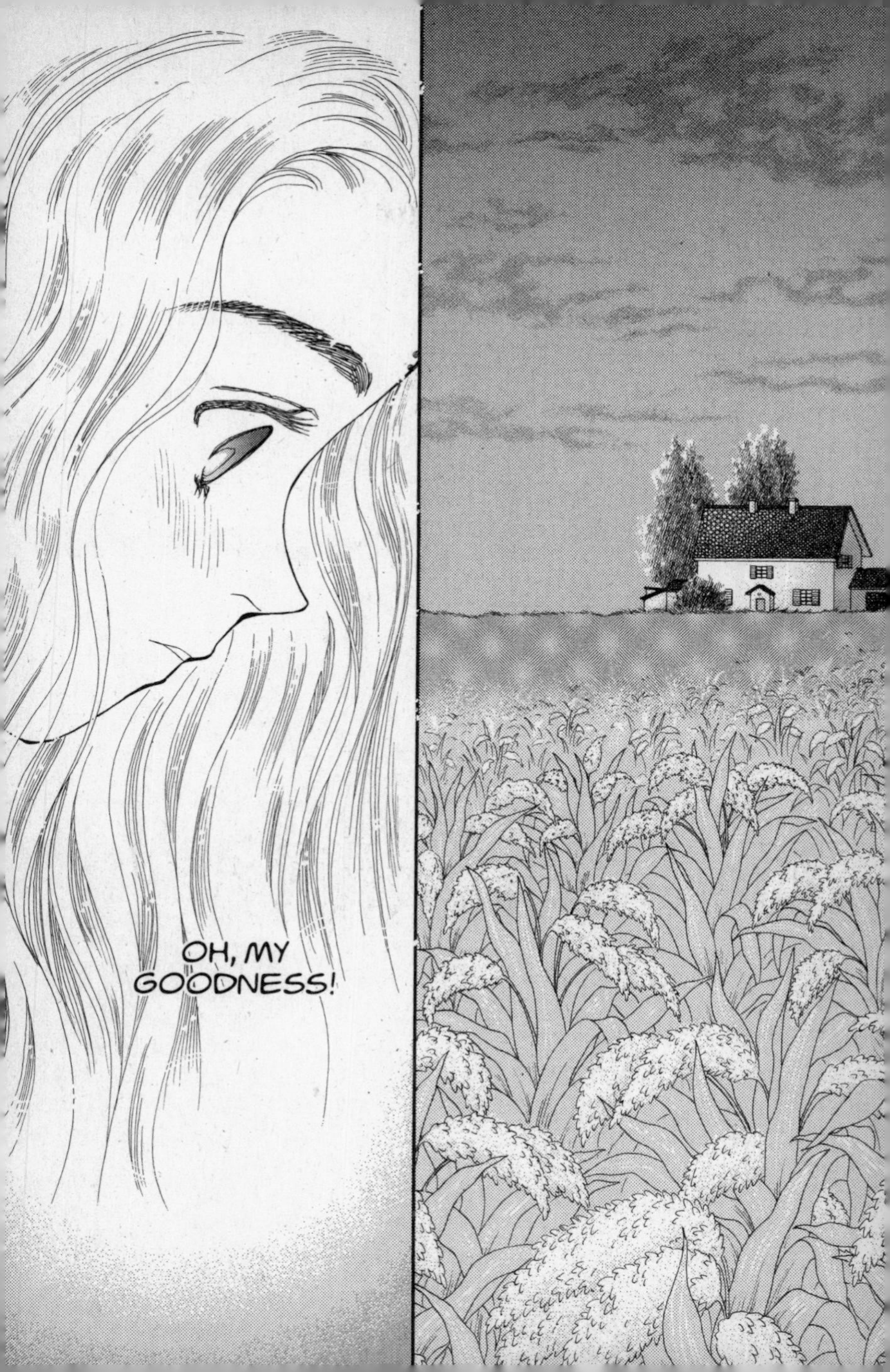
OH, MY GOODNESS!

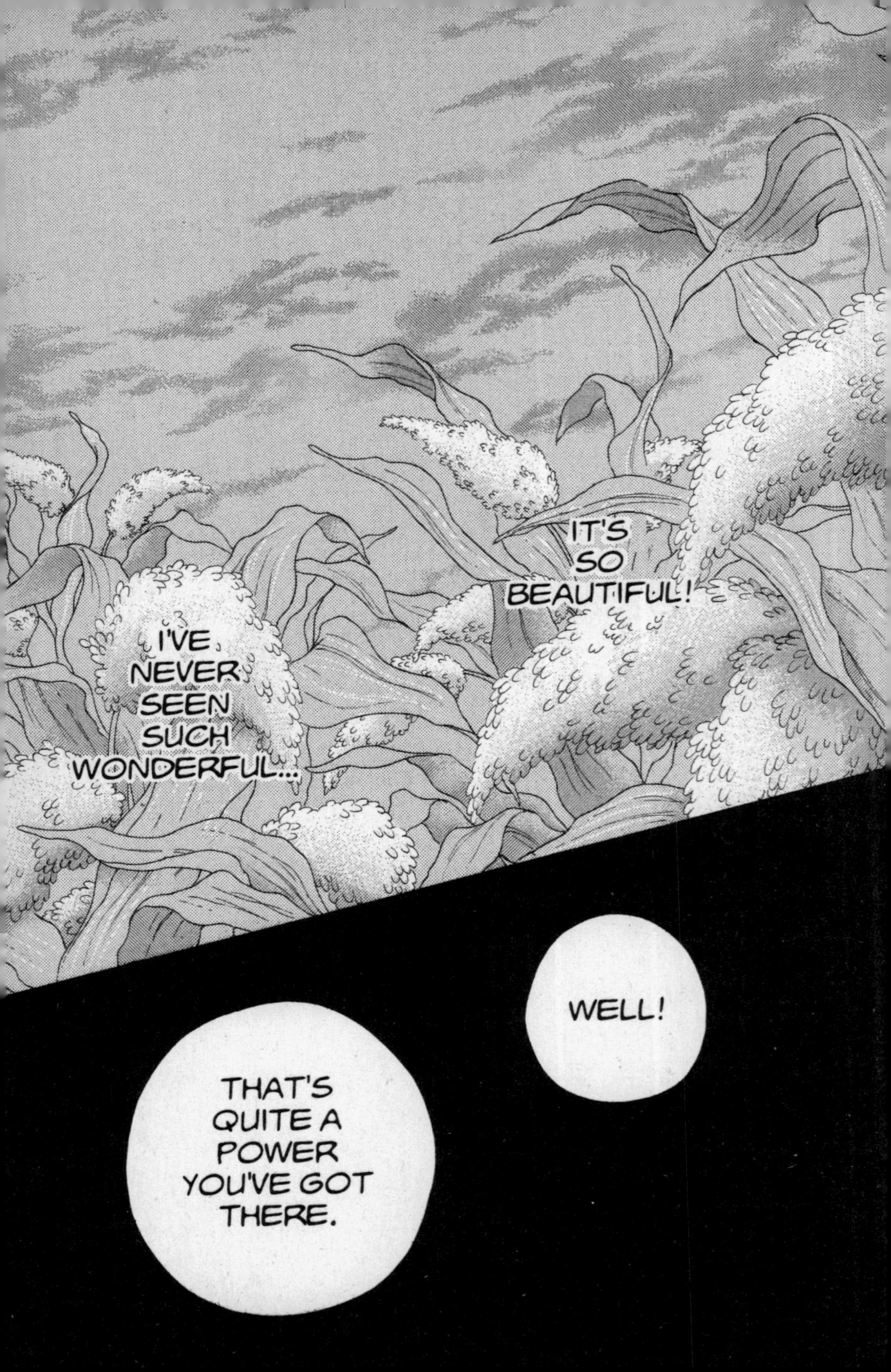
IT'S SO BEAUTIFUL!
I'VE NEVER SEEN SUCH WONDERFUL...
WELL!
THAT'S QUITE A POWER YOU'VE GOT THERE.

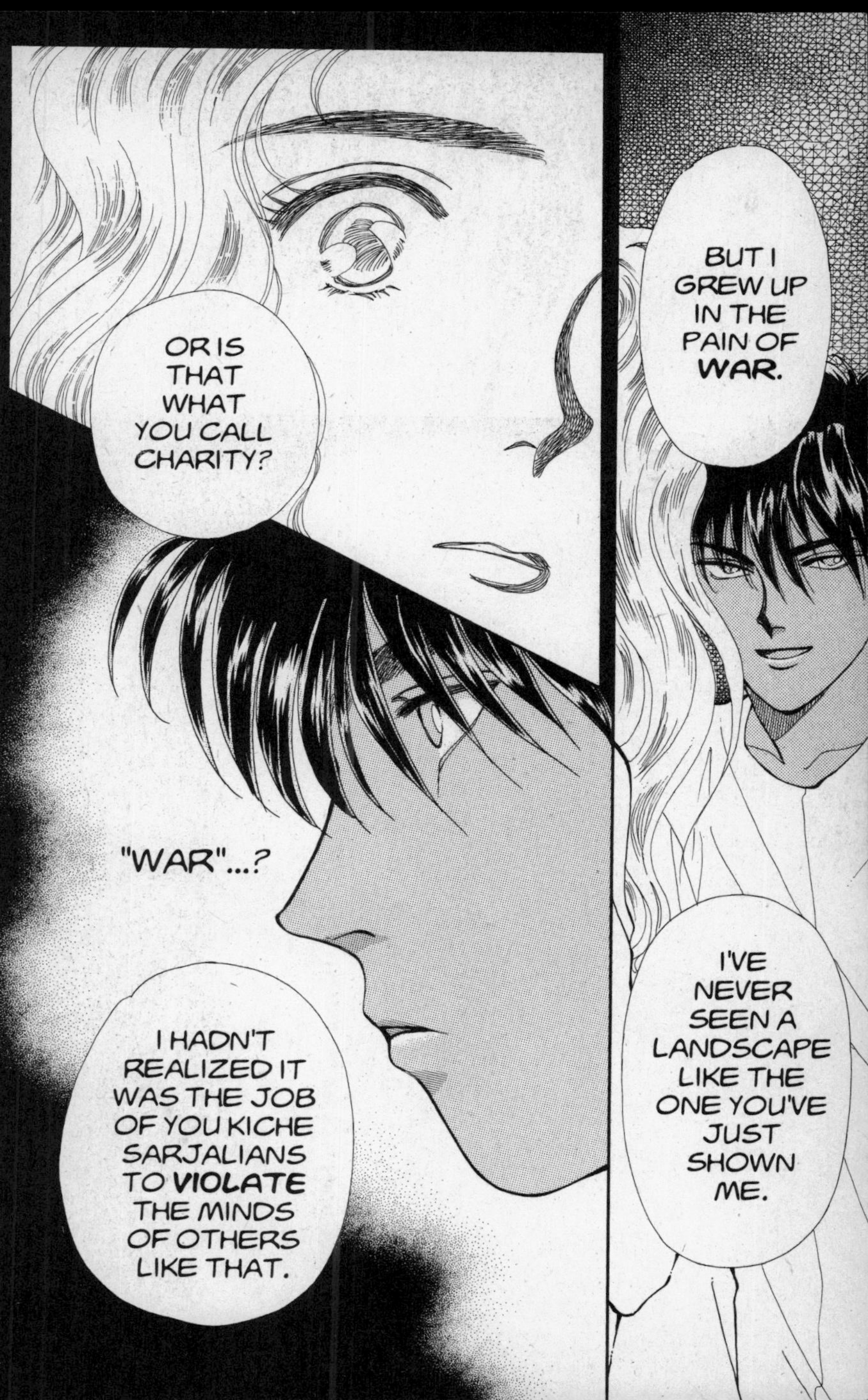
BUT I GREW UP IN THE PAIN OF WAR.
I'VE NEVER SEEN A LANDSCAPE LIKE THE ONE YOU'VE JUST SHOWN ME.
OR IS THAT WHAT YOU CALL CHARITY?
"WAR"...?
I HADN'T REALIZED IT WAS THE JOB OF YOU KICHE SARJALIANS TO VIOLATE THE MINDS OF OTHERS LIKE THAT.

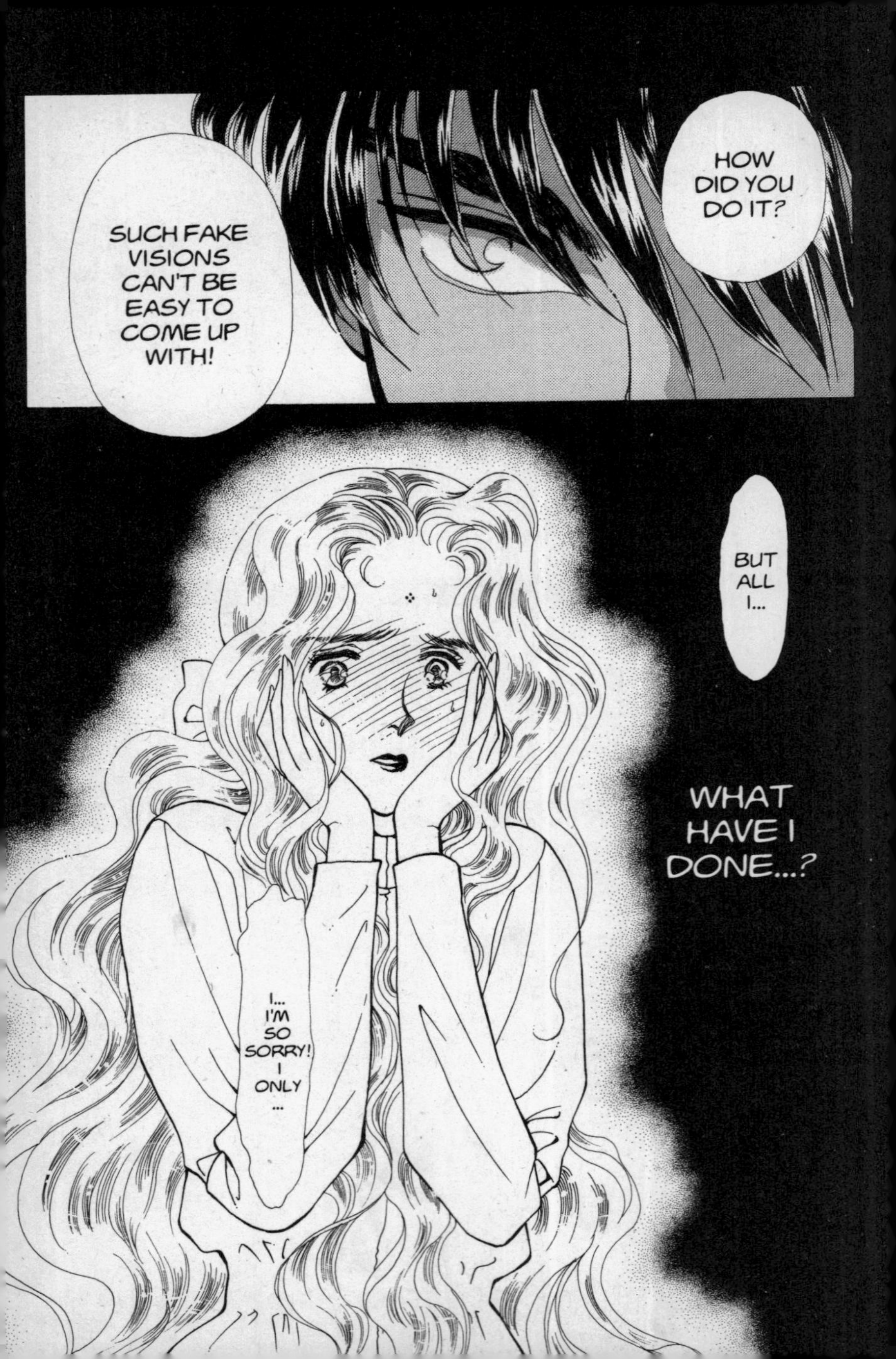
HOW DID YOU DO IT?
SUCH FAKE VISIONS CAN'T BE EASY TO COME UP WITH!
BUT ALL I...
WHAT HAVE I DONE...?
I... I'M SO SORRY! I ONLY ...

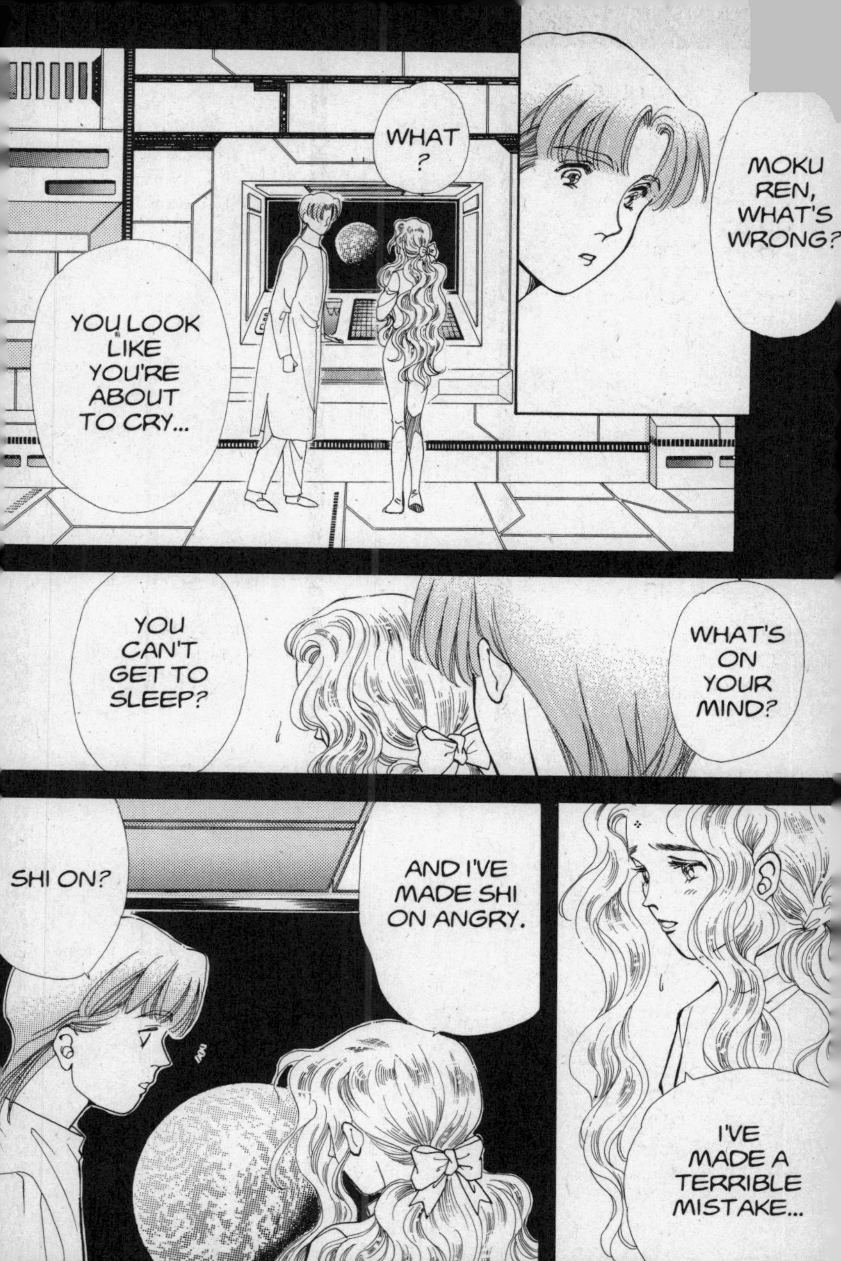
MOKU REN, WHAT'S WRONG?
WHAT ?
YOU LOOK LIKE YOU'RE ABOUT TO CRY...
WHAT'S ON YOUR MIND?
YOU CAN'T GET TO SLEEP?
I'VE MADE A TERRIBLE MISTAKE...
AND I'VE MADE SHI ON ANGRY.
SHI ON?

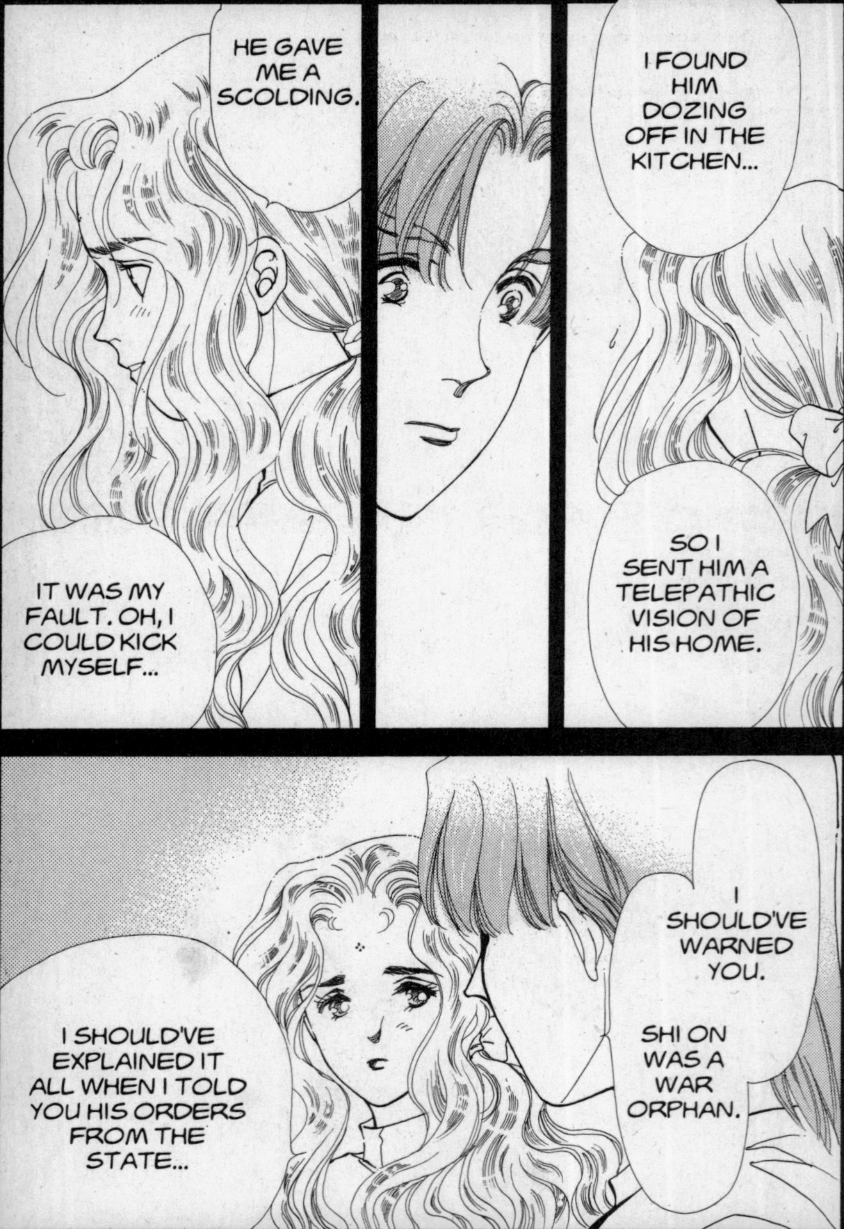
I FOUND HIM DOZING OFF IN THE KITCHEN...
SO I SENT HIM A TELEPATHIC VISION OF HIS HOME.
HE GAVE ME A SCOLDING.
IT WAS MY FAULT. OH, I COULD KICK MYSELF...
I SHOULD'VE WARNED YOU.
SHI ON WAS A WAR ORPHAN.
I SHOULD'VE EXPLAINED IT ALL WHEN I TOLD YOU HIS ORDERS FROM THE STATE...

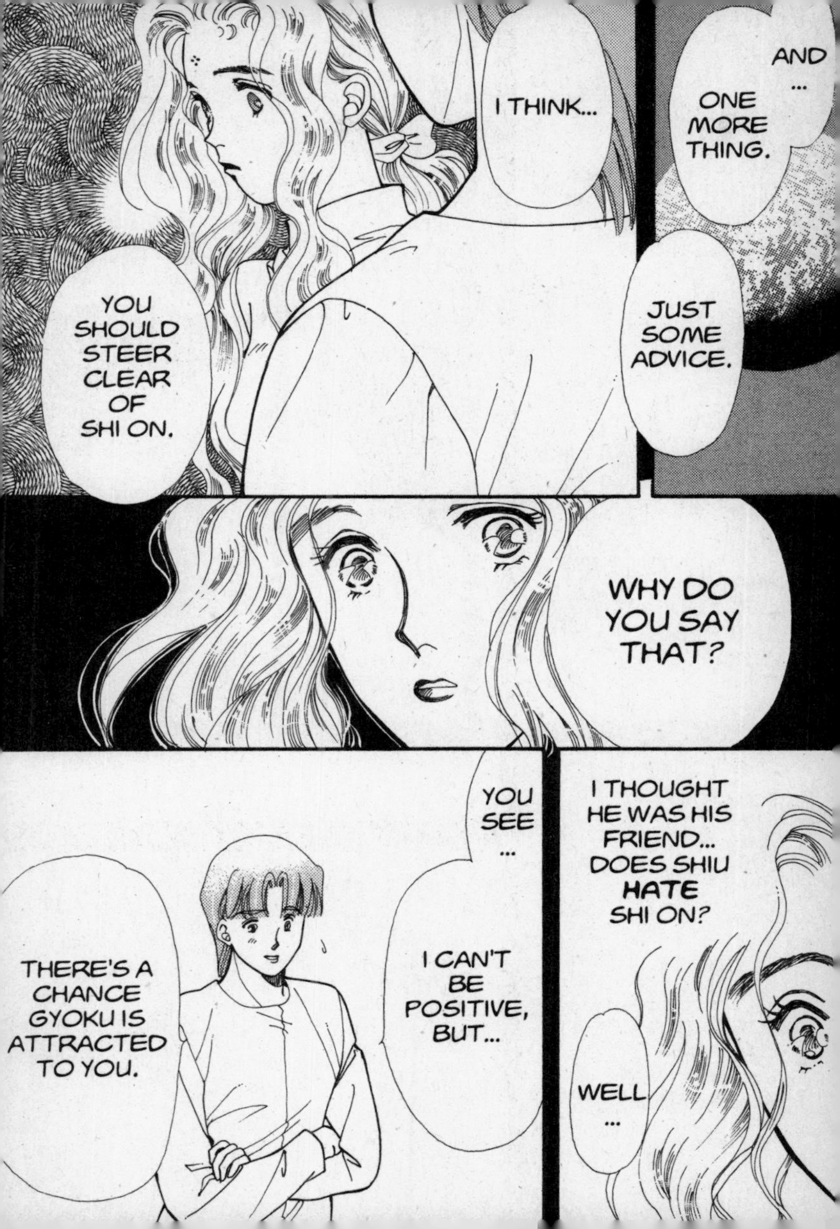
AND... ONE MORE THING.
JUST SOME ADVICE.
I THINK...
YOU SHOULD STEER CLEAR OF SHI ON.
WHY DO YOU SAY THAT?
I THOUGHT HE WAS HIS FRIEND... DOES SHIU HATE SHI ON?
WELL...
YOU SEE...
I CAN'T BE POSITIVE, BUT...
THERE'S A CHANCE GYOKU IS ATTRACTED TO YOU.

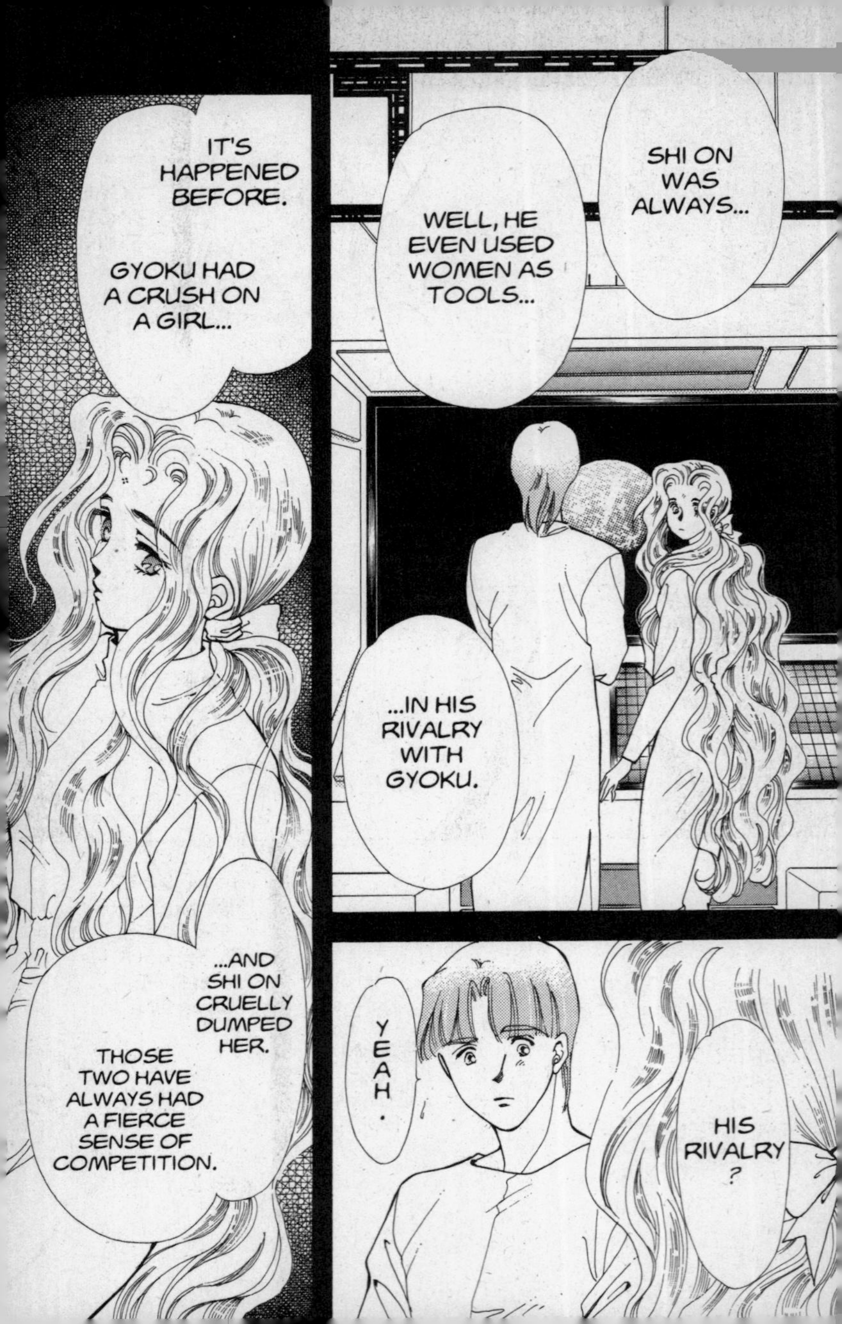
SHI ON WAS ALWAYS...
WELL, HE EVEN USED WOMEN AS TOOLS...
...IN HIS RIVALRY WITH GYOKU.
HIS RIVALRY?
YEAH.
IT'S HAPPENED BEFORE.
GYOKU HAD A CRUSH ON A GIRL...
...AND SHI ON CRUELLY DUMPED HER.
THOSE TWO HAVE ALWAYS HAD A FIERCE SENSE OF COMPETITION.

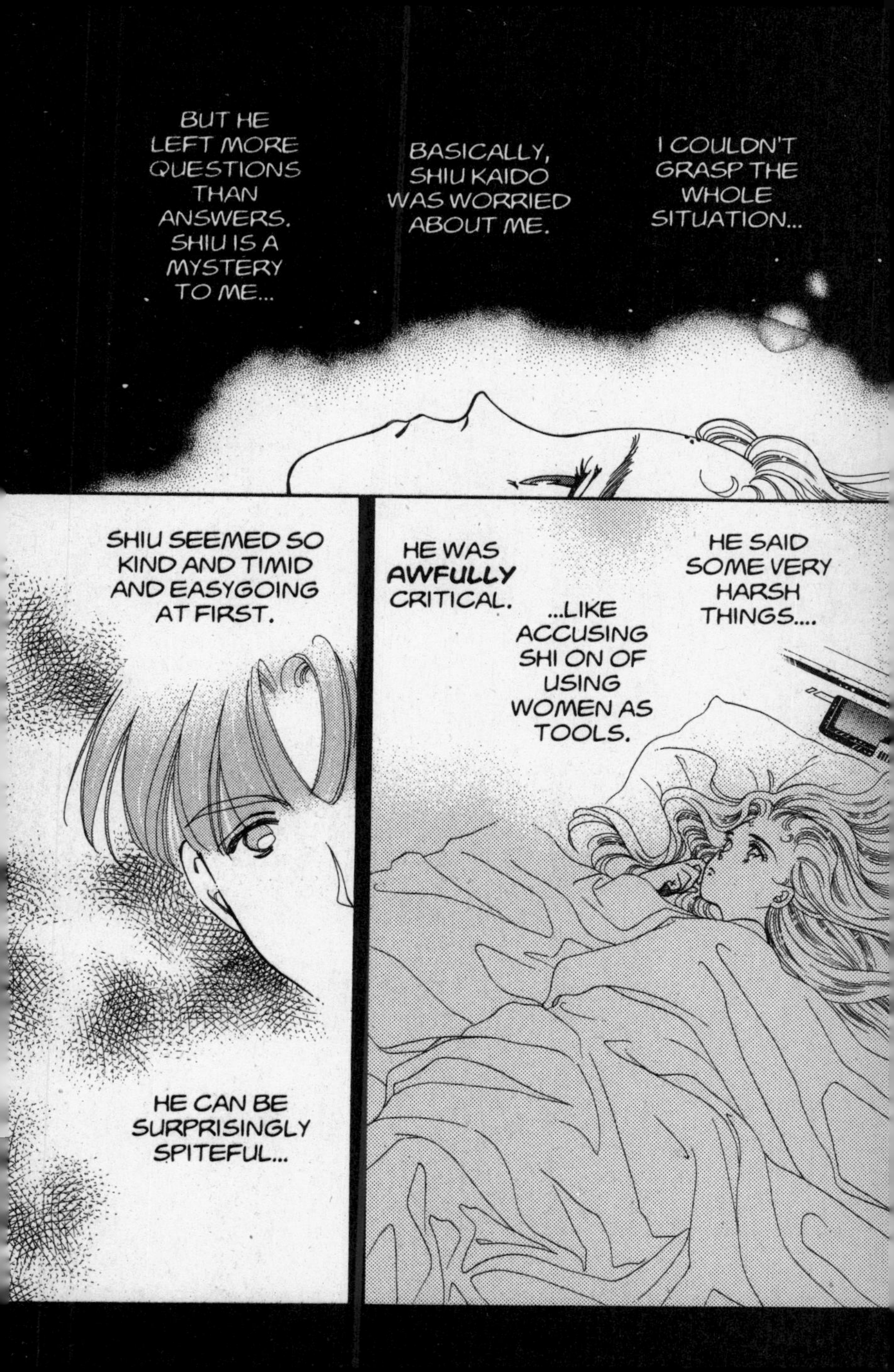
I COULDN'T GRASP THE WHOLE SITUATION...
BASICALLY, SHIU KAIDO WAS WORRIED ABOUT ME.
BUT HE LEFT MORE QUESTIONS THAN ANSWERS. SHIU IS A MYSTERY TO ME...
HE SAID SOME VERY HARSH THINGS....
HE WAS **AWFULLY** CRITICAL.
...LIKE ACCUSING SHI ON OF USING WOMEN AS TOOLS.
SHIU SEEMED SO KIND AND TIMID AND EASYGOING AT FIRST.
HE CAN BE SURPRISINGLY SPITEFUL...

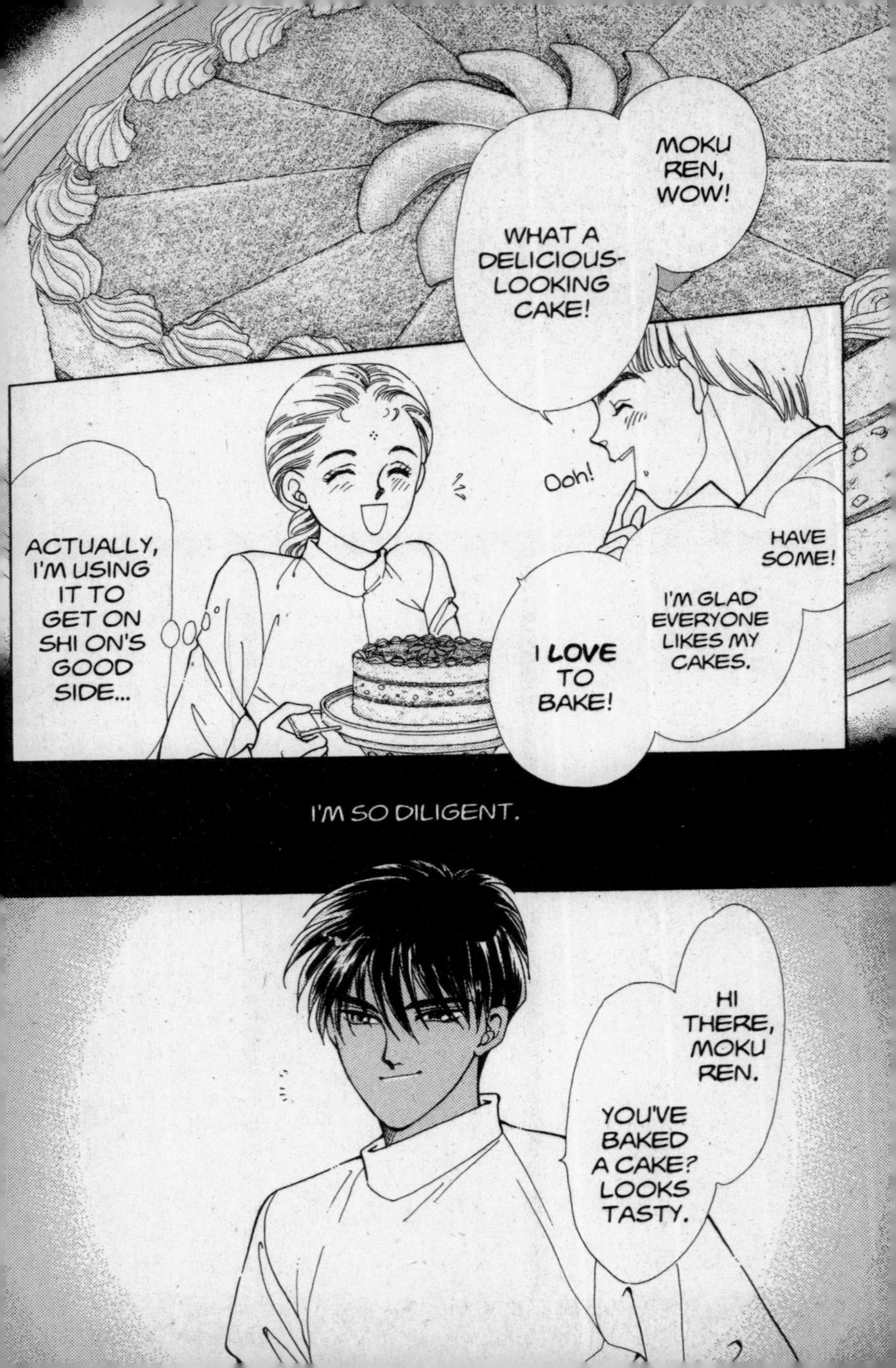
MOKU REN, WOW!
WHAT A DELICIOUS-LOOKING CAKE!
Ooh!
HAVE SOME!
I'M GLAD EVERYONE LIKES MY CAKES.
I **LOVE** TO BAKE!
ACTUALLY, I'M USING IT TO GET ON SHI ON'S GOOD SIDE...
I'M SO DILIGENT.
HI THERE, MOKU REN.
YOU'VE BAKED A CAKE? LOOKS TASTY.

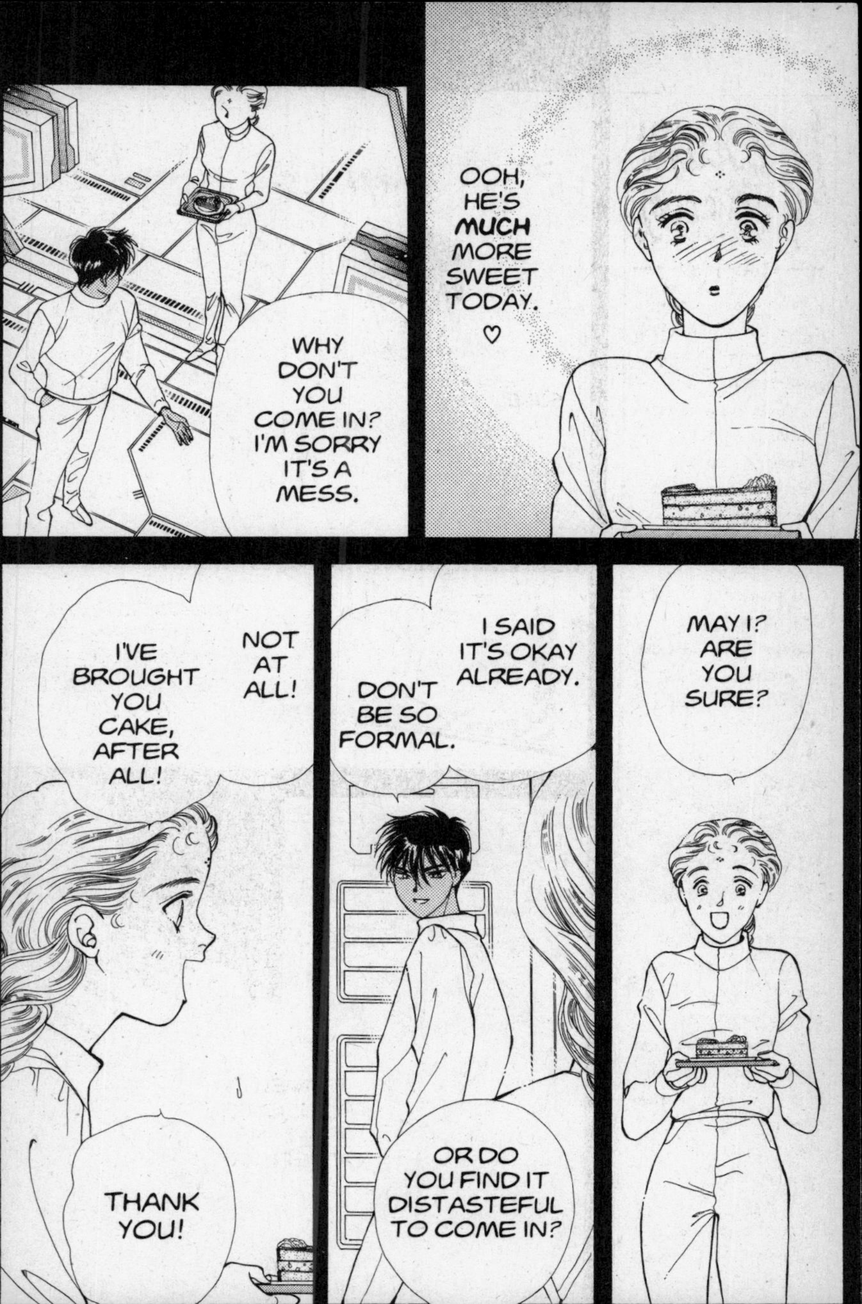

OOH, HE'S MUCH MORE SWEET TODAY. ♡
WHY DON'T YOU COME IN? I'M SORRY IT'S A MESS.
MAY I? ARE YOU SURE?
I SAID IT'S OKAY ALREADY.
DON'T BE SO FORMAL.
OR DO YOU FIND IT DISTASTEFUL TO COME IN?
NOT AT ALL!
I'VE BROUGHT YOU CAKE, AFTER ALL!
THANK YOU!

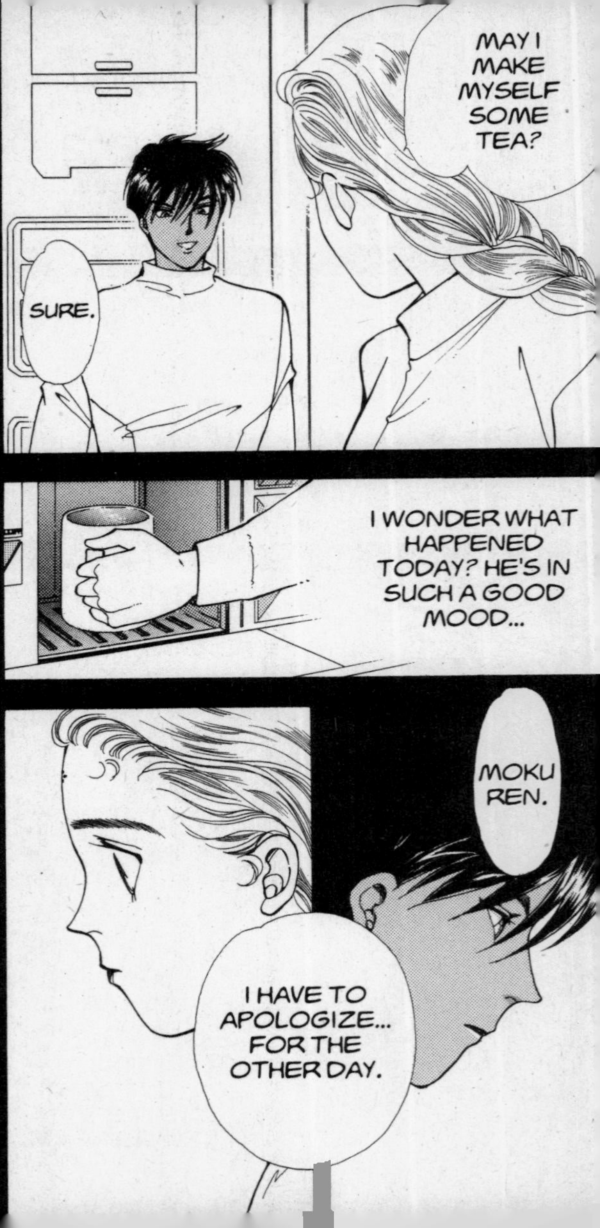
MAY I MAKE MYSELF SOME TEA?
SURE.
I WONDER WHAT HAPPENED TODAY? HE'S IN SUCH A GOOD MOOD...
MOKU REN.
I HAVE TO APOLOGIZE... FOR THE OTHER DAY.

1/4 COLUMN NONSENSE

PART 13

Anyway... this calico kitty is very cute, pretty, and mischievous!

I've named her Tammy, after Tomonori, since I had also adopted him in late October... I used to call him "Tommy" for short. The name also comes from Debbie Reynolds's song "Tammy." I really love this song. Why do I always end up adopting a cat in October? And in my entryway this time, no less.

Uh-oh, is this the final column? Oops, I expected there to be more. Everyone, keep your feet firmly on the ground, reach high for the stars, and be sure to take care of yourselves!

Goodbye! Have a Happy New Year!
Oct. 20, 1992

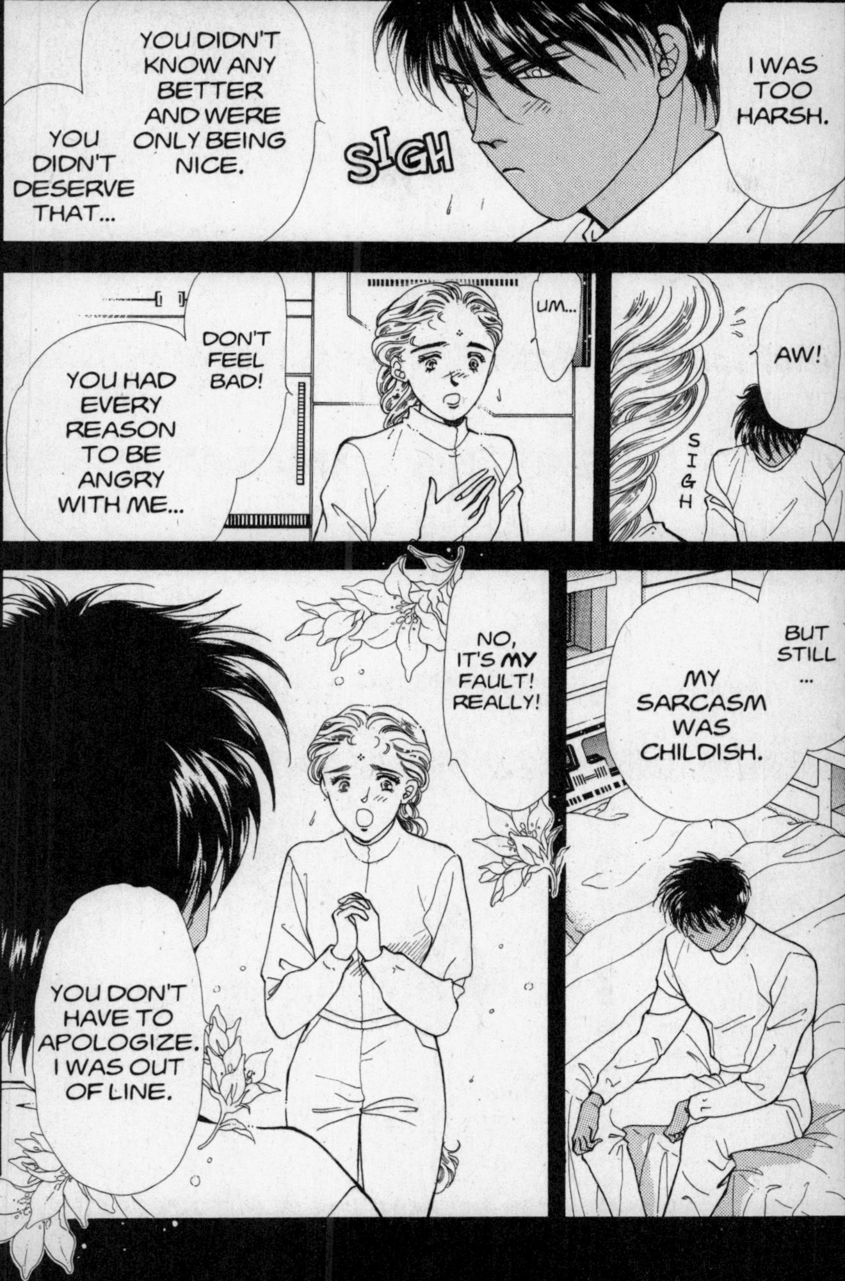
I WAS TOO HARSH.
SIGH
YOU DIDN'T KNOW ANY BETTER AND WERE ONLY BEING NICE.
YOU DIDN'T DESERVE THAT...
AW!
SIGH
UM...
DON'T FEEL BAD!
YOU HAD EVERY REASON TO BE ANGRY WITH ME...
BUT STILL...
MY SARCASM WAS CHILDISH.
NO, IT'S MY FAULT! REALLY!
YOU DON'T HAVE TO APOLOGIZE. I WAS OUT OF LINE.

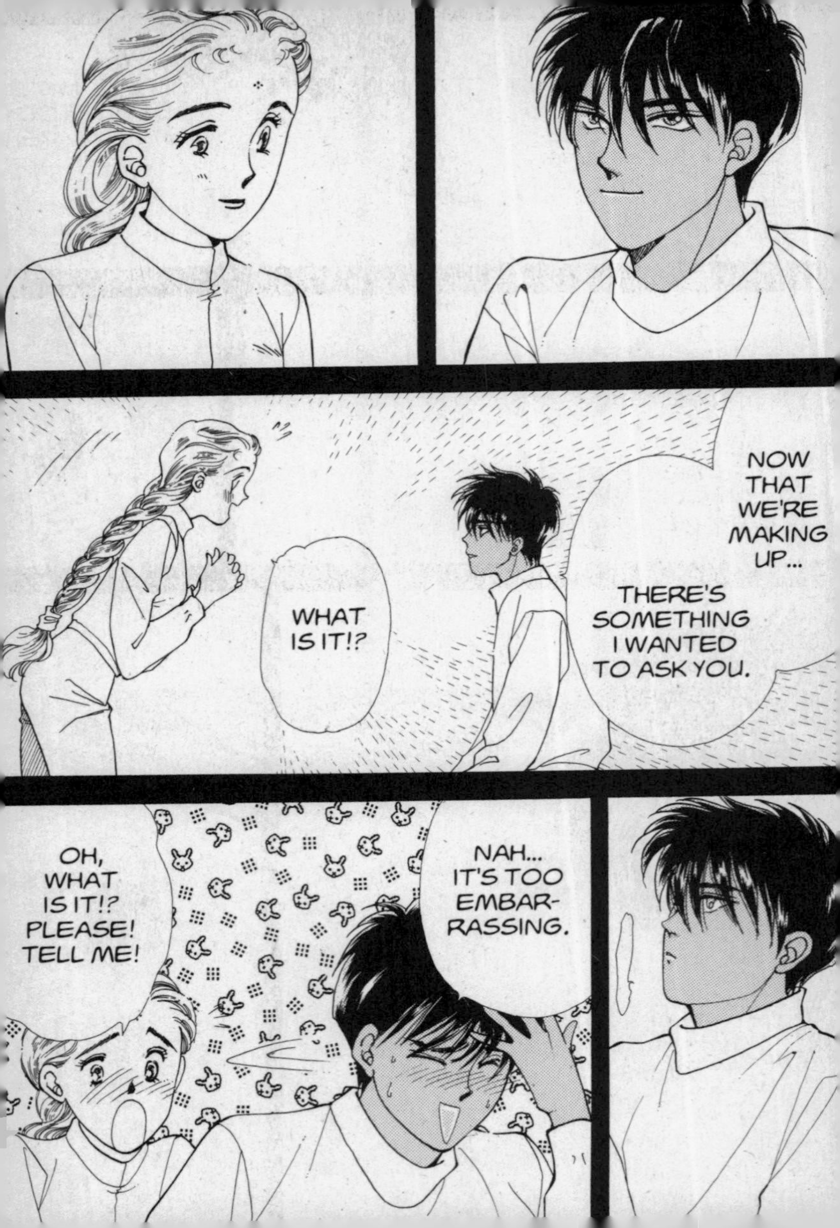
NOW THAT WE'RE MAKING UP...
THERE'S SOMETHING I WANTED TO ASK YOU.
WHAT IS IT!?
NAH... IT'S TOO EMBARRASSING.
OH, WHAT IS IT!? PLEASE! TELL ME!

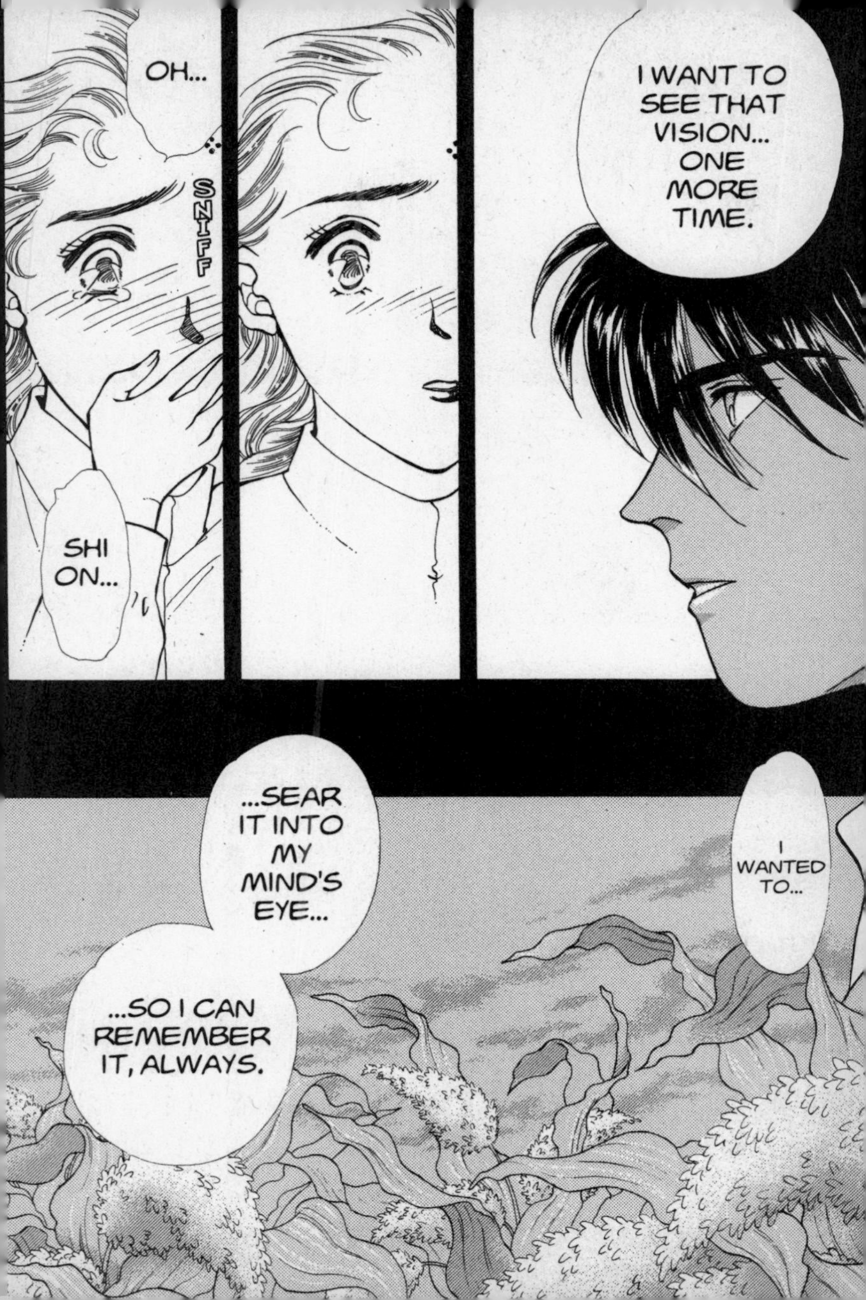
I WANT TO SEE THAT VISION... ONE MORE TIME.
OH...
SNIFF
SHI ON...
I WANTED TO...
...SEAR IT INTO MY MIND'S EYE...
...SO I CAN REMEMBER IT, ALWAYS.

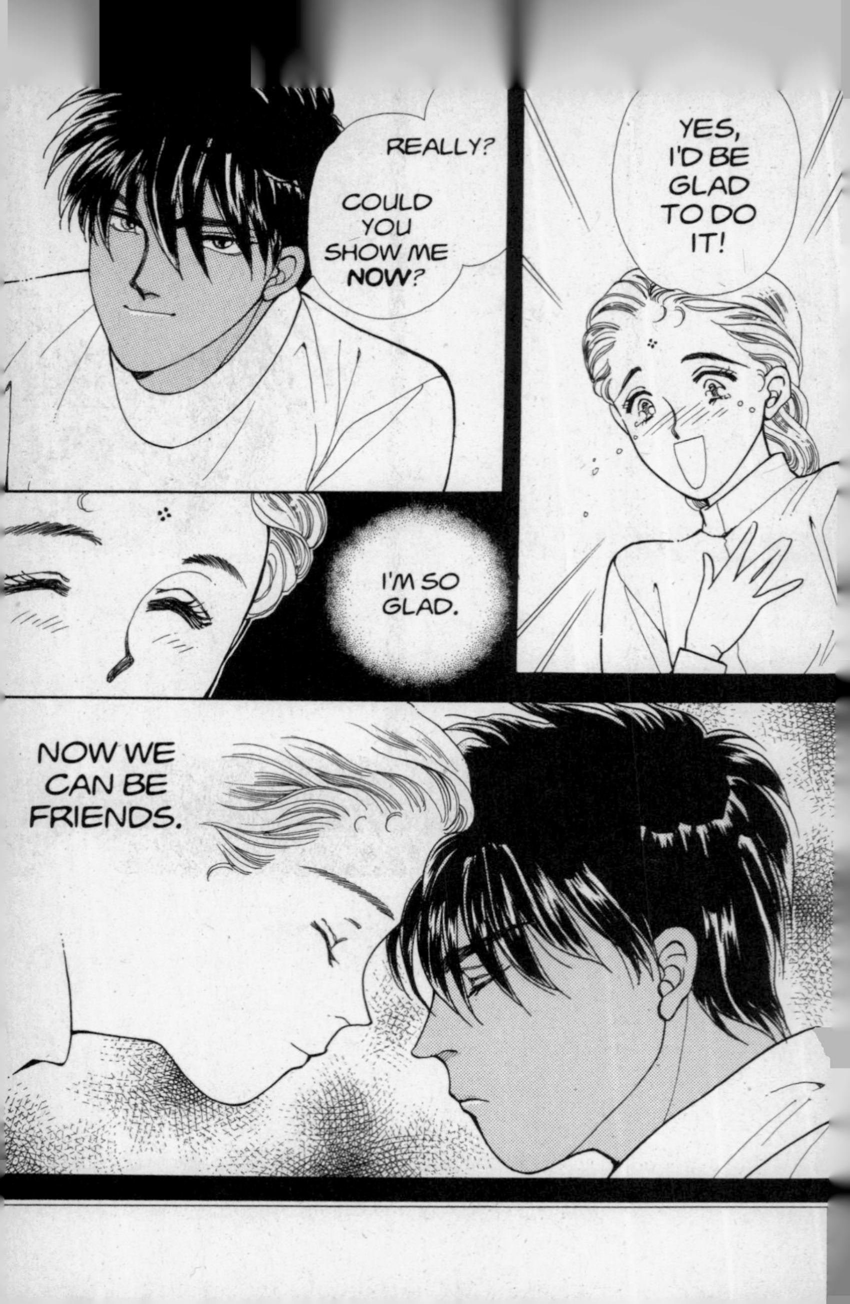
REALLY?
COULD YOU SHOW ME NOW?
YES, I'D BE GLAD TO DO IT!
I'M SO GLAD.
NOW WE CAN BE FRIENDS.

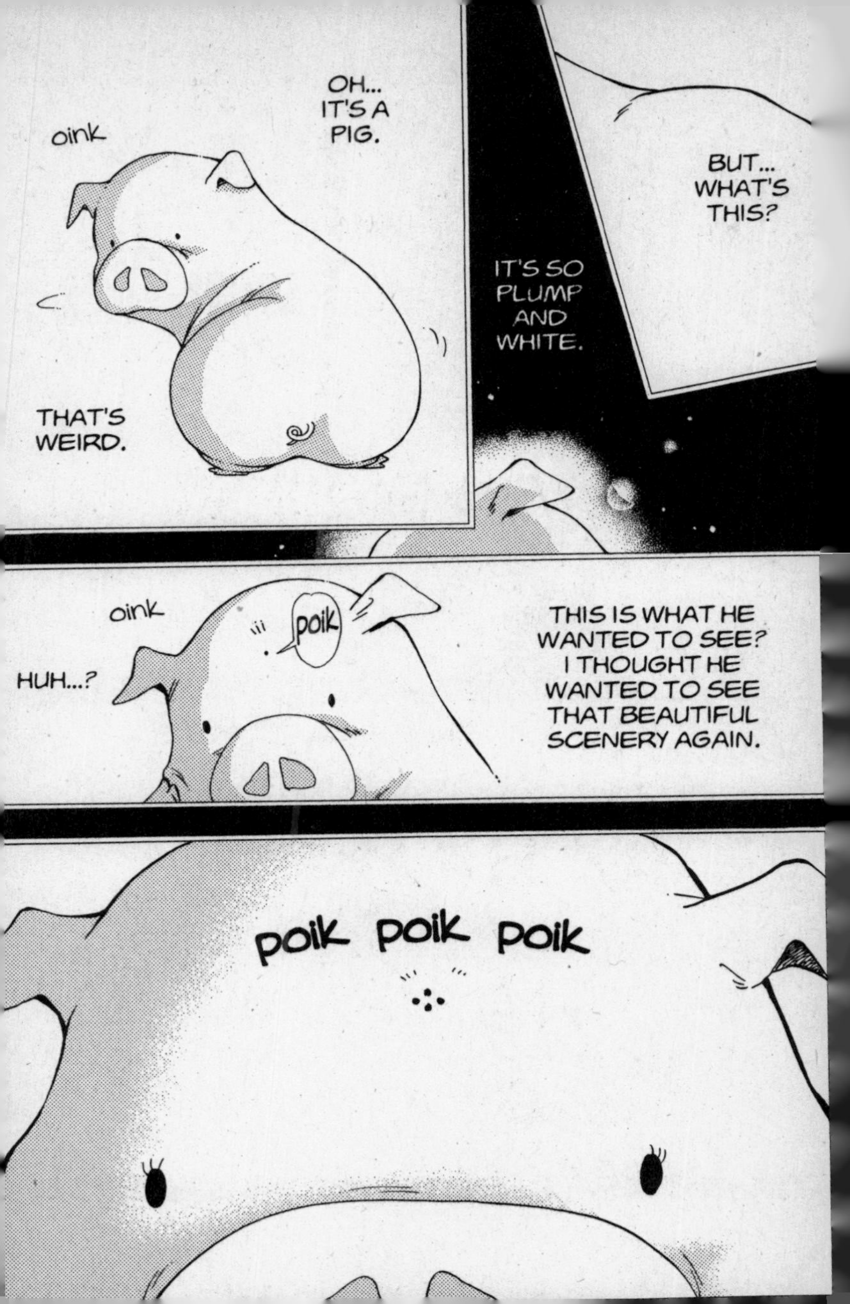
BUT... WHAT'S THIS?
IT'S SO PLUMP AND WHITE.
OH... IT'S A PIG.
oink
THAT'S WEIRD.
THIS IS WHAT HE WANTED TO SEE? I THOUGHT HE WANTED TO SEE THAT BEAUTIFUL SCENERY AGAIN.
poik
oink
HUH...?
poik poik poik

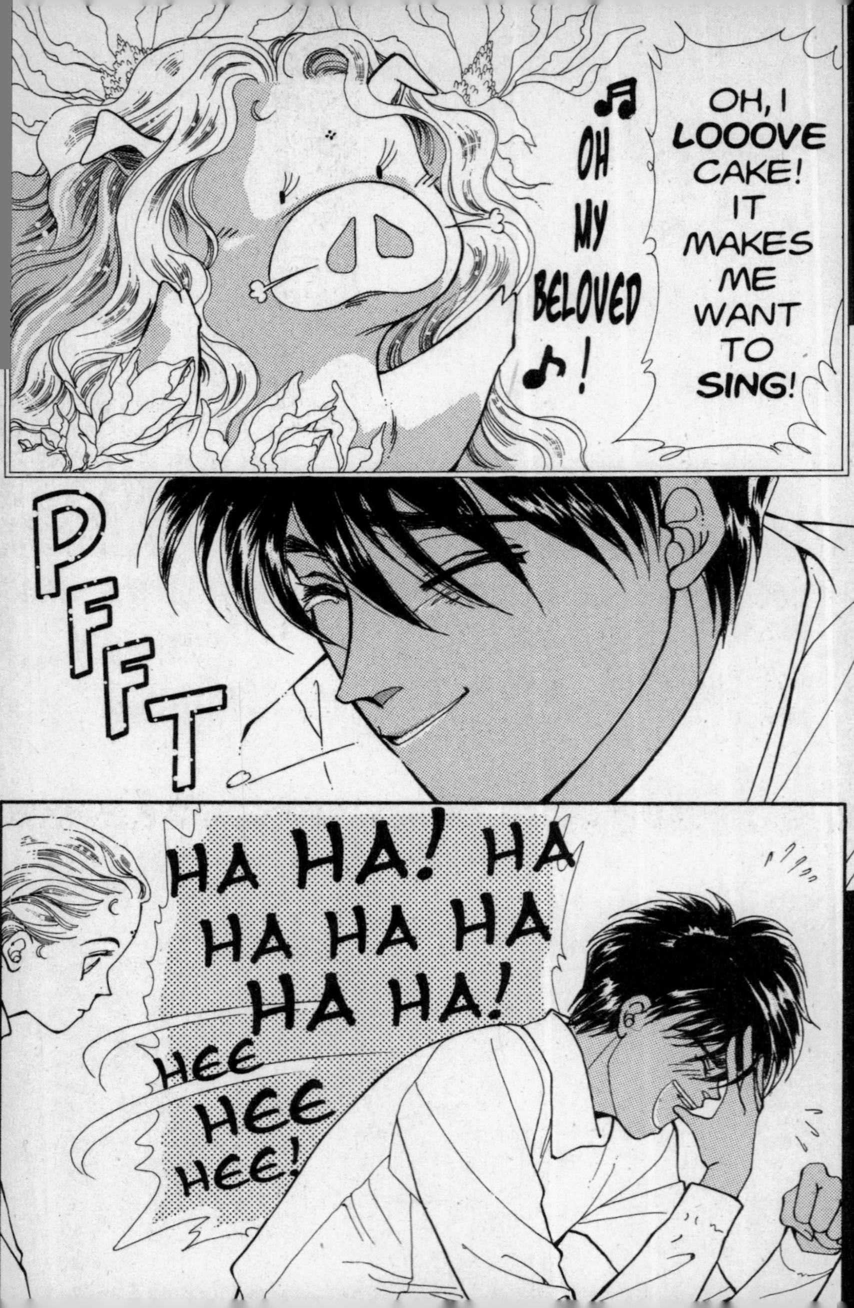
OH, I LOOOVE CAKE! IT MAKES ME WANT TO SING!
♪ OH MY BELOVED ♪!
PFFFT
HA HA! HA HA HA HA HA HA HA!
HEE HEE HEE!

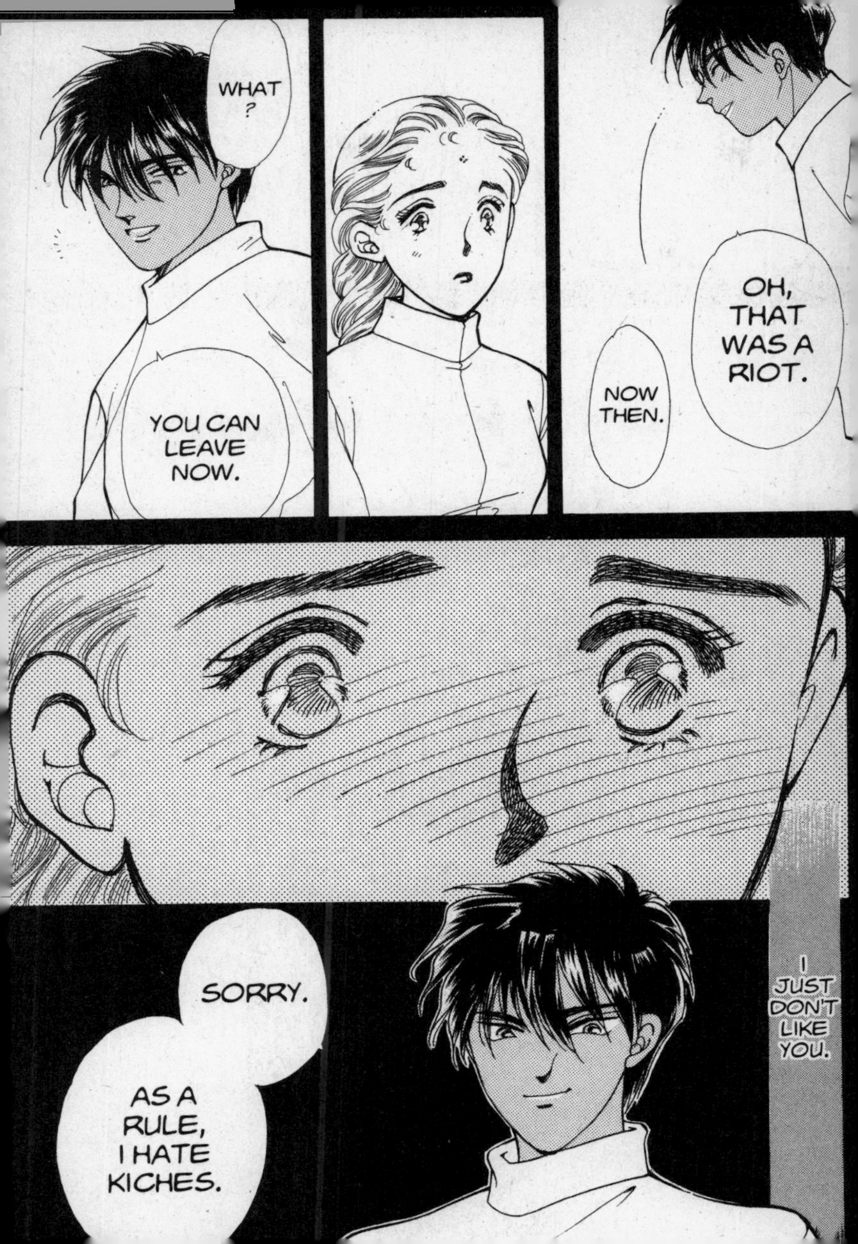
OH, THAT WAS A RIOT.
NOW THEN.
WHAT ?
YOU CAN LEAVE NOW.
I JUST DON'T LIKE YOU.
SORRY.
AS A RULE, I HATE KICHES.

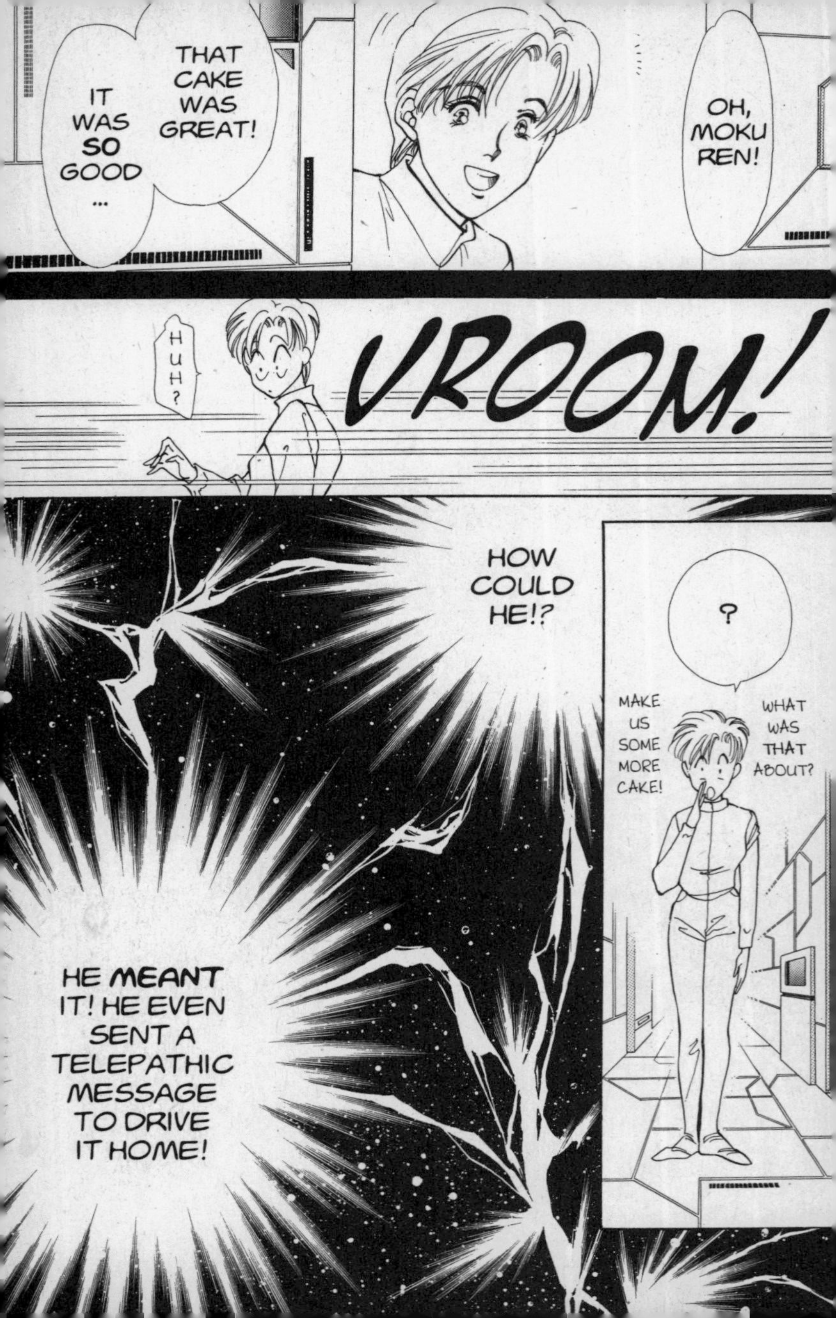
OH, MOKU REN!
THAT CAKE WAS GREAT!
IT WAS SO GOOD ...
VROOM!
HUH?
?
WHAT WAS THAT ABOUT?
MAKE US SOME MORE CAKE!
HOW COULD HE!?
HE MEANT IT! HE EVEN SENT A TELEPATHIC MESSAGE TO DRIVE IT HOME!

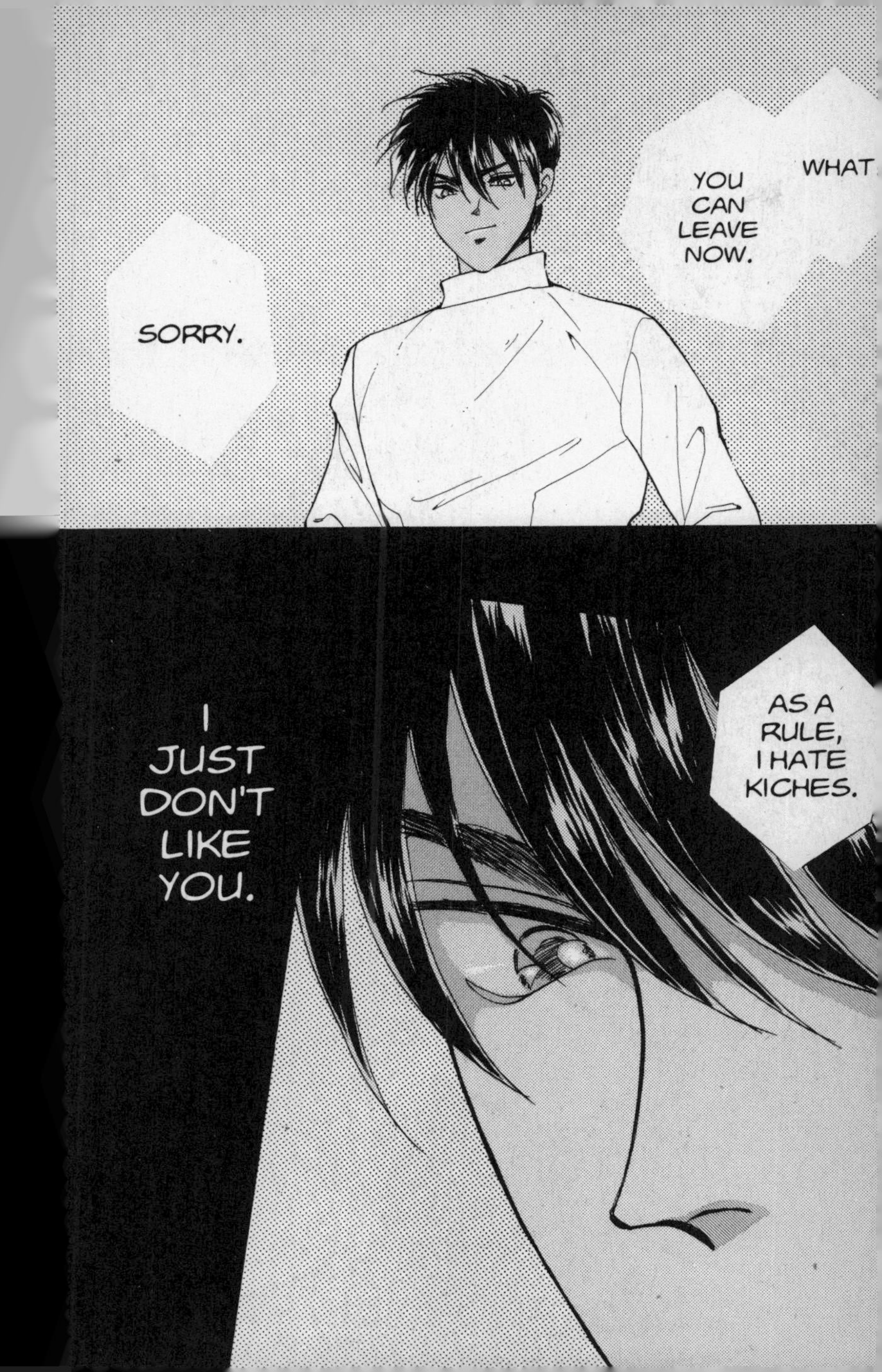
WHAT
YOU CAN LEAVE NOW.
SORRY.
AS A RULE, I HATE KICHES.
I JUST DON'T LIKE YOU.

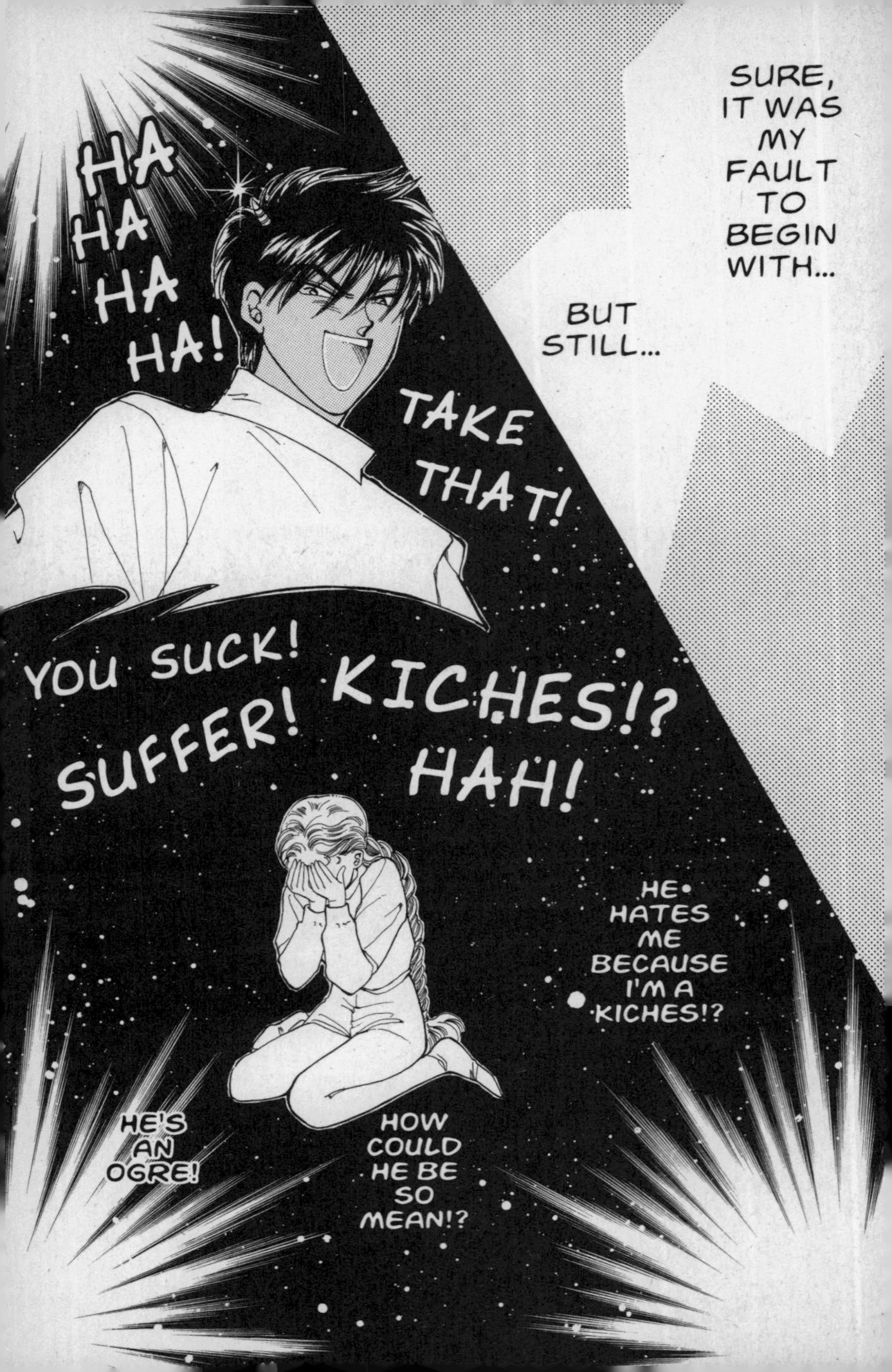
SURE, IT WAS MY FAULT TO BEGIN WITH...
BUT STILL...
TAKE THAT!
HA HA HA HA!
KICHES!? HAH!
YOU SUCK!
SUFFER!
HE HATES ME BECAUSE I'M A KICHES!?
HOW COULD HE BE SO MEAN!?
HE'S AN OGRE!

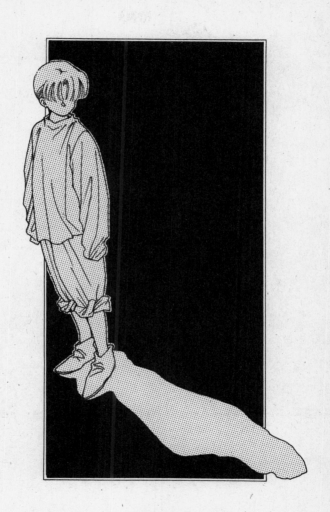

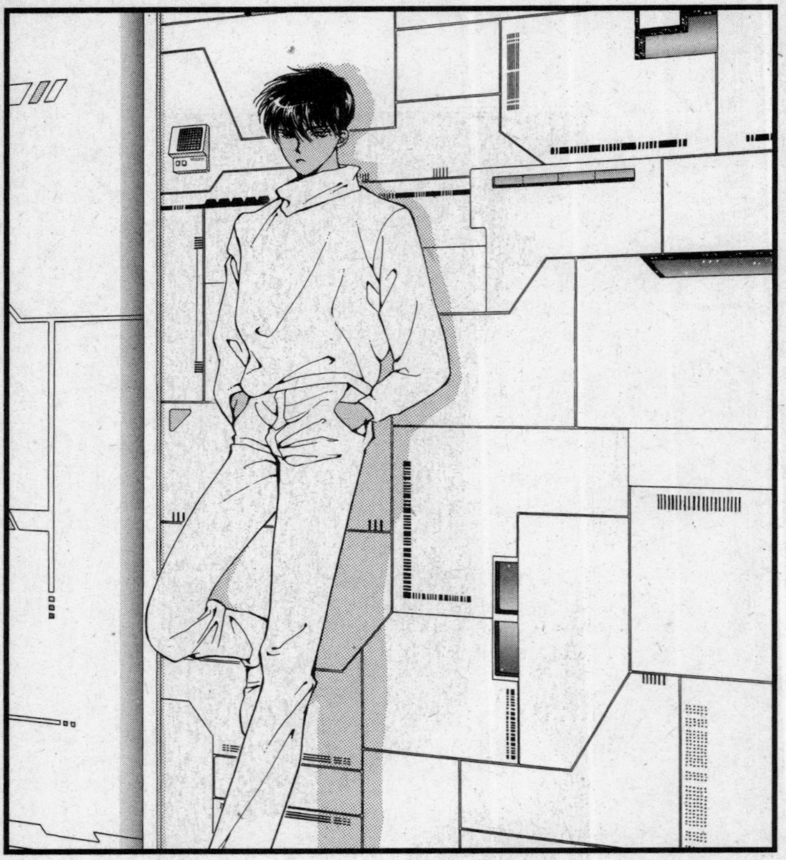

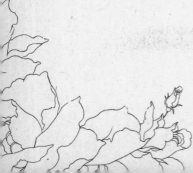

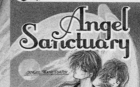

The Power of a Kiss

Soon after her first kiss, Yuri is pulled into a puddle and transported to an ancient Middle Eastern village. Surrounded by strange people speaking a language she can't understand, Yuri has no idea how to get back home and is soon embroiled in the politics and romance of the ancient Middle East. If a kiss helped get Yuri into this mess, can a kiss get her out?

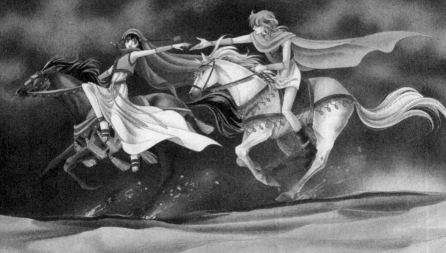

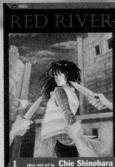

RED RIVER™

Start your graphic novel collection today!

ONLY $9.95!

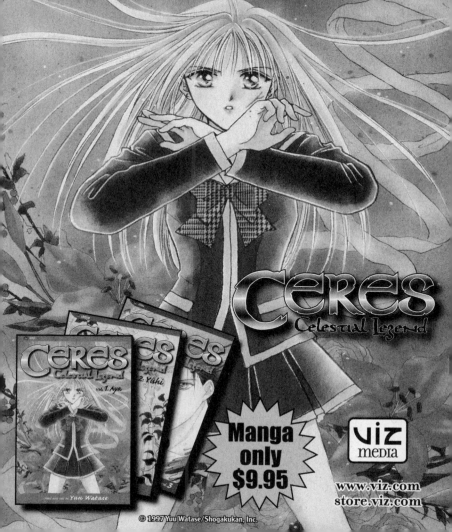

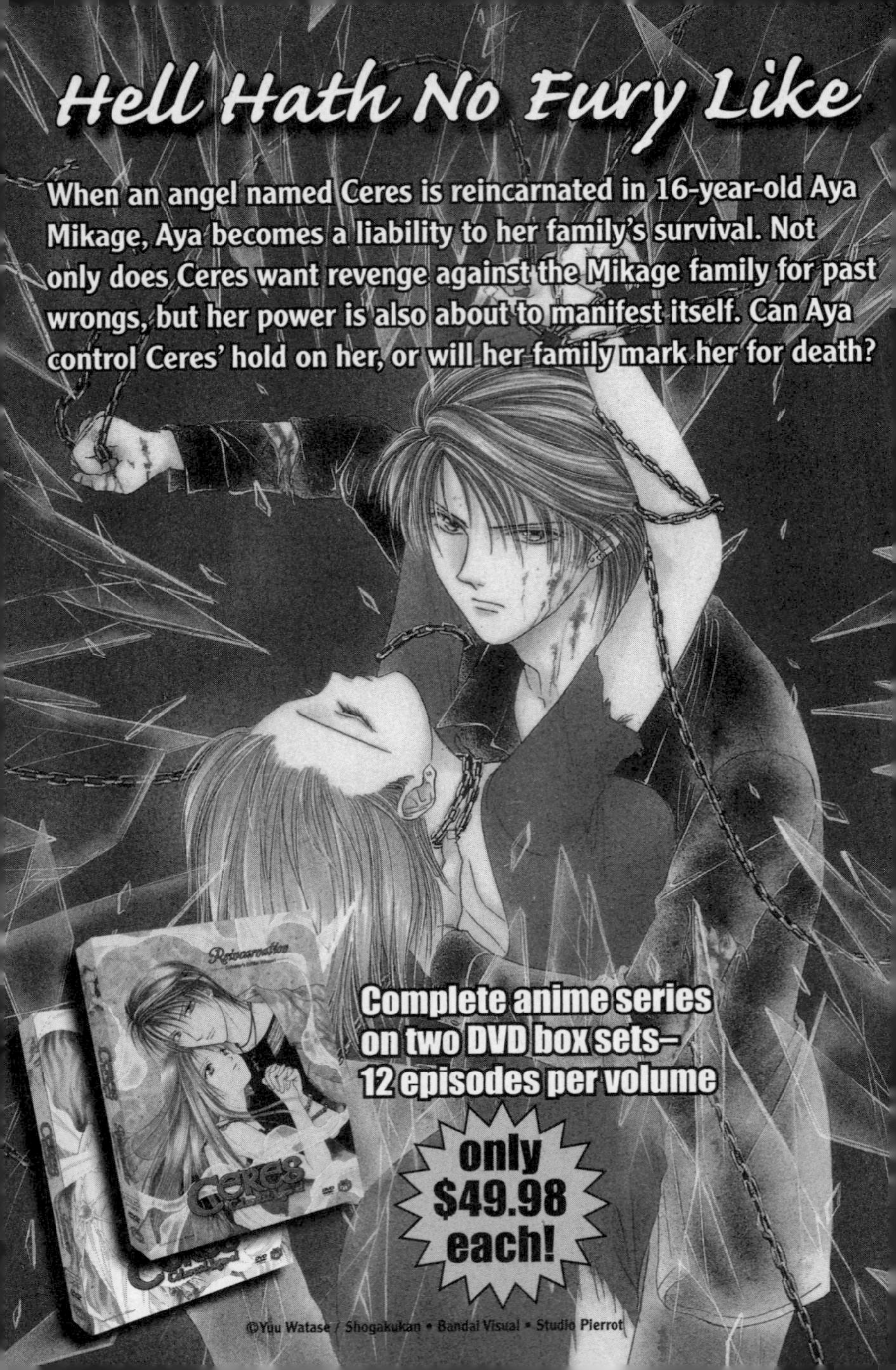
Hell Hath No Fury Like
When an angel named Ceres is reincarnated in 16-year-old Aya Mikage, Aya becomes a liability to her family's survival. Not only does Ceres want revenge against the Mikage family for past wrongs, but her power is also about to manifest itself. Can Aya control Ceres' hold on her, or will her family mark her for death?
Complete anime series on two DVD box sets– 12 episodes per volume
only $49.98 each!
©Yuu Watase / Shogakukan • Bandai Visual • Studio Pierrot

STEAMBOY
Vol. 1
Ani-Manga™
Conceived & Directed by
KATSUHIRO OTOMO
Ani-Manga™
$19.99

STEAMBOY
By Sadayuki Murai • Original Concept by Katsuhiro Otomo
Translated by Naoko Amemiya
Hardcover
$17.99

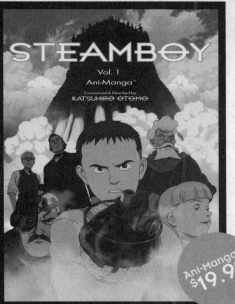

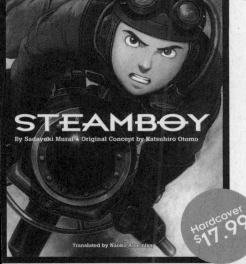

LOVE SHOJO? LET US KNOW!

☐ Please do NOT send me information about VIZ Media products, news and events, special offers, or other information.

☐ Please do NOT send me information from VIZ' trusted business partners.

Name: _____

Address: _____

City: _____ State: _____ Zip: _____

E-mail: _____

☐ Male ☐ Female Date of Birth (mm/dd/yyyy): ___ / ___ / ___ (Under 13? Parental consent required)

What race/ethnicity do you consider yourself? (check all that apply)

☐ White/Caucasian   ☐ Black/African American   ☐ Hispanic/Latino

☐ Asian/Pacific Islander ☐ Native American/Alaskan Native ☐ Other: _____

What VIZ shojo title(s) did you purchase? (indicate title(s) purchased)

_____

What other shojo titles from other publishers do you own? _____

_____

Reason for purchase: (check all that apply)

☐ Special offer   ☐ Favorite title / author / artist / genre

☐ Gift   ☐ Recommendation   ☐ Collection

☐ Read excerpt in VIZ manga sampler ☐ Other _____

Where did you make your purchase? (please check one)

☐ Comic store   ☐ Bookstore   ☐ Mass/Grocery Store

☐ Newsstand   ☐ Video/Video Game Store

☐ Online (site:_____) ☐ Other _____

How many shojo titles have you purchased in the last year? How many were VIZ shojo titles?
(please check one from each column)

SHOJO MANGA	VIZ SHOJO MANGA
☐ None	☐ None
☐ 1 – 4	☐ 1 – 4
☐ 5 – 10	☐ 5 – 10
☐ 11+	☐ 11+

What do you like most about shojo graphic novels? **(check all that apply)**

☐ Romance ☐ Drama / conflict ☐ Fantasy
☐ Comedy ☐ Real-life storylines ☐ Relatable characters
☐ Other ______________________________

Do you purchase every volume of your favorite shojo series?

☐ Yes! Gotta have 'em as my own
☐ No. Please explain: ______________________________

Who are your favorite shojo authors / artists? ______________________________

____

What shojo titles would like you translated and sold in English? ______________________________

____

THANK YOU! Please send the completed form to:

NJW Research
ATTN: VIZ Media Shojo Survey
42 Catharine Street
Poughkeepsie, NY 12601

Your privacy is … **poses only and will not be sold or otherwise di**…

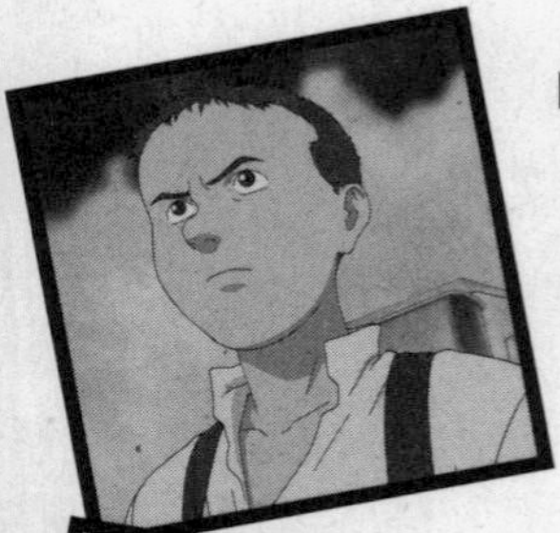

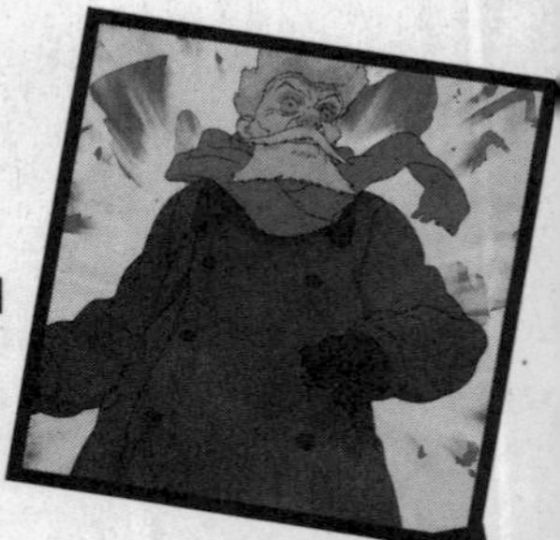

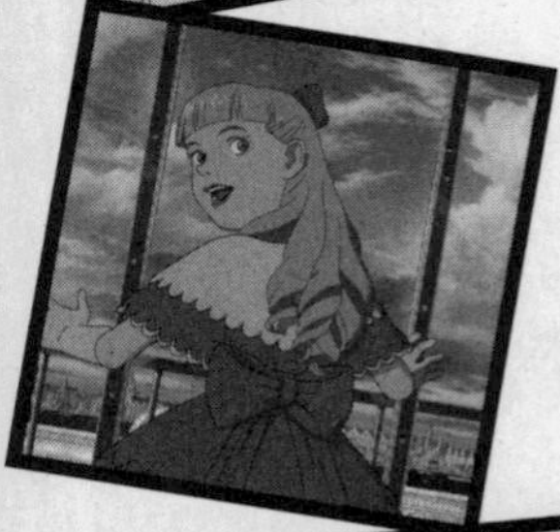

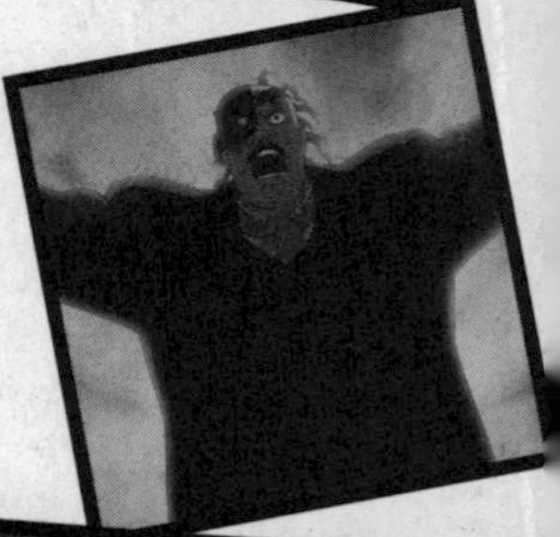

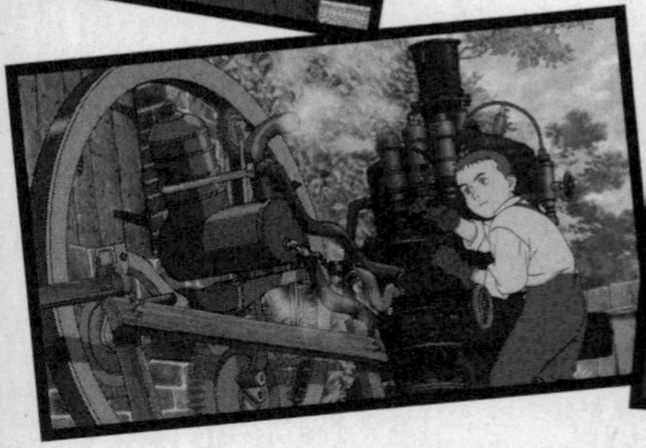

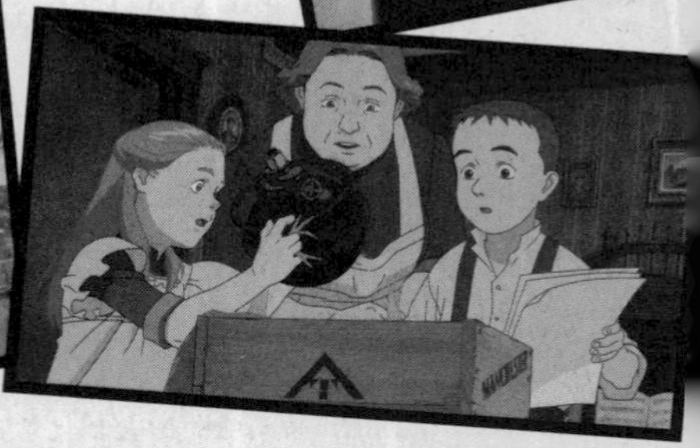

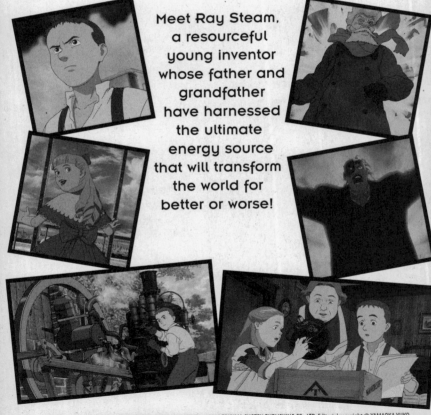

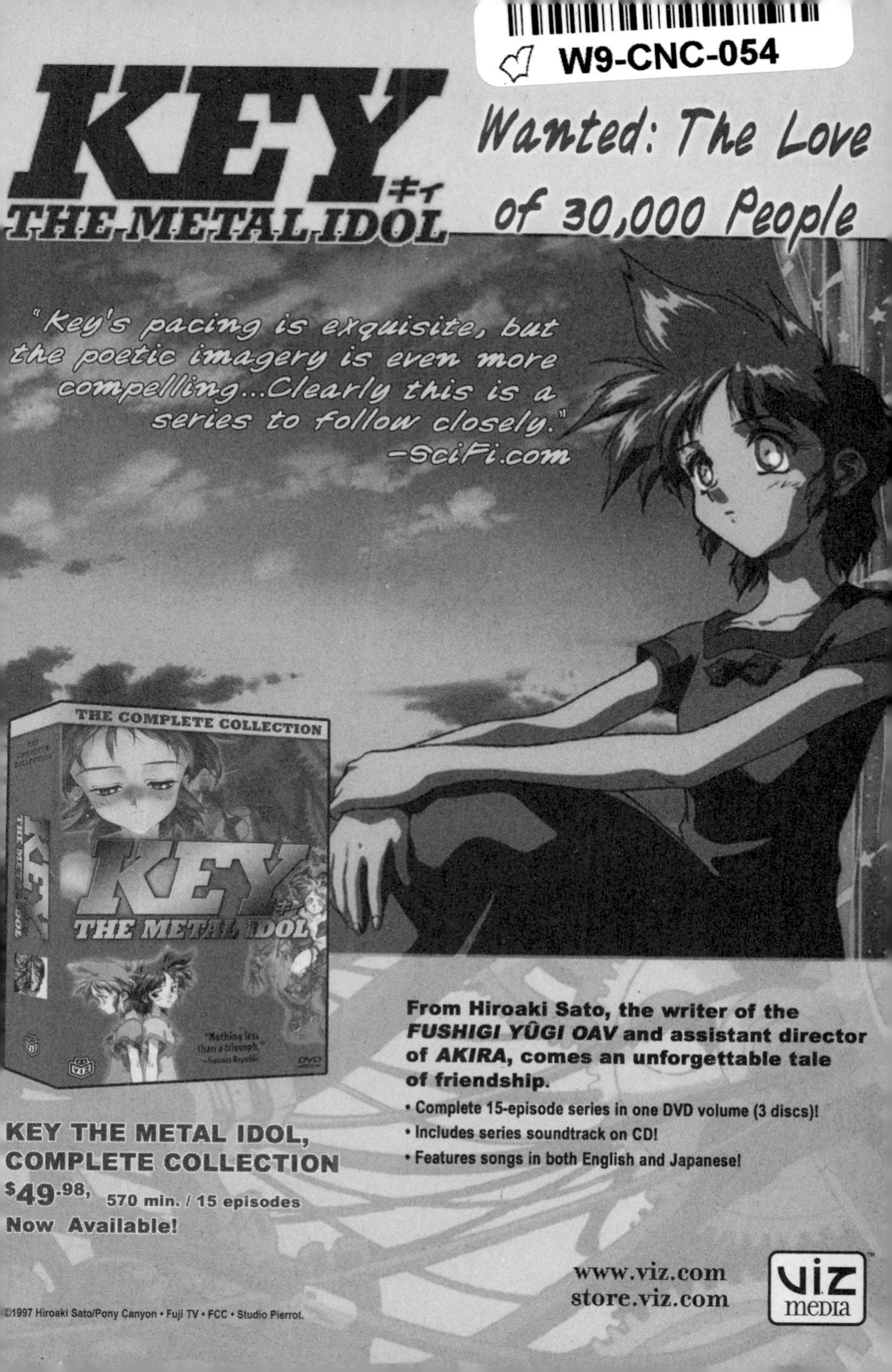
W9-CNC-054
KEY キィ THE METAL IDOL
Wanted: The Love of 30,000 People
"Key's pacing is exquisite, but the poetic imagery is even more compelling...Clearly this is a series to follow closely." -SciFi.com
THE COMPLETE COLLECTION
KEY キィ THE METAL IDOL
"Nothing less than a triumph."
DVD
From Hiroaki Sato, the writer of the FUSHIGI YÛGI OAV and assistant director of AKIRA, comes an unforgettable tale of friendship.
• Complete 15-episode series in one DVD volume (3 discs)!
• Includes series soundtrack on CD!
• Features songs in both English and Japanese!
KEY THE METAL IDOL, COMPLETE COLLECTION
$49.98, 570 min. / 15 episodes
Now Available!
www.viz.com
store.viz.com
VIZ MEDIA
©1997 Hiroaki Sato/Pony Canyon • Fuji TV • FCC • Studio Pierrot.